Courtesans at Table

Courtesans at Table
Gender and Greek Literary Culture in Athenaeus

Laura K. McClure

ROUTLEDGE
NEW YORK AND LONDON

Published in 2003 by
Routledge
29 West 35th Street
New York, NY 10001
www.routledge-ny.com

Published in Great Britain by
Routledge
11 New Fetter Lane
London EC4P 4EE
www.routledge.co.uk

Routledge is an imprint of the Taylor & Francis Group.

Library of Congress Cataloging-in-Publication Data

McClure, Laura, 1959–
    Courtesans at table : gender & Greek literary culture in Athenaeus /
    Laura K. McClure.
        p. cm.
    Includes bibliographical references and index.
        ISBN 0-415-93946-1 (HB) — ISBN 0-415-93947-X (PB)
    1. Athenaeus, of Naucratis. Deipnosophistae. 2. Athenaeus, of
    Naucratis—Characters—Women. 3. Women and literature—Greece—Athens.
    4. Dinners and dining—Greece—Athens. 5. Dinners and dining in
    literature. 6. Athens (Greece)—In literature. 7.
    Women—Greece—Athens. 8. Prostitutes in literature. 9. Courtesans in
    literature. 10. Sex role in literature. I. Title.
    PA3937.M26 2003
    938'.509'082—dc21
                                                        2003013105

For my parents

Contents

Acknowledgments

This book could not have been written without many conversations and many kinds of support, beginning with my home institution, the University of Wisconsin at Madison. Particular thanks are owed to the Graduate School of the College of Letters and Science for providing generous funding for this project at several critical junctures, and to the Institute for Research in the Humanities for a semester's leave. Colleagues in the Classics department deserve special mention for their support. I would especially like to acknowledge Patricia Rosenmeyer for her sustained collegiality and encouragement; her willingness to read most, if not all, of my work over the years has been a unique blessing. William Aylward and Nick Cahill endured with good grace, and considerable expertise, my pestering them with questions about material culture. Conversations with Susan Lape and Angela Pitts stimulated my thinking about representations of gender and Athenaeus' Hellenistic sources. I am grateful to Leslie Kurke for sharing her manuscript on Machon, and to Cathy Keesling for her essay on monuments of courtesans in Greek sanctuaries. Madeleine Henry and the other, anonymous referees for the press provided helpful suggestions on various drafts of the manuscript. Thanks also to Alex Pappas for her work in the trenches, checking references, and proofreading in the final stages of manuscript preparation.

Lastly, my deepest gratitude to my family for their forbearance, and especially to my husband, Richard Heinemann, for conversations about Walter Benjamin, literary theory, and the Konstanz Imperia, as well as for his gracious tolerance of my sustained inattention during the writing of this book.

Madison, Wisconsin
December, 2002

A Note on Abbreviations

I have tended to use Latinized versions of Greek titles and names, particularly where they are well-established and familiar to readers. For less common titles and authors, as in the case of some of the comic plays, I have preserved a spelling closer to the Greek original. The result is not always consistent, and may at times seem arbitrary. I have avoided using a Greek font where possible; on a few occasions it has been necessary to include it to clarify a point. Instead, I have provided English translations, with important words or phrases included in a transliterated version in parentheses. Unless otherwise noted, all translations are my own. Names of authors, titles of texts, and major scholarly works are abbreviated in accordance with the list in *The Oxford Classical Dictionary*, 3d ed. (1996), pp. xxix–liv. Abbreviations for the most frequently cited editions appear below.

CAF	Kock, T. (ed.). 1880–88. *Comicorum Atticorum Fragmenta.* Vols. 1–3. Leipzig.
Choricius	Foerster, R. and E. Richtsteig (eds.). 1929. *Choricii Gazaei opera.* Leipzig.
FGrH	Jacoby, F. (ed.). 1923–58. *Die Fragmente der griechischen Historiker.* Berlin.
FHG	Müller, C. (ed.). 1841–70. *Fragmenta Historicorum Graecorum.* Vols. 1–4. Paris.
Gnom.	Sternbach, L. (ed.). 1963 *Gnomologium Vaticanum e Codice Vaticano Graeco.* Berlin.
Gow	Gow, A. (ed.). 1965. *Machon: The Fragments.* Cambridge.

Jensen	Jensen, C. (ed.). 1963. *Hyperidis Orationes sex cum ceterarum fragmentis.* Stuttgart.
KA	Kassel, R. and C. Austin. (eds.). 1983— *Poetae comici Graeci.* Berlin.
Körte	Körte, A. (ed.). 1953–55. *Menandri quae supersunt.* Vols. 1–2. Leipzig.
LGPN 1	Fraser, P. M. and E. Matthews (eds.). 1987. *Lexicon of Greek Personal Names. Volume I. The Aegean Islands, Cyprus, Cyrenaica.* Oxford.
LGPN 2	Byrne, S. and M. Osborne (eds.). 1994. *Lexicon of Greek Personal Names. Volume II. Attica.* Oxford.
PLG	Bergk, T. (ed.). 1882. *Poetae Lyrici Graeci.* Leipzig.
PMG	Page, D. 1962. *Poetae Melici Graeci.* Oxford.
Preller	Preller, L. (ed.). 1964. *Polemonis Periegetae Fragmenta.* Amsterdam.
Sandbach	Sandbach, F. (ed.). 1991. *Menandri Reliquiae Selectae.* Oxford.
Spengel	Spengel, L. (ed.). 1856. *Rhetores Graeci.* 3 vols. Leipzig. [Repr. Frankfurt am Main: Minerva, 1966].
Thalheim	Thalheim, T. (ed.). 1901. *Lysiae Orationes.* Leipzig.
TGF	Nauck, A. *Tragicorum Graecorum Fragmenta.* 2nd ed. Leipzig.
TrGF	Snell, B., R. Kannicht, and S. Radt (eds.). 1971—*Tragicorum Graecorum Fragmenta.* Göttingen.
Wehrli	Wehrli, F. (ed.). 1974. *Hermippos der Kallimacheer.* Basel.

Introduction

A beautiful woman, yes, arrayed in a thousand splendors, Is a sumptuous table
where many sup and take their fill. . . .[1]

This book is concerned with the representation of courtesans, or *hetaeras,*
in the Greek literary tradition, from the perspective of the late second
century writer, Athenaeus. It is thus both a diachronic and a synchronic
study of these figures and their deployment across genres and periods. Although the heyday of courtesans belonged to a specific literary and cultural matrix, classical Athens in the fourth century B.C.E., our fullest
accounts paradoxically come from a much later period and context, fictional and scholarly works composed by Greek sophists living in the
Roman Empire in the second century C.E. Lost are most of the fourth-century prosecution and defense speeches constructed around courtesans,
little remains of the genres of Middle and New comedy, and none of the
extant fragments fully illustrates the importance of this character type to
the genre. Even more distressing has been the total loss of the Hellenistic
and later prosopographies of Athenian courtesans that apparently chronicled their names and nicknames, their liaisons with famous men, and
their witty quips. Still in circulation in the late second century C.E., these
lost discourses nonetheless played a critical role in formulating the representations of courtesans among Second Sophistic authors such as Lucian,
Alciphron, and Athenaeus.

Arguably the most extensive treatment of these figures occurs in Book
13 of the *Deipnosophistae* of Athenaeus, a compendium of Greek literary
passages concerned with the symposium, or drinking party, in all its aspects and composed at the end of the second century C.E. The symposium
and its banter furnish a dramatic context for the quotation of thousands
of classical and Hellenistic literary sources. Entitled *Peri Gynaikōn* (On

1

Women), Book 13 contains an extensive collection of quotations relating to ancient conceptions of women, gender, and sexuality. The section mentions, at least in passing and sometimes at great length, almost all of the major extant accounts of hetaeras from all periods of Greek literature, as well as many others now lost to us. The courtesans of Athenaeus reflect a diverse array of literary genres disseminated over several centuries; at the same time, many aspects of their representation remained remarkably constant throughout this tradition. As a literary and social type produced and put into circulation by classical Athenian authors, the courtesan held special interest for Second Sophistic writers, who lived and wrote under Roman rule and yet continued to stress their close identification with Hellenic culture. As constructions of Greek speaking sophists living in Asia Minor, Egypt, and elsewhere in the Roman Empire, the hetaeras of the Second Sophistic reflect contemporary concerns with self-representation and display, nostalgia for the classical past and its importance for negotiating self-identity.

A comprehensive modern study of courtesans in ancient Greece has yet to be written (Kampen 1996: 153, n. 49), and indeed, such an undertaking lies outside the scope of the present work. Limited discussions of the social history of hetaeras, largely based upon their literary representation, are found in Licht's (=Brandt) *Sexuality in Ancient Greece* (1932; [first published as *Sittengeschichte Griechenlands,* 1925–28]), and Hauschild's treatise on Greek comedy, *Die Gestalt der Hetäre in der griechischen Komödie* (1933), both written well before the establishment of gender studies and contemporary critical theory. Most of this research relies heavily on Book 13 of Athenaeus' *Deipnosophistae* and tends to interpret its discourse literally as an accurate account of Greek hetaeras and their lives. Even quite recent scholarship reflects this prejudice, as, for example, Dimakis's account of their liaisons with orators.[2] For such scholars, the hetaera is viewed as the first "liberated woman," a desirable, refined companion, capable of discoursing on a broad range of philosophical subjects. But as subsequent chapters demonstrate, this view of hetaeras rests on a superficial and uncontextualized reading of Book 13 of the *Deipnosophistae*, and thus cannot be taken as an accurate assessment of the lives of actual courtesans, nor even of the Greek literary tradition.

A recent surge of interest in courtesans and prostitutes among classical scholars has led to a fuller consideration of their representation in Greek art, their status as commodities traded in the marketplace of men, and their discursive deployment in the democratic city-state.[3] The fact that prostitution has figured prominently in many larger projects of cultural criticism attests to its pivotal importance for understanding ancient constructions of gender, sexuality, and political ideology. Halperin, following upon Dover, elucidates the political repercussions of male prostitution in classical Athens in a chapter of *One Hundred Years of Homosexuality* (1990). More recently, Davidson's *Courtesans and Fishcakes* (1997) analyzes prostitution as a major aspect of the consuming passions privileged and regulated by Athenian men of the classical period. Finally, Kurke, in *Coins, Bodies, Games and Gold* (1999), devotes two chapters to the subject of hetaeras, in which she distinguishes the hetaera from the brothel worker to show how the conflict of aristocratic and democratic political ideology played itself out in the drinking parties of Athenian men.

These studies have largely focused on the role of hetaeras, and prostitution more generally, in the cultural discourses produced by Athenians during the archaic and classical periods, with little attention to the role of Second Sophistic writers, particularly Athenaeus, in transmitting and shaping them. Although Davidson in *Courtesans and Fishcakes* acknowledges his debt to Athenaeus, whom he excavates for evocative classical quotations on the pleasures of the table, he almost completely disregards the literary and cultural matrix in which these quotations are embedded.[4] At the same time, classical scholars have increasingly come to recognize the importance of Athenaeus' oeuvre for all aspects of classical study, as evidenced by the publication of Braund's and Wilkin's *Athenaeus and his World* in 2000. And yet, apart from Henry's essay, "Athenaeus the Ur-Pornographer," few contributors to the volume mention issues of gender and sexuality. My project attempts to bridge this gap by considering not only aspects of literary structure and characterization that frame the discourse on hetaeras in Book 13 of the *Deipnosophistae*, but also the cultural processes at work behind these representations. What representational modes and textual strategies informed Second Sophistic discourses about hetaeras? How did such a socially marginal figure as the hetaera become so culturally central by the late second century C.E.? How do courtesans as realized by these late writers transmit and negotiate issues of intellectual heritage and political identity?

The Courtesan as Fetish

A theoretical framework for formulating a response to these questions is found in contemporary cultural theory, exemplified by the recent materialist analyses of Davidson and Kurke. These scholars stress the function of courtesans and other prostitutes as commodities in classical Athens:

> Commodity exchange establishes a relationship between *objects*, a relationship in terms of price. Commodities are interchangeable, easily measured and compared, their quantity and quality can be broken down into units, often units of currency. (Davidson 1997: 110)

Davidson uses the concept of commodity exchange to argue for a discursive distinction between the hetaera and her brothel counterpart, the porne (terms discussed more fully at the end of this chapter). The hetaera participates in and embodies an economy of gift exchange which maintains, rather than severs, the connection between individuals: she seduces and persuades, providing her services in exchange for gifts, and always holds out the possibility of refusing her favors; indeed, "the very name hetaera—'companion' 'friend'—is ambiguous, a euphemism."[5] In contrast, the discourse of the porne, the hetaera's faceless, nameless brothel counterpart, involves a type of commodity exchange that continually depersonalizes and reifies, exemplified by crass transactional names such as Didrachmon and Obole, both terms for Attic currency (Davidson 1997: 118–9).

Although Kurke fundamentally accepts Davidson's view, she interprets these two discourses from a political perspective, reading them as expressions of the conflict between competing aristocratic and democratic ideologies in the late archaic period.[6] She argues that the invention of the category of hetaera by the aristocratic elite served as a means of deliberately mystifying and de-commodifying her status in archaic Greece. In contrast, commercial transactions involving money, such as the patronage of a porne (brothel worker), represented a debased and debasing, but characteristically democratic, activity:

> The constitution of this category within the framework of aristocratic gift exchange enabled the complete occlusion of the explicit, monetarized economics of the public sphere. In this respect, the *hetaira-pornē* binary functioned just like the opposition of metals and money, to define and differentiate the sympotic world from the public space of the agora and elitist discourse. (Kurke 1999: 185)

Kurke nonetheless admits that hetaeras themselves could be subject to commodification, functioning, at least on Attic vases, "as so much sympotic furniture, like couches and pillows—objects to serve the needs of the male symposiasts" (Kurke 1999: 186). Indeed, the practice of slavery in antiquity meant that some people, normally those of foreign birth, could be turned into commodities. Cohen suggests that servile status differentiated the brothel worker and other types of prostitutes from the hetaera in classical Athens. The name of hetaera therefore may have advertised "the calling of a free person, an honorific perhaps over ostentatious for a formerly enslaved worker" (Cohen, 2002). While her new professional designation may have served to veil the commodity status of the hetaera, she nonetheless continued to be viewed as a commodity in the literary tradition.

An important but often overlooked aspect of the commodity in these discussions is its function as a fetish, that is, its illusory appearance, the mystical character that veils its use-value: "fetishism . . . attaches itself to the products of labor as soon as they are produced as commodities."[7] Nowhere is this more apparent than in the case of the courtesan, whose labor turns her body into a thing of use, and yet continually disguises her commodity status; a similar process is at work in her literary representation. Benjamin in his *Passagen-Werk* (Arcades Project), a materialist analysis of the Arcade phenomenon in fin de siècle Paris, directly applies the concept of the fetish to the prostitute: she is not only the original wage laborer, but an allegory for the act and process of commodification:

> The whore is, fundamentally, the incarnation of a nature suffused with commodity appearance. She has even intensified its power of delusion insofar as, in commerce with her, an always fictive pleasure arises. . . .[8]

The prostitute functions first and foremost as a cultural sign that carries symbolic value: her deployment as a sign simultaneously calls attention to her artificiality and fictiveness, while at the same time concealing her commodity status. The fetish as realized through the prostitute belongs to the world of illusory appearances that conjure loss and the transitory unity of the past:

> In the prostitute, the fetish assumes the illusion (appearance) of an authentic experience recalling in the male subject the image and feeling of a happy past. Through the fragmentation of the female body and the semiotization of the female genitals in prostitution, woman represents . . . the fragmented experience of reality and modernity . . . and supports the appearance of "once upon a time it was beautiful." (Rauch 1988: 82)

The courtesans of Athenaeus' *Deipnosophistae*, fragmented into a series of names and nicknames, jokes and quotations, similarly serve as potent reminders of a lost golden age of literary production and unified cultural identity. The genres that comprise Athenaeus' discourse on courtesans in Book 13, particularly Middle and New comedy, had largely been eclipsed by the rise of rhetoric at the end of the second century C.E. Athens had long since ceased to function as a political power, while the hetaera as a social type was on the verge of extinction; her brief flowering, as a literary figure and historical entity, had ended well over four hundred years earlier. Only the pleasures of literary collection, not authentic production, remained for authors like Athenaeus. In this regard, the literary hetaera uniquely embodies the decadent aesthetic of Second Sophistic literature, with its preference for artifice; such an aesthetic stresses "the primacy of artifice over nature, the value of cosmetic ornament, the sense of art as an enchanting fakery, a surface play of masks and disguises" (Bernheimer 1993: 63).

By the Second Sophistic period, the hetaera fashioned by multiple literary discourses is thus not a historical entity, but a cultural sign; she achieves the same cultural status as art objects or literary works. In her capacity as a fetish, the hetaera serves as the medium for the male subject's projections, particularly his desire to be whole and immortal (Rauch 1988: 78). The literary hetaera of the Second Sophistic on the one hand reminds her audience that the representational system in which she is rendered is dead, or at least on the verge of extinction, while at the same time evoking the archetypal myth of wholeness. The supreme symbol of this unity, for Greek writers in Imperial Rome, was classical Athens. Because lost, this past could only be recovered through its fragments, through the literary quotations and allusions that figure so prominently in Second Sophistic texts, through the ruins of Greek monuments and architecture that confronted Greek inhabitants of Imperial Rome on a daily basis, through the desire to reclaim and preserve a pure linguistic Atticism. In the Second Sophistic period, Greek courtesans, whether deployed as fictional characters, as in Alciphron or Lucian, or in Athenaeus' literary museum, engender narratives that in turn substitute "a context of perpetual consumption for its context of origin" (Stewart, S. 1993: 135). Dislocated from her original context, the hetaera in Athenaeus serves as a metonymical construction, an object of substitution and a vehicle of nostalgia that both recalls the original loss and yet simultaneously distances the subject from that for which it longs.

The concept of nostalgia provides a theoretical framework for understanding the importance of Attic *paideia* for Athenaeus' oeuvre in Chapter 1, and for Second Sophistic literature more generally. Rather than dismissing the text as a hopelessly disjointed and fragmentary discourse loosely organized around sympotic topics, the chapter attempts to show that quotation merits special attention as a literary strategy for confronting problems of authenticity and origin, cultural identity and dislocation during the second century C.E. After briefly exploring the social and political context of the Second Sophistic, the chapter elucidates the genres and authors of particular relevance to Atheneaeus' discourse on courtesans, including Middle and New comedy, the *Chreiae* of Machon, and the Hellenistic courtesan treatises. While disembodied from their original contexts, these quotations do not simply float randomly through Athenaeus' text, but rather are broadly anchored to a rhetorical structure organized around a series of antitheses, beginning with the contrasting speeches of the two main characters, the grammarian Myrtilus and the philosopher Cynulcus.

This is not to suggest that Athenaeus in Book 13 of the *Deipnosophistae* has constructed a coherent, well-organized account of courtesans in the Greek literary tradition; indeed, the primary speech of Myrtilus is often disjointed and difficult to follow, involving abrupt shifts of topic, tangential comments, and numerous interruptions. Because an overarching organizational principle, whether based on topic, literary genre, author, or individual courtesan, is rarely in evidence in Book 13, the remaining chapters of this book consider the major textual strategies, representational modes, and cultural trends that influenced Athenaeus' discourse on hetaeras. Chapter 2 considers the names and pseudonyms of hetaeras, over 150 of which are mentioned in Book 13, and the Hellenistic courtesan treatises that shape this discourse. Indeed, the public naming of hetaeras in the comic theater or the law courts contrasted them with respectable Athenian women in the classical period by advertising their notoriety and sexual availability. But rather than individuating these women, names actually served to obscure their identities, especially given that multiple names are commonly associated with a single woman. Instead, such names emphasized their status as commodities by comparing them to animals and evoking their use value. Although de-emphasized by Athenaeus, the names of hetaeras conjured a discourse of invective targeted against notorious men, provided the fodder of jokes, or served as artifacts to be assembled and classified by Alexandrian scholars. By the Second Sophistic period, however, the names of hetaeras evoked nostalgia for Hellenic *paideia* and a bygone Attic past.

The witticisms of hetaeras, as reflected in the *Chreiae* of Machon as well as in the anecdotal collections of authors such as Lynceus and Aristodemus, serve as the focus of Chapter 3. These jokes combine obscene puns and sophisticated literary allusions to temporarily challenge or invert social hierarchies, comically exposing the pretensions of philosophers, poets, and other celebrated figures. They borrow from the Socratic tradition the convention of the learned courtesan, whose literary sensibility is exceeded only by the sophists at Athenaeus' table. Whether or not Athenian hetaeras actually exhibited this degree of *paideia*, they are paradoxically represented as erudite purveyors of Attic language and culture. And yet, like the names that form such a prominent focus of Book 13 of the *Deipnosophistae*, the comic quip reflects yet another aspect of the fetishization of the hetaera that begins in the Hellenistic period. Instead of fully developing the hetaera as a character, anecdotalists such as Machon excerpted and collected her sayings in a process that already evoked nostalgia for a fleeting era.

Chapter 4 examines narratives about the bodies of hetaeras found in Book 13 of the *Deipnosophistae* and the Hellenistic emphasis on spectacle and rhetorical display that informs them. As comic characters, as models for art works, and as figures who allegedly exhibited their naked bodies at religious festivals and in the law courts, courtesans are represented as playing a significant role in the performance culture of classical Athens. The collective experience of performance and public display brought a theatrical vocabulary to the narratives and dramatic texts that shaped Athenaeus' discourse on hetaeras. The prevalence of hetaeras as characters in Middle and New comedy in the fourth century, as well as their role as entertainers at the symposium, similarly contributed to the view of hetaeras as consummate performers who constructed themselves wholly through artifice. For ancient authors, the bodies of courtesans thus provided a convenient metaphor for literary artifice, epideictic display, and rhetorical persuasion from the classical period through the late second century C.E.

Just as narratives about the bodies of courtesans inserted them into the culture of viewing that characterized the Hellenistic cultural landscape, so, too, accounts of their sanctuaries, monuments, and dedications put them on display, as shown in the final chapter. This spectacle commonly occurs in a context of religious viewing, where the hetaera is conflated with her patron goddess Aphrodite and her commodity status is stressed. Indeed, the revenues of courtesans' bodies are frequently represented as financing their monumental buildings and extravagant dedications. By the time of Athenaeus, however, these monuments had largely disappeared, preserved only through the historiographic and periegetic sources. Although public monuments became increasingly common among the Hellenistic queens, their association with courtesans almost always involves transgression, as if parodying normative conventions of religious dedication. In contrast, the public commemoration of heroic courtesans is represented as preserving the community and even political ideology. For Second Sophistic readers, these monuments and the hetaeras they celebrated conjured the classical past fragmented into literary ruins both familiar and strange.

Although this book begins and ends with Book 13 of the *Deipnosophistae,* it draws on the external literary tradition to elucidate as fully as possible significant aspects of Athenaeus' discourse. Indeed, the continual juxtaposition of quotations from utterly distinct time periods, genres, and authors necessitates recourse to texts outside the *Deipnosophistae,* and the modes of representation and textual strategies they deploy. This is especially true of the very terms for prostitutes used by Athenaeus: to understand what he means by the word hetaera, it is necessary to consider its appearance in the Greek literary tradition as a whole. As recent feminist critics have noted, prostitution is a much-contested social category; its broadest meaning is the sale of sexual services, but it can also refer to a variety of other types of arrangements. In ancient Greece, as in most cultures, a broad range of terms alluded to women who made themselves sexually available to men in exchange for economic support and who operated outside the structure of legitimate marriage. Although Athenaeus states that his work will concern hetaeras, he also makes frequent reference to the porne (brothel worker), the pallake (concubine), the auletris (flute player), along with other performers and entertainers, and the eromene (mistress), terms that will be more fully elucidated in the following section.

Ancient Greek Terms for Prostitutes

We have hetaeras for pleasure, pallakes for the everyday care of our bodies, and wives for the bearing of legitimate children and for being trusted guardians of the house. ([Dem.] 59. 122 = Ath. 13. 573b)

Most scholarly discussions of Greek terms for prostitutes, both ancient and modern, begin with Apollodorus' statement on the differences between the hetaera and the pallake in the epigraph above; indeed, Athenaeus concludes his own discussion of terminology with this passage. Ogden has taken it as evidence for the absolute distinction between legitimate wives and all other women, a distinction that revolves around the production of legitimate children.[9] For Vernant, and later Davidson, the assertion serves the opposite function, acknowledging, rather, the desire for a clear delineation and, at the same time, its impossibility (Vernant 1980: 47; Davidson 1997: 73). Outside of Apollodorus' formulation, however, absolute distinctions are hard to find, a situation complicated by the fact that there is as yet no systematic study of these terms in ancient Greek (Brown 1990: 248–9).

Indeed, Apollodorus neglects a range of Greek terms for prostitutes used by Athenaeus, most notably porne and eromene, as well as the various types of slave entertainers associated with the symposium.[10] It is noteworthy that the orator refers several times to Neaera as a hetaera, only once describing her professional activities as *peporneumenē* (whoring, [Dem.] 59. 107. 5).[11] Given the conspicuous absence of the term in this oration, one might wonder how a second major debate among scholars of Greek prostitution has been constituted around the dichotomy of hetaera and porne, as discussed in the preceding section.[12] While these analyses provocatively illuminate some of the major cultural tensions at work in archaic and classical Athens, their lack of detailed attention to prostitution nomenclature sometimes contributes to an over-determined dichotomy between the hetaera and the porne that has subsequently enmeshed scholarly debate.[13] I will argue in the first part of this section that while the two terms were discernibly distinct for the Greeks, they did not demarcate a binary opposition; in the majority of cases, different terms overlap and absolute distinctions are rare. By the time of the *Deipnosophistae*, most of the classical and archaic vocabulary for prostitution is subsumed under the more general rubric of eromene (mistress).

Analysis of Greek Terms for Prostitutes

Century BCE	8th	7th	6th	5th	4th	3rd	2nd	1st
Works Surveyed	14	27	48	192	281	204	104	100
hetaera	0	0	1	57	201	60	21	27
porne	0	4	2	51	134	24	42	95
pallake	3	0	1	43	20	11	4	60
eromene	0	0	0	64	76	32	9	19
auletris	0	0	0	32	58	19	4	6
Totals	3	4	4	247	489	146	80	207

As this table shows, terms for prostitutes do not enter the mainstream of Greek literature until the fifth and fourth centuries.[14] A few scattered instances of porne and pallake occur in the Homeric poems and archaic lyric and iambic poetry of the seventh and sixth centuries, while the terms hetaera, eromene, and auletris are notably absent. A single pre-classical reference to hetaera is found Aesop's fables, a corpus that has its origins in the sixth century, but was probably not written down until much later.[15] In the Homeric poems, pallake refers to a concubine, a woman of servile status whose children would not have been recognized as legitimate, and one who was probably purchased through trade rather than acquired as the spoils of war.[16] The term porne and its cognates appear in archaic lyric, mostly in the context of invective: the earliest reference, Archilochus (F328 *PMG*), as well as a slightly later iambic fragment of Hipponax (F104 *PMG*), identify the porne with the cinaedus, and with pathic behavior generally. Anacreon similarly uses the compound, "willing whores," to heap violent abuse on a lower class figure, one Artemon (388 *PMG*), a tradition that continued into the classical period in Attic Old comedy and oratory.[17] In Alcaeus, the word porne occurs three times, apparently without invective, two in a badly damaged fragment that moralizes about the dangers of patronizing prostitutes, "what one gives to a prostitute (*pornai*) might as well be thrown into the waves of the gray sea" (Alcaeus 117b *PMG*; trans. Campbell).

In the late fifth and early fourth centuries there is a huge increase in instances of prostitution terminology, mainly due to the flowering of the comic and rhetorical genres and their debt to the tradition of iambic invective. In the late fifth century, the majority of instances of hetaera appear in oratory (19), followed by comedy (14), and about half again in both history and philosophy. The prose writers appear to have preferred the more euphemistic term hetaera during this period, as porne and its cognates never appear in Plato and only rarely occur in oratory. The bulk of the allusions are found in Attic comedy, a genre known for its coarse and collo-quial language. By the mid-fourth century, however, references to the term hetaera quadruple, and those to porne double, a significant increase even taking into account the larger extant corpus. Instances of hetaera are split evenly among fourth-century comedy and oratory with around 60 occur-rences in each genre, while the number of references in both philosophical (non-Socratic) and historical texts increases substantially, to 37 and 21 re-spectively. Porne and its cognates appear eight times in philosophical texts and 16 in historical sources; for comedy and oratory, the numbers are roughly 50 for each. Fourth-century trends are somewhat skewed due to the vast number of references to the words hetaera and porne and their cognates in the pseudo-Demosthenic speech, *Against Neaera*, and in Aeschines' *Against Timarchus.* These two orations serve as the basis of the discussion that follows because they represent the most extensive accounts of prostitution from the classical period. The frequency with which this vocabulary appears in fourth-century comic fragments reflects the impor-tance of prostitutes in the literary tradition and their use in the discourse of invective. However, because almost completely fragmentary, this corpus is of limited use in defining the semantic ranges of many of the terms.

Distinguishing the Hetaera from the Porne

Already in the classical period, there is significant "slippage" between the terms hetaera and porne, as Kurke has observed (Kurke 1999: 178). Clearly, porne is what a speaker resorts to when he wants to insult a woman, or her male relatives, while hetaera is a more euphemistic term.[18] And yet, as com-fortable as that distinction sounds, the two terms are frequently applied to the same woman, even in the classical period. Moreover, it is evident that in some cases a porne or even an auletris could eventually evolve into a het-aera. The word hetaera has a broad range of meanings and often encom-passes many of the other names for prostitutes, applying by turns to those under the control of a pornoboskos (brothel keeper), to the wealthy and fa-mous courtesans of Athenaeus, as well as to slaves and other poor women.[19]

The term hetaera, the feminine form of *hetairos* (male friend), denoted a woman who was maintained by one man, or occasionally two, in ex-change for his exclusive sexual access to her; typically she did not reside in his home, at least not when respectable women were present.[20] Only in a couple of contexts does *hetairos* refer to a woman's male lover: so the speaker of Semonides' iambic fragment 7 represents the donkey woman as willing to make love to any *hetairos* who comes along (*pros ergon aphrodi-sion/elthont' hetairon,* Sem. F7. 49), while the maiden of the love duet in Aristophanes' *Ecclesiazusae* uses it of the youth who courts her (*ouch hēkei moutairos*, Ar. *Eccl.* 912).[21] The use of hetaera to describe a woman who offers sexual services in exchange for pay, first occurs, with a modifier, in Herodotus' account of Rhodopis, a significant figure for Chapter 5:[22]

> And this king left behind a pyramid much smaller than his father's, its sides form a square, each side of which measures two-hundred and eighty feet in length; half made of Ethiopian stone. Some Greeks say that it belongs to the hetaera Rhodopis. . . . She was originally from Thrace, slave (*doulē*) to Iadmon, a Samian man of Hephaestopolis, and the fellow-slave of Aesop, the story teller. . . . Rhodopis was brought to Egypt by Xanthes of Samos, but having come to ply her trade (*kat' ergasian*), she was released for a lot of money (*eluthē chrēmatōn megalōn*) by a Mytilenian man, Charaxus, son of Scamandronymus and brother of Sappho the Melic poet. (2. 134–5)

This early passage is instructive in isolating some of the salient characteristics of hetaeras in ancient Greece, at least as reflected by the literary tradition. Read in conjunction with the Lydian narrative at 1. 93–94, it suggests that the Athenian imaginary strongly identified prostitution with foreigners and slaves; such women typically hailed from East Greece, the island of Samos and cities in Asia Minor. Rhodopis' intimate association with a famous man, Charaxus, the brother of the poet Sappho, distinguishes her from the common slave prostitute. The story may also indicate that the woman evolved from a porne—the phrase *kat' ergasian* implies work in a brothel—into an independent hetaera, released from servitude through the patronage of one man, and thus capable of an expensive public benefaction.

These activities confer upon the hetaera a distinct and celebrated name, "All the Greeks knew the name of Rhodopis, and later, the name of Archidice became a notorious subject of song (*aoidimos*) throughout Hellas" (*kai hoi pantes Hellēnes Rhodōpios to ounoma*, Hdt. 2. 135). While the hetaera Rhodopis and her counterpart Archidice are individuated by their famous names and public notoriety, the other prostituted girls in Herodotus are nameless: unnamed are the Lydian daughters who sell their bodies to finance their dowries (*porneuontai*, 1. 93, and *kataporneuousi*, 1. 94), as is the daughter of Cheops who sat in a brothel (*oikēma*, Hdt. 2. 126) to finance a monumental building.[23] This early account of prostitution sets the stage for subsequent discourses on courtesans: the hetaera is often of foreign birth and may begin her career as a slave; she is later released from the exclusive control of a slave owner or brothel keeper; she has a measure of wealth, enough to make a public benefaction; she consorts with illustrious men; and she is distinguished by a famous name.

For some ancient commentators, including Athenaeus, hetaera and porne referred to the same type of woman, only the former served as a euphemism for the latter. Plutarch credits Solon with this invention, stating the Athenians resorted to euphemisms out of a distaste for inelegance:

porne thus became "hetaera," taxes "donations," and prisons "domiciles" (*tas men pornas hetaeras, tous de phorous suntaxeis . . . oikēma de to desmōtērion kalountas,* Plut. *Sol.* 15. 3). Dionysius of Halicarnassus makes a similar point in his discussion of the application of the nickname Lupa (she-wolf) to prostitutes. Whereas such women were once known as "those who earned their living from sex" (*tais mistharnousais taphrodisia*), now they are addressed by the more respectable name of hetaeras (*hai nun euprepestera klēsei hetairai prosagoreuontai*, Dion. Hal. *Ant.* 1. 84. 4). Athenaeus in Book 13, drawing on a play by Menander, gives a similar account of the meaning of the word hetaera:

> And they call the women who take money "hetaeras" (*tas mistharnousas hetairas*), and the act of taking pay for intercourse "to serve as a hetaera" (*to epi sunousiais mistharnein hetairein*), not so much with reference to the true sense of the word, but for greater decency (*pros to euschēmonesteron*). So Menander, while distinguishing in the *Parakatatheke* male friends from hetaeras, says:
>
>> You have done a deed befitting not male friends (ἑταίρων), by Zeus, but hetaeras (ἑταιρῶν), for although the letters are the same, they make this form of address exceedingly improper. (*ou sphodr' euskhēmon,* 571d–e)

The speaker clearly understands hetaeras as women who accept money for their services, rather than simply gifts; but the name conceals the crass economic aspect of their activities. Because "hetaera" cannot be distinguished from "male friend" in the genitive plural case except by a change of accent, a play of words that appears elsewhere in Book 13 (567a), the term by definition functions as a euphemism.[24] The point of the Menandrian passage appears to be that this euphemism has become so familiar that it has adversely impacted the masculine form of the word.

In fragment of Anaxilas' *Neottis* quoted by Athenaeus, the word hetaera similarly serves as a euphemism that veils the commodity status of its bearer, and is thus distinguishable from the porne:

> A: But if someone who has a measure of wealth
> freely (*pros charin*) renders a service
> to those asking for certain things,
> from this act of *hetairia* she receives the name of hetaera.
> And so in this instance, you happen to be in love
> not with a porne, as you say,
> but a hetaera. But is she really so simple?
> B: She's quite clever (*asteia*), by Zeus!
>> (Anaxilas, Neottis F20 KA=572b)

The allusive language—the woman renders her services for an unspecified favor to unnamed men requesting things unmentioned—reinforces the idea put forth by Plutarch and Dionysius of Halicarnassus that the term hetaera functioned as a euphemism for porne, imbuing this figure with the semblance of respectability. Her activities, partners, and status are elusive and often difficult to pin down: at the very least, the hetaera can be recognized by the refined demeanor (*tropois*, 572a) that advertises her as respectable and at the same time equivocates. The hetaera who is an *astē* (of citizen class) gives the profession a good name (Antiphanes *Hydria* F210 = 572a), while the "real" hetaeras (*peri tōn ontōs hetairōn*), in contrast to the false, are capable of an "honest love" (*philian adolon*, 571c).

Although not explicit in the passage of Herodotus discussed above, a major difference between the hetaera and porne involved the number and types of their relationships. The hetaera expected relative permanence in her liaisons with men and professed fidelity to him.[25] An anecdote from the Hellenistic poet Machon describes the hetaera Mania as cohabiting with a pancratiast named Leontiscus "in the manner of a wedded wife" (*monos gametēs tropon gunaikos*, Machon 219–20 = 578f); her affair with another man, moreover, is referred to as an act of feminine adultery (*moicheomenēn*, Machon 222 = 579f). In this respect, the hetaera shared common ground with the pallake: "there is no clear dividing line between a courtesan who is installed as one man's mistress, perhaps for quite a long period, and any other woman who happens to live with a man without being married to him" (Brown 1990: 249). However, the concept of a mistress, designated by the term *erōmenē*, does not appear to have been fully developed until the late fourth century B.C.E. Davidson even goes so far as to suggest that the visual inaccessibility of the great hetaeras rendered them closer to wives than to their brothel counterparts.[26] Literary sources speak of their refined behavior (571f–572a; Lucian *Dial. meret.* 6. 3) and the attempts of procuresses to confer respectability on their charges by referring to them euphemistically as daughters ([Dem.] 59. 19). In *Against Neaera*, Neaera and Stephanus view her cohabitation with him as an opportunity to increase their revenues: her changed status not only permits her to charge higher fees, it also provides an opportunity for extortion since her clients can potentially be charged with adultery ([Dem.] 59. 41).

The expected longevity of the hetaera's relationships is also seen in the practice of military consorts: according to Xenophon, hetaeras, not pornae, followed the Greek army.[27] A hetaera could thus be difficult to distinguish; indeed, Apollodorus' allegations that Nicarete could command more money for her charges by passing them off as free women ([Dem.] 59. 19), or that Neaera could earn more as the pseudo-wife of Stephanus suggests as much. Since keeping house with a man (*sunoikia*) did not invoke the privileges of citizenship, a woman in such partnerships was probably more or less accepted by the community as a common law wife without regard for her origin (Post 1940: 446). For this reason, the prosecutors of two surviving orations that deal directly with women of questionable sexual status, Neaera in pseudo-Demosthenes 59 and the mother of the girl in Isaeus 3, have difficulty providing direct proof of their prostitutional activities.

The term porne originally denoted a brothel slave and often is distinguished from the hetaera by the number and anonymity of her partners, as well as by the fact that she could not choose them; she sells herself to "anyone who wishes her."[28] Although the term porne has commanded considerably less attention from classical scholars, on the assumption that its meaning is more transparent, a glance at Lysias' *On a Wound by Premeditation* shows its semantic complexity. The speech concerns a contractual dispute between two men over the ownership of a porne (*pornēs anthrōpou*, Lys. 4. 9). The same woman is described both as a freed woman (*eleutheran*, 4. 12) and as a co-owned property (*hautē de hupērkhe koinē*, 4. 16) put to torture for legal evidence, like a slave (*basanistheisēs*, 4. 17; *doulē*, 19). Conversely, the acceptance of all customers applies to the hetaera in a speech by Isaeus (*tōi bouloumenōi*, Isaeus 3. 13. 1) and to Neaera in the same-name speech (*emistharnei tōi boulomenōi*, [Dem.] 59. 23).

References to porne/pornos as a noun in the classical period are typically feminine, with a great majority of these occurring in comedy; the verbal form, in contrast, tends to refer to male prostitutes. The brothel keeper, pornoboskos, however, was normally male, although there is a reference to one pornoboskousa: Antigone, once one of the most gifted courtesans of her time, is said to continue to practice as a procuress after her retirement (Hyp. 3. 2–3).[29] Nicarete, the original owner of Neaera, certainly brokers young girls, but she is never actually called a pornoboskousa. The masculine form, pornos, is the term most frequently applied to males engaged in sex for pay: in one of Xenophon's dialogues, Socrates describes the pornos as one who offers his beauty and wisdom for money to anyone who wishes (*tōi boulomenōi*), an assertion that sets up an identification between sophistry, prostitution, and trade (Xen. *Mem.* 1. 6. 13).[30] A similar distinction with regard to the length of the sexual liaison obtains for male prostitutes: verbal cognates of *hetairein* describe a more exclusive relationship, even suggesting cohabitation with one person, while *porneuein* suggests multiple partners. To describe Timarchus' long-term affair with Misoglas, with whom he lived, Aeschines uses a form of *hetairein* but switches to *porneuein* when speaking of his promiscuous liaisons with a series of other lovers as he moved indiscriminately from house to house (Aeschin. 1. 51–52). By plying his trade in the houses of citizens, Timarchus in effect turned them all into brothels.

There is thus a spatial discrimination between the hetaera and the porne: the former belongs to the private domicile where she goes to entertain; the porne, on the other hand, abides in a public place which men must leave their houses to patronize. Perhaps this distinction underlies Apollodorus' graphic description of Phrynion's public copulation with Neaera ([Dem.] 59. 33); in so doing, he treats her as a porne, not a hetaera. Similarly, Neaera's cohabitation with Stephanus effectively turns their house into a brothel:

> In addition to this he brought forth the law which does not permit one to be taken as an adulterer who has to do with women who sit in a brothel (*ep' ergastriou kathōntai*) or who openly sell themselves (*pōlōntai apopephasmenōs*); for this, he said, is what the house of Stephanus is, a house of prostitution. (*tēn ergasian*, [Dem.] 59. 67)

The example of the slave girl Alce in Antiphon similarly confirms this distinction: a pallake while resident in Philoneus' house, she will be placed in a brothel as a porne unless she regains her master's affections (Ant. 1. 14. 4). Conversely, disgrace attached to married men who took hetaeras into their own homes where respectable women were present, even after the death of a wife (Dem. 40. 9); the fact that Alcibiades does so is viewed as reasonable grounds for divorce ([Dem.] 59. 22; Andoc. 4. 14; Patterson 1990: 55 n. 61). Concern for respectability even provoked some men to remove their grown sons from the house in order to install their hetaeras, as in the case of Hyperides (Ath. 13. 590c). Similarly, Lysias lodged his hetaera with a friend, "out of respect for his wife" (*aischunomenos tēn te gunaika*, [Dem.] 59. 22), just as Charisius does in Menander's *Epitrepontes.* The lack of spatial stability parallels the unstable social identity of both the hetaera and the porne: while the porne inhabited brothels and streets, the hetaera and the auletris brought this part of the city into the homes of citizens, but never permanently.

In addition to charges of citizen prostitution, the accusation of fraternizing with a porne or hetaera comprised a major portion of inflammatory abuse in fourth-century oratory.[31] Indeed, Athenaeus describes the ridicule the Athenian general Timotheus incurred for having a hetaera mother (*skōptomenos*, 577b), while the charge of conceiving children with whores represented a routine form of political invective in oratory (Dem. 54. 26; Aeschin. 2. 177). The keeping of a hetaera, on the other hand, suggested not only depravity but also prodigality as such relationships could be expensive, presumably quite a bit more than patronizing brothels: so the speaker in *Against Phormio* attacks Antimachus by alluding to his fondness for hetaeras and slave attendants (Dem. 36. 45; cf. [Dem.] 59. 29–30).[32] In an inheritance dispute, Callistratus lambastes Olympiadorus for keeping a citizen woman as his hetaera, whose freedom he has purchased (*gunaika men astēn*, Dem. 48. 53–4), instead of a lawful wife. Her expensive taste in jewelry and clothing illustrates the prohibitive cost involved in keeping a hetaera, and the prodigality of their paramours. So the extravagant Pytheas in one of Demosthenes' letters is taken to task for keeping not one, but two hetaeras (Dem. *Epist.* 3. 30).[33]

Hetaeras and prostitutes are also depicted as profligate in Attic oratory: Timarchus squanders the wages of his *porneia* on female flute players and hetaeras (Aeschin. 1. 42. 6, 75. 9, 115. 4), while Stephanus and Neaera use the revenues of their adultery scam to finance an expensive lifestyle ([Dem.] 59. 42–3). To the cliché of prostitution and profligacy, the philosophical writers added debased political ideology: for them, consorting with hetaeras symbolized not only a lack of masculine self-control but a corrupt society (Xen. *Mem.* 1. 5. 4; *Oec.* 1. 13. 3; Pl. *Phaedr.* 240b). In Plato's *Republic*, the hetaera embodies the prodigality of the city of luxury, its banquets (*truphōsan polin*, Pl. *Rep.* 373a), and even tyranny; indeed, Socrates accuses the tyrant of being closer to his hetaera than to his own mother (*Rep.* 574b–c).

From a linguistic standpoint, prostitution is often represented as an activity for males, but not a state of being. So the prostitutional proclivities of Timarchus, and the laws governing them, are described by the verbs *hetairein* (to serve as a companion)[34] and cognates of *porneuein* (to sell), including *peporneumenos, porneusthai,* and *peporneusthai*;[35] in fact, the noun *pornos* is only used three times in reference to him (Aeschin. 1. 70. 4, 123. 2, 130. 3). The term *hetairein* in connection with male prostitution seems to have had a legal meaning, since the earliest uses commonly allude to the alleged prostitution of male citizens (Andoc. 1. 100. 2; Lys. 14. 41. 5), as do those of the fourth century.[36] Aeschines repeatedly appeals to this law in *Against Timarchus*: "If any Athenian shall have prostituted his person, he shall not be permitted to become one of the nine archons . . ." (*hetairēsē*, Aeschin. 1. 21; cf. 21. 30. 7). Yet Aeschines virtually collapses the distinction between *hetairein* and *porneuein* in *Against Timarchus*, equating *peporneumenos* and *hētairēkōs* in a list of those persons not permitted to address the Athenian Assembly (Aeschin. 1. 29; cf. Dem. 19. 233. 8). The use of verbs rather than nouns to define the prostitutional activities of citizen males may indicate that their status as prostitutes was considered unnatural and only temporary.

In contrast, the verbal form *hetairein* is never used for female prostitution in the classical sources: indeed, throughout Pseudo-Demosthenes' *Against Neaera*, the formulation *hōs hetaira ousa* or simply *hetaira ousa* reinforces the idea that prostitution for women was not considered an activity, or profession, but a state of being.[37] Similar phrasing is used in Isaeus' *On the Estate of Pyrrhus*, an inheritance dispute that revolves around the legitimacy of a daughter, whose mother may have been a hetaera; the phrase *hōs ex hetairas ousan* that recurs throughout the speech suggests legal terminology (3. 52, 55, 70, 71). Only a few instances of the verb *porneuein* apply to females in fourth-century literature: Neaera is described as "whoring her way through Hellas," as mentioned above; as the other two

examples occur in fragmentary form, they are difficult to assess: a fragment of Hyperides speaks of Timandra, presumably the hetaera linked to
Alcibiades, as whoring (*peporneukuias*), while a fragment of the historian
Theopompus contains the word *porneumenas* (*FGrH* F227. 8).[38] The fact
that Athenaeus and his sources occasionally use the verb *hetairein* to refer
to the activities of women may indicate a weakening of the semantic range
by the late second century C.E.[39]

While the terms hetaera and porne in the archaic and classical period
were semantically distinct, they did not always designate a binary opposition. The terms and behaviors of either category could be applied to the
other; in the case of Attic oratory, a hetaera could be accused of acting like
a porne, or even be designated a porne, to call into question her status as a
freed woman. Moreover, a porne, with the help of a male patron, could
eventually transcend her servile origins and become a hetaera. By the time
of Middle and New comedy, however, the terms hetaera and porne appear
to have become interchangeable: a fragment of Anaxilas' *Neottis* quoted by
Athenaens at one moment describes Plangon, Sinope, Gnathaena, Nannion, Phryne, and Theano as hetaeras, and at another, as pornae (558a–d).
Another speaks of a hetaera residing in a brothel with other "courtesan
whores" (*porneion esti, polutelōs Adōnia/agous' hetaira meth' heterōn
pornōn chudēn*, Diphilus F43. 39–40 KA). Athenaeus also does not always
draw a sharp distinction between the two terms, although one of the main
speakers in Book 13, the philosopher Cynulcus, clearly formulates his invective around a contrast between high-priced courtesans and brothel
whores. And yet his speech shows a continual slippage in terminology. For
instance, in attributing the outbreak of the Peloponnesian War to prostitutes, the philosopher alludes to the Megarian Simaetha and two of Aspasia's women as *hetaerides*, even though the passage he adduces, from
Aristophanes' *Acharnians* (Ar. *Ach.* 524–29 = 569f–570a), calls them pornae. More will be said about the structure and characterization of Book 13
in the next chapter.

The Pallake

The term pallake/pallakis does not occur with anywhere near the frequency of the words hetaera and porne in the classical period: while 43 instances are found in the fifth century, there are only 20 in the fourth
century. The word appears most often among the prose writers, the historians Herodotus and Xenophon, as well as among the Attic orators. It
seldom occurs in comedy, and probably for this reason does not appear
with any great frequency in Athenaeus.[40] The fact that almost all of the references to this word in Book 13 appear in Larensis' encomium of wives
suggests that they were more closely associated with wives rather than

prostitutes. As Brown observes, a pallake was not necessarily a prostitute, that is, a woman who offered sex for pay, although a hetaera could become a concubine; the determining factor appears to have been the expected permanence and exclusivity of the relationship (Brown 1990: 249 and 263, n. 38). The pallake resided within the household, although only in the absence of a wife (*pallakēn echein endon*, [Dem.] 59. 118); her presence in a man's house probably distinguished her from the hetaera and the porne.[41] It might be argued that the pallake was not in fact a prostitute, but a common law wife without citizen status, since she was typically of slave or foreign origins (Patterson 1990: 55 and n. 61). Plutarch, following Cratinus, refers to Pericles' mistress, Aspasia, as a pallake and not a hetaera, probably for just this reason.[42] To the Athenian imagination, the pallake conjured the exotic and polygamous practices of foreigners, particularly the Persians. Almost a third of the fifth-century references occur in Herodotus, where concubinage is represented as a distinctly Persian, although not indigenous, custom. Herodotus maintains that the Persians adopted the practice of concubinage, along with polygamy, from another, unspecified culture; he further states that both the Egyptians (Hdt. 2. 130) and Scythians kept concubines (Hdt. 4. 71).

Most concubines mentioned in classical literature are represented as the captives of war: they accompanied the Persian army on its expedition into Greece (Hdt. 7. 83, 187), and after its defeat, were divvied up among the Greek soldiers (Hdt. 9. 76). Xenophon describes the Median capture of highborn women, not only wives but also concubines, brought back as the spoils of war (Xen. *Cyr.* 4. 3. 1). As captives, concubines were typically foreigners: Herodotus states that the offspring of a Lycian man and his concubine, a *xenē* (foreigner), was not considered legitimate because the Carians only recognized matrilineal descent (Hdt. 1. 173). Similarly, all of the pallakides mentioned by Xenophon are in the possession of foreign kings and leaders, including the satrap Pharnabazus (Xen. *Hell.* 3. 1. 10), Cyrus (Xen. *Anab.* 1. 10. 2), and the Hyrcanian king (Xen. *Cyr.* 5. 2. 28). The supplication of Pausanias by one of Pharandates' concubines shows that such women could be Greek:

> Save me, your suppliant, O King of Sparta, from captive slavery (*aichmalōtou doulosunēs*)! . . . . by birth I am Coan, the daughter of Hegetorides, son of Antagoras; in Cos the Persian captured me, taking me by force! (*biēi de me labōn en Kōi eiche ho Persēs*, Hdt. 9. 76)

Yet pallakides were not always spear captives: Phronime, mother of the stammering Battus, was the abandoned daughter of a Cretan ruler taken in by the man entrusted with killing her (Hdt. 4. 155), while Cambyses' request for Amasis' daughter in marriage only thinly disguises his intention to keep her as his concubine (Hdt. 3. 1).

Although concubinage may have been considered a foreign custom, its incorporation into the social fabric of classical Athens is well attested in oratory. Such women could be slave or free, foreign or Attic. The speaker of Lysias 1 argues that the law against adultery applied equally to the lawful wife and to the pallake (Lys. 1. 31). Demosthenes 23 also makes reference to this law, but modifies the term pallake with the phrase, "kept for the procreation of free children" (Dem. 23. 53. 5). These statements may allude, in Patterson's view, to pre-Solonian legal structures in which the offspring of the concubine could be considered legitimate although unequal members of the paternal household (Patterson 1990: 54). Similarly, the speaker of Isaeus 3 refers in general terms to men, presumably not slaves or foreigners, "who give their own women as concubines" (Is. 3. 39. 4–6). And in a plot worthy of tragedy, the hapless slave pallake of Antiphon 1 unwittingly poisons her master rather than risk losing his affections (1. 14, 16, 19). Notably, the concubines of oratory and comedy do not play any part in political invective, probably because they were viewed as closer to wives than to prostitutes.

Athenaeus also locates the origins of concubinage in Asian despotism, beginning with Priam's polygamy in Homer's *Iliad*. He argues that the Greeks never practiced concubinage, or at least did not condone it. In contrast, the Persian queens tolerated large numbers of concubines, "because the king rules his wife as a despot (*despotēn*) and is worshipped by the concubines, or at any rate they prostrate themselves before her" (*thrēskeuesthai*, 556b). Athenaeus then contrasts Hecuba's tolerance for Priam's multiple partners with Greek condemnation of the practice, citing the displeasure felt by Phoenix' mother for his father's concubine (Hom. *Il.* 9. 447–57); moreover, he adduces in support of his argument the fact that Homer does not attribute a concubine to Menelaus (556d). The concept of concubinage as a form of polygamy practiced by non-Greeks, particularly the Asian dynasts, reappears in connection with the Persian king Darius. He is said to have brought 360 concubines along with him on military campaigns (557b); among his inventory of captured goods numbered 329 musician concubines (608a). Athenaeus repeats Herodotus' account of Amasis' refusal to give his daughter in marriage to Cambyses because he feared she would become his pallake (560d). Similarly, he cites Xenophon's account of "the concubine of Miletus," presumably Aspasia the Younger/ Milto who accompanied Cyrus the Younger on his campaigns (576d). Last but not least, the Persian Oxyartes had as his concubine Timosa (609b). Only two references to the term pallake in connection with Athenian practice appear in Book 13 of the *Deipnosophistae*. Both deal with orators: a comic fragment from Strattis refers to Lagisca as the pallake of Isocrates (592d)—although she is elsewhere described as a hetaera—and the generalizing statement from Demosthenes' *Neaera* quoted at the outset of this section (573b).

The Auletris and Other Female Entertainers

In addition to hetaeras, other types of prostitutes played an important role at the symposium: the auletris (flute player), citharist (cithara player), psaltria (harpist), orchestris (dancer), and mousourgos (singer) not only provided musical accompaniment or acrobatic entertainment during the party, but also probably engaged in sexual activities with symposiasts.[43] Such women are sometimes designated by the term hetaera when modified by a noun describing their specific specialty, e.g., the *orchēstris hetaira* of Metagenes (F4 KA = 571b); in contrast, the *pezē hetaira* (pedestrian, Eupolis F184 KA) is a prostitute who does not play an instrument.[44] Female tumblers, *thaumatopoioi*, could also be prostitutes, since Matro uses the word of *pornae* (Ath. 4. 137c).[45] Another female servant of the symposium was the *oenochoousa* (cup bearer); according to Polybius as quoted by Athenaeus, Philadelphus employed Cleino as his cup bearer and set up images of her in Alexandria wearing only a short tunic and holding a rhyton (drinking horn) in her hand (576f).[46]

Although some of the most illustrious of the third- and fourth-century courtesans were flute players, like Lamia (577c) and Nanno (597a), in general they approached the status of the porne because they hailed from the brothel.[47] One of Theophrastus' characters speaks of instructing a servant to bring an auletris from the brothel (and so under the supervision of the *pornoboskos*) "that all of us might be entertained by her playing and be made glad" (*euphrainōmetha*, Theophr. *Char.* 20. 10). In Menander's *Epitrepontes*, Smikrines refers to the psaltria Habrotonon as a porne (646) who is expected to provide sexual favors to her clientele (431–41; Brown 1990: 249 and 263 n. 40). In Menander's *Perikeiromene*, the slave Daos explains to Moschion that in seducing Glycera, he must approach with caution as she is "no auletris, no wretched porne" (Davidson 1997: 82 and 329 n. 27). A few comic fragments similarly allude to flute girls offering their services to men on the streets, suggesting that they were not simply hired for their musical abilities alone.[48] An obscene joke about the orator Demeas recorded by Athenaeus plays on the association between flute playing and fellatio, presumably an extra service offered by the auletris at the symposium:

> You know that the orator Demades fathered Demeas from a flute-playing hetaera (*aulētridos hetairas*). Hyperides once silenced him as he snorted on the speaker's platform, saying: "Won't you be quiet, young man? You've got a bigger 'blow' (*to phusēma*) than your mother!" (591f)

Philocleon's entreaty to the auletris in Aristophanes' *Wasps* involves the same type of innuendo (Ar. *Vesp.* 1344–9). While the auletris, like the porne, may have been identified with casual sex and brothel slavery, she could escape her origins and gain a more enduring attachment much like the pallake. So Philocleon in Aristophanes' *Wasps* states that he will make the flute player his concubine, once he has freed her (*lusamenos hexō pallakēn*, Ar. *Vesp.* 1353).

The word auletris does not enter the Greek literary tradition until the late fifth century; most allusions occur in a sympotic context, whether in comedy, philosophical prose, or vase representations.[49] In Xenophon's *Symposium*, the Syracusan brings with him an auletris, an orchestris "able to do wonderous things," and a boy skilled at the cithara and dancing, with emphasis given to the youth and beauty of the latter (Xen. *Symp.* 2. 1. 3). In a reversal of normal sympotic protocol, Socrates dismisses the flute player at the beginning of Plato's *Symposium* with the words, "Let her play to herself, or if she wishes, to the women within" (Pl. *Symp.* 176e). The departure of the auletris signifies a shift to serious and sober conversation, while her return at the end of the dialogue, accompanied by Alcibiades and his revelers, marks a restoration of drunken festivity (*Symp.* 212c–d). A passage from the Hippocratic corpus similarly underlines the close association of the auletris with the symposium: one man allegedly suffered from a fear of flute girls, becoming frightened whenever he heard the sound of the flute at a symposium (Hippoc. *Epid.* 5. 81. 2). Like hetaeras and pornae, flute girls were associated with dissolute pleasures (Aeschin. 1. 42. 6, 75. 9) and youthful degeneracy (Isoc. *Areopagiticus* 48; *Antid.* 287), indulgences to be disdained by philosophers (Pl. *Theatetus* 173d).

The Eromene

The vocabulary of prostitution in Athenaeus and the Greek literary tradition also includes a neglected term that does not come into widespread use until the late fourth century: eromene (beloved) refers to the mistress, normally a hetaera, of a famous literary or political figure. While the word does not strictly allude to a prostitute, it often occurs in conjunction with other prostitution vocabulary: Lamia is thus a hetaera, an auletris, and the eromene of Demetrius Poliorcetes. The more familiar term *erōmenos*, the masculine passive participle of *eran* (be in love with), applies to the subordinate partner, normally a prepubescent boy, in the homoerotic relationship idealized by Socratic discourse. The vast majority of these references occur in philosophical texts, with some treatment in the comic poets and the orators; the paucity of instances in these latter two genres would suggest that calling a person an *erōmenos* did not constitute an insult.[50] In fact, the exclusive occurrence of this term in Aeschines' *Timarchus* markedly contrasts *erōmenoi*, "men who are loved chastely" (*tous dia sōphrosunēs erōmenous*), with those who practice brothel prostitution (*peporneumenous*, Aeschin. 1. 159).

The feminine eromene hardly appears at all in the classical period; an early example is found in Herodotus' account of Cambyses' incestuous love for his sister. A special dispensation from the royal judges allows him to circumvent Persian law and marry her, his eromene (*tote men dē ho Kambusēs egēme tēn erōmenēn*, Hdt. 3. 31). Not until Middle and New comedy does the term occur with any regularity: a fragment of Anaxippus speaks of a youth's mistress as devouring his patrimony (*meirakion erōmenēn/ echon patrōian ousian katesthiei*, Anaxippus F1. 31–32 KA = Ath. 9. 404c). It may refer to one of the twin courtesans in a fragment of the *Dis Exapaton* described as well-born and persuasive (*tēn kalēn te kagathēn/ idein erōmenēn an hed[e]ōs kenos/ pithaneuomenēn*, *Dis Exapaton* 92).[51] In the *Misoumenos*, it applies to Thrasonides' citizen concubine; in his invocation to night, the estranged soldier yearns for his eromene (*exon katheudein tēn t' erōmenēn echein*, A9 Sandbach).[52] In *Perikeiromene*, a play that concerns Glycera, a citizen foundling believed to be a hetaera, Moschion longs for a message from her, his putative eromene, but in actuality his sister, with her terms for a rendez-vous (*para tēs erōmenēs*, Men. *Pk.* 549 Sandbach). Another fragment, variously attributed, appears to speak of purchasing a "dainty eromene" (*habran gar antōnoumenos/ erōmenēn*, *Sicyonius* F1 Sandbach). The plot of Alexis' *Agonis* or *Hippiskos*, according to Athenaeus, concerned a young man who displays his wealth to his eromene, probably the hetaera Agonis (6. 230b).[53] Finally, in another Menandrian fragment, a speaker emphatically states that a father should neither make threats against his son nor conceive a passion for his eromene (*oudepot' alēthes ouden outh' huiōi patēr eiōth' apeilein out' erōn erōmenēi*, F663 Körte). Likewise, in Theophrastus' *Characters*, the man with bad timing serenades his eromene while she is sick (Theophr. *Char.* 12. 3. 1). Although eromene often refers, somewhat euphemistically, to hetaeras or putative hetaeras, citizen or foreign, it also denotes the lower-class counterparts of stock male characters, such as soldiers, for whom they exhibit a special affection.

The term eromene fits well with the obscure and often transitional status of most females in New comedy (Hunter 1989: 87). After all, Glycera undergoes several status changes in the course of *Perikeiromene*, "from a citizen by birth, to foundling, to concubine, *de facto* wife, imagined hetaira, to citizen once again" (Henry 1985: 76). It also accords with the emphasis on heterosexual union characteristic of New comedy, and the move away from the idealized pederasty promulgated by the philosophical texts. The eromene, and the hetaera, whether originally of foreign or citizen birth, provided a means for representing a new type of heterosexual courtship precluded by the ideology of female seclusion.[54] The new focus on the eromene at the end of the fourth century could reflect prevailing social trends in which restrictions placed on women may have became more relaxed, providing greater opportunities for female education and increased participation in public life (Pomeroy 1977).

In Athenaeus, the term eromene denotes the exclusive relationship of a woman, normally a hetaera, with a famous paramour (see Appendices III and IV); it occurs most frequently in the historiographical sources concerned with Persian kings or Hellenistic monarchs, but also in the context of Attic oratory. While some of the named mistresses, especially those connected with the Hellenistic monarchs, like Mysta, seem to have been exclusively referred to as eromenae, many, we are explicitly told, were also hetaeras or other types of prostitutes (see Appendix III for specific terms).[55] Curiously, most of these appear to have been flute players, as opposed to hetaeras, such as Mnesis, Potheine, the Samian Bacchis, and the notorious Lamia, or other entertainers at court, like the orchestris Philinna, the actress or mime Myrtion, and the wine pourer Cleino. But a few hetaeras, such as Leme and Leaena II are also called eromenae.

The term frequently crops up in Athenaeus' discussion of the orators and their mistresses, a phenomenon that shows the laxity with which the author deploys prostitution terminology. Although eromene is never found in extant oratory, it is nonetheless liberally applied by Athenaeus to the loves of the orators: for example, Metanira is called the eromene of Isocrates and Lysias, while the original source, pseudo-Demosthenes' *Against Neaera*, designates the latter orator as her *erastēs* (lover, [Dem.] 59. 21 = 592c). Similarly, Athenaeus adduces Lysias' *Against Philonides* as evidence that Nais functioned as the eromene of Philonides (Lys. F245 = 592c) and *Against Neaera* for proof of Nicarete as the eromene of Stephanus (593f). Neaera, in turn, is alleged to have been the eromene of several men, including Xenoclides the poet, Hipparchus the actor, and Phrynion (593f). Quoting Gorgias, the author of a Hellenistic courtesan treatise, Athenaeus similarly refers to the hetaera Leme as the eromene of the orator Stratocles (596f). Possibly Athenaeus, through the character of Myrtilus, attempts to imbue these liaisons with respectability by resorting to the word eromene instead of some of the more explicit terms for prostitutes discussed above. After all, even though Athenaeus attempts to construct an encomium of hetaeras, he must draw upon many sources that originally intended to work the opposite effect, as will be seen in the next chapter. It is more likely that Athenaeus' use of this term reflects his dependence on intermediary Hellenistic sources such as those of Hermippus, Idomeneus, and the various courtesan treatises, in which such terminology would have been commonplace.

Conclusion

The semantic distinctions in ancient Greek prostitution terminology, while never precise, had clearly eroded by the time of Athenaeus. So we find Lagisca alluded to as the eromene and pallake of Isocrates (592b–d) and as a hetaera (586e) who prostitutes herself as a porne (*porneuomenē*, 586e). Nemeas is simultaneously referred to as an auletris, a porne, and a hetaera (*hetairousa*, 587c). The celebrated Lais II is designated an eromene (588c), a hetaera, a spear captive (*aichmalōtos*, 588c), and a common whore (*koinē pornē*, 588e) while Lamia appears as an auletris (2. 101e; 3. 128b; 577c, 577d–f; 14. 614f), a porne (14. 614f), and an eromene (2. 101e; 3. 128b). Even an auletris could be designated a hetaera, or a hetaera an auletris, as in the case of the mother of Demades, or Boa, the mother of Philetaerus (577b), a practice that contradicts the identification of this figure with the porne in the classical period. Although these terms might at times be carelessly deployed in the *Deipnosophistae*, differences in social and economic status and in the activities ascribed to hetaeras and their brothel counterparts persist, and in fact, even structure some of the arguments in Book 13, as will be seen in the next chapter.

The ambiguity of prostitutional nomenclature both in the earlier periods as well as at the end of the second century C.E. reinforces the idea that courtesans and other types of prostitutes were outsiders with a transient and marginal social status. To be sure, citizen status even for Athenian males could be equally difficult to ascertain in some cases, and thus a source of considerable anxiety during the classical period (Patterson 1990: 45). Nonetheless, the social identity of prostitutes tended to be particularly fluid in the Greek literary tradition, if not in everyday life. Neaera, for example, began life as a slave and a foreigner in the house of Nicarete, then worked as a slave courtesan. After being sold two times, she assumed guardianship of herself and functioned as a free courtesan (*eis eleutherian,* [Dem.] 59. 40, 45; *autēn autēs kurian,* 46) until she began cohabiting with Stephanus "like a wife" (*autos de gunaika autēn hexōn*), or pallake ([Dem.] 59. 118, 122). Similarly, the fictional character Chrysis in Menander's *Samia* temporarily works as a free courtesan at Athens (Men. *Sam.* 21, 25 Sandbach), but later becomes the "hetaera wife" of the citizen Demeas (*gametēn hetairan,* 130 Sandbach). Later in the play, however, another character refers to her as a pallake, presumably because of her long-term liaison with Demeas (508 Sandbach). The reversibility of her position is underscored by the abuse Demeas heaps upon her when he wrongly suspects her of seducing his son, calling her a *chamaitupē* (ground beater, modifying *hē anthrōpos*, Men. *Sam.* 348 Sandbach), and threatening to turn her out on the streets (Men. *Sam.* 390–394 Sandbach). Such women could not always be distinguished from common law wives and thus lacked a precise legal and social vocabulary to define them. The hetaera's mutable and fluid identity made it easy for the literary tradition to transform her into a cultural sign that could embody a broad range of literary, social, political, and discursive issues from the archaic period to the late second century C.E. and beyond.

CHAPTER 1

Genres of Courtesans:
Athenaeus and Literary Nostalgia

Austro-Hungary is no more. I do not want to live anywhere else. . . . I shall live
on with the torso and imagine that it is whole.[1]

Nostalgia—the longing for a remote past and its imagined wholeness, figured by Freud as fragmented statuary—has long been considered the hall-
mark of Second Sophistic discourse.[2] Nostalgia cultivates distance and
therefore cannot ᴜe sustained without loss; at the same time, it is always
ideological in its quest for an absent past that has "never existed except as
narrative."[3] Nostalgia for classical Athens, not a lived experience but an
idealized, scholarly past found in libraries and monuments, fragments and
ruins, emerged as a central aspect of the construction and negotiation of
self-identity in the changing political environment of the first and second
centuries C.E., when Greeks in the eastern half of the empire confronted
the permanence of Roman dominion and the temporal remoteness of Hellenic power.[4] For Greeks living under Roman rule, identification with the
classical past, whether through the Greek language or Hellenic culture
more generally, afforded a sense of privilege and political empowerment.[5]

Nostalgia for an idealized past arguably did not originate in the Second
Sophistic period, but emerges as a consistent feature of the Greek literary
imagination from as early as Homer, from Nestor's evocation of past martial glories in Book 11 of the *Iliad*, to Demosthenes' late classical longings
for the glorious lost empire of fifth-century Athens.[6] To the sacralization of
public monuments, relics, and records already underway in the fourth century B.C.E., the Second Sophistic writers added an almost fetishistic preoccupation with the collection, preservation, and circulation of commentary

on the ruins and fragments of the classical past.[7] Although the writers of the Second Sophistic reconstituted Greece as an imaginary whole in their writings, the stark ruins of classical monuments confronted them on a daily basis with irrevocable loss. The fetishization of fragments, whether of classical monuments, or literary texts, provided a means of obliterating "the traumatic memory of the shattering of Greece" (Porter 2001: 84). Nowhere is this process more evident than in the text of Athenaeus, which overwhelms the reader with hundreds of disembodied quotations from the Greek literary tradition.[8] A similar process is at work in Book 13 of the *Deipnosophistae*, where the desire to recover an authentic Attic past is displaced onto the figure of the courtesan who is in turn fragmented and fetishized into a series of names, jokes, and monuments.

The foundations of the Second Sophistic movement can be traced to Alexander the Great's conquest of the east, Persia, and Egypt, and the subsequent dissemination of Hellenic culture and language throughout the ancient world. The consciousness of a golden era forever lost coupled with the consolidation of Hellenic power and its administration through the Antigonid, Seleucid, and Ptolemaic dynasties stimulated an unprecedented amount of scholarly activity geared at preserving, classifying, imitating, and transmitting the Greek literary past. Scholars like Aristophanes of Byzantium, with their burgeoning interests in lexicography, contributed to the privileging of Attic Greek language and literature in the educational system. At the same time, interest in the realia of classical Athens accompanied the study of language and literature (Bowie 1970: 28–9) with the result that local histories, prosopographies, and other scholarly works on Attic culture began to appear.

During the late Republic, Rome's expansion of its Mediterranean empire contributed to the decline of the Hellenistic Greek kingdoms. But the Greek city-state still remained intact in the east as the basic political unit and continued to be locally governed even under Roman rule. By the period of the Second Sophistic, the cities of old Greece, including Athens and those in Asia Minor, had become important urban centers of the sophistic world, while rural dwellings declined. This new "Greekness," it must be emphasized, was not always Attic, arising as it did from Asiatic cities such as Smyrna and Ephesus, a region associated in the classical period with decadence, luxury, and courtesans, a point discussed more fully in the next chapter.[9] Literary sources such as the Greek novel reflect these political and social changes, contrasting the Greek city as the center of Hellenic civilization with the barbarism of the countryside.[10] So, too, the return of the hetaera as a prevalent literary figure during this period signals the new emphasis on urbanism, a trope arguably as old as the origins of human civilization.[11]

For authors such as Tacitus and Juvenal, Greeks living in the eastern half of the empire represented an inversion of Roman values: over-civilized, obsequious, sexually perverse, and disingenuous in their way of life, they represented a threat to Roman stability. Roman administrators in the Greek east thus viewed their task as no less than moral reform, "saving imperial Greeks from their characteristic vices" (Woolf 1994: 124). According to Dionysius of Halicarnassus, the Romans, under the rule of the Augustan principate, were even responsible for salvaging and re-appropriating classical Greek oratory, which had yielded to a vulgar, histrionic, and deceptive rhetoric after the death of Alexander. The expansion of classical culture beyond Hellas to barbarian places is viewed as "the decline of civilization itself" (Gabba 1982: 46). Asianism became identified with the rhetoric of the masses, while Atticism became the intellectual property of the Greek elite, for whom Roman dominion enabled a resurgence of classical ideals (Gabba 1982: 47). In a compelling passage, Dionysius even goes so far as to represent Asianism's conquest of Greece as a hetaera that destroys the family estate and denigrates the free, lawful wife:[12]

> The ancient and indigenous Attic Muse, deprived of her possessions, had lost her civic rank, while her antagonist, an upstart that had arrived only yesterday from some Asiatic death-hole, a Mysian or Phrygian or Carian creature, claimed the right to rule over Greek cities, expelling her rival from public life. (Dion. Hal. *De ant. orat.* 1. 1. 4–5; trans. Usher)

Dionysius here plays on the association of hetaeras, and sophists, with Asia Minor, a trope reversed by Athenaeus in Book 13 of the *Deipnosophistae*, for whom the Euripides-quoting hetaera serves as a purveyor of pure Attic classicism, an idea explored more fully in Chapter 3.[13] As a cultural sign, the hetaera can convey a broad range of ethnic and cultural inflections because of her fluid social and political identity.

Roman culture, with the exception of law and the gladiatorial games, appears to have had little impact in the east, where strong Greek cultural identity persisted, in contrast to the Gallic and Hispanic cultures (Woolf 1994: 116); as a consequence, Roman emperors made little attempt to romanize this area. From the Roman perspective, the Greek inhabitants themselves asserted and celebrated a continuity with the past, to the extent that "Roman literary culture and education, so closely imitated and acquired at such a high price by westerners, was in the east generally ignored and occasionally reviled" (Woolf 2001: 117). While Greco-Latin bilingualism became the mark of Roman elite identity, the Greek elite of the eastern half of the empire did not absorb into their education specific elements of the Latin tradition, although they did incorporate architectural and other material elements.[14] The Romans had a sense of civilization and of their imperial mission, while the Greeks maintained a strong sense of continuous cultural and ethnic identity. The late Roman republican aristocracy had already appropriated the Greek cultural myth of a civilizing process at

work amid barbarians; this myth "provided Romans with one way of justi-
fying and understanding their experience in the Western provinces."[15] According to Pliny, it was the destiny of Romans to unite scattered realms and
disparate tongues to give *humanitas* to man.[16] Roman identity did not
stress common ancestry but rather membership in a political and religious
community; their political legends emphasized the progressive incorporation of outsiders into Roman society (Woolf 1994: 121).

Although Athenaeus has little to say about the fusion of Greek and
Roman cultures in the late second century C.E., his interest in the classical
past identifies him with contemporary issues of identity, *paideia*, and nostalgia.[17] Bowie's formulation that the political marginalization of Greeks
living in the Roman empire led to an increased need to assert their connection to an idealized classical past has continued to inform most studies of
the period.[18] Through literary activity, the Greeks of Imperial Rome paci-
fied their feelings of alienation and dislocation by reconnecting with the
Hellenic past.[19] Bowie theorized that the cultural activities of upper-class
Greeks during the Second Sophistic period expressed their discontent with
Roman rule and perhaps "fostered the illusion in some that a cultural
resurgence would somehow bring with it a restoration of political power
and independence."[20] Swain essentially seconds this view in his portrait of
elite Greeks living under Roman rule:

> In our period it was Rome—now permanently established as their political mas-
> ter and cultural rival—which particularly challenged them to say who they were.
> This is surely a key reason behind the intensified awareness of their Greekness. It
> also accounts for its mode of expression. For since Greek identity could not be
> grounded in the real political world, it had to assert itself in the cultural domain
> and do so as loudly as possible. (Swain 1996: 89–90)

Both Bowie and Swain in my view draw too sharp a distinction between
Roman dominion and Greek subordination: in the blurring of cultural,
ethnic, and temporal boundaries that characterizes Second Sophistic literary activity, no absolute, unified identity for either culture emerges.[21] And
it should be remembered that "Greekness" in this period was infused with
Asiatic permutations and in that sense bore little resemblance to the construction of political and literary solidarity prevalent in classical Athens.

In contrast, Gabba has emphasized the cultural and political symbiosis
of the Greeks and Romans during the late second century C.E. Rather than
feeling oppressed by Roman rule and alienated from their past, some
Greeks actually profited from their dependence upon the Romans. The ad-
ministrative branch of the Roman empire provided a stable power base for
Greek elite, helping them to acquire influence while excluding or subordi-
nating the uneducated masses (Gabba 1982: 48–49). Linguistic purity—
exemplified by the character of Ulpian in Athenaeus' *Deipnosophistae* (3.

97c–e)—and knowledge of classical *paideia*—demonstrated by all of the interlocutors at Athenaeus' table—served as a status-markers that distinguished the elite, educated classes, both Greek and Roman, from everyone else.[22] Through a shared intellectual heritage and mythology, Greek and Roman cultures became fused to such a degree that Dionysius of Halicarnassus could assert Greek origins of Roman foundation through the figure of the Corinthian Demaratus. These Hellenic ideals paved the way for Imperial Roman society; indeed, as Gabba has argued, the glorification of Greece could only occur "within the framework of an acceptance of Rome's empire" (Gabba 1982: 64–5).

Certainly, being Greek under Rome did not simply signify an ethnic identification, but a "stake in the empire-wide aristocratic competition for status," negotiated by education and self-display (Whitmarsh 2001: 273). Moreover, this identity was not stable but had to be continually renegotiated through literary and rhetorical activity. In contrast to classical Athens, identity for urban Greeks living under Roman rule was not constituted by political enfranchisement in the polis (Arist. *Pol.* 1253a1–4; Whitmarsh 2001: 271). Instead, self-identity was increasingly based on celebrity performance and rhetorical posturing before a broad public and exemplified by the widespread popularity of the *epideixis* or rhetorical display (Bowie 1970: 6). The display speech borrowed from Greek New comedy its interest in *ethopoeia*, the delineation of stock character types that could easily be translated across cultural and temporal boundaries. Athenaeus' *Deipnosophistae* provides a stunning example of this type of literary *epideixis* in its depiction of competitive sophists anxious to display their compendious literary knowledge.

Epideictic display reflected the mechanics of rhetorical education in the late empire, in which pupils learned basic exercises of speech construction (*progymnasmata*), preliminary essays in narration (*mythos, diegema*), description (*ecphrasis*) and argument, comparison, and praise and blame. The content drew on stock fictitious events and circumstances, which, according to van Groningen, "diverted attention from reality and enclosed a spiritual vacuum within the four walls of a classroom."[23] Rhetorical literature, exemplified in the Severan period by authors such as Alciphron and Athenaeus, aimed both to entertain and to amaze listeners with displays of erudition.[24] Praise and blame speeches had a particularly strong influence on the formation of this literature; handbooks encouraged speakers to take liberties with the encomium, presenting negative qualities in as positive a light as possible. This technique is exemplified in the humorous praise of worthless or lower things, known as the paradoxical encomium, that originates in Gorgias' *Helen* but takes on new life in the Second Sophistic period: witness Libanius' praise of the unworthy Thersites, Lucian's Fly, Fronto's encomia of Sleep (Haines vol. 2. 12–8), Smoke, and Dust (Haines vol. 1. 38–44), and Favorinus' glorification of Quartan Fever (Aul. Gell. *NA* 17. 12. 3ff.).[25] As the final section of this chapter demonstrates, Myrtilus' discourse on courtesans in Book 13 of the *Deipnosophistae* makes use of just this rhetorical technique.

Declamations on fictitious topics, both historical and judicial, often set in classical Athens, had become standard components of rhetorical education by the beginning of the principate; a century later both rhetors and sophists displayed their skills in public performances that began to vie with the theater in popularity.[26] Herodes Atticus declaimed in Agrippa's theater at Athens, while others performed in the great sophistic centers of Smyrna and Ephesus. By the second half of the second century C.E., a group of important sophists, including Athenaeus, had emerged from the Greek city of Naucratis, a trading post on the Nile Delta and the place where Sappho's brother allegedly fell in love with a local courtesan.[27] Sophists were normally of good birth, possessed of considerable means and thus could make benefactions that would elevate them to the highest ranks of Roman society, e.g., the equestrian and senatorial orders.[28] The category of sophists encompassed both rhetors and philosophers, although its use appears to have been restricted to only very accomplished speakers.[29]

These "second" sophists exemplified the importance of *paideia* in defining elite identity. Through *paideia*, the elite were bound together by a common set of civilizing ideals that separated them from the lower classes (Anderson, G. 1993: 8). In his autobiographical work *Dream*, Lucian, born between 115–125 C.E. at Samosata, a city of Roman Syria, allies himself with a personified *Paideia* who promises to rescue him from a life of menial labor (cf. Lucian *Som.* 9–13; Swain 1996: 309). The literary and cultural activities of the Second Sophistic period therefore belonged almost entirely to upper-class Greeks: "The leading idea was that the ancients were the ones to emulate: their works had to be properly interpreted, as the only possible sources of knowledge and guidance."[30] Erudition, whether it took the form of language purism, or a general knowledge of the Hellenic past, helped strengthen elite Greek identity in Imperial Rome.

As literary figures, hetaeras were uniquely adapted to the Second Sophistic milieu. Their chameleon-like status as both Asiatic and Attic, their pervasive association with urban life, as well as their widespread and continuous appearance in rhetorical and comic genres throughout the Greek tradition made them well suited to conveying contemporary concerns with cultural identity, *paideia*, and tradition.[31] As stock comic characters, they had a broad cultural appeal and translated well across cultural boundaries, while the decline in drama intensified interest in conventional *ethopeia*, in which courtesans figured prominently.[32] Their marginal social status also appealed to the aesthetic of sophistic paradox, which made them disseminators of classical Athenian heritage and contemptuous mockers of philosophers and other pretentious intellectuals.

The new emphasis on marriage as mutually fulfilling, a trend influenced by the rise of Stoicism in the Greek novel, may have also contributed to their popularity in literature (Swain 1996: 120–1). For this reason, hetaeras commonly figure in conventional sophistic debates about heterosexual versus homosexual love, exemplified by Plutarch's *Essay on Love* and Achilles Tatius' *Leucippe and Clitophon,* in which the hero states he has frequented prostitutes in his defense of the erotic charms of women (2. 35–38). In Lucian's *Amores,* the Platonic ideal of homosexual love is shown to be untenable; similar debates frame Books 5 and 13 of the *Deipnosophistae,* as I will show below.[33] Swain argues that the shift from homosexual to heterosexual orientation during the Second Sophistic period resulted from the decreased importance of marriage for political advancement in the Roman empire; contracted on a voluntary basis, marriages could now promote equality and mutuality. The courtesan, with her obscure social status, by turns possessing the refinement of a respectable matron and yet sexually available, served as the perfect literary vehicle for representing heterosexual desire as early as the comedies of the late fourth century. So Plutarch in his *Table Talk* commends New comedy with its hetaeras as a genre that awakens desire for one's wife, since it does not depict any eros for boys.[34]

Athenaeus and the Literary Symposium

Athenaeus' oeuvre belongs to the body of rhetorical literature from the Severan period, making him a contemporary of Philostratus, although the precise dating of the *Deipnosophistae* has provoked much debate.[35] The author also wrote a history of the Syrian Kings (5. 211a), and a commentary on Archippus' *Ichthyes* (Fishes), a comic play (7. 329c). The text of the *Deipnosophistae* survived from late antiquity to the Middle Ages as one manuscript, the Marcianus Codex, a mutilated copy of the original work, probably divided into fifteen books by Athenaeus himself.[36] The extant manuscript lacks all of Books 1 and 2, most of 11 and portions of 15.[37] A late Byzantine epitome, made from a better text than Marcianus, survives in four copies, which omit some of the original quotations and conversational exchanges, and most of the source attributions.[38]

By the time of Athenaeus, the literary symposium had become a well-developed genre, or as one scholar put it, "an overdetermined literary event, freighted with a rich cargo of allusion," along with conventional characters, debates, and discourses.[39] In Book 13, for example, Athenaeus alludes to three earlier sympotic works, including Plato's *Symposium,* and two more obscure sources, Persaeus of Citium's *Sympotic Notes,* and the courtesan Gnathaena's *Table Manners.* The genre originates in the classical period with the Socratic symposia of Plato and Xenophon, or even earlier, in the salacious after-dinner story of the adulterous Aphrodite which Odysseus tells to the Phaeacians in the *Odyssey* (Hom. *Od.* 8. 266–369). As a literary genre, the symposium encourages joke telling, risqué anecdotes, and comic action as a foil to serious philosophical discussion. Even in Plato's *Symposium,* Aristophanes' jester-like hiccup (*gelōtopoios,* Pl. *Symp.* 185c–e; 189a–b) and Alcibiades' drunken entrance with an auletris (Pl. *Symp.* 212d) interrupt an otherwise serious (and sober) round of speechifying.[40] This combination of seriousness and humor also characterizes Xenophon's *Symposium,* in which Socrates proposes to recount not only the serious deeds of great men (*kalōn kagathōn*) but also the things done in jest (*tais paidiais,* Xen. *Symp.* 1.1).[41] While the epitomator claims that Athenaeus evokes or imitates this Socratic tradition (*zelōi Platonikōi,* 1. 2a), the endless preoccupation with the trifles of table and the repeated criticism of the Cynics for their rejection of pleasure leaves little room for serious philosophical discussion, suggesting instead an ironic parody of its literary antecedents.[42]

From the genre of the *deipnon,* of which no complete example survives, Athenaeus seems to have borrowed his parodic catalogues of sympotic accoutrements, and perhaps also some of his discourse on hetaeras. As a poetic genre, the *deipnon* has exemplars in Timachidas of Rhodes, Numenius of Heraclea, Hegemon of Thasos, and Matro of Pitane, a parodist of the fourth century B.C.E. The latter composed a work entitled *Deipnon Attikon* (Attic Dinner Party), an eroticized account of the delicacies of the table delivered as an epic parody and apparently already an obscure work by the time of Athenaeus. He excerpts it at 4. 134d–137c.[43] Matro's *Deipnon* featured stock comic characters such as the parasite, the cook, the slave, and the prostitute.[44] The *deipnon* of Hegemon, another parodist mentioned by Aristotle with a possible floruit of the late fifth century B.C.E. also featured similar parodic characters (Martin, J. 1931: 157). Several prose versions of the *deipnon* genre are mentioned by Athenaeus, including that of the fifth-century author Chaerephon (6. 244a); the *Deipnetikai Epistolai* (Dinner Letters) of Lynceus of Samos, a writer of *apomnemoneumata* important for Book 13, and Hippolochus the Macedonian.[45]

The reconstruction of learned conversations, nascent in the symposia of Plato and Xenophon, found special favor among writers of the second century C.E. Aulus Gellius' *Attic Nights* recounts such sophistic feats as Favorinus' lengthy exegesis on the Greek names of winds, and Herodes' extensive quotation of Arrian's "Epictetus" in response to an pretentious table mate (Aul. Gell. *NA* 2. 22.1–27; 1.2; Anderson, G. 1997: 2177). In contrast to the considerable rhetorical and philosophical finesse exhibited by the speeches in Plato's *Symposium*, these narratives are motivated by a sophistic obsession with epideictic display and literary showmanship. So the epitomator informs his readers that the *Deipnosophistae* recounts the fine sayings of educated men, "men most learned in every kind of *paideia*. . . . Not one of their excellent sayings (*tōn kallistōn*) has Athenaeus failed to remember" (1. 1a–b). The conversation takes place among gentlemen (*kaloi kai agathoi*), intent on speaking in an elegant and orderly fashion (*kosmiōs*), without the distractions of flute and dancing girls (3. 97a–b). As the purveyors of the Greek literary tradition made available by public and private libraries, the symposiasts deliver disquisitions rather than engaging in dialogues, they recite decontextualized "fine sayings" and itemized catalogues rather than rhetorically well-crafted speeches. Indeed, the epitomator immediately makes us aware of the fact that this is a *book*, not a conversation:

> For he has placed in his book an account of fishes, explaining their uses and their names and derivations; also vegetables of all sorts and every kind of animal; historians, poets, philosophers, musical instruments, and numerous kinds of jests. . . . (1. 1b)

The historians and poets alluded to in this passage are not actual characters, but references and quotations mentioned by all of the various speakers at Athenaeus' table. The author creates for his readers a veritable library replete with bibliographers and librarians, who come to the table with huge bundles of books (1. 4b), little speeches (*logaria*, 8. 331b–c; 6. 270d), and promises of lending scrolls to one another (556b).[46] Indeed, one speaker at the beginning of Book 13 mentions that he will send to one of his fellow diners a book by Hieronymous of Rhodes that mentions an Athenian decree on bigamy (556b).

Although Athenaeus sets the banquet at the home of the Roman Larensis, he rarely alludes to any aspect of Roman culture, thereby collapsing any sense of cultural or ethnic distinction.[47] A conversation at dinner between Athenaeus and the young Timocrates—probably a fictional character meant to evoke the philosophy teacher of the sophist Polemo—who wants to hear reports of the banquets of Larensis, forms the narrative framework (1. 2a).[48] Indeed, almost all of the books begin and end with an exchange between Athenaeus and Timocrates (Wilkins 2000: 23). Athenaeus further borrows from the sympotic tradition several stock characters, including the host, entertainers such as musicians and clowns; doctors; the uninvited guest; the weeper; and the heavy drinker.[49] Noteworthy is the absence of hetaeras or female entertainers, such as the auletris, and the amorous couple, a role played by Socrates and Alcibiades in Plato's *Symposium*. The guest list includes a range of historical and fictitious personages, or aggregates of both: the narrator Athenaeus, the Roman host Larensis, the addressee Timocrates, the doctor Galen, and the

Atticist pedant Ulpian.[50] All are "sophists" in the sense that they represent the learned professions. Their facility for display and their role as encyclopedic authorities identifies them with the most generally acknowledged characteristics of Imperial sophists.[51] Moreover, the intermingling of historical personages, quasi-historical names, and purely fictitious individuals creates a seamless realm of Greek *paideia*, not bound to any specific time or place.

The largest professional category represented at Athenaeus' table is that of the grammarians: Aemilianus Maurus; Arrian, referred to as "the great Roman sophist" (*megalosophistēs*, 3. 113a–d); Myrtilus, the primary speaker after Ulpian and Cynulcus, and the encomiast of hetaeras in Book 13; Palamedes the Eleatic lexicographer (9. 397a); Philadelphus of Ptolemais, a silent participant (1. 1d); Plutarch of Alexandria, who, according to Kaibel, might have dominated book 12, where no speakers are assigned; Varus, who delivers a speech on pickled fish (3. 118d–e); and Zoilus. The party also includes four doctors, stock figures in sympotic literature beginning with Eryximachus in Plato's *Symposium* and a real-life convention of the second century C.E. (Baldwin 1977: 43): Rufinus of Nicaea, mentioned in name only (1. 1f); Daphnus of Ephesus; Dionysocles; and Galen.[52] The physicians do not participate much in the conversation, perhaps reflecting Athenaeus' disdain for the profession stated in Book 15: "If it were not for the doctors, there would not be anything more insipid than grammarians" (15. 666a).[53]

The banquet includes four philosophers, who are not always distinguishable from the grammarians; the major exception is Cynulcus, the nickname of Theodorus (4. 160d), the Cynic opponent of Ulpian and second most frequent speaker. Other philosophers are the polymaths Democritus and Pontianus, both of Nicomedia (1. 1d); and Leonidas of Elis, who is praised, along with a few of the grammarians, as an elegant critic.[54] Also at table are two musicians, Alceides of Alexandria (4. 174b–185a) and Amoebeus (14. 622d–23d); one jurist, Masurius, also a well-known polymath and poet with a specialty in Archilochian satire, as well as proficient in music (14. 623e); and one gourmand, Magnus, described as having a passion for the table (*philotrapezos*, 3. 113e). Magnus is possibly a Roman, and the only guest not formally associated with a profession (Baldwin 1977: 44–5).

According to the epitomator, the plan of the discourse reflects the abundance of the feast, and the arrangement of the books, the courses of the dinner (*hē tēs biblou diaskeuē tēs en tōi deipnōi*, 1. 1b). In Lukinovich's words, "each episode of the banquet has been constructed by the author around the discussion for which it is the pretext."[55] The main courses start appearing at the end of Book 5, while the meal concludes and the symposium begins midway through Book 10 (Wilkins 2000: 23). To summarize the topics: the literature of food, food and drink in Homer, and wine, occupy Book 1; in Books 2–3, the symposiasts turn to appetizers and bread; Book 4 deals with the organization of meals and music; in Book 5, the subject is lavish display and luxury; Book 6 concerns parasites and flattery; Books 7–8 introduce the subject of entrées, beginning with fish, and followed by meat and poultry in Book 9; the talk of food raises the subject of gluttony, and more wine, in Book 10; Book 11 covers cups and Book 12, social behavior; Book 13 praises erotic love; and in Book 14, the conversation shifts to music and desserts, then to wreathes and perfume in Book 15.[56] The *Deipnosophistae* also contains a large number of digressions on sympotic elements, presented as inventories, including drinking cups (11. 465c–504c), fish (7. 276e–8. 334f; 337b–348a), gluttons (10. 411a–18d) and hetaeras, the subject of Book 13 (571a–610b). Athenaeus even provides a humorous parody of the most famous example of the genre, the Homeric catalogue of ships (5. 203e–9e; Lukinovich 1990: 268).

Genres of Courtesans: Athenaeus and the Literary Quotation

Even as recently as Dihle, the standard view of Athenaeus' *Deipnosophistae* as an encyclopedic compilation with little literary merit, valuable only for its thousands of quotations of lost sources—particularly Middle and New comedy—has prevailed.[57] Indignant critics have characterized the work as "swollen" (Bowie 1985: 682); "a great gallimaufry" (Relihan 1992: 227); "a most peculiar piece" (Dihle 1994: 345); "a garrulous orgy of philosophical pedantry" (Anderson, G. 1993: 72); and a "Sargasso sea" (Henry 1995: 153 and n. 1). In dismissing Athenaeus as a collector of quotations strung together by a fragile narrative thread, these scholars have paid little attention to the possible meanings of his disjointed and fragmentary discourse and the larger narrative context in which these quotations are embedded.[58] To grapple with Athenaeus is to confront problems of quotation and collection, authenticity and origin, cultural identity and dislocation.

The hundreds of authors and texts quoted in the *Deipnosophistae* reflect the contemporary subject matter of the schools, including Homer, tragedy, oratory, Plato, Xenophon, and historians of the early Hellenistic period. For the most part, Athenaeus identified authors and works precisely, and then rendered quotations as accurately as possible.[59] In some places, he appears to be copying straight from a literary text. Some of the briefer quotes may have been taken from intermediaries such as glossaries and commentaries, and are, in effect, quotations of quotations. Many of the classical sources were probably transmitted by various Hellenistic treatises: so when Athenaeus refers to the famous trial of Phryne, he relies on the Hellenistic biographer Hermippus who in turn borrowed from Idomeneus of Lam-pascus, rather than on the original speech of Hyperides (590d–e). This amassing of sources may reflect the historical patterns of ancient libraries, from city or court libraries to the Roman private collections of mostly old Greek books, and exemplified in the text by the Roman host, Larensis.

Like the epigram and the proverb, the literary quotation functions as "a piece of free-floating discourse that speaks to all times and places" (Stewart, S. 1993: 53); in Athenaeus, it decontextualizes discourse and creates a timeless, imaginary space detached from contemporary political life. Even quotations from quite different genres, authors, and periods lose their authenticity and become strangely homogeneous in the fabric of Athenaeus' narrative. Moreover, the privileging of classical and Hellenistic sources further contributes to the aura of an authoritative, canonized Greek literary space far removed from the present, as does the very obscurity of many of the quotations. In her work, *On Longing*, Susan Stewart provocatively illuminates the paradox of the literary quotation:

> The quotation appears as a severed head, a voice whose authority is grounded in itself, and therein lies its power and its limit. For although the quotation now speaks with the voice of history and tradition, a voice "for all times and places," it has been severed from its context of origin and of original interpretation, a context which gave it authenticity. Once quoted, the utterance enters the arena of social conflict. . . . It is no longer the possession of its author; it has only the authority of use. (Stewart, S. 1993: 20)

Athenaeus engages in a similar paradox: by removing the quotation from its original context, he renders it timeless and universal; at the same time, its attribution to a particular author imbues it with a degree of cultural authority. Quotation also very literally engages in the arena of social conflict as speakers compete for discursive status; through this process, they reconstruct classical Athens and its literary tradition and yet simultaneously diminish the totality of that imaginary in a continual process of restoration and disillusionment.[60]

Quotations in Athenaeus serve another important function, and one not always fully appreciated by his contemporary readers: however fragmentary, they reflect the constraints and biases of their genres and original contexts (for a list of works appearing in Book 13, see Appendix I). So the ostensible quarrel between the philosopher Cynulcus and the grammarian Myrtilus that frames Book 13 about erotic proclivities is simultaneously a war of genres, realized in fragments of texts, between the "high" philosophical genres and the "low" genres of courtesan treatises, Greek comedy, and sundry erotica. Moreover, the polemical nature of many of the sources slants the representation of courtesans in significant ways and substantially hinders access to historical women. Before turning to the quarrel it-self, and to the structure of Book 13 more generally, it is necessary to con-sider the different genres that Athenaeus draws upon to construct his discourse of courtesans. He borrowed from a broad range of texts and gen-res, mostly from late classical and early Hellenistic Athens, including comic poetry, oratory, historiography, prosopography, collections of anecdotes, and periegetic works.[61]

Central to Athenaeus' enterprise is Greek comedy of all periods; one diner boasts of having read and excerpted more than 800 titles of Middle Comedy (8. 336d).[62] To 57 poets Athenaeus attributes more than 800 plays; the most important are Anaxandrides, Antiphanes, Alexis, Eubulus, and Timocles.[63] Because so many Middle and New comedies featured hetaeras as characters, the genre is especially important to Book 13, and to scholarly discourse about them more generally.[64] The popularity of hetaeras in this genre in turn influenced the biographical tradition and its numerous ac-counts of the amorous liaisons of comic poets with hetaeras, such as that of Diphilus and Gnathaena, since ancient biographers often equated the lives of poets with their literary subjects (Lefkowitz 1981 and 1983). Athenaeus himself provides a good example of this process in his discussion of the lyric poets (13. 600f–604f). That Attic old comedy did not develop courtesans as literary characters as fully as Middle and New comedies, but rather alluded to historical women as part of its political humor, explains the smaller num-ber of references to this genre in Book 13.[65] Generally speaking, Athenaeus most often draws on the comic plays for their prosopographical references, as a resource for hetaeras' names, and to a lesser extent, for their extended descriptions of their lives and the men with whom they consorted.

With no complete play extant, the fragments of Middle comedy are dif-ficult to assess; in the case of New comedy, one must rely only on Menan-der's fragmentary corpus, since his only complete play lacks a hetaera.[66] The genres of Middle and New comedy replaced the obscenity of Attic old comedy with innuendo and a focus on legitimate marriage, and contained less of the political critique so central to Aristophanes.[67] Play titles suggest the representation of contemporary types, manners and pursuits; virtually all of the stock comic figures—soldiers, courtesans, parasites, pimps, cooks, angry or avaricious old men—can be identified in the fragments and titles of Middle comedy. Although it is frequently difficult to distin-guish historical from fictitious courtesans in the comic fragments, the shift away from mythic titles and plots after 350 B.C.E. toward plays named after contemporaries does suggest at least some of the characters were drawn from real life.[68]

Many of the plays of Middle and New comedy alluded to actual hetaeras well known to their contemporary Athenian spectators, although it is often difficult to link these characters directly to historical individuals. For example, the title character of Alexis' *Opora* could have been either a "caricature of a real person," like the heroines of Eubulus' *Clepsydra* and *Nannion* and Timocles' *Neaera*; a deglamorized or faded goddess that symbolized the vintage; or a fictive persona (Arnott 1996: 596–600). On the basis of Webster's principle that one may assume a play is named after a historical person "if a suitable contemporary is known to exist," at least some of the over forty titles of Middle and New comedy found in Book 13 can be correlated to historical hetaeras.[69] Numbered among those cited by Athenaeus are *Clepsydra*, *Chrysilla*, and *Nannion* by Eubulus; Philip's *Nannion*; and the *Anteia* by either Eunicus or Philyllius (567c). The two plays entitled *Neaera* by Philemon and Timocles and Epicrates' *Antilais* are especially intriguing because of their parallels in oratory. The plays appear to have been produced after the prosecutions of these hetaeras, recounted in [Demosthenes'] *Against Neaera*, discussed more fully in the last chapter, and Lysias' *Against Lais*, of which we have only the title and exiguous fragments. An even stronger case can be made when a courtesan is linked to a specific historical person, but even then the connections between the titles of comic plays and those of orations can only be conjectured. Whatever the case, it is clear that both genres drew on the same cultural prosopography for their material.

Other comic play titles may have alluded to fictional hetaeras in their use of generic names, nicknames, or other terms associated with them. Thus the titles of Menander's *Chrysis*, *Phanion*, and *Thais* may reflect common female names, which, like the comic mask, identified their fictional characters as hetaeras (Webster 1974: 94). *Neottis* (Chick), the title of separate plays by Anaxilas, Antiphanes, and Eubulus, probably also featured a fictional hetaera, given that there is no known real hetaera of this name. Webster speculates that it dealt with the rescue of a young hetaera from her pimp by a lover (Webster 1952: 26). Similar are the *Thalatta* plays of Diocles and Pherecrates, and the *Opora* (Harvest) of Alexis. Eubulus' *Stephanopolides* (Wreath Sellers), Menander's *Auletris*, and Posidippus' *Ephesia*, all play on occupations or regions associated with hetaeras. It is possible, too, that the plots of Antiphanes' *Halieuomene* (Female Fish Monger) and Philtaerus' *Cynagis* (Huntress), may have revolved around hetaeras, given their association with gender inversions, and the number of fragments from these plays that feature prostitutes. The centrality and significance of names and naming in Attic comedy of all periods renders it an important source of material for the Hellenistic grammarians and their treatises on courtesans, as will be seen below.

Another major genre that influences Athenaeus' discourse on hetaeras is Attic oratory; but instead of examining the charges against the women or the content of the speeches, Athenaeus simply mines them for names (see

Appendix III). The material also provides an opportunity to expatiate on the liaisons of orators and hetaeras, a favorite defamatory technique among the fourth century demagogues and a theme of later historians. Although Attic oratory typically alluded to known contemporaries, the genre frequently combined fact with fiction; even in the case of historical personages, the orators fabricated characteristics or circumstances to serve their rhetorical ends.[70] To judge from the titles found in Book 13, a large number of these speeches revolved around the defense or prosecution of hetaeras, although most of these are now lost. One might speculate that at least some of these speeches were showpieces ultimately meant for entertainment rather than for the courts. Certainly the eulogies of *Lagis* by Cephalus and *Nais* by Alcidamas mentioned by Athenaeus exemplify the importance of hetaeras as subjects of epideictic oratory.

The trial of Aspasia, in which she was prosecuted by the comic poet Hermippus for impiety and for procuring free-born women for Pericles, probably served as the prototype for the representations of courtesans in fourth-century oratory, although she herself was mostly likely a *pallake*.[71] The most famous extant speech from a courtesan trial, to which Athenaeus alludes several times, is Apollodorus' prosecution of Neaera depicted in pseudo-Demosthenes' *Against Neaera*. The speech mentions not only Neaera, using the contemptuous phrase *Neaira hautēi*, it also identifies several other women of ill-repute, including the procuress Nicarete and the seven girls whom she employed, presumably courtesans-in-training; Neaera's daughter, Phano; as well as the names of four of her servants. Other courtesan speeches mentioned by Athenaeus but now lost include Hyperides' *Against Aristagora* (Hyp. FF5–6 Jensen), Lysias' *Against Lais* (F59 Thalheim), and a group of speeches related to the trial of Phryne.

Like Aspasia before her, Phryne was accused of impiety for introducing a foreign cult centered on Isodaitos (Cooper 1995: 305–306 and n. 9). As discussed more fully in Chapter 4, Hyperides' *Defense of Phryne* (FF171–80 Jensen) and its disrobing scene later became quite famous in the rhetorical tradition. Athenaeus' derived his account of the oration at 590d–e from the third century biographer Hermippus (not the comic poet), who had in turn adapted the story from Idomeneus' polemic on the Athenian demagogues (Cooper 1995: 304). Other prosecution speeches mentioned by Athenaeus include *Against Phryne* by Aristogeiton, and another *Against Phryne* composed for Euthias by Anaxamenes, neither of which is extant. The attribution of prosecution speeches against Phryne to several different authors suggests that they may not have been intended for the law court, but as rhetorical exercises or some other form of *epideixis*. Such notorious trials became fodder for comedy, as we saw above; in a fragment of Posidippus, *Ephesia* (F13 KA = 591f), the poet describes Phryne as clasping the hand of each of the jurors as she wept in supplication for her life, a description which suggests that the disrobing scene may have been a later invention.[72]

Other speeches are cited by Athenaeus for including the names of historical courtesans: in *Against Androtion*, the orator alludes to Phanostrate and Sinope, the hapless prostitutes victimized by the rapacious defendant (13. 585f–86a; cf. Dem. 22. 56). Similarly, Hyperides mentions the names Nannion and Nemeas in *Against Patrocles* (587a; cf. FF141–42 Jensen), while *Against Aristagora* appeared to have contained a virtual who's who of Athenian hetaeras, including Lais, Metanira, Ocimon, Philyra, Phryne, and Stagonion (587d; cf. FF13, 24).[73] The orator in Lysias provides a similar array of names in his lost courtesan speech, *Against Lais*, which made reference, again according to Athenaeus, to the hetaeras Antheia, Aristoclea, Hippaphesis, Lagisca, Lais, Psamathe, Scione, and Theocleia (586e). Hetaeras are also mentioned in several of Lysias' extant speeches including Oia/Anticyra in *Against Medon*, Medontis in *Against Axiochus*, and Nais in *Against Philonides* and Eirenis in Lycurgus' only extant speech. Given the tendency of ancient biographers to cull the facts of their subjects' lives from their literary works, it is no surprise to learn that liaisons with courtesans are frequently attributed to orators, especially Demosthenes and Hyperides, just like the comic poets.

Athenaeus also drew extensively in Book 13 from fourth-century and Hellenistic historians, a category that includes genres of biography, prosopography, paradoxography, and periegetic literature. From these sources, he borrowed not only the names of famous courtesans, but information about their liaisons with various men, particularly the Hellenistic monarchs, their heroic actions, and the monuments and dedications connected with them. Apart from Theopompus and Polemon, a majority of these authors appear to have been Peripatetics associated with the circles of Aristotle and Theophrastus. Interest in paradoxography, such as fantastic animal tales, as well as a fascination with ethnography and geography, permeates the work of Peripatetic writers such as Clearchus of Soli, as well as Duris, among whom there are close parallels, and Hieronymus of Rhodes (Kebric 1977: 28–9). The moralizing tendencies evident among these authors, especially their interest in the details of wanton luxury, may also explain the presence of courtesans in their works.

Duris and his brother Lynceus studied under Theophrastus, who occasions several references in Book 13 in connection with his erotic treatise (*Peri tōi Erōtikōi*). This work is cited as a source for various topics, although none explicitly concerned with hetaeras: female beauty contests at Elis (609f), female competitions of *sophrosynē* (modesty) and housekeeping (610a), the fourth century tragic poet Chaeremon's comparison of eros to drinking (562e), and the sexual expertise of Amasis of Elis (567b). Another

Peripatetic, Clearchus of Soli (320 to 250 B.C.E.), a contemporary of Duris and Lynceus, recorded proverbs and paradoxes, and composed sensationalist biographies and erotica. Athenaeus also mentions his erotic treatise (*Peri tōi Erōtikōi*), which bears the same title as that of his mentor Theophrastus, several times in the course of Book 13. The work dealt with subjects such as beauty (564a–b), the excessive passion of great men for their mistresses, including Gyges (573a), Pericles (589d), and the poets Antimachus and Lamynthius (597a), and even the sayings of courtesans (605d). To judge by his comment about the sexual incontinence of Epameinondas of Thebes, the work may have had a moralizing tone (590c). Like his contemporaries, Clearchus had a fascination with paradox and marvels, which are described at 606c.

Another Peripatetic, Hieronymus of Rhodes (290 to 230 B.C.E.), was an Antigonid court apologist best known for his history of the successors of Alexander; although far older than Duris, he may have written in reaction to the latter's anti-Macedonian polemic (Kebric 1977: 46 and n. 85). From his oeuvre, Athenaeus borrows a reference to a decree allowing men to marry two wives (556b), stories about the erotic inclinations of the tragic poets Euripides (557e) and Sophocles (604d), as well as an account of the origins of pederasty (602a–b). Idomeneus of Lampascus (325 to 265 B.C.E.), a friend of Epicurus and also a contemporary of Duris, wrote in an anecdotal manner similar to the Peripatetics (Kebric 1977: 42–3). Athenaeus draws on his work for the story about Themistocles' yoking of four hetaeras to a chariot, an anecdote also found in Matro's *deipnon*, as well as his work on Athenian demagogues that detailed the licentiousness of orators such as Hyperides (590d) and Demosthenes (593f), as discussed above. The Peripatetic Satyrus (fl. 3rd century), known for his entertaining historical fiction, composed a set of biographies entitled *Lives* that Athenaeus mined for stories about famous wives, including those of Socrates (573c) and Philip of Macedon (599c–d), as well as a fictionalized exchange between the philosopher Stilpo and the courtesan Glycera.[74]

The lively stories of the fourth-century historian Theopompus of Chios (b. 378/7) also contributed to Athenaeus' discourse on hetaeras.[75] They deal with dedications made by various men on behalf of their mistresses (605a–d), on the prayers of Corinthian hetaeras in times of civic crisis (573d), and on the beauty of Xenopeitheia, the mother of Lysandridas (609b). Much of this work marshals hetaeras in service of an anti-Macedonian discourse, in a manner similar to Duris' anecdote about courtesans and flute players at the courts of Demetrius and Lysimachus. So the hetaeras Pythionice (595a–c) and Glycera (586a, 595a–d) are deployed to expose the incontinence of the Macedonian ruler Harpalus; the story of Pythionice's *mnēmata* will be considered more fully in Chapter 5.

Another historian important for the discourse on hetaeras is Phylarchus, the principle historical source for Athens during the years 270 to 220, and a popular writer among authors of the first and second century C.E.; Dionysius of Halicarnassus, for example, praises his pure Attic style (Dion. Hal. *Comp.* 4). Influenced by Duris, his oeuvre exemplifies "tragic history," a historical subgenre that borrowed from tragic drama narrative strategies such as heroic actions, reversals of fortune, and moral lessons (Kebric 1977: 15). Phylarchus, in particular, received condemnation from Polybius for his sensationalist and digressive mode (Polyb. 2. 56–63). Perhaps for this reason he did not scruple to omit hetaeras from his work: from him, Athenaeus derives his accounts of the heroic actions of courtesans that resulted in the rescue of their lovers (593c–e), and the licentious and beautiful but unmarriageable Pantica (609c). His interest in *mirabilia* contributes stories about the loyalty of a dolphin toward his rescuer and an elephant's affection for a human baby to Athenaeus' section on animal marvels.

Last, but not least, the periegetic writer Polemon of Ilium (fl. 190 B.C.E.) supplied Athenaeus with information about courtesans and material culture, especially his works concerned with dedications and monuments at Delphi, Sparta, and Athens.[76] Polemon documented inscriptions, such as the decree forbidding hetaeras to be named after sacred festivals (587e), described the painters of courtesans (567b), their statues and dedications, such as that of Cottina at Sparta and her bronze dedicatory cow (574c), and the porch at Sicyon established by Lamia (577c), stories that will be examined in more detail in Chapter 5.

One other obsolete genre that plays a very significant part in Athenaeus' discourse on hetaeras is the Hellenistic treatise on courtesans, the only surviving fragments of which are preserved in Book 13 of the *Deipnosophistae.* These most likely evolved from comic prosopographies, such as the *Komoidoumenoi* (Comic Characters) of Herodicus the Cratetean twice mentioned by Athenaeus. Both of Herodicus' references deal with the derogatory nicknames of hetaeras (586a, 591c), as did treatises of the Alexandrian lexicographers.[77] At one point Athenaeus states that lists of well over 130 names and nicknames had been compiled by these scholars (583d); he himself mentions over 150 (see Appendix III). The tracts also included other biographical information about hetaeras, such as their famous lovers—a scrap of Gorgias' treatise mentions the orator Stratocles in connection with Leme (596f)—or their witticisms. The only fragment we have of Callistratus' treatise does not discuss nicknames but rather describes Phryne's role in rebuilding the demolished walls of Thebes in 316 (*FGrH* 348 F1 = 591d).

That these treatises originated in Alexandria, among a close circle of scholars, may explain their apparent homogeneity.[78] The taxonomy of courtesans rather bizarrely accompanied the study of Attic grammar, since Aristophanes of Byzantium (c. 275–180 B.C.E.), a scholar who played a prodigious role in the development of Atticism and the Hellenistic interest in lexicography, also composed a courtesan tract. Reared in Egypt and associated with Callimachus, Zenodotus, and Machon, Aristophanes was above all a grammarian; he produced an edition of the *Iliad* and established a system of lectional signs, to mark breathings, quantities, and accents. His greatest achievement, however, was the arrangement and classification of the lyric poets, particularly Pindar (Fraser, P. 1972: 1. 459–60). His pupil, Callistratus (c. 2nd C. B.C.E.), produced a work on courtesans, as did other members of his circle, including the grammarians Ammonius and Apollodorus of Athens. The former is said to have composed a *Komoidoumenoi* (*FGrH* 350 F1–4), while the latter, according to Athenaeus, expanded and improved that of Aristophanes of Byzantium (*FGrH* 244 F208 = 583d–e). Antiphanes the Younger, a contemporary of Apollodorus, composed yet another courtesan treatise. The popularity of the genre continued into the early second century C.E., the date of Gorgias of Athens' treatise, from which Athenaeus borrows a couple of lines about Leme, and may have been reflected in a lost treatise on famous prostitutes attributed to the Roman Suetonius (fl. ?69–122? C.E.).[79]

The largest literary excerpt in Book 13 concerned with hetaeras belongs to Machon's *Chreiae* (Anecdotes), an account of their witticisms at table, quoted verbatim by Myrtilus from 577d–583d. This poem, and similar works cited in Book 13, such as Lynceus' *Apomnemoneumata* (Memorabilia) and Aristodemus' *Geloia Apomnemoneumata* (Amusing Memorabilia), exemplify the Hellenistic interest in collecting and disseminating anecdotes drawn mostly from an oral tradition; normally they featured stock characters accessible to a diverse and increasingly international audience (Dalby 2000: 379). Although it is unclear exactly how this body of work became transmitted to Athenaeus, it is likely that he consulted many of the same sources as Aelian, Plutarch, Diogenes Laertius, and Pollux (Hawley 1993: 76).

Machon, mentioned elsewhere in Athenaeus by Democritus, the philosopher from Nicomedia (Machon F8 Gow), and by Cynulcus (F11 Gow), was a comic poet, a native of Corinth or Sicyon, and the teacher of Aristophanes of Byzantium. He spent most of his life at Alexandria, where his comedies were produced, although some of his witticisms, particularly those featuring Lamia and Demetrius Poliorcetes, may have originated at Sicyon (Griffen 1982: 162). The *Chreiae* of Machon depicted as one of its character types historical and fictional courtesans engaged in sympotic raillery with stock characters such as actors, artisans, athletes, and dramatic poets. Its subject matter and style suggest the influence of both Attic Old and New comedy, although the vocabulary is prosaic and colloquial;

even the meter approximates prose rather than poetry (Gow 1965: 22–3). The sources of Machon's anecdotes have yet to be determined, although it is clear that some of the stories experienced broad circulation; some probably had a literary basis.

Other sources for the witticisms of hetaeras in Book 13 include the *Apomnemoneumata* (Memorabilia) of Lynceus, comic poet, friend of Menander and the brother of Duris (probably 583f, 584b–585f); the *Geloia Apomnemoneumata* (Amusing Memorabilia) of Aristodemus (possibly 13. 585a); and a work of Hegesander.[80] These quasi-historical anecdotes provide some of the earliest literary treatments of courtesans outside Greek comedy. Because some of the courtesans' *chreiae* are attributed to multiple authors—for example, Machon assigns one anecdote to the courtesan Mania (263 Gow = 578e) that Lynceus elsewhere attributes to Gnathaena (584c)—it is likely that there was a well-established oral tradition in circulation. As discussed more fully in Chapter 3, whether Machon took his anecdotes from Lynceus remains open to question.[81]

Book 13 and the Discourse on Hetaeras

The sympotic genre demands an erotic discourse and Athenaeus provides one in Book 13, the only section of the *Deipnosophistae* designated by a special title, *Peri Gynaikōn* (On Women; for an outline of the structure of the book, see Appendix II). This title, however, is misleading: the book mainly concerns hetaeras, and the low genres that feature them, as the opening anecdote playfully suggests:

> When the comic poet, Antiphanes, Timocrates my friend, was once reading one of his plays to King Alexander, the latter made it clear that that he did not like it at all. The poet said, "For the man who likes this play of mine must have dined often at contribution-dinners, and, even more often, he must have received and given blows over a courtesan." (*peri hetairas*, 555a)

Book 13 also uncharacteristically begins with an invocation to a Muse, Erato, patron of erotic poetry, whom the narrator summons for help recounting his "erotic catalogue" (*ton erotikon . . . katalogon*, 555b). This poetic invocation in effect parodies the Homeric catalogue by juxtaposing low with high genres, the marginal figure of the hetaera with her highborn lovers. Indeed, the book's dramatic structure assumes the form of a quarrel between competing discourses, represented by its two central interlocutors, the grammarian Myrtilus and Cynulcus the philosopher. Actual hetaeras, however, do not materialize, as do musicians (4. 174b; 14. 622d), jesters (14. 613d), and even parasites (6. 224c), elsewhere in Athenaeus' text. Instead, they are introduced through the quoted snippets of Middle and New comedy, Attic oratory, biography, historiography, and the anecdotal collections discussed above.

Reflecting the influence of contemporary rhetorical education, Athenaeus structures Book 13 around a series of antitheses: thesis is followed by antithesis, speeches of praise by speeches of blame, encomium by invective. For example, the host Larensis begins by juxtaposing an encomium of wives (555c–557e) with an invective against hetaeras (557e–558e), concluding with a gnomic statement about their dangers: "there is no beast more ruinous than a hetaera." Leonidas responds in turn with an invective against wives (*psegein*, 557f–560b), followed by praise of the woman "purchased for her ways" (*ōnēteos*, 559a–b). The philosophers' praise of eros (561a–563c) is answered in turn by an invective against their penchant for boys (563d–565f). Much later in the dialogue, an encomium of Aphrodite, "the golden" (599f), symmetrically balances the earlier praise of eros.

This shifting series of antitheses, in which all types of women are classified as either good or bad, prefigures and indeed structures the major dramatic device of Book 13, the quarrel between the Cynic philosopher, Cynulcus, and the grammarian, Myrtilus. The dispute is over the attractions of women versus those of boys, a conventional sophistic topos of the period, as we saw above, and one in which courtesans figured prominently.[82] It is one of several stock quarrels in the *Deipnosophistae*, almost all of which feature Cynulcus sparring with various interlocutors, including Ulpian (3. 96f–104c; 6. 270c), Ulpian, Myrtilus, and Pontianus (4. 121e–127d), and Magnus (4. 160d–165b). In these debates, one side engages in specious, involved, and hypocritical arguments, while the other manifests "a fastidious and sterile accumulation of scattered scraps of information" (Lukinovich 1990: 266 and n. 14). By this device, Athenaeus use the sophistic paradox to parody the pretensions of philosophers and grammarians and to ridicule the behavior of intellectuals at banquets, a trope prefigured by Aristophanes' *Clouds* and many other comic poets.[83] The quarrel between Myrtilus and Cynulcus is similarly structured by antithesis: the philosopher begins with an invective against high-priced hetaeras, the *megalomisthoi*, which is answered by Myrtilus' encomium of their virtues (571–610a). Each of these speeches, in turn, contains a central antithesis: so Cynulcus in his argument against hetaeras praises the convenience of brothel workers, while Myrtilus uses his glorification of hetaeras to deliver an invective against philosophers.

Cynulcus' Invective against Hetaeras

Cynulcus exemplifies the stereotype of the impoverished philosopher who despises Atticist learning and civilized society in general, even though his speeches contain as many arcane quotations and intellectual oddments as those of his tablemates. He frequently serves as the target of humor at Athenaeus' table, as when the assembled guests deride his use of the word "conch" (*kongchos*, 4. 159f) in his encomium of lentils. Dio Chrysostom portrays Cynic philosophers as ubiquitous urban figures who begged on street corners, told coarse jokes, and used foul language.[84] The doctrine of the Cynics encouraged above all the rejection of all intellectual culture, encompassed by the word *paideia* (Branham and Goulet-Cazé 1996: 22–5). Two central concepts informed Cynic philosophy, the license to speak as one wished in public (*parrhēsia*), and the right to commit shameless public acts (*anaideia*), activities that served to expose the pretensions of contemporary life (Dudley 1998: 28–9). This flagrant disregard for convention infused Cynic literary works, such as Menippean satire and even obscene verse, and allowed them to deface tradition.[85] Through the figure of Cynulcus, Athenaeus continually satirizes philosophers even as he conflates Stoic, Cynic, Epicurean, and other schools of philosophical thought (3. 98f–99b; 563d–e).[86]

Cynulcus contributes to the dialogue a diatribe against high-priced courtesans, the *megalomisthoi*, by which he designates the wealthy, famous hetaeras of the law courts and the comic stage, and to whom these speeches and plays gave their titles (567c–d), in response to Leonidas' invective against wives.[87] The term *megalomisthoi* is deliberate: it unveils or rather exposes the commodity status that is normally concealed by the name of hetaera. Drawing on numerous comic sources, he compares the hetaera to Pandora: she is a great evil (*kakon . . . mega*, 567d), greedy, inaccessible, and physically repellent, a money trap that paralyzes any man who frequents her (567e–568d). Since she knows how to hide her imperfections and enhance her attractive features, her appearance is illusory and fetishistic, a mask that easily deceives men (568a–d). Because of her prohibitive expense, the philosopher advises Myrtilus to embrace instead "those who stand before the brothel" (*epi tōn oikēmatōn*, 568e). Such women offer a refuge from the perils of adultery and costly hetaeras (568f–569c). Indeed, brothels should be viewed in a positive light, as civic institutions that provide a sexual outlet other than adultery for young men (569e–f). Worse yet, hetaeras spawn quarrels among men, and even incite war: so Aristophanes in the *Acharnians* (Ar. *Ach.* 524–29) attributes the outbreak of the Peloponnesian war to a squabble over hetaeras in a comic inversion of the theft of Helen (569f–570a). Lastly, he reminds Myrtilus that old age frequently reduces once elusive, beautiful courtesans, such as Lais II, to the status of a brothel slave (570c–d). Throughout his invective, Cynulcus links high-priced courtesans with scholarly sophistication, indeed, with Attic *paideia* and lexicographical exegesis; by de-glamorizing Attic hetaeras, the philosopher in effect exposes the educated discourse of his interlocutor as morally and intellectually bankrupt.

Through Cynulcus, we are introduced to the character of Myrtilus: the latter embraces or typifies contemporary ideas of *paideia*, the love of obscure quotation combined with nostalgia for Greek literary forms and institutions. Like Aristophanes of Byzantium and the other writers of courtesan treatises discussed above, Myrtilus is a professional grammarian (*grammatikos*). He is also an old man (608f), from Thessaly (1. 11b; 7. 308b; 13. 568d; 15. 677a), although he once resided as a sophist in Corinth, a Greek city famous for prostitution, like Athenaeus' own Naucratis (567c; 573c). The fact that his father was a cobbler (*krepidopoios*), a profession linked with sophists and demagogues in Attic Old comedy and in the Socratic dialogues, suggests his lower class origins (568e). It is fitting, therefore, that Myrtilus is named after a poet of Attic Old comedy (556e) and that most of the references to hetaeras occur in his lengthy speech (563d–610b), given the prominence of these figures in the comic genres. He is thus identified not only with his comic namesake but also with the crude *bōmolochos* of Attic old comedy (comic buffoon; 566e):

> "Do you dare to say this to me?" Not "being rosy-fingered," according to Cratinus, but rather having one leg made of cow dung, while you carry around the shank of that poet, your namesake, for you always dine in wineshops and public houses. . . . But there, O Sophist, you associate constantly not with male friends (ἑταίρων) but with courtesans (ἑταιρῶν), having around yourself not just a few procuresses, and always carrying around the sorts of books written by Aristophanes, Apollodorus, Ammonius, Antiphanes, even Gorgias of Athens, all of whom have written treatises entitled *On Athenian Courtesans*. O what lovely learning you have! (*kalēs polumathias*, 566e–67b)

Cynulcus has altered a quotation of the comic poet Cratinus and borrowed the image of the cow dung leg from Aristophanes (*boltinon skelos*, Ar. *Ran.* 294–95) to turn his rival into a comic character unworthy of epic epithets like "rosy-fingered." In Cynulcus' view, Myrtilus' knowledge originates in the rankest sector of the city, in the taverns and public houses, venues associated only with the lowest social class, since "not even a slave would dare to eat or drink in a tavern" (566f). For this reason, the grammarian is concerned with low (*bōmolocheuesthai*) rather than high (*semnunesthai*) literary genres. Playing on the semantic ambiguities of the term hetaera in the genitive plural case, a Menandrian pun discussed in the introduction, Cynulcus draws a connection between moral and intellectual depravity. Myrtilus not only consorts with hetaeras and their madames, but even studies them by reading courtesan treatises and viewing erotic paintings by painters such as Pausias, Aristides, and Nicophanes. These activities earn him the title of *pornographos* (567b), the first use of this word in ancient Greek, and, later, that of *erōtomanēs* (love-mad, 599e).[88] And surely it is no coincidence that Cynulcus makes the first reference in Book 13 to Attic oratory, a genre in which the charge of consorting with hetaeras served as a common means of slandering one's opponents.

In addition to his identification with the comic buffoon, Myrtilus also evokes the Alexandrian lexicographers who developed prosopographies of famous Athenian courtesans and other comic characters. Cynulcus makes patent the association when he addresses him as *grammatikōtatos* (supreme grammarian, 570b), an epithet also applied to Aristarchus, a pupil of Aristophanes of Byzantium (15. 671f). According to a passage of Plutarch's *Table Talk*, only the grammarian can fully explain the identities of persons named in comedy (Plut. *Mor.* 712a; Henry 1995: 156 n. 11). Thus the main activity of Myrtilus consists of glossing the names of hetaeras: he informs his pupils that a reference to Ocimon in a comedy of Eubulus is the name of a hetaera (567c). His references to over 150 courtesans' names, more than those recorded in the Hellenistic courtesan treatises, likens his discourse to that of his Alexandrian predecessors. Moreover, his speech is repeatedly characterized as a catalogue: "In all this, my friends, I think I have constructed for you, not without effort, a catalogue of lovers" (*tōn erōtikon . . . logon*, 599e). The allusion to an "erotic catalogue" evokes the "catalogue of beautiful women" (*tōn kalōn gunaikōn katalogon*) initiated at 590c. That the speech begins and ends with the verb *katalegein* (to arrange) further evokes the idea of a prosopographical list: "I will recite for you, Cynulcus, a kind of Ionian discourse" (*katalexō de soi, Kunoulke, Iōnikēn tina rhēsin*, 573b; *tosauta tou Murtilou hexēs katalexantos*, 610b).

The interest in names that defines the grammarian's profession is not in itself objectionable to the philosopher; what rankles him are the sources of these names, the comic genres, sensationalist historiography, like that of Phylarchus, and courtesan treatises:

> "Erudition (*polumathēmosunēs*)—there is nothing more empty than this," said Hippon the atheist. But even the godlike Heracleitus says, "Erudition does not teach common sense." And Timon also said, "There is nothing more empty than boasting of erudition." For what is the use of all these names, you grammarian (*ō grammatike*), more to wear down (*epitripsai*) rather than to make moderate (*sōphronisai*) your listeners? (610b–c)

In this passage, the goal of literature is common sense (*noon echein*) for the Cynic philosopher, not *paideia*; from an ethical standpoint, it is moderation (*sōphronisai*) rather than the indulgence in pleasure. To name all of the Greek heroes shut up in the Trojan horse—names found in the *Ilioupersis* of Sacadas of Argos—or the companions of Odysseus devoured by the Cyclops, or the Laestrygonians, poses the proper sort of intellectual challenge, one that Myrtilus cannot meet (610d–e). Rather, the grammarian can only quote Phylarchus on the absence of hetaeras and flute girls in the towns of Ceos (*FGrH* 81 F42 = 610d). Scholarly exegeses on prostitutes exemplify, for the philosopher, the corruption of contemporary rhetorical education, and stigmatize the grammarian as debauched and ill-bred.

Myrtilus' Encomium of Hetaeras

This section attempts to isolate some of the major strands of Myrtilus' often disjointed defense of courtesans as they relate to his larger argument, the importance of courtesans in transmitting Hellenic *paideia*. His speech thus exemplifies the contemporary rhetorical strategy of the paradoxical encomium, in which negative characteristics are portrayed in a positive light. In fashioning an encomium of hetaeras from the same tradition as Cynulcus, Myrtilus must de-emphasize their role as objects and agents of invective and abuse; thus he omits details of their prosecutions while glamorizing their liaisons with famous men. This skewed discourse has had a direct impact on contemporary interpretations of Greek hetaeras as cultured and liberated women, and yet its role in forming this view has been almost completely overlooked by classical scholars. To avoid overwhelming the reader with minutiae, my discussion will focus on just a few of the main themes that recur throughout the speech and which form the bases of subsequent chapters. While this approach may run the risk of making Myrtilus' speech appear too unified, or of omitting some important details, it nonetheless attempts to elucidate its main internal structure and methodology (for a summary of the major points, see Appendix II).

Myrtilus begins his refutation of Cynulcus' invective against the *megalomisthoi*, the high-paid courtesans, with an invective against the philosopher's lack of *paideia*: "How stupid you are, and boorish, and given to foul language!" (571a–b). As mentioned above, his assault on philosophers perversely assumes the form of an encomium of hetaeras that enumerates their virtues. In his discourse, the grammarian de-emphasizes the commodity status of hetaeras, rarely mentioning money and often alluding to them enphemistically as as eromenae (mistresses); he also minimizes or omits any negative representations of their characters. He distinguishes courtesans from other types of prostitutes, contrasting the "real" hetaeras—those capable of an affection without deception (*adolos philia*), whom Cynulcus has just reviled (*loidorein*, 571c)—with mere entertainers, such as dancers (*orchēstridas . . . hetairas*) and flute girls. True to his profession, the grammarian begins with an analysis of the word hetaera: he argues that the name confers respectability rather than notoriety. Hetaeras are the only women addressed by the title of *philia* (friendly) and derive their name from Aphrodite *Hetaera*, "she who brings companions together, male and female" (571d–e); freeborn women and girls refer to close friends as "hetaeras," as does Sappho in one of her fragments. Only later does the term become a euphemism for women "who hire themselves out" to men (*tas mistharnousas hetairas*, 571d). The euphemism of the hetaera's name extends also to her appearance and manners, to her pleasant flattery and refined demeanor at table; in this regard, she resembles a legitimate citizen wife more than a prostitute (572a). In contrast, the boy lover of the philosophers, the *philosophomeirakiskos* (572c), is compared to a *pornos*, a common whore.

To the respectability of the hetaera at table, Myrtilus adds their religious importance as agents of Aphrodite, a goddess worshipped throughout eastern Greece and Asia Minor in her capacity as patron of hetaeras (572d–e). He mentions several shrines in honor of Aphrodite Hetaera or Porne, to be discussed more fully in Chapter 5, as examples of the courtesan's importance in ancient Greece. Instead of causing wars, hetaeras may promote civic welfare during times of crisis, as when a band of Corinthian hetaeras averted the Persian invasion by means of their supplication (573d). They are public benefactors, using their wealth to make dedications to the gods (574d–f). The section on love at first sight (575a–576b), in which Myrtilus chronicles famous romances, not only supports his argument in favor of heterosexual eros, but possibly also attempts to imbue the love of hetaeras with a degree of respectability.

A central focus of Myrtilus' encomium is the famous men with whom hetaeras have consorted: as Appendix IV shows, these were mostly political figures such as orators and monarchs, but they could also be poets and philosophers. This discourse begins at 576c, and continues, with various interruptions, to 599c (see Appendix II). Hetaeras often gave birth to remarkable children, such as the Athenian archon Themistocles, son of the courtesan Habrotonon; the general Timotheus; and the king of Pergamum, Philetaerus (577b–c). Athenaeus mentions a large number of hetaeras in connection with the Macedonian kings, known for their polygamy.[89] Among the Hellenistic leaders implicated with courtesans, three in particular stand out: Demetrius Poliorcetes and Ptolemy Philadelphus for the number of their mistresses, and Harpalus for the lengthy accounts of his extravagant love for the courtesans Pythionice and Glycera.[90]

The Macedonian general, Harpalus (d. 324), friend of Alexander the Great, enjoyed not only a reputation for whoring, but for political corruption as well, falling under suspicion of bribery at Athens in 324 B.C.E. His stint in Babylonia around 330 probably explains his persistent association with hetaeras, for he controlled the treasuries of the satraps and reputedly lived a decadent lifestyle. According to Athenaeus, Theopompus in his *Letter to Alexander* took Harpalus to task for his *akolasia*, adducing as an example Pythionice's grandiose funerary monument (*mnēmeion*, 595a) that stood just outside of Athens (594e–595c). The attribution of the epithets *tridoulos* and *tripornos* to this courtesan must be understood in this defamatory context: not only did the ruler show a slavish devotion to his mistress, his frequent association with courtesans called into question his own moral character.

According to Athenaeus, the Alexandrian ruler Ptolemy II Philadelphus (308–246) had the greatest number of mistresses among the Hellenistic monarchs (576e–f). Theocritus refers to him as *erōtikos* (Theocr. 14. 61), the same word Myrtilus uses of himself at 599e. Athenaeus names as his partners Didyme, Bilistiche, Cleino, Agathocleia, Stratonice, and Myrtion, and alludes to many others (576e–f).[91] The king also appears to have had a penchant for dedicating monuments to them: we hear of a memorial for Stratonice near Eleusis and images of the oenochoousa, Cleino, established around Alexandria. Demetrius Poliorcetes (336–283) of Macedon enjoyed a similar reputation for womanizing. Not only did he have an enduring passion for the Attic *auletris* Lamia, he fell in love with Leaena II "and countless others" (577d). According to Plutarch, he claimed Lamia, daughter of Cleanor of Athens, from among the abandoned luxuries of Ptolemy I Soter after the battle of Salamis in 306 (Plut. *Demetr.* 16. 3). Although much older, Lamia so mastered him with her charm that Demetrius immediately declared his exclusive devotion to her and the two eventually had a daughter together named Phila.

The persistent association of multiple Athenian courtesans with the Hellenistic monarchs may have been a backhanded attempt on the part of some of the Athenian historians to discredit them and their rule by implicating them in a corrupt and profligate way of life, including polygamy. Indeed, in his introduction to the lives of Demetrius and Antony, Plutarch portrays both men as bibulous, profligate, amorous, unstable and subject to swift reversals of fortune. On the other hand, the prominence of hetaera-mistresses among the Hellenistic monarchs may also reflect the increasing importance of women in legitimating royal children during the Hellenistic period and contemporary reservations about their new role (Ogden 1999: 177–178). Stories of mistresses and prostitutes ascending to the throne enact an anxiety over the potential for relative outsiders to control major centers of power and ultimately to affect the course of dynastic succession. Although an association with hetaeras typically signals the profligacy or depravity for men, Myrtilus inverts this tradition by adducing them as evidence for the respectability and broad public influence of these women.

Myrtilus also pays special attention to the names of courtesans as they figure in Attic oratory and comedy (585f–587f), a subject to be discussed more fully in Chapter 2, as well as to the accounts of their liaisons with the men who defended them in court (590b–593a). The latter section may have originally been longer, given Harpocration's fuller treatment of these women in his *Lexicon of the Ten Orators*. Athenaeus trawled the speeches of orators such as Hyperides, Isocrates, Lysias, and Stephanus, for names of hetaeras and then borrowed from Idomeneaus and other Hellenistic biographers accounts of their scandalous affairs. As we saw above, hetaeras loomed large in charges of prodigality waged by the orators; their company could also suggest effeminacy, as in the case of Demosthenes, a man "uncontrolled in sexual matters" (*akolastos . . . peri aphrodisia*, 592e–f). The legendary promiscuity of Alcibiades incites one comic fragment to describe him as *habron* (delicate, 574d; cf. 535a–b). We hear also that Demetrius of Phalerum, in love with the Samian courtesan Lampito, liked to be called by her name and the nickname Chairitoblepharos (Pretty Eyes, 593f).[92] Myrtilus predictably downplays the content of these speeches, since the genre often represents courtesans as vehicles of abuse and his rhetorical purpose is rather to construct an encomium of their virtues. While ostensibly concerned with oratory, this section actually deploys the genre as a springboard for a lexicographical analysis of the names of famous hetaeras and their liaisons, while minimizing its defamatory content.

In addition to serving as the subjects of oratory, hetaeras are also romantically linked to several of the orators (590b–593a). Myrtilus gives as an example the licentious Hyperides, who ejected his son Glaucippus from the paternal household in order to install Myrrhine, "the most costly of all the hetaeras" (*polutelestatēn*, 590c), along with a succession of others, including Phila and his putative clients, Aristagora and Phryne. So, too, the modest Isocrates kept Metanira as his mistress, as did Lysias, who later maintained Lagisca in his old age. In connection with the same orator, we also hear of Phryne and her public nudity at the Eleusinia, the baring of her breasts at her impiety trial and Praxiteles' marble statue of her at Delphi (590d–592f). An inscription naming her as the daughter of Epicles of Thespiae at Delphi provides an opportunity to discuss her nicknames and those of a homonymous hetaera (591c–d), as well as to emphasize her great wealth. The legendary profligacy of Demosthenes, including the children resulting from his unions with hetaeras and his fondness for boys, caps the section (592f). The hetaeras maintained by Demetrius of Phalerum, Stephanus, and Lysias lead to a digression on the hetaera Neaera and all of the men with whom she was linked, including Xenoclides the poet, Hipparchus the actor, as well as Phrynion (593f–594a). Again, the charges against Neaera set forth in this oration and its defamatory content are predictably omitted. Like most of the stories that attach hetaeras to famous men, these fancifully, and probably fictively, conflated the subject matter of the authors with their biographies, e.g., because orators defended courtesans, they must have patronized them.

Myrtilus also chronicles famous encounters between hetaeras and another class of professionals, philosophers: Leontion, the lover of Epicurus, is said to have consorted openly with men in the garden even after she had taken up the study of philosophy (588a–c). Lais II of Hyccara is linked with the philosophers Aristippus and Diogenes the Cynic, the orator Demosthenes, and the painter Apelles; she later met her death at the hands of women wielding footstools in Thessaly (588c–589b). Socrates is known to have conversed with the courtesan Theodote (588d) and Aspasia, the pallake of Pericles (589d–f), while Aristotle kept Herpyllis as his mistress and Plato Archeanassa, the Colophonian courtesan (589c–d). Courtesans, the grammarian argues, have inspired poetic texts: Antimachus and Lamynthius both composed poems entitled *Lyde*, one in elegiac couplets, the other in lyric meters, in honor of their courtesans (597a–599b). The *Leontion* of Hermesianax, another literary work that commemorates a courtesan, recounts literary affairs between poets and their characters or muses: Homer and Penelope, Sappho and Alcaeus, Mimnermus and Nanno, Theano and Pythagoras, Socrates and Aspasia (597b–599b).

The association of hetaeras with poets and philosophers leads to a consideration of their literary sophistication and clever conversation at table. Hetaeras like Nicarete of Megara and Bilistiche of Argo earn praise (*eudoxos*) for their high birth and remarkable erudition (*paideia*, 596e). They are cultured and witty, as evidenced by a lengthy passage from the *Chreiae* of Machon (577d–582cd), and the anecdotes of Lynceus (583f–585f), Hegesander (584f), and Aristodemus (585a). Prominent among these are the risqué witticisms of the courtesans Mania (578c–579d), the crone Gnathaena (579e–81a), and her daughter or granddaughter, Gnathaenion (581a); in this capacity, we also hear of Glycera (584a, 585d–e), Nico (582f, 583c–d, 584f), Callistion (583a, 585c), and Phryne (583c, 584c–d, 585e). In almost all of these anecdotes, the hetaera uses coarse humor to repel the sexual advances of a lover; typically she is a crone, a figure crudely eroticized in Aristophanic comedy. Some of these jokes even involve a high degree of literary sophistication, as we shall see in Chapter 3. In all of these accounts, Myrtilus stresses the courtesan as a consummate purveyor of Attic heritage and learning.

The grammarian also describes the self-sacrificing and heroic actions of hetaeras that save their lovers or defend their cities: Eirene, the courtesan of a son of Ptolemy II Philadelphus, lost her life along with him as they attempted to elude his enemies (593a–b). Danae saved Sophron's life by revealing another hetaera's plans for his murder; as a punishment, her rival threw her from a precipice to her death. Similarly, Mysta allowed herself to be sold into slavery after the defeat of her lover Seleucus, with whom she eventually reunited. And although tortured by the henchmen of Hippias,

Harmodius' Leaena I died without uttering a word in order to further the cause of democracy (596f). Modeled on tragic heroines, these salvific courtesans refute the claim that they are treacherous, rapacious, and unfaithful.

The hetaera that emerges from Myrtilus' discourse is a creature utterly distinct from that crafted by Cynulcus, even though both speakers draw from the same literary tradition. Whereas the philosopher portrays them as physically repulsive, rapacious, deceitful, and of low status, the grammarian plays up their importance in shaping and transmitting the cultural legacy of Athens. Educated, wellborn, and wealthy, these hetaeras defend their cities and their lovers; they wittily quote Euripides at the symposium; they are public benefactors, the subject of art works and dedications, the muses of poets, and the mothers and mistresses of generals, kings, and orators. In constructing this discourse, Myrtilus deliberately downplays their vilification as objects of contempt and mockery and vehicles of abuse in the literary tradition. Cleansed of invective, Myrtilus' hetaera serves as the embodiment of Athenian cultural heritage and Hellenic *paideia*. Indeed, she is marshaled at the end of the grammarian's speech as a moral authority that condemns the hypocrisy of philosophers and their penchant for boys:

> Take care, you philosophers who enjoy a passion contrary to nature and sin against the goddess of love (*hoi para phusin tē Aphroditēi chrōmenoi kai asebountes eis tēn theon*), take care that you are not destroyed in the same way. For even boys are handsome, as long as they look like a woman, as the courtesan Glycera, in the account given by Clearchus, once alleged. (*gunaiki*, 605d)

Myrtilus here brings back into his discourse the voice of the hetaera, silent since 599b, to reinforce his condemnation of philosophers: she is made to convert their homoerotic proclivities into the compulsory heterosexuality of the grammarian. Indeed, this allusion to Glycera introduces the final theme of the speech, a diatribe against philosophers.

A passage on animal *mirabilia*, mortal love affairs with animals (605a–607a), leads Myrtilus to his final insult: philosophers are worse than beasts in their rejection of pleasure, "for it is fitting to make mention of *aphrodisia* while drinking" (*peri aphrodisiōn harmoston einai en tōi oinōi mneian poieisthai*, 607b). Erotic matters, not syllogisms, ought to be the topic of conversation at the symposium. And if symposiasts cannot turn their minds away from philosophy, flute players and dancing girls are required. In an account of a famous symposium of Antigonus Gonatas, the entry of a chorus line of almost naked orchestrides causes a riot of vulgarity "over the wonderful sight" (607c–d). At the same party, a philosopher refuses to allow a flute girl to sit next to him, but then ends in a drunken brawl with another man after a bidding war for her favors (607e). Last, but not least, we are told that another philosopher, one Polystratus of Athens, also known as the "Etruscan," and a pupil of Theophrastus, enjoyed clothing himself in the garments of flute girls. In all of these instances, the hetaera unmasks the pretensions and hypocrisies of intellectuals and turns them into objects of comic mockery and contempt. Myrtilus marshals this potent cultural sign in just the same way, using the hetaera to critique the Cynic lifestyle. Through her, he has reduced his opponent to the level of the eponymous dog, snarling and voracious, abject and naked, roofless and without hearth (611d). In a book preoccupied with names and naming, Myrtilus lives up to his comic name: his risqué and scurrilous discourse challenges that of the philosophers, exposing their intellectual pretensions and hypocrisy, and giving the grammarian the last word:

> And now I will end my speech against you and the other Cynic dogs with a line of the tragic poet Aristarchus: "Not making a beginning in these things, but as an avenger" (*tad' ouch' huparchōn, alla timōroumenos*). (*TrGF* 73 F3 = 612f)

Conclusion

The purpose of this chapter has been to situate Book 13 of the *Deipnosophistae* in its cultural and literary context and to show the complexity involved in interpreting its representations of the Greek hetaera. While issues of cultural identity do not engage Athenaeus as directly as some of his contemporaries, the longing for a classical Greek past is clearly felt in his oeuvre. This nostalgia surfaces in his use of quotation, the literary equivalent of ruined monuments, and his construction of a timeless literary space cleansed of ethnic and political identity and populated by quasi-historical characters who cannot be fully correlated to real people. In structuring Book 13, Athenaeus also deploys conventional rhetorical forms, such as antithesis, paradox, and stock debates: through the quarrel over erotic proclivities between the pedantic grammarian Myrtilus and the moralizing Cynic philosopher, the author forges a dramatic structure capable of supporting the numerous fragmentary accounts of hetaeras. Most of the discourse on hetaeras occurs in the speech of the grammarian, which simultaneously functions as an encomium of hetaeras and as an invective against philosophers. The speech is an epideictic tour de force that marshals quotations about hetaeras, drawn from comedy, oratory, historiography, and anecdotes, to fabricate, in effect, a version of the Alexandrian courtesan treatise with its focus on names and nicknames. Throughout his speech, Myrtilus implicitly links together the sophist and the courtesan as symbols of contemporary urban life and decadent *paideia*. Like the dining sophists, they are strongly identified with Asia Minor, yet they ventriloquize the Attic past. They engage in the witty banter of the symposium, even quote with precision famous dramatic passages, trumping their fictive interlocutors, and yet they retain their status as outsiders or low others. They share a facility for display and masquerade and yet they never perform at Athenaeus' table.

CHAPTER 2

The Women Most Mentioned: The Names of Athenian Courtesans

All the Greeks knew the name of Rhodopis, and, later, the name of Archidice became the subject of song throughout Hellas.[1]

As we saw in the last chapter, the names of famous courtesans attracted much interest in the classical world, from fourth century Attic orators and comic poets, to the Alexandrian scholars who catalogued them, and later, to the Greek sophists of Imperial Rome. Given the fascination with hetaeras' names and nicknames exhibited by the grammarian Myrtilus in Book 13 of the *Deipnosophistae* and the Hellenistic treatises that shape his discourse, it is somewhat surprising that so little scholarly attention, apart from Schneider's list in Pauly-Wissowa's *Realencyclopädie* in 1913, has been given to this subject.[2] The first part of this chapter examines the range of names, given in Appendix III, associated with hetaeras in Book 13 and their possible meanings for Athenaeus and the earlier tradition. Although publicly named, such women were not necessarily individuated or fully identified; closer scrutiny reveals a widespread use of homonyms, nicknames, or professional names, both generic and particular, as well as inconsistencies from author to author. In the literary tradition, the names of hetaeras conjured a discourse of invective targeted against notorious men, provided the fodder of jokes, or served as artifacts to be assembled and classified by Alexandrian scholars. In Athenaeus, the names of hetaeras function as yet another literary commodity through which discursive status is negotiated, even as they evoke nostalgia for a bygone Attic past.

The Problem with Names

As a grammarian, Myrtilus specializes in the elucidation of obscure names, especially those found in Attic Middle and New comedy. His speech in effect improves upon the lists of his Alexandrian predecessors that catalogued vast numbers of courtesans' names. In their initial exchange, the philosopher Cynulcus elaborates on the sophist's lexicographical abilities:

> The beautiful erudition (*polumathia*), my dear friends, of our grammarian here, who does not even conceal his meaning, but always candidly quotes the words of Eubulus' *Cercopes*:
>
> "I went to Corinth. There somehow sweetly
> nibbling some Ocimon (Basil), I came to ruin (*diephtharēn*);
> and there idle talk overpowered (*katelērēsa*) my cloak."
>
> (Eubulus, *Cercopes* F53 KA= 567b–c)

Not only is Myrtilus made to quote an obscure comic passage verbatim, he is represented as providing a gloss on the name Ocimon worthy of a Hellenistic grammarian. In Cynulcus' view, the ability to perform such scholarly exegeses stigmatizes the grammarian as pedantic and vulgar; indeed, the philosopher later takes him to task for neglecting the epic tradition in favor of debased erotic texts (610b).

Most of the exegeses on names, particularly secondary names, occur in the quotation of Machon's *Chreiae* (577d–583d) and in the section on oratory (585f–587f). Elaboration of a hetaera's name or nickname appears to have been a secondary focus of Machon's *Chreiae* as evidenced by the story of how Mania (Crazy) acquired her name. Her original name was apparently Melissa, a fairly common Attic name for women and one not strictly associated with courtesans.[3] The difficulty of attributing a primary name to Mania, or "that which belonged to her from infancy" (*to men oun huparchon eutheōs ek paidiou autēi Melitt' ēn onoma*, 578c), is illustrated by Plutarch's assertion that she was originally called Demo, a name attributed to many other courtesans (Plut. *Demetr.* 27; s. v. *Demo* in Appendix III).

> But perhaps one of my present hearers may ask,
> and with good reason, too, whether an Attic woman
> was ever addressed as or recognized by the name of Mania.
> For it is shameful (*aischron*) for a woman to have a Phrygian name,
> especially for a hetaera from the very center of Greece,
> shameful that the city of the Athenians did not prevent it,
> a city where all men are improved. (578b–c)

This passage strikingly insists that the hetaera called Mania, a known ethnic, was Attic, not foreign, and that such a misnomer would not have been tolerated by the Athenians. Indeed, there is evidence of a Phrygian Mania from the Troad around 413 B.C.E.; she was a queen to Zenis, the acting satrap of Aeolia then under the control of Pharnabazus.[4] To Atticize the name, Machon goes on to explain it as arising from the exclamations of admirers, "It's crazy (*mania*) how beautiful Melissa is!" and her own habit of crying "Crazy!" in response to a joke or in praising or blaming someone. The hetaera's lovers purportedly renamed her after this habit, even though the name itself contains a long alpha, while the word for madness a short one, an inconsistency that occasions yet another explanation (578d; Ogden 1999: 246). This type of punning is characteristic of ancient accounts of the names of hetaeras; it also appears in the jokes attributed to them, as we shall see in Chapter 3. Moreover, the peculiar insistence on the Attic origins of these names at least partially explains why such catalogues were of interest to the Alexandrian scholars and their Second Sophistic imitators.

In the section that follows the quotation of Machon, Myrtilus discusses the names of hetaeras found in oratory, drawing on the Hellenistic courtesan treatises as well as on comic and historical genres. For example, we learn that the Sinope mentioned by Demosthenes in *Against Androtion* had as her secondary name Abydus, according to Crates' *Komoidoumenoi*; in addition, she appeared in several comedies, including those of Antiphanes, Alexis, and Callicrates (585f–5856a). Sometimes Athenaeus, as ventriloquized through Mytrilus, editorializes about the reliability of his sources. For instance, after quoting a passage from Lysias' lost speech, *Against Lais*, the grammarian remarks that the orator incorrectly wrote Antheia for Anteia:

> "Philyra, at least, stopped whoring (*porneuomenē*) when she was still young, and so did Scione, Hippaphesis, Theocleia, Psamathe, Lagisca, and Antheia." Perhaps for Antheia, we should write Anteia. For we cannot find in any author the name Antheia recorded as that of a courtesan, whereas from Anteia an entire play takes its title, as I have said above (567e), the *Anteia* of Eunicus or Philyllius. And the writer of the *Speech against Neaera* also mentions her. (586e)

The earlier reference to the name Anteia does not occur in Myrtilus' speech, however, but in that of Cynulcus, implying that the use of the first person pronoun should be ascribed to the narrator rather than to the grammarian. The numerous parallels adduced between oratory and Middle and New comedy, particularly those of Menander, Philetaerus, and Theophilus (587e–f), throughout this passage show that the same cultural prosopography informed both genres.

Deviations from Athenian naming customs also elicit comment in this section; as in Machon's anecdote about Mania, Myrtilus worries about the plausibility of the name of an Attic auletris:

> The auletris Nemeas is mentioned by Hyperides in *Against Patrocles*. Concerning her, it is worth wondering how the Athenians allowed the porne to be addressed in this way, using the name of a very respected festival (*endoxotatēs*). For it was forbidden not only for women working as hetaeras (*hetairousais*), but even other female slaves (*alla kai tais allais doulais*), to adopt (*tithesthai*) such names, as Polemon says in his work *On the Acropolis*. (Polemon F38 Preller = 587c)

The practice does not appear exceptional: Athenaeus mentions many hetaeras named after festivals. A hetaera called Isthmias is mentioned elsewhere in Book 13 (587e, 593f), as are the names Pannychis, Olympia, and Pythionice. The passage elides the distinction between the porne/auletris and the hetaera, equating all of them with slavery and perhaps even implying that such women chose their professional names themselves. It further suggests that the regulation of names, even for individuals of marginal status, was a matter of civic importance in classical Athens.

The punning encountered in Machon's account of the names of courtesans also appears to have been popular among their Alexandrian chroniclers. From Aristophanes of Byzantium's treatise, we learn how the hetaera Oia acquired the name of Anticyra (Hellebore):

> In the speech *Against Philonides*, an action for forcible seizure, Lysias, if the speech is genuine, mentions also the hetaera Nais, and in *Against Medon*, an action for bearing false witness, Anticyra. Now this was an epithet (*epōnumon*) given to the courtesan; for her principal name (*kurion*) was Oia, as Aristophanes says in his work *On Courtesans*, alleging that she was called Anticyra either because she drank together with men driven mad by passion (*parakinousi kai memēnosin*), or because the doctor Nicostratus, adopting her, left her a large amount of hellebore after he died, but nothing else. (586e–f)

Plant names, such as Ocimon (Basil), Corianno (Coriander), Herpyllis (Creeping Thyme), and Sisymbrion (Mint) are also commonly applied to hetaeras. Anticyra alludes to the region where the plant, the hellebore, grew in abundance. Like that of Mania, her naming devolves from her sympotic activities and the men with whom she consorted. Part of the joke here is the medicinal effect of plant as a cure for madness; hence the doctor supplies the men at the symposium with the proper remedy for their love-sickness.

The nickname of Nannion, a courtesan mentioned in Hyperides' *Against Patrocles*, involves a similar type of pun: she was called Aix (Goat) because she consumed (*exanalōsai*) the tavern keeper, Thallus (Sapling, 587a). As goats, Myrtilus explains, "delight in saplings" (*thallōi chairousin hai aiges*), the Athenians prohibited them from grazing on the Acropolis (587a). The pun implicit in the name of the tavern keeper invites an excursus about feeding a *thallos* to a young goat in a lost play by Sophocles. The same name and anecdote, along with a reference to Sophocles, are also reiterated by Machon in connection with the courtesan Nico, who reputedly "devoured" (*katephagen*) her lover Thallus the Great (582f). A scholion that glosses a reference to goats and eating in Aristophanes' *Plutus* as an obscene double entendre suggests a similar meaning at work in this nickname.[5]

The anecdotes discussed above illustrate some of the complexities involved in interpreting the names of hetaeras.[6] On the surface, a celebrated name appears to have differentiated the *megalomisthos* hetaera from her nameless brothel counterparts, a distinction observed in Herodotus' narratives of prostitution discussed in the introductory chapter. However, this is not the case: the public naming of hetaeras, especially their nicknames, actually obscured their identities, turning them into sexual commodities or fictional entities. For instance, it is often impossible to determine the actual names of hetaeras, since most of them had more than one: the name given to them at birth, and a secondary or professional name. Some names associated with courtesans appear to have been generic, or perhaps even slang terms for hetaeras, such as Corone (Crow), Aphye (Sardine), and possibly Aix (Goat); taken alone, they could imply that a woman worked as a courtesan. Another problem is widespread homonymity: two different women with the same names may have become conflated, such as Demo, a hetaera simultaneously associated with three generations of Antigonids (578b).[7] Or one courtesan may have been wrongly differentiated into two, an explanation that may account for the confusion surrounding Phryne Saperdion (Little Fish) and Phryne Clausigelos (Teary Laughter, 591c). Occasionally the same woman is referred to by different names, as in the case of Demo by Plutarch and Melissa-Mania by Machon (578a–b; Plut. *Demetr.* 27), or the courtesan referred to by Sappho as Doriche and whom Herodotus later calls Rhodopis (Hdt. 2. 135; cf. 596c). Athenaeus similarly alludes to a favorite hetaera of Alcibiades both as Damasandra and Timandra (574e and 535c, respectively; for the latter, cf. Plut. *Alc.* 39) while a scholion to Aristophanes' *Plutus* (179) calls her Epimandra. Two names used by the same courtesan, such as Melissa-Mania, may not be correctly identified as belonging to one person. Moreover, the same names tend to be used for hetaeras from generation to generation with the result that all of the major hetaeras, such as Lais II, Leaena II, and Phryne, have doublets, a woman with the same name but associated with a different historical period, region, or nickname. Textual corruption and letter confusion such as that found in the pairs Lais and Nais and Anteia and Antheia further obscure matters.

Finally, and perhaps most critically for historians of women, the presence of the same names in multiple genres makes it almost impossible to disentangle actual women from their fictive counterparts. One assumes that the names of hetaeras found in oratory corresponded directly to actual women resident in Athens during the period of their production; however, the equation is less clear in the case of the comic plays, most of which are very fragmentary. To what extent do the named women of Middle and New comedy refer to historical women, as they frequently do in Attic Old comedy? And how does the widespread use of nicknames and slang terms complicate this picture? By the time of Athenaeus, multiple authors, genres, and periods had facilitated, and obscured, the transmission of the names of hetaeras in the literary tradition. Even historical figures had become embellished by anecdote and comic fiction, only to emerge in authors like Lucian and Alciphron as fully realized comic tropes evocative of classical Athens and its cultural milieu. The process of turning the hetaera into a fetish, whether on the comic stage or the law court, began with the name.

The Names of Athenian Women

The Athenian practice of omitting the names of reputable, living women from the public record, especially in oratory, is by now a commonplace of classical scholarship.[8] Pericles' famous advice to women widowed by the Peloponnesian war has long served as the starting point for discussions of the discursive exclusion of women in classical Athens (Thuc. 2. 45. 2).[9] Orators avoided mentioning the names of living women whose reputations they wished to protect, referring instead to their male relatives or guardians, while at the same time never failing to name women of questionable character. But the names of respectable women could be publicized after their death and many survive in sepulchral inscriptions from classical Athens.[10] The most common type of inscription for citizen women gives the woman's name along with a man's name in the genitive, normally her guardian; in most cases, this appears to have been her father, and only secondarily, her husband (Vestergaard et al. 1985 [1993]: 183–5). The rare appearance of metronymics on inscriptions, a subject almost entirely neglected by scholars, invites speculation about the social status of these women, and will be examined more closely at the end of this chapter.

The names given to citizen girls at Athens did not differ in large part from those of their male counterparts except that they were feminine in form, and as such covered the same semantic range (Golden 1986: 249). There were a few types of names that may have been distinctly feminine, those that described qualities, characteristics, or tasks uniquely associated with women, such as Malthace (Soft), Canthara (Pure), Titthe (Nursemaid), or Samacion (an article of female clothing). Although these names are obviously feminine, they do not fully disclose the social status of their bearers.[11] Neuter diminutives such as Boidion (Little Calf), Callistion (Little Beauty), and Chrysion (Goldie) also typically occur among women's names, as well as among hetaeras and slaves. Yet another category appears distinct from the names assigned to males, names formed from abstract feminine nouns. An anecdote from Philostratus' *Life of Apollonius* illustrates this practice: when stopped on his way out of Mesopotamia by a customs official, who asked him to declare his "goods," Apollonius replied:

> "I am taking with me Sophrosyne (Moderation), Dikaiosyne (Justice), Arete (Virtue), Egkratia (Continence), Andreia (Courage), and Akesis (Discipline)." And in this way he uttered a number of feminine names. The other, already seeing his own gain, said, "You must then declare these female slaves (*doulas*)." Apollonius answered, "Impossible, for they are not female slaves (*doulas*) that I am taking out with me, but respectable ladies (*despoinas*)." (Philostr. *VA* 1. 20; trans. Conybeare)

Names formed from feminine abstractions may have suggested the qualities or characteristics the Athenians wished to encourage in girls, and as such contributed "to a tendency to depersonalize and objectify women."[12] Naming practices facilitated social control in classical Athens not only with regard to women but also in relation to slaves and prostitutes, as we saw in the discussions of Mania and Nemeas. In the anecdote above, the customs official's initial reaction upon hearing these names suggests that such abstractions more properly belonged to female slaves, a category of women that often served as prostitutes.

In many cases, hetaeras' names did not differ at all from those of Athenian citizen women. Schneider in his entry "Hetairai" in *Real Encyclopädie* concludes that only 10% of the 300 names included in his list could be termed "Hetäresnamen." This remark certainly applies to many of the hetaeras' names found in Book 13 of Athenaeus (see Appendix III). Many appear to have been common Athenian names that would not have marked the bearer as a hetaera.[13] Archedice, Archippe, Euphrosyne, Melissa, Nicarete, Phile, and Plangon are all attested numerous times on Attic funerary reliefs, in family groupings, from the classical through the Hellenistic periods.[14] Similarly, many other names attributed to hetaeras appear to have been popular women's names in archaic and classical Athens: Aristagora, Aristocleia, Demo, Glycera, Malthace, Myrrhine, Nico, Pamphila, Phanostrate, Stratonice, Theano, and Theodote. Even the names Callistion, Chrysis, and Mania, names associated with well-known courtesans in Athenaeus, occur over ten times in Attica during the classical and Hellenistic periods.

Attic Identity, Foreign Birth

The title of the Hellenistic courtesan treatises, *On Athenian Courtesans* (*Peri tōn Athēnēsi Hetairidōn*), sometimes shortened to *On Courtesans*, suggests that such women were Athenian, or at least bore Atticized names. Indeed, Myrtilus assumes as much when he exclaims, just before referring to these works, "Our beautiful Athens produced such a quantity of courtesans . . . . a throng such as no populous city ever yet had!" (*hai gar kalai hēmōn Athēnai tosouton plēthos ēnegkan hetairōn*, 583d). And while Athenian men may have kept courtesans from Asia Minor in classical Athens, the Hellenistic dynasts clearly preferred courtesans from cities in Old Greece. Thais, connected first with Alexander, then with Ptolemy I Soter (576d), Harpalus' Pythionice and Glycera (Diod. Sic. 17. 108. 4–6), Lamia and Leaena II, the lovers of Demetrius Poliorcetes, all were said to have been of Attic origin.[15] In fact, Athenaeus records that Lamia had a citizen father, Cleanor of Athens (577c; cf. Diog. Laert. 5. 76); another, Euphrosyne, was the daughter of a fuller, one who cleaned and manufactured clothing, a profession ridiculed by Aristophanes as lower class.[16] Bilistiche purportedly traced her descent from the Atreids, although she could have come from Macedon.[17] Thais' citizen status and Athenian patriotism, in Athenaeus' view, explain her pivotal role in the burning of the palace at Persepolis (576d–e), a story discussed more fully in Chapter 5. None of these accounts, however, can be taken as secure evidence for hetaeras of Attic birth or citizen status, but suggest, instead, how fully these women had became identified with classical Athens and Hellenic *paideia* by the third century B.C.E. In emphasizing their Attic origins, the Hellenistic monarchs and their biographers may have attempted to infuse their courts with the glamour of classical Athens, and, as we saw in the last chapter, they may have served a similar function among the Second Sophistic writers.

In contrast, their names suggest that most hetaeras were probably not of Attic birth but worked or resided in Athens; indeed, the designation *Attikē* in Athenaeus may only mean that these women hailed from Athens.[18] The orator of *Against Neaera* repeatedly harps on the courtesan's status as a foreigner because of its implications for citizenship (*xenē*, [Dem.] 59. 14. 17 and *passim*). Chrysis in Menander's *Samia* is said to have moved from Samos to Athens to work as a free courtesan (Men. *Sam.* 21, 25 Sandbach). Schneider and others maintain that an influx of hetaeras from Asia Minor to Athens in late sixth and early fifth centuries, facilitated by an increase in long-distance trade, brought women like Aspasia of Miletus to the city.[19] Indeed, the widespread representation of prostitutes on sympotic vases during the last quarter of the sixth century would seem to support their appearance in Athens just prior to the democratic revolution of 508 B.C.E.[20]

Many of the names attributed to hetaeras in Athenaeus, beyond those commonly given to citizen women as discussed above, suggest non-Attic origins. The following names are seldom attested in Attica, but are found somewhat more commonly in the Aegean islands, Cyprus, and Cyrenaica: Antheia, Archeanassa, Bittis, Boa, Cottina, Lais, Laodice, Leaena, Lyca,

Lyde, Megiste, Mnesis, Nais, Nannion, Nausion, Nicostratis, Nysa, Sige, Sinope, Stagonion, Telesis, Thallusa, and Thaumarion. Two of these names, Laodice and Myrto, are associated with Jews from various periods, while Lais occurs eight times in Cyrenaica, lending support to the traditional view that some of these women had their ethnic origins in or were identified with the ancient Near East.[21] Similarly, popular hetaeras' names formed from the roots habro*, myrt*, and lamp* occur with some frequency in these regions. The name Rhodopis, found as an inscription on an Attic cup by Makron, is found in Asia Minor and may possibly reflect the influx of hetaeras from this region in the early fifth century.[22]

Many of the hetaeras mentioned by Athenaeus are said to originate in Asia Minor. Medontis, for example, came from Abydus, a Mysian city on the Asiatic side of the Hellespont colonized around 700 B.C.E. by the Milesians, but more than two centuries later under the control of the Athenian empire and known for the licentiousness of its women (12. 525b). Ionian cities produced the courtesans Archeanassa and Leontion of Colophon, Plangon and Aspasia the Elder of Miletus, and Aspasia II of Phocaea. Within a mile of the Ionian coast, the island of Samos had a long association with courtesans, including Bacchis, Lampito, and Myrrhine, one of Demetrius Poliorcetes' courtesans (593a). The hetaera named "Sappho," the doublet of the lyric poet, was said to have originated in Eresus, a city on the island of Lesbos, about six miles northwest of Asia Minor. The courtesans Eirene, Danae, and Laodice all hailed from Ephesus on the western coast of Asia Minor, while Boa reputedly came from Paphlagonia in the north. The common name of Lyde, an ethnic, earns one woman the epithet barbaros (597a). Moreover, in an observation cribbed from Herodotus (Hdt. 2. 135), Athenaeus alludes to several courtesans as originating in Egypt, in particular Archedice (although not an Egyptian name), Doriche or Rhodopis, Didyme, and Neitetis. He even singles out his hometown of Naucratis for the beauty and celebrity of its hetaeras (endoxous de hetairas kai epi kallei diapherousas, 596b).

The use of place names for courtesans is attested as early as Attic Old comedy with Aristophanes' two references to Cyrene (Ar. Ran. 1325–1328; Thesm. 98); the practice shows the close association of prostitutes with urban centers and ports of trade. According to Athenaeus, the aging Sinope had as her sobriquet, Abydus, the name of a prosperous town on the Black Sea, at that time in a state of decay (12. 524f), and the birthplace of Medontis, as we saw above. Other courtesans with the names of cities include Anticyra, a Phocian port and the name of the region famous for its hellebore; Scione, a hetaera who lived in the time of Themistocles, and the name of a town in northern Greece, as well as Nysa and Olympia. Naming a hetaera after a river, as in the case of Tigris (590a), also belongs to this category. Whereas many of the names and sobriquets of hetaeras indicated their foreign origins, if not in reality at least in the Greek imaginary, their meanings for Athenians of the late archaic and classical periods are difficult to gauge. The attribution of place names to hetaeras may have paradoxically evoked their servile status, as slaves were normally foreigners and designated by depersonalizing ethnic terms. At the same time, they may have conjured, at least for Athenians in the late archaic period, the glamour and luxury of Asia Minor, an association that may have in turn reinforced, as Kurke believes, aristocratic ideology.[23] By the late classical period, however, such women were considered an expensive democratic luxury that only the very wealthy could afford; thus Socrates in Plato's *Republic* associates them with the decadent "city of pigs" that he modeled on the late Athenian democracy (Pl. *Rep.* 373a). By the time of the Second Sophistic, however, there is a pronounced tendency to regard all famous hetaeras of the classical and early Hellenistic periods as Athenian.

The Names of Hetaeras

Although many of the names mentioned by Athenaeus do not differ substantially from those of respectable women, others appear to diverge, some radically, from standard Athenian naming practices of the classical and early Hellenistic periods. Indeed, the spectators of New comedy probably could have distinguished the character of the hetaera not only by her mask, but also by her name. The naming practices of hetaeras differed in many respects from those of respectable Athenian women: first, they had a public dimension because they were heard by men, in the comic theater, in the lawcourts, and on the streets. Second, it was common for a hetaera to have more than one name (and not so for respectable women); indeed, in the case of common female names, these secondary names probably helped differentiate hetaeras from women of the citizen class, thereby denoting their marginal and mutable social status. Of course, it is not always easy to recognize a nickname; strictly speaking, one can only be verified when another name is also attributed to the same woman (see the table below for a complete list). Phryne (Toad), for instance, was originally called Mnesarete (591e), the courtesan Mania, Melissa (578c–d), Leme, Phylacion (probably not itself an actual name as it nowhere appears among Attic inscriptions), and Aspasia II, Milto (576d). The speaker of *Against Neaera* may wish to imply that Phano, the daughter of Neaera, was also a hetaera when he claims that her original name was Strybele (*tote men Strubēlēn ekaloun, nuni de Phanō*, [Dem.] 59. 50; cf. 594a; note that Athenaeus alludes to her as Strymbele). Indeed, the name Neaera (possibly from *neiaira*, belly) itself may have been a nickname, as it is nowhere attested in inscriptional sources.

The attribution of nicknames to notorious individuals, to politicians as well as to more marginal figures such as courtesans and parasites, appears to have been standard practice in classical Athens. As Plutarch observes, this custom often obscured the real names of individuals for later authors (Plut. *Mor.* 401b). In his discussion of parasites, Athenaeus states that such names were given in "derisive jest" (*epichleuei paizontes*) and were frequently based on physical attributes: so one Koniortos (Dustcloud) earned his name from his unkempt and dirty appearance (6. 238d). Other parasites took their nicknames from the delicacies they sponged off the tables of their sympotic hosts: Karabos (Crayfish), Skombros (Mackerel), and Semidalis (Cake Flour, 6. 242d). For these stock sympotic figures, as with hetaeras, such names converted them into objects of sympotic and comic mockery and fixed their place in the social order. Athenaeus typically designates these secondary names with the verb *epikalein*; other terms include simply *onoma* or *onomazein* (Gnome, 245d; Phryne/Sestus, 591c), and more exceptionally, *epōnumon* (Anticyra/Oia; 586f; cf. Aphye, 586a–b). His assertion that Milto later changed her name (*metonomasthēnai*) to Aspasia, probably in emulation of Pericles' concubine, suggests that hetaeras may have adopted new names upon entering their profession.

Attic Old comedy and oratory are filled with the derogatory nicknames of historical persons. Aristophanes uses them to turn his contemporaries into objects of comic abuse: the appellation Kolearchos (sheath rump) punningly identifies Clearchus as a pathic while the name Timarchus becomes a byword for male prostitution.[24] Pathics in general tended to have pet names such as Lamb and Raven, as well as more eroticized terms.[25] In oratory, nicknames comprised a form of political abuse, although they appear to have been well-known sobriquets, not just literary inventions. We find, for example, Archedemus, the Glamon (Blear-Eyed; Lys. 14. 25), a popular leader who pushed for the prosecution of the commanders after Arginusae in 406 B.C.E., and the name Kyrebion (Bran) given to the execrable Epicrates (Dem. 19. 287). Humorous nicknames are represented as something of a fad among the sons of the elite (*kaloi kagathoi*) taken to task in Demosthenes' *Against Conon*: they patronize hetaeras and refer to themselves as Ithyphallos (Erection) and Autolekythos (Beggar, Dem. 54. 14). Demosthenes himself was known as Battalus or Batalus (Aeschin. 1. 131), "a scurrilous epithet of debauchees or stammerers."[26] Aeschines attributes this name to Demosthenes in a context of abuse, where he describes the latter's effeminacy and transvestism, while elsewhere, he uses it in connection with his sexual incontinence (Aeschin. 1. 131, 2. 99; cf. Dem. 18. 180).

As public figures and frequent targets of invective in both comedy and oratory, hetaeras and other prostitutes attracted such sobriquets as early as the late archaic period. Numerous Attic vases from the late sixth century to the middle of the fifth century depicting hetaeras are accompanied by name inscriptions. In the early period, many of these appear to have been nicknames that related to their activities or "Handwerk," as Peschel calls it.[27] A stamnos by Smikros (Brussels A717) names one figure Choro (Dance), another Helike (Screw), a word that may refer either to a dance move or to a sexual position, and Rhode, a name with eastern associations that alludes to feminine beauty.[28] These more euphemistic names contrast the cruder sobriquets found on other vases: Syko, the name inscribed above a flute player on a red figure kelch krater by Euphronius (Munich Antikensammlungen 8935/8945. 6. 8950) calls attention to her sexual availability, as the term *sukon* (ripe fig) denotes the pudenda muliebra.[29]

A red figure psykter by Euphronius similarly depicts several figures whose names denote their professional activities (Hermitage Museum B644): Agape (Love) symbolizes the amorous encounters of the symposium, Palaisto (Wrestler) plays on the Greek association between athletic and sexual activity, while Secline, a name also found on a red figure kalpis (Brussels Mus. Royaux R351), perhaps encourages her partner to recline.[30] A red figure cup depicting a sympotic orgy (Berlin Staatliche Museen 3251) names one of the figures Corone, a generic literary term for hetaeras discussed more fully below.[31] Peschel argues that in using these names, vase painters in the late sixth century referred to real women, more or less well-known in Athens at the time; and yet such scenes should not be understood as portraits, but as generic sympotic tableaux given particularity through realistic names.[32]

Fewer hetaeras' names are found on vases produced during the middle of the fifth century; whereas the earlier names reflected the women's professional activities, these later vases employ more euphemisms, using generic names that are less explicitly sexual (Peschel 1987: 183). For example, the name Oenophile (Wine Lover) given to one hetaera on a lekythos (London British Museum 1922. 10.–1.1) evokes her function as a sympotic symbol rather than as a sex object; indeed, Athenaeus, citing Gorgias, gives Paroinos (Drunken with Wine) as a generic name for courtesans. Another sympotic vase, a red figure cup by the Brygos Painter (London British Museum E 68), ascribes the names Nicopile and Callisto to two women; the latter perhaps has an echo in Callistion, the name given to one well-known fourth-century Athenian hetaera mentioned by Athenaeus (583a; 585b). By the second half of the fifth century, such vase inscriptions disappear almost entirely, and along with them, the practice of ascribing nicknames to vase representations of hetaeras; indeed, only three examples of hetaeras' names are found and these probably allude to real people: a red figure dinos in Ferrara (Museo Archeologico Nazionale 9380 T11 C VP 701) contains the names Apenris, an auletris, and Cleanoe, while a red figure stamnos in the British Museum names another auletris Cleodoxa (London British Museum E 454).

Similar types of nicknames are associated with the celebrated courtesans mentioned in Book 13 of the *Deipnosophistae*. The table below gives 24 secondary names of courtesans along with their purported primary names; in fact, fully 22 of these names come from Athenaeus, and most of these from Book 13.[33]

Nicknames of Hetaeras

Secondary Name	Translation	Primary Name	Reference
Abydus	Asian City	Sinope	Ath. 586a
Aix	Goat	Nico, Nannion	Ath. 582e–f, 587a
Anticyra	Hellebore	Hoia or Oia	Ath. 586f
Axine	Ax	Lais	Ael. VH 12.5; 14. 35
Aphye	Anchovy	Nicostratis, Stagonion	Ath. 586a–b
Clausigelos	Teary Laughter	Phryne	Ath. 591c
Clepsydra	Waterclock	Metiche	Ath. 567d
Corone	Crow	Theocleia	Ath. 583e
Cynamyia	Dog Fly	Nicion	Ath. 157a
Didrachmon	Two Drachmas	Phylacion	Ath. 596f
Gnome	Judgement	Unknown	Ath. 245d
Hys	Sow	Callistion	Ath. 583a
Leme	Rheum	Phylacion	Ath. 569f
Lychnos	Lamp	Synoris	Ath. 583e
Paroinos	Drunken	Unknown	Ath. 583e
Parorama	Oversight	Phylacion	Ath. 596f
Pasiphile	Loved by All	Plangon	Ath. 594c–d
Phtheiropyle	Lousegate	Phanostrate	Ath. 586a
Proscenion	Stage	Nannion	Ath. 587b
Ptochelene	Begging Helen	Callistion	Ath. 585b
Saperdion	Little Fish	Phryne	Ath. 591c
Sestus	Fleecer	Phryne	Ath. 591c
Scotodine	Vertigo	Nicostrate	Ath. 467e
Theatrotoryne	Stage Pounder	Melissa	Ath. 157a

A majority of professional names for hetaeras derive from the animal kingdom; Leaena, Leontion, and Lais all have as their root the Greek word for lion and possibly play on the erotic lioness *schēma*.[34] Hippe (Mare), Hippaphesis (Starting Post of a Race Course), and Synoris (Pair of Horses) all allude to equestrian metaphors for sex, well illustrated by an epigram of Asclepiades (*Anth. Pal.* 5. 203) that depicts a hetaera sitting astride her lover, a position much sought-after but frequently denied by hetaeras on the grounds that it was degrading, if we are to believe Machon (cf. 581d–e).[35] Hippe's *erastēs*, the one who fed the livestock at Demetrius Poliorcetes' court, rounds out the sexual joke (583a–b). Similarly, a scholion to Aristophanes' *Ecclesiazusae* 1021 explains the reference to the mythical mares of Diomedes as prostitutes who wore men out with their lovemaking. Hys (Sow), the sobriquet of the courtesan Callistion, evokes the scene in Aristophanes' *Acharnians* where the starving Megarian attempts to prostitute his two young daughters as "piggies" for a bag of salt, playing on the meaning of the word *choiros* (Ar. *Ach.* 764–823).[36] The nickname Goat applied both to Nannion and to Nico underscores the rapacious sexuality of the hetaera, evoking the discourse of loss and waste that contact with her engenders.

The many names that refer to birds or fish may have served as slang terms or generic descriptors of hetaeras, especially since they so often appear in comic texts.[37] Neottis (Chick) may have been a colloquialism for a prostitute, given the numerous plays with this title, and Epicrates' reference in his *Antilais* to the courtesan in her youth as a "young chick" (*neottos kai nea*, Epicrates, *Antilais* FKA = F3. 11 KA = 570c). Similarly, a fragment by Eubulus describes courtesans as birds that ensnare or deceive their customers (*tas paleutrias*, Eubulus, *Pannychis* F82 KA = 568e), while another by Ephippus depicts a hetaera as kissing with an open mouth, like a sparrow (*strouthias*, Ephippus, *Empole* F6 KA = 571f). Philataerus' *Cynagis*, a play which possibly takes its title from the name of a hetaera, mentions Corone (Crow) and Cossyphe (Blackbird) as generic nicknames for courtesans (F9 KA =587f). The name Corone, in particular, appears frequently in connection with hetaeras and in the visual tradition as well, as we saw above; Athenaeus attributes it to Theocleia (583e).[38] Given their association with luxury and the symposium, fish figure prominently in the naming of hetaeras, as well as of parasites.[39] Aphye (Anchovy) serves as a generic term for prostitute in Hyperides' *Aristagora*, a name later applied by Apollodorus to the sisters Stagonion and Anthis, because they were "light of color, thin, and had large eyes" (*leukai kai leptai ousai tous ophthalmous megalous eichon*, Hyp. F24 Jensen = 586b). Antiphanes in his courtesan list also gives this name to Nicostratis (586b). Archippus' play, *Ichthyes* (Fishes), invites a direct comparison of the pleasures of the table with those of the bed in its depiction of an auletris and a hetaera named after fish: Atherine (Smelt) and Sepia (Cuttlefish, 7. 329c).[40] Athenaeus, citing Apollodorus, distinguishes the two Phrynes by means of their nicknames: one is called Clausigelos (Teary Laughter) and the other Saperdion (Little Fish, 591c).[41] Other generic names for courtesans include Ocimon (Basil, Eubulus F53 KA = 567a), Galene (Calm, Philetaerus F9. 6 = 587f), and Opora (Harvest, Alexis FF169–70 = 567c).[42] Paroinos, the nickname of an unnamed woman in Gorgias' list (*epiklētheisan*, 583e), probably also represents a common term, since it appears as a generic descriptor of hetaeras in Antiphanes' *Lyde* (F144 KA = 445b–e) and evokes the role of the hetaera at the symposium like the names inscribed on vases. Indeed, the drunkenness of hetaeras was, according to Athenaeus, a commonplace of the comic tradition (587b).

Some of the other secondary names play up the commercial aspects of the hetaera: one of Leme's nicknames, Didrachmon (For Two Drachmas), advertises her required fee while Metiche's *nom de guerre*, Clepsydra, alludes to the clock used to time her dalliances.[43] Others underscore the dangers of conducting business with courtesans: one of the Phrynes earned the sobriquet Sestus (Fleecer), according to the orators, "because she sifted and stripped those who slept with her" (*onomazomenēn Sēston kaleisthai dia to aposēthein kai apoduein tous sunontas autēi*, 591c), while the name Ptochelene (Begging Helen), calls attention to the economic perils of their commerce. Proscenion (Stage), the other nickname of Nannion, not only identifies her with theatrical illusion and cosmetic artifice, ideas discussed more fully in Chapter 4, but alludes to the commodity status of her body:

> Nannion was called Proscenium because she had a pretty face (*prosōpon asteion*) and wore golden ornaments and expensive clothing, but when divested of these, she appeared very unattractive. (*aischrotatē*, 587b)

The name commodifies both aspects of Nannion's appearance, her clothing, and her nakedness: while her costly garments flaunt the price of her body, her nudity marks it as an object available for men. The explanation of Phanostrate's nickname Phtheiropyle (Lousegate) similarly dehumanizes and commodifies the hetaera:

> Concerning Phanostrate, Apollodorus in his work *On Athenian Courtesans* says that she was nicknamed Lousegate because she picked lice off herself (*ephtheirizeto*) as she stood (*hestōsa*) at the door. (*thuras* A or *pulas* CE, 586a)

Whether she stood at the door or the gate, the name vividly advertises her status as a commodity, since the participle *hestōsa*, especially in association with *pulē*, recalls the activities of brothel whores.[44] Another group of names function either as terms of endearment or emphasize the amorous activities of hetaeras: Glycera, Glycerion, Phila, Philinna, and Potheine. The names formed from the stem *lamp**, Lampas, Lampito, Lampyris, or related in meaning, like Lychnos (the nickname of Synoris) and Thryallis (Wick), also allude to the sexual activities of hetaeras, as lamps are frequently invoked in Greek and Latin love poetry as the witnesses of love-making.[45] And more crudely, names such as Lenaetocystus (Crotch Press?) and Ischas (Fig) speak directly to the hetaera's sexual services just as some of the names inscribed on Attic vases.

The Names of Slaves

One cannot understate the extent to which many of the names associated with courtesans evoked those of slaves. Myrtilus' discussion of the inappropriateness of the name Nemeas for an auletris indicates that such names could be used of slaves.[46] The passage indicates not only that many prostitutes were in fact slaves, a point that has already been well established by scholars, but that Athenian naming practices reflected and even reinforced this status. For example, names based on abstractions that related to "the situation, qualities, or defects of the subject" (Garlan 1988: 28) typified the names of female slaves, as the anecdote of Philostratus quoted at the beginning of the chapter strongly suggests. The same type of name is also applied to hetaeras, e.g., Eirene (Peace), Euphrosyne (Mirth), Galene (Calm), Opora (Harvest), Peitho (Persuasion), and Sige (Silence).[47] To this category belong names based on economic transactions, such as Didrachmon and Obole. Names derived from ethnics also typically belonged to slaves:

> The Athenians would either name their slaves after the peoples from whom they were imported, like 'Lydos' or 'Syros', or give them names which were common in those countries, like 'Manes' or 'Midias' for a Phrygian, or 'Tibios' for a Paphlegonian. (Strabo 7. 3. 12)

In Attic Old and New comedy, Mania is a slave name, while the names Lyca, Lyde, and Grymea all have servile associations. The length to which Machon must go to argue for the Attic origins of the hetaera Mania's name shows how strongly the Athenian imaginary would have associated it with a foreigner. Many of the hetaeras' names discussed above, especially place names, ethnics, feminine abstractions, and nicknames based on commerce and social function, readily fit into one or more of these categories, strengthening the probability that many of these names denoted or derived from a servile social status.

Although Myrtilus rarely alludes to the servile status of courtesans, given his focus on wealthy and celebrated women, he occasionally mentions stories of enslavement or captivity. Lais II, born in Sicilian Hyccara, purportedly first traveled to Corinth as a spear captive of the Sicilian expedition, and then later went to Athens (*aichmalōtos genomenē*, 588c). The Samian courtesan Bacchis, an auletris and the eromene of an anonymous Colophonian youth (594b–c, 595a), is referred to as the female slave of the Thracian procuress Sinope, while Pythionice, in turn, is said to have been her slave, an impossibility given that slaves could not own property. From a narrative perspective, Pythionice's lowly origins as a triple slave and triple porne, "a woman who had been shared by all who desired her at the same price for all," surely enhances the story of her precipitous ascent to the role of Harpalus' revered consort (595b–c). Similarly, the hetaeras Anteia, Aristocleia, Isthmias, Metanira, Neaera, Nicarete, Phila, and Stratola are all mentioned as the slaves of Casius of Elis (the latter name is probably a corruption of Charisios, cf. [Dem.] 59. 18–20). Hyperides is said to have purchased this Phila, or a homonymous woman, and kept her as freed woman (*eleutherōsas*), eventually putting her in charge of his household (590d). Even Rhodopis, the first woman to be called a hetaera in the Greek literary tradition, began life as the slave of a Samian man, along with the storyteller Aesop (Hdt. 2. 134).[48] But on the whole, Athenaeus de-emphasizes the connection between prostitution and slavery, choosing instead to focus on the wealthy and economically independent hetaeras, the *megalomisthoi*, and their liaisons with famous men.

While neither Athenaeus nor Demosthenes mention how these slave hetaeras acquired their names, Athenian custom dictated that their owners would have named them, since "the slave was an outsider who brought no rights with him from the society he came from, and had no claims on the host society which maintained him. . . . he had no name apart from that which his owner chose to give him."[49] Because the names of slaves could be changed at several critical junctures in their lives, including at birth into slavery within a household, at manumission, or upon the passing of a manumitted slave into the local population, they were generally more mutable than those of citizen men. The widespread use of secondary names by hetaeras, coupled with the Athenian law cited by Polemon forbidding prostitutes and female slaves to assume the names of important festivals, indicates that perhaps the women themselves selected their professional names to mark their entry into the profession. For citizens, in contrast, names and naming comprised a primary means of stabilizing and perpetuating the patrilineal household.[50] This even held true for citizen women, whose public naming on funerary monuments reinforced the integrity of their natal households by continuing to affiliate them with their fathers even after marriage and death.[51] The names of hetaeras, in contrast, conveyed their marginal and mutable social status as figures outside the control of a male oikos.

The Use of the Metronymic

In the earlier discussion of Athenian naming practices, it was observed that metronymics accompanied a small percentage of women's names on funerary inscriptions, instead of the more typical formulation of the father's name in the genitive case. According to Ogden, of the approximately 70 instances of the metronymic in private inscriptions from throughout the Greek world, only 17 are male. He hypothesizes that the metronymic typically occurred in the context of women's cults, especially those in which the mother-daughter relationship had a primary significance, such as that of Demeter and Kore, or else indicated sacerdotal status, a profession that may have been transmitted from mother to daughter (Ogden 1996: 94–5). Metronymics also occur with regularity in spells and curses, "the only significant body of documentary evidence for women's language in the Greek world" (Ogden 1996: 95). Among the Alexandrian poets, identification of speakers by the maternal line appears with regularity in domestic genre scenes; indeed, an epigram of Nossis alludes to the poet's mother as "Theophilis, daughter of Cleocha" (Nossis, *Anth. Pal.* 6. 265).[52] This usage may reflect a gender-specific speech practice of actual women.[53] More important for our study, however, the metronymic appears to have had a specialized use among courtesans: a procuress in one of Herodas' poems refers to herself as "Gyllis, the mother of Philaenis," the putative author of a Hellenistic sex manual (Herod. 1. 5).

Athenaeus regularly refers to the matrilineal descent of his courtesans. We hear of Damasandra or Timandra, mother of the Lais II and of Theodote (535c; 574e); Nannion, mother of Corone II (587b); and Corone I, the mother of Callistion (583a); the Epicurean Leontion, the mother of Danae (593b–d); Gnathaena, mother or grandmother of Gnathaenion (585a); and Thalassis, mother of Glycera (586c). Nannion's daughter, Corone II, earned the sobriquet "Grandma" because of her inherited profession: "Now there was a daughter of Nannion named Corone who acquired the name Tethe (Grandmother) because of her triple prostitution" (*ek triporneias*, 587b), a phrase that may indicate descent from a prostitute mother. The speaker of *Against Neaera* repeatedly refers to Phano as "the daughter of Neaera" ([Dem.] 59. 51, 55, 59, 63, 67, 72) and accuses Stephanus of passing off "daughters of hetaeras" as his own ([Dem.] 59. 13).[54] The threat posed by Neaera's acquittal, that the daughters of citizen men could become whores and that married women might turn into hetaeras, perhaps plays on the idea of prostitution as an intergenerational practice handed down from mother to daughter ([Dem.] 59. 113). Another speech uses the phrase "born of a hetaera" to discredit one daughter's claim of legitimacy (*ex hetairas ousan*, Isaeus 3. 48, 52, 55 and *passim*). So, too, in Plautus' *Cistellaria*, the procuress Syra speaks of bearing a daughter from a transient union and of training her in the arts of prostitution (Plaut. *Cist.* 39–41).

A joke attributed to Diogenes plays on the obscure paternity of the offspring of prostitutes: upon seeing the son of a hetaera casting a stone at a crowd, he quipped, "Take care lest you strike your father" (Favorinus, *Rhet.* F112. 1). Based on this observation, the rare appearance of a metronymic in the inscriptional evidence suggests, especially in the cases of names known to have been associated with hetaeras, that such women were prostitutes and their fathers unknown. One inscription from the fourth century B.C.E. refers to Callistion (IGii² 11793 (PA8109a)) as the daughter of Nicomache, perhaps the "Crow" of Machon's anecdote (Machon 433 = 583a). Another fourth-century inscription for a woman named Aspasia describes her as the daughter of Mania, also the name of a famous courtesan (IG ii² 10892 (PA 2635a)). Similarly, Malthace is referred to as the daughter of Magadis (IG ii² 12026). Another woman bearing a name commonly associated with courtesans, Galene, is modified by the metronymic Polycleia.[55] Given the prevalence of prostitution as a female occupation transmitted from generation to generation in the literary sources, it is likely that many of the metronymics found on funerary inscriptions can be explained as referring to courtesans or other type of female prostitute.

Conclusion

The use of the metronymic to refer to courtesans, and the absence of paternal names, shows just how far outside normative Athenian social hierarchies the hetaera and her brothel counterparts lived. The same ambiguities are found in the Greek terms that identified them, as we saw in the introductory chapter. Just as slave names reflected a mutable and rootless existence, so the surplus of sobriquets for individual courtesans and their shifting attributions calls attention to their lack of personal identity and social stability. The woman referred to as Leme (Rheum), also known as Didrachmon (For Two Drachmas) and Parorama (Oversight), and by her "real" name, Phylacion, actually recedes under these multiple layers of signification, becoming only a series of derogatory and fictionalizing terms.[56] Similarly, the identity of the hetaera Callistion is subsumed by her denigrating nicknames, Hys (Sow, 583a) and Ptochelene (Beggar Helen, 585). The use of pseudonyms meant that such women were always multiply signified, and thus never fully individuated, even in the classical period.

Names, whether birth names or derogatory nicknames, stigmatized and fictionalized hetaeras both in the context of symposium as well as on the comic stage, erasing them as historical subjects and constructing them as objects of male discourse. The preservation and collection of these names by the Alexandrian prosopographers must be viewed as central to the project of fetishizing an idealized Hellenic past through the decontextualization of names, characters, and quotations, a process also evident in the *Deipnosophistae.* The literary tradition assimilated these figures to the intellectual and literary environment of the late classical period, even to the extent of Atticizing patently non-Attic names and minimizing their servile status. Within the context of Book 13, the characterization of Myrtilus as a grammarian preoccupied with the glossing of obscure courtesans' names exemplifies, as well as parodies, the *paideia* of contemporary sophists, with their love of literary collection. For these practitioners of pure linguistic Atticism, the process of fetishizing the hetaera, whether at the sympotic table or on the comic stage, began with the name.

CHAPTER 3

The Witticisms of Courtesans and Attic *Paideia*

A certain courtesan said to the woman who reproached her with the charge that she did not like to work or touch wool, "Yet, such as I am, in this short time I have taken down three webs."[1]

Just as the names and nicknames of courtesans attracted scholarly interest in the Hellenistic period, so, too, their witticisms were circulated in anecdotal and poetic compilations such as the *Chreiae* of Machon, excerpted at 577d to 583d of Book 13 of the *Deipnosophistae*. Because easily severed from their original context and adapted to a new one, these sayings may be viewed as a form of literary quotation that fetishizes the figure of the hetaera, and through her, the Greek literary tradition. Not only do their witty quips demonstrate the lofty erudition of courtesans capable, like Athenaeus' banqueters, of quoting Euripides chapter and verse, they signify their status as sympotic performers who transmit Attic *paideia* and Greek literary culture. At the same time, the witticisms of hetaeras involve a verbal dynamic in which obscene punning and literary quotation threaten to disrupt normative class and gender categories while placing the hetaera in discursive control.[2] Whether in the symposium and its public correlative, the comic theater, or in Athenaeus' literary banquet, the hetaera's witty speech provokes the trangressive laughter of temporary license.[3] As ventriloquized by Myrtilus, this parodic, carnivalesque discourse inserts into the conversation of respectable men a risqué jesting that comically exposes and denounces the pretensions of philosophers.[4]

Flattery, Riddles, and Double-Entendres

Although Athenaeus does not include any female characters in his *Deip-nosophistae*, hetaeras probably engaged in verbal exchanges with their male clientele at the symposium in the form of poetic and rhetorical improvisa-tion, philosophical discussion, *chreiae*, and verbal games, as well as provid-ing theatrical entertainment (Xen. *Symp.* 2. 2; Pl. *Symp.* 176e).[5] This skilled repartee probably required of the most elite courtesans a basic literary ed-ucation; indeed, some were even said to have written literary treatises of their own. Another function of their conversation was to entertain and draw men's minds away from the everyday concerns of business and polit-ical life. In his opening defense of "real" hetaeras (*tōn ontōs hetairōn*, 571c), Myrtilus emphasizes their value as genteel entertainers whose charming conversation brightens the spirits of their clientele:

> And then if one of us happens to come in feeling troubled,
> she greets him with pleasing flattery (*ekolakeusen hēdeōs*);
> she kisses him, not squeezing her lips close together,
> as if he were her enemy, but opening her mouth
> as sparrows do; she sits him down, she soothes and gladdens him,
> and soon takes away all his trouble and makes him happy again.
> (Ephippus, *Empole* F6 = 571e–f)

Making pleasant conversation appears to have comprised a major portion of the hetaera's art: Socrates also mentions delightful speech as one of the hetaera's many tools of seduction (*ho ti an legousa euphrainois*, Xen. *Mem.* 3. 11. 10). The Hellenistic poet Machon similarly describes a courtesan as "being well equipped in speech and conversation" (*phōnēi d' homiliai te kechorēgēmenē*, Machon 198 = 578c). In one of Lucian's dialogues, the successful hetaera not only smiles frequently but also provides her clients with clever *homilia*, verbal and sexual companionship (*prosomilousa dexiōs*, *Dial. meret.* 6. 3). A lover in one of Alciphron's letters praises the flattering blandishments and the Siren-like conversation of his hetaera (*homiliais*, Alci-phr. 4. 11. 7). The talk of hetaeras on the Greek comic stage is typically filled with endearments: in one fragment quoted by Athenaeus, brothel workers at-tract customers through their use of flattering diminutives, calling old men *patridia* and young men *appharia* (569c).[6] So also the Athenian courtesan Philaenium in Plautus' *Asinaria* is described as speaking *verba blanda* (525).

This conversation involves multiple levels of signification: in a fragment of Anaxilas quoted by Larensis at the beginning of Book 13, the prostitute's brazen self-advertisement is simultaneously riddling, flattering, and obscene:

> It is possible to call every porne a Theban Sphinx;
> they chatter not in simple language, but in riddles,

about how sweetly they like to love and kiss and come together.
And one says, "Let me have a four-footed bed or chair";
another, "Make it a tripod"; still another, "A two-footed little girl."

(Anaxilas, *Neottis* F22. 22–26 KA = 558d)

Here the hetaera (the word is used later, and interchangeably, with porne) recasts the riddle solved by Oedipus ("What walks on four feet in the morning, two feet in the afternoon and three feet in the evening?") into an obscene advertisement of her sexual expertise. Riddles, defined by Athenaeus as "a problem put in jest" (*griphos problēma esti paistikon*, 10. 448c), regularly accompanied drinking at the symposium and often alluded to the accoutrements or conditions of the drinking party.[7] But here the hetaera cleverly parodies the literary tradition, reducing the tragic predicament of Oedipus to a vulgar joke.

There is also a tradition of females propounding riddles. New comedy features a mother-daughter pair riddling about sleep in a fragment of Alexis' *Hypnos* (10. 449d–e) and Sappho's famous riddle about a letter (10. 450e– 451b). Likewise, Cleobolina, the daughter of one of the seven sages, tells a riddle about an *aulos* (Plu. *Mor.* 150e–f). At the Adonia, three Samian girls pose an obscene riddle about a phallus while drinking (Diphilus F49 KA = 10. 451b); courtesans at the symposium probably propounded similar riddles for the amusement of their guests.[8] Anaxilas in the quotation above may have drawn on the tradition of prostitutes as riddle-tellers who use their fawning speech—double in meaning and potentially obscene—to entice clients. Because the riddle teller manipulates "the normal borders of referential speech" and thus controls access to meaning, the hetaera through her conversation could be viewed as temporarily attaining discursive mastery over her interlocutors.[9] For this reason, one supposes, the mock legal contract portrayed in Plautus' *Asinaria* prohibits the Greek courtesan Philaenium from speaking in double meanings (*verbum . . . perplexabile*, 793).

According to Myrtilus, the hetaera's ability to manipulate meanings and deliver witty double entendres results from *paideia*, a masculine familiarity with the Athenian literary tradition:

> Other hetaeras also thought highly of themselves, getting an education (*paideias antechomenai*) and devoting their time to learning (*tois mathēmasi chronon apomerizousai*). For this reason they were quick at rejoinders. (583f)

As discussed in previous chapters, all of the speakers at Athenaeus' table, even Cynulcus, strive to exhibit *paideia*, knowledge of Attic Greek literature and language. This erudition also characterizes high class courtesans: Nicarete of Megara is well born (*ouk agennēs*), even of good parentage (*alla kai goneōn heneka*) and very desirable on account of her education (*kata paideian eperastos*); she even reputedly studied philosophy with Stilpo (596e). The fictive hetaera Thais in one of Alciphron's letters claims that she has studied and discoursed with various Socratic philosophers (*autē para toutois escholaka kai pollois dieilegmai*, Alciphr. 4. 7. 5–6), although she calls herself a follower of Epicurus. The relationship of philosophers and courtesans will be discussed more fully toward the end of this chapter.

These learned hetaeras are represented as engaging on equal discursive footing with their male interlocutors, even, at times, turning the tables on them through their witty repartee.[10] Courtesans like Gnathaena are described by Athenaeus as "exceedingly quick in her answers" (*sphodra d' ēn euthiktos pros tas apokriseis*, 583f) and "very adept and not unsophisticated in her replies" (*sphodra emmelēs d' ēn panu hē Gnathaina kai ouk anasteios apophthegxasthai*, 585b). Mania is similarly termed *asteia* in her responses (*asteia tis apokrinasthai*, 578e), while the auletris Lamia is said to be "quick and sophisticated" in her rejoinders (*sphodra euthiktos kai astikē pros tas apokriseis*, 577d). The latter example is of special interest: the word *astikē* is actually Schweighäuser's emendation for *attikē*, the reading of all three manuscripts, suggesting perhaps an affinity between this type of verbal sophistication and Atticism more generally. Indeed, in a fragment of Anaxilas, the designation *asteia* distinguishes the hetaera from her brothel counterpart, the porne (Anaxilas F21 KA = 572b), while in Theocritus' *Idyll* 20, a hetaera describes her kisses as *astika* (citified, Theoc. *Id*. 20. 4) as she mocks the rude manners of a country bumpkin (*agroikōs*). For Aristotle, the category of *ta asteia*—apophthegms, puns, and double entendres—comprise an important aspect of male rhetorical training (Arist. *Rh*. 1411b–1413b), and in fact, such clever remarks could earn a defendant acquittal in the Athenian lawcourts.[11]

On the Roman side, Philaenium in Plautus' *Asinaria* utters *dicta docta* (525) in addition to her blandishments, while the *Saturnalia* of Macrobius inserts the witticisms of the Emperor Augustus' daughter Julia into a fictional Roman dinner party mostly concerned with the discussion of Vergil. Two of Julia's jokes turn the tables on her male interlocutors, even subverting, as Richlin has argued, Augustan moral discourse.[12] Her risqué double entendre, "I never take on a passenger unless the ship is full (e.g., unless pregnant)" (Macrob. *Sat*. 2. 5. 9), resembles in some respects the obscene jokes of Athenaeus' courtesans. And yet her table talk is characterized as *eleganter* (2. 5. 6) and earns the admiration of her male audience (*mirantibus*, 2. 5. 2; *mirarentur*, 2. 5. 9). While some of the witticisms of hetaeras may indicate an unusual degree of education, especially in the case of those that quote verse, most in fact revolve around obscene meanings and temporary inversions of the social order. In this regard, they reflect the influence of comic discourse and its function as social and literary parody, rather than historical reality.

Hetaeras as Poets and Poets as Hetaeras

Lascivious books and songs tended to be associated with feminine names.[13]

The idea of the learned hetaera finds corroboration in the tradition that ascribes to hetaeras sympotic verse and prose treatises on the symposium and various erotic subjects. Only one poetic sample survives, a fragment of Herodicus Cratetean, attributed to the fifth-century pallake, Aspasia of Miletus, and quoted by Larensis in his vilification of the Socratics in Book 5 of the *Deipnosophistae* (219c–d).[14] In the fragment, the woman, described by Larensis as Socrates' *sophē* teacher of rhetoric, advises the philosopher how to win the affections of a boy. Here Aspasia assumes the role of *erōtodidaskalos* (teacher of eros, 219d), a term applied to Myrtilus elsewhere in Book 13:

> Socrates, I see that desire for the son of Deinomache and Cleinias
> has bitten your heart. If you wish to have your pleasure in boys,
> pay attention. Do not ignore my message, but listen.
> It will be much better for you. For as soon as I heard,
> my body was suffused with the glow of joy,
> and weeping not unwelcome fell from my eyelids.
> Restrain yourself, filling your heart with the conquering Muse,
> with her help you will conquer him. Pour her into his desiring ears.
> For she is the beginning of love in both parties. With her help,
> you will master him, offering to his ears bridal gifts for his heart.
> (*PLG* 2. 288 = 219c–d)

The fragment parodically figures the philosopher, legendary for his self-restraint, as unable to control his passions while simultaneously portraying the pallake in the mold of Diotima, as both priestess of love and teacher of rhetoric.[15] It also inverts the role played by Socrates in the *Memorabilia* (Xen. *Mem.* 3. 11–12), in which he advises another courtesan, Theodote, on how to attract clients. The repetition of verbs for hearing and the emphasis on the ears seems to imply an almost Gorgian model of persuasive power. The fact that the verse assumes a non-sympotic metrical form, that of dactylic hexameter, the meter of epic poetry, may suggest philosophical parody.

The prose tradition attributed to courtesans consisted of erotic works and sympotic tracts. Elephantis, a courtesan of Alexandria, allegedly composed a sex manual which the emperor Tiberius kept at his country estate for ready reference during orgies (Suet. *Tib.* 43). Athenaeus further mentions works by Nico of Samos and Callistrate of Lesbos that advised readers on the mechanics of seduction (5. 220f).[16] Philaenis was the name of the author of a licentious volume on *aphrodisia* mentioned by Athenaeus in connection with the cookbook of Archestratus (8. 335c–e; 10. 457e).[17] A badly damaged papyrus from Oxyrhynchus preserves part of this manual, which concerned itself more with the arts of seduction than with sexual *schēmata*, according to Lobel, and in apparent contrast to that of Elephantis.[18] As with the fragment of Herodicus, the hetaera's words engage in genre parody.

> Philaenis, daughter of Ocymenes of Samos, has written this book for those who want to lead their life with scientific knowledge (*meth' historiēs*) and not haphazardly (*mē parergōs*). (P. *Oxy.* 2891)

The discrepancy between the idea of scientific enquiry and the book's subject matter has led to the conclusion that the manual was intended as a parody of "the preface of Herodotus and other authors of serious literature" (Tsantsanoglou 1973: 186). The author later advises the seducer to be good-looking but to wear his hair in a simple fashion so that the woman will not think that he paid too much attention to it (Tsantsanoglou 1973: 188–89); sections on flattery, kissing, and one on the modes of love apparently followed (West 1996: 20–21). West argues that the female names attached to these manuals were actually pseudonyms for male authors (1996: 21). Their Samian and Lesbian origins, two places legendary for the dissolute behavior of their women, fit with literary fantasy rather than historical reality (cf. Plut. *Mor.* 303c). Tsantsanoglou also cites in support of this argument the epigram of Aeschrion that attributes the treatise of Philaenis to an Athenian sophist named Polycrates intent on denying her status as a prostitute (*oude dēmōdēs*, Anth. Pal. 7. 345; cf. Dioscurides 7. 450).[19] In the latter view, the pseudonymous manual of Philaenis offers a parody of historical writing meant to travesty traditional stylistic features of the genre (Tsantsanoglou 1973: 194). And yet it is equally possible that the epigram may have been intended as a rhetorical exercise, an apology for a notorious woman, much like Gorgias' encomium for Helen.

Athenaeus provides the only example of a non-erotic philosophical treatise composed by a hetaera, the *Nomos Sussitikos* (Table Manners) of Gnathaena. This work outlined, also probably parodically, sympotic protocol for her lovers and imitated similar treatises by philosophers (*kata zēlon tōn ta toiauta suntaxamenōn philosophōn*, 585b). According to Callimachus' *Pinax*, it amounted to 323 lines, and began, "The rule here written down is equal and fair to all" (*hode ho nomos isos egraphē kai homoios*, 585b).[20] The stress on equality, seen also in the inclusion of courtesans in the circle of Epicurus below as well as in the some of the stories of their monuments, reinforces the notion of status inversion, genre parody, and the erosion of class boundaries generally associated with hetaeras in the literary tradition.

Many ancient writers, including Athenaeus, allege that some of the women poets were hetaeras, or at least behaved like them, beginning with Sappho.[21] In his brief study of Greek women poets, West identifies the poets Charixena, Glauce, Nossis, and Theano as hetaeras, mainly because of their association with erotic or sympotic verse. The proverbial Charixena, alluded to by one of the crones at the end of Aristophanes' *Ecclesiazusae*, reputedly was an auletris and author of erotic verse; by the time of Theopompus, she had become a by-word for old age.[22] In the case of Glauce of Ceos, who entertained Ptolemy II Philadelphus at his court, her profession as a citharist indicates that she, too, might have been a hetaera (West 1996: 26–27 and 43). West also revives Reitzenstein's suggestion that the early Hellenistic poet Nossis was a hetaera on the basis of her praise of Aphrodite in one of her epigrams (*Anth. Pal.* 5. 170).[23] He argues that her origins in Locri, a place famous for its loose women and erotic musical tradition, known as "Locrian songs," point to her status as a courtesan.[24] According to Athenaeus, the Locrians prostituted their daughters (*hetairismōi*, 12. 516a) while the songs of their women were said to incite adultery (*moichikai*, *PMG* 583 = cf. 14. 639a). Although Locrian songs belonged to a folk tradition and were thus anonymous, the genre is attributed to another female author, Theano of Locri, the name of the legendary Pythagorean, either the wife or daughter of the philosopher, and also possibly the name of a courtesan in Book 8 of the *Deipnosophistae* (see Appendix III).[25]

Athenaeus identifies other female poets with hetaeras, although he does not specifically designate them as such: the Spartan poet Megalostrate from the time of Alcman is described as a *poiētria* able to attract lovers by means of her hetaera-like skill at conversation (*dia tēn homilian tous erastas proselkusasthai*, 600f).[26] This reference occurs in a rather literal discussion that equates the erotic behavior of the lyric poets with their poetic personae and thus cannot be taken very seriously: just as the male lyric poet is termed *akolasios*, so the female poet is analogized to the hetaera. Athenaeus attempts to clarify a similar conflation of female poet and hetaera by distinguishing between the archaic poet Sappho and a courtesan of the same name (596e; cf. Ael. *VH* 12. 19). A collection of *skolia* (drinking songs) that were well known in Athens by the middle of the fifth century, is attributed to the lyric poet Praxilla (594a). Aristophanes parodies two of them, and the first four words of a third appear on part of a vase from around 470 B.C.E.: "You who look out of the window, so beautifully/ a maiden's head above yet a woman below" (*PMG* 754 = Campbell F754).[27]

The attribution of drinking songs to Praxilla likewise prompts Campbell to conjecture that she was a hetaera, although West rejects this view, contending instead that the poet must be the fictionalized creation of a male author.[28]

Although a few literary works were attributed to hetaeras, not one of the women poets is actually called a hetaera; rather, scholars have marshaled as evidence either their professions as musicians or the types of songs they composed. In fact, far more women poets were reputed to have been priestesses, especially at Delphi.[29] The exiguousness of the evidence makes it difficult, if not impossible, to determine the actual status of these women. Whatever the case, it is clear that the ancients, especially later authors such as Athenaeus, found plausible the idea that courtesans and flute players composed sympotic and erotic verse, as well as acquired a high level of literary education not normally considered appropriate to ancient women. Certainly among the Romans of the early principate and later, the learned woman had become synonymous with sexual promiscuity: knowledge of Greek and Latin literature, verse composition, and witty conversation branded elite women such as Sempronia and Julia as prostitutes.[30]

Sympotic Mockery

Greek comic conventions associate raillery or crude jesting (*skōmmata*) with lower class characters such fish-wives, inn-keepers, prostitutes, and parasites, as well as with the symposium.[31] The latter two figures often appear as subversive members of court and table, where they direct their derisive humor against their patrons, their paramours, and even each other. This type of raillery comprises one of the key components of the drinking party, together with songs, drinks, garlands, perfume, and sweetmeats (Alciphr. 4. 14. 3). So a mother advises her courtesan daughter not to laugh too readily at table (*kagcharizein rhadiōs*, Luc. *Dial. meretr.* 6. 3), like the two hetaeras who tease their lovers as they process to a pastoral symposium in one of Alciphron's letters (*ta men gar allēlas eskōptomen ē tous erastas*, Alciphr. 4. 13. 2). Their activity is referred to as *paidia* (4. 13. 3), a type of verbal play also associated with the sophists at Athenaeus' table, and with parasites. Later in the letter, a hetaera mocks (*kōmōidēsasa akolastōs*) a jeering bystander in response to his obscene pun on *sukas*, a metaphor for the female genitals in Middle comedy and later literature: "Lucky is that place where you are going, since it will have lots of figs!" (Alciphr. 4. 13. 3).[32] The hetaera's mockery, denoted by the participle *kōmōidēsasa*, temporarily figures her as in discursive control. Instead of serving as the typical object of comic and sympotic abuse, she is represented as fashioning

her own comic discourse to put her interlocutor in his place.[33] The structure of this exchange typifies those found between hetaeras and their clientele in Book 13 of Athenaeus, in which their sexual humor ridicules the
uninvited sexual advances of various men (e.g., Mania, Machon 245 =
579c; Gnathaena, Machon 322 = 580f).[34] They also turn their raillery
against each other: Gnathaena and Mania insult each other with their
quips (*loidoresthai*, Machon 215 = 578e–f),[35] and elsewhere a hetaera
threatens to get even with her friends not in the usual manner, through
mockery and slander (*en skōmmasin oude blasphēmias*, Alciphr. 4. 6. 7), but
by other means.

The hetaera's male sympotic counterparts included parasites, flatterers,
and the *gelōtopoios* or clowns who paid for their dinners with jokes (14. 614c;
cf. Xen. *Symp.* 1. 14–15).[36] The parasite may have been somewhat lower on
the social scale in comparison to a wealthy hetaera: Phryne, for instance, had
her own parasite, Gryllion (591e). Like the hetaera, the jester had a repertoire
of mocking jests or insults, *loidoria* and *skōmma* in classical prose, to produce
laughter, as well as parodied tragic and comic scenes that included the imitation of various types of characters.[37] In Book 8 of the *Deipnosophistae*, the
musician Stratonicus plays a similar role and not insignificantly he also figures as the subject of nine anecdotes from Machon's *Chreiae* (Machon
91–167 Gow = Ath. 8. 348e–349f). His witticisms are embedded in Cynulcus'
lengthy speech about fish (8. 347d–352d) that begins with a well-known riddle recast as an insulting joke directed at a rival musician (8. 347f), two kinds
of speech genres associated with hetaeras. His humor also involves puns,
double meanings, sexual innuendo, and the unconventional use of proverbs,
idioms, or quotations (8. 351a–b; Gilula 2000: 426–7). The musician's verbal
facility resembles that of the hetaera; he, too, always has a ready quip (*peri tēs
eustochias autou tōn apokriseōn*, 8. 348d). At the same time, Stratonicus, with
his sharp tongue and clever rejoinders, shares a vision similar to that of
Athenaeus' dinner guests, a penchant for humorous word play, literary quotation, and verbal competition, all reflecting a cosmopolitan perspective.

The masculine character of the hetaera's jesting is further seen in her
similarity to these male figures at table, particularly the *kolax*, the flatterer
or parasite, who makes a lengthy textual appearance at Athenaeus' table in
Book 6 (6. 234d to 262b). At the banquet and on the comic stage, such figures both ridicule their superiors while also serving as the targets of their
jokes, as a parasite in a play of Epicharmus states: "There I am elegantly
witty and I cause much laughter and I praise my host" (6. 235f–236a).
Menander's *Kolax* also characterizes the function of the parasite at the
symposium as *paidia*, to laugh loudly, to mock others and to drink a lot
(*hadron gelasai, skōpsai tin', empiein polun*, 6. 258e). Alexis in his *Poietai*
describes one famous Athenian parasite, a certain Eucrates nicknamed

Korydos (Lark), as simultaneously the joke teller and the butt of humor, "Yes indeed, I want to be laughed at and always to say funny things" (*panu toi boulomai/ houtos gelasthai kai geloi' aei legein*, 241d). The fact that the Lark had a reputation for prostituting himself (*hos edokei peporneusthai*, 241e) further underscores his similarity to the courtesan; even his derisive nickname contributes to his objectification, as do those of the courtesans Phtheiropyle, Leme, and Hys, discussed in the last chapter. Indeed, a joke that conflates the high cost of the Lark's sexual services with the price of a thrush (6. 241e) plays on the parasite's sexual availability in much the same way as jokes made about and by hetaeras.

The verbal license afforded by the context of the symposium and the temporary inversions it effects are seen in an anecdote about Philip of Macedon and his parasite: when the king made a joke at his parasite's expense, the latter responded with a role-inverting quip, "Then shall I not maintain you (instead of the other way around)?" (*eit' ouk egō se, ephē, threpsō*, 6. 248e). The subversive aspects of this humor did not always sit well with its patrons: a miscalculated joke that playfully poked fun at Arsinoë, the wife of Lysimachus, had a disastrous result. Telesphorus, a member at court, embedded a derisive jab against the queen, who was prone to vomiting, in a tragic reference to Euripides' *Antiope*: "You are starting trouble by bringing in this vomiting woman (*kakōn katarcheis tēnd' emousan eisagōn*, F184 TGF² = 14. 616c). Altering *tēnde Mousan* (this Muse) to *tēnd' emousan* (this vomiting woman), Telesphorus foolishly exposed Arsinoë's embarrassing sickness.[38] The hazards of court humor are amply illustrated by his punishment: locked in a cage like an animal, he starved to death— possibly an apt penalty for a sponging dinner guest. In Book 13 of the *Deipnosophistae*, hetaeras similarly adapt tragic verse to expose the foibles of their interlocutors, inverting social status within the context of the vignettes that feature them, only their meanings are frequently obscene.

The Laughter of Hetaeras

The mockery of hetaeras is often accompanied by derisive laughter, denoted by the verb *gelan*; such laughter is also characteristic of the *kolax* (Theophr. *Char.* 2. 4). In Athenaeus, the verb rarely occurs in connection with women; indeed, all feminine examples refer to hetaeras and most occur in Book 13. The word conveys not pleasure or happiness, but masculine scorn or arrogance.[39] Theocritus' *Idyll* 20 represents a hetaera as alternately enticing and mocking a simple herdsman, a scene that concludes with violent laughter at the rustic's expense (*sobaron m' egelaxen*, 20. 15). In Athenaeus, the close connection between the hetaera's laughter and her masculine insolence is seen in Lais' laughing response to Euripides' insult (*hē de gelasas' apekrithē*, 582d). The laughter of the courtesan Nico, who quips that Sophocles' boy favorite, Demophon, should take her ass and give it to Sophocles (*hē de gelasasa*, 582f), also shows a comic mastery of the situation even as it contributes to her own commodification. Similarly, the courtesans Lamia and Mania mock and reject sexual advances not only with their jokes, but also with their derisive laughter (*gelasasa*, Machon 184 = 577f; Machon 255 = 579d).

The subversive and aggressively masculine aspects of the hetaera's laughter are tangible in another anecdote. In Book 9, we find the appropriately named Gnathaena (Jaws) indulging in cooked testicles at a banquet. While the other women politely pretend not to notice this obscene feast (*ēkkizeto*), "man-slaying" Gnathaena heartily guffaws (*hē d' androphonos Gnathain' anagelasasa*) as she snatches up two of them and gulps them down (Philippides, *Ananeosis* F5 KA= 9. 384e). The laughter of hetaeras has a subversive effect: here it clearly induces anxiety in Gnathaena's (male) interlocutors, connected as it is with her predatory sexuality and prodigious appetite, potentially emasculating men even as it seduces them.

The only other anecdote about female laughter outside Book 13 similarly encapsulates its parodic and subversive function. The courtesans Melissa and Nicion are described as laughing at the humble fare, the bowls of lentil soup, set before them at a symposium of Cynic philosophers:

> After a burst of laughter (*gelōtos*), the stage-pounder Melissa and that dog-fly Nicion entered; for these were very well known courtesans. Glancing around with wonder at the things placed before them, they laughed (*egelōn*). And Nicion said, "Don't any of you beard-gatherers (*geneiosullektadai*) eat fish?" (4. 157a–b)

This scoffing hetaera strongly resembles some of Athenaeus' banqueters: not only does she bring comic discourse into the symposium with the word *geneiosullektadai* (cf. *stōmuliosullektidē*, "gossip-gathers," Ar. *Ran.* 841), she goes on to quote the epigrammatist Meleager and the philosopher Antisthenes, a pupil of Socrates and the founder of the Cynics, advising his followers to "take themselves from life" (*exagein heautous tou biou*) for tolerating such food. But the joke is just as much about hetaeras as philosophers; in refusing the delicacies of table, they also implicitly deny the pleasures of courtesans. The laughter of these hetaeras, like those of Book 13, thus parodies the practices and doctrines of the Cynic philosophers, namely their frugal banquets. For the philosopher has just delivered a lengthy account of the ascetic practices of the Cynics, an account that provokes the derisive laughter of everyone at table (*gelasantōn*, 4. 156c). As we have seen in previous chapters, Mytrilus deploys the discourse of hetaeras in Book 13 to much the same end.

The *Chreia* as a Literary Genre

In his quotation of the witticisms of hetaeras, Athenaeus make use of a well-known literary genre, the collections of sayings or anecdotes compiled by a single author, and popular among fourth-century Athenian and later writers. The *chreia* formed the basis for the *apomnemoneumata*, the sayings of a master collected by a pupil, and the *hypomnemata*, a writer's or philosopher's "scrapbook." By the late second century C.E., however, the term *chreia* had a specific, technical meaning and became a regular feature of the *progymnasmata* of the imperial rhetors.[40] Such anecdotes formed part of elementary rhetorical instruction: individuals created personal collections of *chreiae*, a practice that perhaps informs the learned displays of many of Athenaeus' characters. The speakers of the *Deipnosophistae* employ the terms *chreiae, apophthegmata,* and *apomnemoneumata* more or less interchangeably (cf. 8. 348e; 13. 579d, 588a).

As a genre, the *chreia* apparently originated in classical Athens among philosophers, sophists, and other literary figures (Hock and O'Neil 1986: 4–5); Plato even attributes a *chreia* to Sophocles (Pl. *Resp.* 329b–c). It was a favorite Cynic form and was often introduced into the diatribe genre and even verse (Dudley 1998: 111–12). In contrast to maxims or proverbs, *chreiae* depict stock figures such as kings, soldiers, parasites, and courtesans engaged in dialogue in a familiar narrative setting.[41] The form is quite flexible, allowing for alteration, improvisation, and last minute changes of venue and character (Gilula 2000: 429). The literary genre dates at least to the fourth century, according to Diogenes Laertius, who mentions several works entitled *Chreiae* by philosophical authors of this period.[42] It also served as one of the "chief weapons" in the Cynics' arsenal (Dudley 1998: 112); in fact, Diogenes the Cynic himself composed a *Chreiae* (Diog. Laert. 6. 80).[43] According to Diogenes Laertius, this philosopher had a reputation for witty quips that heaped scorn upon his interlocutors (*katasobareusasthai,* Diog. Laert. 6. 24 and *passim*), as in the following:

> Upon seeing an Olympian victor glance repeatedly at a hetaera, he said, "See how the ram, frenzied for battle, has had his neck rung (*trachēlizetai*) by a common girl." (Diog. Laert. 6. 61)

The extreme obscenity found in most of Machon's *Chreiae* has lead to the speculation, correct in my view, that they are meant as a parody of this philosophical and rhetorical tradition; indeed, Gow himself struggles to understand their applicability to rhetorical education ("highly unsuitable for the schoolroom," he remarks).[44] However, it should be noted that one of the school exercises performed on *chreiae* in late antiquity involved passing judgment on an anecdote, refuting it because of its unsuitability or shamelessness.[45]

The telling of *chreiae* by women of learning is found in the story of Hipparchia's putdown of Theodorus, a fellow guest at a banquet. Like the witty hetaera, the wife of the Cynic Crates uses a tragic allusion to rebuff an unwanted advance. When Theodorus attempted to strip off her cloak, Hipparchia purportedly quoted a line of Euripides' *Bacchae*, "Is this she who left behind her shuttles at the loom?" *(hautē 'stin hē tas par' histois eklipousa kerkidas*, Diog. Laert. 6. 97–98 = Eur. *Ba.* 1236). The witticism both displays her knowledge of *paideia* as well as justifies her own pursuit of it; much like the hetaeras of Machon, she deflects the advances of her interlocutor with this remark.[46] Clearly, such witticisms were expected of philosophers at table, and even of their female companions: Lynceus' account of one of Phryne's rejoinders illustrates the technique of philosophical parody at work in the genre. To a question (*zētoumenou*) about hanging wreaths at the symposium, Phryne responds, "to guide the soul" (*hoti psuchagōgousin*, 585e), a quip that possibly plays on the *zētēmata* of the Stoics (cf. 553e–554b,15. 670a–e). Certainly, Myrtilus' lengthy quotation of Machon's *Chreiae* functions similarly at Athenaeus' banquet, parodying philosophers and their pretentious discourses, particularly that of Cynulcus.

While it is clear that Machon provides the bulk of the witticisms attributed to hetaeras in the *Deipnosophistae*, the relation of the poet to his predecessors, Lynceus and Duris, remains a mystery.[47] The difference between the two versions of the "stone" joke—Machon attributes it to Gnathaena (578e), Lynceus to Phryne (584c)—militates against the view that Machon borrowed directly from these two authors. Lynceus' anecdotes (583d–585e) are less fully developed than those of Machon, providing little in the way of dramatic setting and characterization; they mostly involve quotidian puns without the graphic obscenity of Machon. The subject matter of Aristodemus' *Geloia Apomnemoneumata*, if we are to judge by Gnathaena's joke about a cistern (*lakkos*), appears to have been much cruder than that of Lynceus. His account features some of the same courtesans as Machon, including Gnathaena (583f, 584b–e, 585a–b), Phryne (584c–d, 585e–f), Nico (584f), Callistion (585c), and Lais (585e); but to these he adds Metanira (584f), Glycera (585c–d), and Thais (585d–e). One other author, Hegesander (fl. 2nd century B.C.E.), who wrote a *Hypomnemata* on Hellenistic court life, featuring parasites, courtesans, and philosophers, also records a witty *chreia* attributed to Metanira (584f), as well as a risqué riposte about Sophocles and the courtesan Archippe (592b).

Tragic Humor, Comic Obscenity

Let us turn now to the actual witticisms of hetaeras as quoted by Myrtilus. Most hinge on an obscene pun that deflects a demeaning sexual request and thus puts the interlocutor in his place.[48] Through this strategy, the hetaera gains discursive control in the sympotic scenario, playing the part of the joke-teller rather than serving as the target of the humor. By placing the discourse of hetaeras in Myrtilus' mouth, Athenaeus portrays him as deploying an erotic and comic discourse that disrupts the orderly progression of sympotic conversation; he plays the part of the *bōmolochos*, the buffoon of Attic Old comedy. Just as the courtesans he ventriloquizes, Myrtilus turns the tables on Cynulcus and wins a putative discursive victory, reducing his competitor to a mere "dog" (611c–d). At the same time, he strengthens the identification of the courtesan with classical Athenian culture, already observed in the Atticizing of their names, and thus analogizes her to the sophist as a purveyor of Attic *paideia*.

The late fourth-century courtesan Gnathaena had the widest reputation for her humor; she also allegedly composed the literary treatise, *Nomos Sussitikos* (Table Manners), as we saw above; her jokes are characterized by coarse language and excessive crudity. Other examples of her wit occur in the *Apomnemoneumata* of the Samian Lynceus (584b) and in the *Geloia Apomnemoneumata* of Aristodemus (585a). Her special gift perhaps reflects her status as a crone, a character type frequently associated with scurrilous joking in Attic Old comedy; indeed, at one point she is referred to as "almost a coffin" (*homologoumenē soros*, 580c).[49] Such verbal talents apparently ran in the family, as her granddaughter or daughter, Gnathaenion (little Gnathaena), is also quoted numerous times in Book 13.[50] Many other rejoinders are attributed to the quick-witted Lamia, the auletris associated with Demetrius Poliorcetes.

The numerous witticisms that involve tragic allusions not only reinforce the association of *paideia* with the Greek hetaera, they perversely transform the hetaera, an outsider and normally a foreigner, into the purveyor of classical Athenian literary culture. The Latin literary tradition reinforces this idea in the mock contract staged between Philaenium and Diabolus in which she is warned, "And let her use no language except Attic Greek" (*neque ulla lingua sciat loqui nisi Attica*, 794). The parodic send-up of Oedipus' riddle in the fragment of Anaxilas discussed above exemplifies the genre, in which a hetaera is made to burlesque a tragic idea or even to parody tragic language. For example, Gnathaena, asked to pay the expenses for a drinking party in advance, replies to the slave messenger of her lover Andronicus, the tragic actor, "Cursed slave, what word hast thou spoken!" (*olomene paidōn, ephē, poion eirēkas logon*, 584d), a line from an unattributed tragic play (F837 *TGF*). Here pure Attic speech is put in the mouth of the person least likely to quote it, a foreigner and outsider. The gesture is doubly ironic as every speaker at Athenaeus' table is represented as negotiating his own identity in relation to this same cultural past.

Most of the hetaera's tragic rejoinders revolve around an obscene double meaning and borrow much from the comic technique of tragic parody. The first *chreia* quoted by Myrtilus depicts the auletris Lamia as delivering a ribald riposte to the infamous Macedonian king, Demetrius Poliorcetes:

> After Leaena had executed a certain position (*schēma*)
> extremely well and had found favor with Demetrius,
> they say Lamia also once rode gracefully atop (*kelētisai*) the king,
> and thus won his praise. And she retorted as follows,
> "In view of that, take on Leaena too if you like!
> (*pros tauta kai Leainan, ei boulei, kratei*)."
> (Machon 168–73 = 577d)

The anecdote revolves around two different sexual *schēmata* associated with each hetaera and named after specific animals. The double meaning inheres in the pun on Leaena II, one of the two famous courtesans associated with Demetrius, and the feminine form of the Greek word for lion (*leōn*); it may also refer to the lioness *schēma* in which the woman crouched with her posterior raised, perhaps like the lion ornamenting the tomb in a black figure vase at the British Museum.[51] The specialty of her rival, Lamia, is the antithesis of a lioness pose: for the woman to ride equestrian-style atop the man was considered demeaning, even for courtesans, as shown in the last chapter.[52] On another level, the line itself alludes to the final episode of Euripides' *Medea*, in which Medea says to Jason: "In view of that, call me a lion, if you wish" (*pros tauta kai leainan, ei boulei, kalei*, Eur. *Med.* 1358). But here the hetaera has modified the word at line end from *kalei* to *kratei*. Moreover, the dramatic context of the line reinforces the idea of female discursive dominance: raised aloft in the position of *dea ex machina*, Medea utters these lines over her emasculated husband just before departing in her dragon chariot.[53] The status reversals of gender and class which Lamia's joke plays upon and even temporarily effects are seen in another of Machon's *Chreiae* in which Lamia disdains Demetrius' costly gifts and then openly laughs at him (*gelasasa*) as he crudely handles his member in front of her (Machon 174–87 = 577e). Punning on the perfume he has given her, she tells him that his "scent" smells the most putrid of all (*saprotaton*, Machon 185 = 577f).[54]

In another vignette that features Demetrius, the courtesan Mania makes similar use of tragic allusion when she consents to the king's request for her ass, the most demeaning form of sexual congress in the Greek literary tradition:

> They say that once when king Demetrius asked
> for Mania's ass, she demanded a gift in return from him.

After he had given it, she turned around and after a little while said,
"Child of Agamemnon, now it is possible for you
(*Agamemnonos pai, nun, ekein' exesti soi*)."

(Machon 226–230 = 579a).

Her retort alludes to a passage in Sophocles' *Electra* where the Paedagogus
says to Orestes, "Child, now it is possible for you to see those things for
which you were always eager" (*Agamemnonos pai, nun ekein' exesti soi
paronti leussein, hōn prothumos ēsth' aei*, Soph. *El.* 2). The joke, however,
depends on the omission of the infinitive *leussein* of the original text:
Demetrius does not ask merely to *see* her ass, but rather requests anal intercourse.[55] The anecdote receives additional frisson if one considers that
Mania may be quoting the parodic lines of the wife of the tragic actor
Theodorus who refused to allow him into her bed until he returned victo-
rious from a tragic competition (Gow 1965: 103; cf. Plut. *Mor.* 737b).

Play on tragic phrases similarly occurs in the Gnathaenion's retort to
Gnathaena when the latter pressures her to reconcile with a lover:

Mother, she said, how can I kiss
that good-for-nothing (*to mēden ōphelēma*),
one who wants to possess
under one roof (*stegas*) all hollow Argos as a gift.

(Machon 384–86 = 582a)

The phrase "hollow Argos" comes from a passage in Sophocles' *Oedipus at
Colonus* in which Oedipus curses his son Polyneices (Soph. *OC* 1387; cf.
378), but here it euphemistically refers to her own body. The phrase *to
mēden ōphelēma* may also be taken from a tragedy while *stegos* puns on
house and brothel.[56] By taking a tragic phrase or statement out of context
and imbuing it with obscene meaning, the speaker parodies the tragic
genre in a manner familiar from comedy while at the same time deflecting
the demeaning requests of her clients.

The hetaera's witty recasting of tragic lines has affinities with the literary gamesmanship in which all of the interlocutors at Athenaeus' table engage; not only do they string together one obscure quotation after another
as they vie for discursive victory, they often humorously alter the original
quotation for comic effect. So Cynulcus' revision of a comic line resembles
the hetaera's deliberate misquotation:

Cease your ways, now that you are an old man. For don't you know
that it is *not* sweetest (*ouk estin hēdiston*) to die while screwing,
they way they say Phormisius died?

(Philetaerus F6 KA = 570f)

By inserting a negative at the beginning of the second line, the philosopher attempts to expurgate the comic poet's original words as he exhorts Myrtilus to leave off his amorous pursuits and adopt the ascetic lifestyle of the Cynic philosopher. His negation of the comic message employs the same technique as the jokes of hetaeras and yet strives for quite a different end, the erasure of pleasure.

Elsewhere the courtesan pokes fun at the literary pretensions of dramatic poets and actors, again turning the tables on her male interlocutors. In a joke that apparently made the rounds, Gnathaena bests her lover, the comic poet Diphilus:

> Drinking once at Gnathaena's house, Diphilus remarked,
> "That vessel (*aggeion*) you have is cold (*psuchron*), Gnathaena."
> "That's because we always deliberately put in
> some of your plays," she said.
>
> (Machon 258–61 = 579e).

As a term of literary criticism, *psuchros* denotes something tedious and devoid of humor; so we hear of the "frigid" witticisms of the parasite Eucleides (6. 242b).[57] Although there is no evidence for any obscene usage of *aggeion*, it is nonetheless tempting to interpret both quips as mutual professional put-downs: the poet is taken to task for his flat writing and the courtesan for her lack of erotic ardor.

Indeed, Machon's subsequent retelling of the anecdote implies as much; here the poet represents the rejoinder as an attempt to conceal a different lover's inferior gifts of snow and cheap fish:

> Ashamed that someone might learn about the gifts,
> and being especially worried about Diphilus,
> in case he should pay her back by putting her
> in a comedy (*kōmōidoumenē*). . . .
>
> (Machon 271–273 = 579f)

In this exchange, as in the previous version, the two speakers vie for discursive control: Diphilus through his comedies and his public humiliation of the hetaera, and Gnathaena through her private witticisms at table.[58] After a lengthy preamble, Diphilus delivers the expected punch line,

> "By Athena and the gods," he said,
> "your cistern (*lakkon*) sure is cold (*psuchron*)."
> And she replied, "That's because we always
> deliberately put in some of your prologues!"
>
> (Machon 281–284 = 580a)

The use of *lakkos* here, a word frequently paired with *prōktos* in Attic Old comedy, clearly shows the obscene intent of Diphilus' remark. And yet,

Machon gives the hetaera the last word and thus temporarily places her in
the dominant discursive position. Her joke, in turn, casts the male in a sexually, and grammatically, passive role: Diphilus is said to be loved by her
(*hup' autēs . . . agapōmenos*, Machon 265 = 579e) and is even designated
her most esteemed *erōmenos* (Machon 264 = 579e).[59] Moreover, the coarse
nature of these witticisms may be intended to reflect the crude and explicit
language of Diphilus own plays.[60]

Not only in Machon, but among other authors as well, Diphilus appears as
a repeated target of courtesans' ridicule. In an anecdote ascribed to Lynceus,
Gnathaena berates the poet for his failure in another dramatic competition:

> It once happened that Diphilus, disgracefully defeated in a dramatic competi-
> tion, was "raised" out of the theater (*arthēnai ek tou theatrou*) but he went to
> Gnathaena's house nonetheless. When Diphilus enjoined her to wash his feet,
> she replied, "Why should I, when you come to me not being raised up?" (*ti gar,
> eipen, ouk ērmenos hēkeis*, 583f)

The poet's public humiliation in the theater effects a status reversal, ren-
dering him unworthy of the servile attention that courtesans typically
lavished upon their lovers, a displacement only compounded by the witticism. The joke, which was probably a standard one, plays on the idea of the
poet's literary creation, the hetaera—a stock figure in comedy—"talking
back" to her creator.[61] In another anecdote, Menander, returning home
"down on his luck," perhaps after a similar failure in the theater, endures
the obscene ridicule of Glycera, also one of his own characters. After he rejects the hot milk she offers, the hetaera quips, "Get rid of the upper part
and use what's below" (*apophusa, eipe, kai tōi katō chrō*, 585c). The joke
plays on the double sense of *graus* as old woman and the wrinkled scum
that forms on the surface of boiled milk.

One last anecdote represents an encounter between the fifth-century
hetaera Lais and the poet Euripides, in which she mocks him with a line
from his own play in much the same manner as Dionysus in Aristophanes'
Frogs when he awards the tragic prize to Aeschylus (Ar. *Ran.* 1471). Upon
seeing the poet in a garden with his writing tablet and stylus, the hetaera
engages him in the following exchange:

> Tell me (*apokrinai*), my poet,
> why did you write in your tragedy
> "Away shameful doer (*err' aischropoie*)"?
> Whereupon Euripides, amazed
> at her audacity, said, "What are you, woman?
> Not a shameful doer (*ouk aischropoios*)?"
> And she, laughing (*gelasasa*), retorted,
> "What is shameful, if it does not seem so to the doer?"
> (Machon 405–410 = 582c–d)

As in the earlier parody of Euripides' *Medea*, these lines come from the final scene of the tragedy, when Jason's and Medea's positions are spatially and discursively reversed.[62] Lais asks why Euripides used the word *aischropoios* of Medea in fashioning Jason's scathing denunciation of her (Eur. *Med.* 1346). With *apokrinai*, she invites the poet to deliver his own witticism in this conventional game of ripostes. He responds by turning the tables on the hetaera, but she (literally) has the last laugh by brilliantly responding with a famous line from another of his plays, *Aeolus* (F19 *TGF*). It probably referred to the incest of Macareus with his sister Canace and in any case expressed Euripides' tendency toward moral relativism.[63] We see again the same comic procedure at work: the hetaera uses laughter and witticisms to put a powerful and derisive male interlocutor in his place by using his own inclinations and doctrines against him.

The ability to quote Euripides in the post-classical era may have served as the consummate mark of *paideia*. Plutarch in his account of the Sicilian expedition states that the Sicilians consigned to the quarries all Athenians captured in war, except those who could recite Euripides from memory (Plu. *Nic.* 19. 2).[64] Indeed, as the passage appears to suggest, the tragic verse of Euripides, along with the comic figure of the hetaera, played an important role in the Hellenization of the ancient world from the fourth century onward. The close identification of classical Greek *paideia* with the poetry of Euripides reinforces the image of Lais as a learned courtesan and as the embodiment of classical Athenian culture. In the world of Athenaeus, her quotation of tragic verse affiliates her with the dining sophists and their use of literary quotations in their quest for discursive status.

In addition to tragic poets, the hetaera's humor targets stock lower-class figures such as soldiers, rogues (*mastigias*, 585f), parasites, actors, athletes, and craftsmen, many of whom were conventional characters in Middle and New comedy. In one such story, a deserter, an *automolos*,[65] holds a drinking party for his friends—one assumes these are the free-loading parasites and prostitutes, the *asumboloi*, that so frequently populate the dinner parties of the rich and famous (cf. 572c). The anecdote plays up the foreignness of the interlocutor and the hetaera, juxtaposing his doltish attempt at a joke with her witty command of sympotic *paidia*:

A foreign man, who seemed to be a deserter,
was staying in Athens once, and sent for Mania,
paying her whatever she asked.
To his drinking party, he had invited some others,
those from the city always accustomed to laugh
with their hosts at everything out of gratitude.
He wished to show himself both subtle and witty
(*glaphuros asteios th' hama*), while Mania

bandied about her wittiest remarks (*arista paizousēs*),
even though she often left the room. Wishing to jeer at her
as a scurrying hare, the deserter said, "By the gods,
boys, which of the wild beasts in the mountains
seems to you to run the fastest?"
And Mania answered, "Why the deserter, my good man."
When Mania had entered the room once more after this,
she mocked (*eskōpte*) the deserter and said that once
he had been a shield-caster during an attack.

(Machon 231–46 = 579b)

The adjective *asteios* links the table banter of the parasitic deserter to that
of the hetaera and thus sets up a game of competitive ripostes between
the two. With her verbal play at its "best" (*arista paizousēs*, Machon 238 =
579b)—and note the affinities of *paizein* with the sympotic table banter of
Athenaeus' sophists—the hetaera Mania wins the contest with her witty
solution to the riddle. In Gow's words, she "catches the man's jest, turns it
against him, and embroiders her suggestion" (Gow 1965: 245). Her joke
unmans the deserter by unmasking his martial cowardice while at the same
time giving her a discursive victory as the one who solves the riddle. It
illustrates quite nicely the relation of riddling to mockery in a sympotic
context: both speech acts put the speaker in a discursive control at the expense of the comic target.

Another *chreia* depicts the hetaera Mania as the lover of two rival pan-
cratiasts. Taking up with one pancratiast while serving as the common-law
wife of the other (*gametēs tropon gunaikos*), she incurs the abuse of her
cuckolded "husband" (*moicheuomenēn*). To his complaints, Mania quips:

Darling, don't be concerned. For I just wanted to learn
and ascertain what two athletes, victors at Olympia, could do,
stroke for stroke (*plēgēn para plēgēn*), in a single night.

(Machon 222–25 = 578f)

Here the double entendre resides in the play on *plēgē*, a word that can refer
both to athletic and sexual activity in Attic Old comedy. The sports metaphor effectively turns the hetaera into the athletic victor able to take on two
opponents at once while at the same time giving her the discursive victory.
Gnathaenion deploys a similar equation between sexual and athletic conquest in her response to a passing wrestler (*palaistēs*) in another anecdote.
When he attempted to pass her retinue as she processed to the Peiraeus and
threatened to throw her down if her party did not get out of his way, she
replied, "You poor fool, not you sir! For that is something you have not yet
done!" (*Ô talan, mē dēt', aner;/ oudepote gar tout' esti soi pepragmenon*, Ma-

chon 400–1 = 582c). By mocking his failure as a performer in the public arena, the hetaera's repartee attempts to humiliate and emasculate her interlocutor, much as the anecdotes about Diphilus discussed above.

In another joke that involves multiple status inversions, the aging Gnathaena, now taken up residence with the tragic actor Andronicus, comes out of retirement to offer her services to a bronze smith for a large amount of gold. The low status of this character is indicated by the phrase "being ill-bred and one who works with his hands" (*anagōgos ōn de kai banausos pantelōs* Machon 358 = 581d), and by the fact that he sits around gossiping in a cobbler's shop. When the rumor gets back to Andronicus that the hetaera had engaged in the "horse" position with the bronze smith, a *schēma* she had refused to perform with him (*kathippasthai*, Machon 362 = 581d; cf. *kelētisai*, Machon 171 = 577d), he reviles her (*loidoroumenos*, 581e). In the eyes of the actor, the hetaera's willingness to perform this position with just anyone constitutes an act of subversion, since it elevates the socially marginal figure of the artisan to the level of aristocracy, or at least those who can afford such luxuries (*entruphan*, 581e).[66] The hetaera in effect aids and abets this process of disrupting status boundaries by renting out her body and allowing equal access to all. And yet her final quip to the cuckolded Andronicus restores those boundaries by reasserting her physical and discursive control over this degrading act: "I cleverly contrived to touch the part of his person which projects farthest and is smallest" (*ephilosophēsa th', hin' akron hōs malista kai/ elachiston autou perilabō tou sōmatos*, Machon 374–375 = 581f). The verb *philosophein* injects an element of bathos: the lofty thoughts of the hetaera contrast her degrading sexual activities, while at the same time affiliating her with the philosophical discourse she so frequently is made to parody. The same use of repartee to deflect a client's demeaning sexual demand and to expose his baseness is also found in another of Mania's rejoinders: when a knave (*ponērōn tis*), upon taking her in his turn, asks, "Do you wish to come together from on top or below?" (*poter' anō theleis/ elthous' hama balein ē katō*) she laughingly responds, "On top . . . that you not steal my hair ornament while I am prone" (*gelasas' anō,/ . . . dedoika se/ mē mou propesousēs toumplokion hupertragēs*, Machon 255–57= 579d).

Another anecdote, condemned by Gow as "grossly corrupt and the point hardly intelligible" (1965: 112), seems to contain an obscene pun that functions as a put-down of another marginal character. Upon learning that her partner, a *mastigias*, allegedly received the scars on his back after falling into a funeral pyre, Gnathaena quips, "Yes, by the dear Demeter, and rightly did you flail yourself, since you are over-sexed" (*nai tēn philēn Dēmētra dikaiōs toi deros/ anthrōpe, phēsin, exedarēs akolastos ōn*, Machon 293–294 = 580b).[67] Although Gow rightly points out that the term *akolastos* normally refers to sexual incontinence, he misses the sense of *ekderein*; not only does it mean to flay or skin, but it possibly refers to masturbation, or even homosexual rape, as it does in Attic old comedy.[68] Through her jest, the hetaera exposes not only the rogue's lack of masculine self-control, but also his lower-class status as a criminal worthy of whipping. In another, less graphic anecdote, possibly by Aristodemus, Phryne similarly chides a *mastigias* for insulting her. To his allegation that she had been embraced by many men, she responds, "I am angry at *you* for having so many women!" (585f). Like many of the anecdotes already discussed, the hetaera's jokes invert gender roles, casting her in the role of the male partner.

The puns and rejoinders of older hetaeras, like Gnathaena, may convey their predatory sexuality in a gesture that renders men as the objects of erotic appraisal. Old women are typically depicted as lecherous and prone to obscenity in Greek literature, from Iambe in the *Homeric Hymn to Demeter* to the three crones at the end of Aristophanes' *Ecclesiazusae* (976ff.) who embed obscene double entendres in legal language as they spar over sexual access to the Youth. The elderly Gnathaena delivers some of the coarsest humor in the book in her exchange with another lower class character, a young butcher's boy:

> Upon seeing by chance
> a butcher boy standing at the scales, very pretty (*asteion*)
> and young in age, Gnathaena said, "By the gods,
> boy, the good looking one, tell me,
> how do you do your weighing (*histēs*)?"
> The boy smiled (*meidiasas*) and said,
> "From behind, for three obols" (*kubd' . . . triōbolou*).
> "But who will allow you,
> poor fool, to use Carian measures in Athens
> (*en Athēnais Karikois chrēsthai stathmois*)?"
> (Machon 304–10 = 580d)

The crone's attempt to turn the boy into an object of erotic appraisal is met by a counter proposition which states a price of three obols. As in all of Machon's *Chreiae*, however, the hetaera has the last word as she "measures" the butcher boy against Athenian social and sexual standards in a complex pun that alludes to the sexual perversions of the Carians. In a similar act of objectification, Gnathaena elsewhere ridicules a homely boy, described as skinny and dark (*ischnon panu/ kai melana lepton th'*, Machon 319–320 = 580e) by comparing him to Adonis (*eskōpten eis Adōnin*), a witticism that may allude to the types of jokes uttered by hetaeras celebrating the Adonia.[69]

Philosophers and Courtesans

The masculinized hetaeras of Machon and Lynceus bear little resemblance to the companions who flatter their clients with sweet nothings depicted by Ephippus. Their laughter is raucous, their jokes, while at times sophisticated, are basically crude. They belong instead to a subversive and parodic comic discourse that exposes the objects of their ridicule as depraved and unmanly, lacking in the self-control necessary for participation in the classical Athenian polis. And although these hetaeras inhabit a shadowy demimonde of cobbler shops, marketplaces, private symposia, and gardens, they nonetheless threaten to breach the status boundaries of gender and class by consorting with everyone. In this regard, they resemble other lower class comic characters such as parasites and jesters, figures with whom kings and poets rubbed elbows, and exchanged jokes, at court and table. But in the hands of the comic poets, to say nothing of historians with a flair for the theatrical, association with such marginal figures, female or male, called into question the status and manhood of the men who were their subjects. A similar dynamic obtains at Athenaeus' table: as ventriloquized by Myrtilus, hetaeras' witticisms form the heart of a parodic discourse intended to put Cynulcus, and philosophers generally, in their place.

In so doing, Athenaeus makes use of a well-established tradition, and a popular sophistic paradox, that linked philosophers and courtesans, beginning in fourth-century Athens with the Socratic dialogues of Xenophon and Plato's *Menexenus*. During this period, both types of professionals belonged to a large class of itinerant specialists that provided education and entertainment to an increasingly international clientele, one that also included cooks, actors, and artists (McKechnie 1989). In Xenophon's *Memorabilia* (3. 11. 1–18), a work discussed at greater length in Chapter 4, the philosopher both analogizes and contrasts the art of the hetaera with his own profession. Through a dialectical exchange with the historical courtesan, Theodote, he argues that both draw followers to them through their use of persuasion and yet their ends differ: the philosopher pursues truth while the hetaera seeks illusion.[70] The philosopher's laughter (*episkōptōn*) in response to her invitation to "visit often" indicates the light-hearted, ironic tone of the dialogue (Xen. *Mem.* 3. 11. 15–16).

In the *Menexenus*, Socrates ventriloquizes the speech of his "teacher," the pallake Aspasia, much as he does that of the priestess Diotima in the *Symposium*, to deride (*prospaizeis*, 235c) the epitaphios, or public funeral oration, that falsely praises even the lowliest of citizens.[71] This dialogue clearly informs the sympotic verse attributed to her and preserved by Herodicus the Cratetean, discussed earlier in this chapter. When Menexenus expresses incredulity that such a speech could have been composed by a woman (249d), the philosopher invites his interlocutor to hear the speech from her own lips (*akousei autēs legousēs*, 249d). Menexenus' wry response, "I have conversed with Aspasia many times, O Socrates, and know what sort she is" (249d), conflates the hetaera's rhetorical ability with her sexual availability.[72] Although Socrates publicizes Aspasia's authorship of the speech, coyly asserting that she may be vexed with him for broadcasting it (*hē didaskalos, an exenegkō autēs ton logon*, 236c), Menexenus doubts its veracity: "I am grateful to her, *or to whoever it was that repeated it to you*" (249e). This Platonic vignette functions in much the same way as the discourse of hetaeras in Book 13 of the *Deipnosophistae*: it provides the speaker a vehicle for parodying professions and literary genres such as the epitaphios, and the art of rhetoric in general. As deployed by Myrtilus, it parodies philosophical discourse itself.

Abbreviated dialogues between hetaeras and philosophers modeled on this Socratic tradition are widespread in Greek literature of first and second centuries C.E. and exemplify the sophistic love of combining paradox with *paideia* (Anderson, G. 1993: 184–85). Aelian develops an encounter between Socrates and the hetaera Callisto along the lines of Xenophon's account. When the hetaera boasts that the philosopher could not attract any of her clients while she could steal away all of his pupils, Socrates responds:

> Of course you could, because you lead all of your followers on the downward path (*epi tēn katantē*) while I force them to move toward virtue (*aretē*). The ascent is steep and unfamiliar for most people. (Ael. *VH* 13. 32)

The anecdote implicitly equates the professions of philosophy and prostitution while underscoring their divergent moral ends; in the Socratic tradition, however, the philosopher, not the courtesan, has the last word, affirming the truth of his discourse and the speciousness of hers.

Alciphron borrows from the same tradition Thais' letter to Euthydemus, but he wittily inverts the traditional Socratic moral. In the letter, the courtesan competes with a pederastic philosopher for the affections of her lover in a version of the conventional erotic debate that structures Book 13 of the *Deipnosophistae*:

> Do you think a sophist (*sophistēn*) is any different from a courtesan (*hetairas*)? Perhaps inasmuch as the means by which they persuade (*peithein*) are different; but one end—gain (*to labein*)—is the goal for both. (Alciphr. 4. 7. 4)

Thais inverts the claim of the Xenophontic Socrates that the hetaera and the philosopher employ the same technique for different ends; here the techniques are different, but the end is the same. She is also made to argue that the hetaera, not the philosopher, holds the moral high ground: after all, she believes in the gods, trusts in her lover's oaths, and condemns incest and adultery (Alciphr. 4. 7. 4–5). In fact, men in the company of hetaeras, she argues, tend to stay out of political trouble: they do not desire tyranny or sow civil strife, but rather think only of drink and sleep (4. 7. 6). Thais then adduces the example of Socrates and Aspasia to prove that hetaeras know better than philosophers how to teach rhetoric to young men, since the latter purportedly instructed Pericles.

The letter seeks not only to retain the affection of a wayward lover, but to convert him to the Epicurean doctrine of pleasure, "so that after drinking a bit, we might prove to one another the noble goal of pleasure" (*to kalon telos tēs hēdonēs*, Alciphr. 4. 7. 8). In this capacity, Thais plays the role of the wise female advisor earlier exemplified by Diotima and Aspasia in the Socratic dialogues (*kai soi nun malista phanoumai sophē*, Alciphr. 7. 4. 8); but here the courtesan literally acts as the agent of Epicurus' own doctrine, using her own body to entice the sophist toward a life of pleasure. One of Alciphron's parasites similarly marshals the figure of the hetaera to poke fun at a banquet of philosophers: while the Pythagorean recites a short didactic poem, the Epicurean embraces a psaltria, gazing up her as the "solidification of pleasure"; the Cynic, by contrast, publicly urinates, then prepares to have intercourse with a mousourgos in full view of all (Alciphr. 3. 19. 7–9).

The discourse of the wise and witty hetaera in the *Deipnosophistae* similarly parodies the pretensions of philosophers. The technique is encapsulated in a fictionalized exchange between the hetaera Glycera and the Hellenistic philosopher, Stilpo, quoted by Myrtilus. It follows his discussion of courtesans and *paideia* and makes use of many of the conventions discussed above:

> To Stilpo's accusation at a drinking party that she corrupted young men (*diaphtheirousēs tous neous*), as Satyrus says in his *Lives*, Glycera responded, "We incur the same blame, Stilpo. For they say that you corrupt (*diaphtheirein*) all that meet you by teaching them worthless, eristic sophistries (*anōphelē kai eristika sophismata*), while I likewise teach them erotic ones (*hōsautōs erōtika*). It makes no difference, therefore, to people who are utterly destroyed and down on their luck, whether they live in the company of a philosopher or a courtesan (*philosophou zēn ē hetairas*)." (Satyrus *FHG 3*. 164 = 584a)

With a technique similar to that of the witty rejoinder, Glycera deflects the criticism of the philosopher by equating her art with his; indeed, the verb *diaphtheirein* is thematic in descriptions of the harmful effects of encounters with hetaeras (cf. 567c). So also Myrtilus informs us that the Romans expelled their sophists, a term used interchangeably with philosopher in Book 13 and in the Alciphron letter discussed above, on the grounds that they corrupted the youth (610f). Given Stilpo's associations with Socratic and Cynic philosophy, the allusion implicitly equates him with Cynulcus, while casting Myrtilus in the role of the clever hetaera who exposes the pretensions of her interlocutor.

An anecdote about Epicurus and Leontion at the end of Myrtilus' speech about the *paideia* of courtesans shows yet again how the hetaera beats the philosopher at his own game. As a full member of Epicurus' school after it moved to Athens, Leontion had a reputation for erudition: she purportedly refuted Theophrastus in a book and wrote excellent Attic Greek.[73] No better figure could be found with which to mock the philosopher's lack of learning:

> Didn't this same Epicurus have Leontion as his mistress (*erōmenēn*), the woman who had become famous for being a hetaera (*tēn epi hetaireia diaboēton genomenēn*)? Not even when she began to study philosophy (*philosophein*), did she cease being a hetaera (*hetairousa*), but consorted (*sunēn*) with all the Epicureans in the Gardens, and even in full view of Epicurus. (588b)

In this passage, the hetaera embodies the notorious hedonism of the Epicureans while at the same time unmasking the foolishness of the philosopher himself (588a–b). Indeed, detractors of Epicurus and his followers, such as Cicero, deride their practice of including women in their circle and adduce it as evidence of their licentiousness (Gordon 1996: 85). Catalogues of these women attribute courtesan-like names to them, including diminutives such as Boidion, Erotion, Mammarion, and Nicidion, and abstractions such as Hedeia (Gordon 1996: 86). In Myrtilus' account, Leontion's presence in the garden disrupts their contemplative life by means of the very principle of pleasure embraced by adherents and thus turns their own precepts against them, in the same manner as Lais' fictive encounter with Euripides.

In addition to their hypocrisy, the figure of Leontion exposes yet another flaw of philosophers: their putative lack of erudition and *paideia*. Myrtilus attributes to Epicurus the same charge lodged against Cynulcus, a failure to engage with the literary tradition: he is "uninitiated in *paideia*" (*paideias amuētos*, 588a) and given to praise others also "cleansed of all *paideia*" (*katharos pasēs paideias*, 588a). The problem of the philosopher's inadequate education returns at the end of Book 13, when the grammarian accuses his Cynic opponent of hating literature: "Then am I not right in hating all of you philosophers, you who hate the *logoi*?" (*eit' ouk egō dikaiōs pantas humas tous philosophous misō misophilologous ontas*, 610d). The hetaeras' learned witticisms, with their inversions of gender and genres, their paradoxical mix of high and low, tragic and coarse, form the heart of Myrtilus' comic and parodic discourse and is intended to expose the inflated pretensions of the moralizing philosopher. They introduce into Athenaeus' symposium a scurrilous and boisterous discourse that works much like the presence of Leontion in Epicurus' garden. In recounting the witty *chreiae* of courtesans, Myrtilus uses the Cynics' own parodic and shameless discourse against them.

Conclusion

Athenaeus excerpts and develops the witticisms of hetaeras more fully than any other aspect of their representation in Book 13. Allusions to their speech and to their rejoinders portray them as having a literary sensibility exceeded only by the sophists at Athenaeus' table. Whether or not Athenian hetaeras actually exhibited this degree of *paideia* (Neaera, for instance, notably lacked such finesse), they are paradoxically constructed by Athenaeus and the literary tradition as the learned transmitters of Attic language and culture and so resemble the sophists that populate his banquet. Their rejoinders involve a complex verbal dynamic in which the marginal or low other turns the tables on an interlocutor of equal or higher status. In the same way, Myrtilus marshals their discourse to ridicule Cynulcus, and philosophers generally. From a broader perspective, the "fine sayings" of hetaeras evoke, and poke fun at, "the fine sayings of educated men" alluded to by the epitomator in Book 1 of the *Deipnosophistae*. Their use of literary quotation and their playful adaptation of tragic verse make use of some of the same verbal strategies as those of the sophists and philosophers at Athenaeus' table. Moreover, the struggle for discursive control exemplified by the witticisms of hetaeras implicitly mocks and exposes the intellectual environment of Athenaeus and other Second Sophistic writers, in which individuals competed for status through verbal performance.[74]

CHAPTER **4**

The Spectacle of the Body: Courtesans in Performance

She was not so much a woman as a walking work of art, a compilation of symbols
and markers of eroticism, as far removed from a human being as a bonsai
is from a natural tree.[1]

As public figures and sympotic performers, courtesans played a significant role in the "culture of viewing" that constituted Athenian society from the fifth century onward. This visual culture in turn engendered a host of spectacular narratives about the public nudity of hetaeras put on display in the law courts and at religious festivals, or conjured by famous statues, many of which are preserved in Book 13 of the *Deipnosophistae*. In the Hellenistic period, the city boasted, as one tourist put it, "spectacles without interruption," theatrical performances, public monuments, dedications in sanctuaries and elsewhere, mobile works of art, and funerals.[2] This collective experience of performance and public display brought a theatrical vocabulary to the narratives and dramatic texts that shaped Athenaeus' discourse on hetaeras, the "tragic history" of Duris and Phylarchus, as well as oratory and anecdotal collections (Chaniotis 1997: 251). An account of Macedonian court life inserted into Book 14 of the *Deipnosophistae* shows both the influence of contemporary spectacles on these authors as well as the pervasive association of courtesans with theatrical space and performance:

> Demetrius used to say that the court of Lysimachus did not differ from a comic scene (*kōmikēs skēnēs*). For all the characters that appeared in the scene had disyllabic names. He made fun of Bithys and Paris, men who were the most important to Lysimachus, and some of his other friends. From his own court were

107

Peucesteses and Menelauses, and even Oxythemises. Hearing this, Lysimachus said, in reference to the flute girl Lamia, "I have never seen a porne appear in a tragic scene." And when this had been reported to him, Demetrius once more took him up and said, "But any porne at my court lives more moderately than any Penelope at his." (614e–f)

This story shows the pervasive association of the Greek courtesan with comic drama; her presence converts the Macedonian court into a comic stage as a means of ridiculing the foibles of its monarchy. As the anecdote suggests, the prevalence of hetaeras as characters in Middle and New Comedy in the fourth century contributed to their representation as public performers and even as metaphors for theatricality, a process that began with their names.

In all of these contexts, the primary instrument of the hetaera's performance, whether in the symposium, the comic theater, or in art, is the body.[3] Theatricality and self-representation through external markers such as clothing, delivery, gesture, and gait became an important component of male public life in fourth century Athens as well as among the second sophists, after whom Athenaeus' models his symposiasts.[4] As Gleason has shown, the Greek sophists of Imperial Rome indicated character and gender status through movement and posture; a dignified carriage signified a manly speaker, while restless movements and slack limbs conveyed a feminine nature.[5] Courtesans also engaged in this male performance culture from the classical period onward, whether as bodies displayed in the brothel or on the street, or as performers in the theater, the symposium, or even the courts. This public presence in everyday life, combined with their literary representation, contributed to the view of courtesans as consummate performers who constructed themselves wholly through artifice. The bodies of courtesans thus provide a convenient metaphor for literary artifice, epideictic display, and rhetorical persuasion from the classical period through the late second century C.E. As foreigners and outsiders who belonged to no one and yet made themselves available to all, the courtesan's visual and textual signification could more readily be multiplied, manipulated, and continually mediated than that of citizen wives. This chapter explores narratives about the bodies of hetaeras and prostitutes found in Book 13 of the *Deipnosophistae*, and the tradition that informs them, from the perspective of Hellenistic spectacle and rhetorical display. A related form of spectacle connected with hetaeras, public monuments erected in their honor, will be discussed in the next chapter.

Staging the Female Body

Hetaeras and other types of prostitutes performed privately as entertainers and conversationalists at the dinner parties of men; in the theater, they appeared as fictive constructs played by male actors, as the silent abstractions of Attic Old comedy, or the stock characters of Middle and New comedy. Because most of the representations of the bodies of hetaeras in Book 13 come from the comic tradition and "tragic history," they are infused with allusions to stage performance and theatricality. To judge from the fragments, comic passages featuring courtesans often appear to have had a self-referential dimension evocative of modes of theatrical viewing, disguise, and performative illusion. The inclusion of a personified Theoria (Spectatorship) in Aristophane's *Peace*, for instance, demonstrates the strong association of the courtesan with performance and spectacle in the Athenian imaginary from as early as the fifth century B.C.E.(Ar. *Pax* 713ff). Even the verb *theorein* and its cognates equate theatrical viewing with the act of gazing on the bodies of courtesans and prostitutes, both in comedy as well as in narratives about the visual arts.

The comic stage deployed a variety of semi-naked female prostitutes, such as the two women who accompany Dicaeopolis at the end *Acharnians* (1198–1234), the auletris Philocleon attempts to assault in *Wasps* (1326– 1371), Procne in the *Birds* (666–74), and the orchestris summoned by Euripides to entice the Scythian Archer in *Thesmophoriazusae* (1174–1201). Whether hetaeras or other types of prostitutes actually played these roles, or whether they were performed by men in padded clothing, these bodies were visually and verbally exposed in Attic Old comedy.[6] They are often found in scenes that involve "physical acts of inspection and palpitation . . . accompanied by obscene verbal commentaries that make use of highly colored terminology intended to spice the humor of exposure and/or degradation."[7] Considered in this way, the staged nakedness of sexualized females such as Diallage (Reconciliation) and Theoria in Attic Old comedy not only reinforces the idea of the hetaera's body as a general metaphor for spectacle, but as a spectacle offered up for the use and enjoyment of men.

A metatheatrical moment in Aristophanes' *Peace*, a play produced in 421 B.C.E., illustrates how Attic Old comedy conjures the body of the courtesan or prostitute in service of a personified abstraction. At lines 657–661, Hermes escorts the recalcitrant figure of Eirene (Peace) onstage: she angrily refuses to speak before the male spectators (657–661) and averts her gaze (682). Next, the god entrusts to Trygaeus two other mute abstractions, Theoria and Opora, a name associated with courtesans as we saw in Chapter 2, for sexual gratification and propagation (*xunoikōn . . . kusai*, 708–9). The explicit sexual allusions to her anatomy, and to that of Trygaeus, later in the play suggest Opora may be a courtesan (*titthiōn . . . pugēs . . . peos*, 860–870). The same applies to Theoria, who is described as vulnerable to sexual assault (*prōktopentetērida*, 876; 877–879).[8] The men later caution Eirene not to turn away, like a fickle adulteress (*moicheuomenai*, 980), but ask her to show her full form (*apophēnon holēn sautēn*, 987). Similarly, the mute figure of Diallage at the end of *Lysistrata* becomes a map upon which the Spartans and Athenians, sparring over cities inscribed as body parts, can read the geography of a united Hellas (1161–1175). The use of mute female figures—if not actually courtesans or prostitutes, at least strongly suggestive of them—to personify abstract concepts in Aristophanes demonstrates their interchangeability as signs traded in the intellectual marketplace of men.[9]

As figures of substitution, the prostitutes of Attic Old comedy could serve as a metaphor for political deception and theatrical illusion: through them the moral depravities and corruption of contemporary politicians and the degradation of literary genres are signified.[10] At the end of *Thesmophoriazusae*, the depiction of Euripides as a procurer who puts a dancer onstage to distract the loutish Scythian plays up the comic association of the poet with prostitution (Ar. *Thesm.* 1172–1202). In the *Frogs*, Aeschylus compares Euripides' monotonous meters to Cyrene's sexual tricks: "You who compose such things, dare to revile my songs, you who make your music amid the twelve positions of Cyrene" (Ar. *Ran.* 1325–28).[11] Aeschylus similarly denounces Euripides for being a teacher of prostitution (*pornōidikōn*, 1301), that is, putting adulteresses such as Phaedra and Stheneboea onstage (*Ran.* 1043). Moreover, he brings to the stage a whorish muse, "the personification of cheap and decadent versifying and degraded subject matter" (Henry 1985: 29 and n. 55). In all these contexts, whether Attic Old comedy, oratory, or prose, the courtesan embodies the power of persuasion to corrupt and the base rhetorical tricks meant to deceive rather than to edify.

Cynulcus' Praise of Brothels

Although Cynulcus accuses Myrtilus of being a *pornographos*, the philosopher actually constructs the most explicit visual tableau of brothel whores in the book with his invective against high-priced courtesans, a discourse that may be intended to evoke the shamelessness of the Cynics. By contrast, Myrtilus downplays the graphic nudity of hetaeras even as he reports the crude witticisms by which they objectify their interlocutors, and occasionally, even themselves. Given his rhetorical purpose, the praise of exemplary hetaeras, as opposed to brazen pornographic displays, the grammarian fastens instead upon their elusive artifice, their euphemistic naming, their theatricality, and the fetishization of their bodies into art objects and public monuments. According to Cynulcus, the extent to which the prostitute's body could be seen depended on whether she worked the streets or stood before the brothel door; at least, this distinction forms the heart of his discourse against high–paid courtesans and his encomium of the porne. In excoriating hetaeras and praising whores, Cynulcus gives the most explicit testimonia—all of which are drawn from Middle and New comedy—for bodily display in Book 13 of the *Deipnosophistae*. In contrast, the catalogue of Myrtilus focuses almost exclusively on names and words, making little reference to the bodies of hetaeras beyond conventional praise of their beauty. By quoting comic passages concerned predominantly with the display of the prostitutional body, Cynulcus effectively depersonalizes the denizens of Athenian brothels and reduces them to mere bodies easily consumed and discarded by men. In contrast to hetaeras, such women are vulnerable because they can be easily seen, lacking the protection of wealth and powerful men.[12]

He begins with the women "in the brothels" (*tas epi tōn oikēmatōn*, 568d) depicted in a scene of Eubulus' *Pannychis* (Vigil):

> Those song-loving birds of profit (*kermatōn*),
> . . . trained fillies of Aphrodite, stripped for action
> and posted in battle line (*gumnas ephexēs epi kerōs tetagmenas*),
> stand in finely woven garments (*en leptopēnois huphēsin*)
> like the daughters whom the Eridanus waters with its pure stream.
> From them, reliably and securely you can
> buy your pleasure for a small price (*kermatos*).
>
> (Eubulus, *Pannychis* F82 KA= 568e–f)

The metaphorical allusions to birds (*paleutrias*), as well as to fillies (*pōlous*), recall the many ornithological and equine nicknames for courtesans that play up and objectify their sexuality in the Greek literary tradition. The stark repetition of the word *kerma* (gain) in both the first and last lines reinforces the stereotype of the prostitute as greedy and rapacious, while at the same time emphasizing her commodity status.

Another version of this passage, attributed to the *Nannion* of Eubulus, describes brothel whores with almost the same language: the women are "stripped for action" and "posted for battle", they wear transparent clothing, and can be had for little cost. However, this fragment places the emphasis on the male observer through its use of the masculine participle *theōrēsanti* (568f). The verb here as elsewhere analogizes this masculine pornographic gaze to theatrical viewing. A passage of Persaeus of Citium quoted at the end of Book 13 similarly describes scantily clad orchestrides as a "marvelous sight" for the male spectators (*hōs thaumaston ti theama*, *FGrH* 584 F4 = 607d). The verb is also used of the painter Apelles as he gazes on the youthful Lais, future hetaera and model (*theasamenos*, 588c), just as Socrates and his companions behold the beauty of Theodote (*theasomenois*, 588d).[13] As objects of the male gaze, the bodies of hetaeras are analogized to a form of spectacle simliar to that experienced in the theater or even in a religious context.

For Cynulcus and the comic poets he quotes, the visibility and availability of the brothel prostitute inverts the seclusion of respectable wives, who cannot be seen, "or if seen, cannot be seen clearly" (*has d' out' idein est', outh' horōnt' idein saphōs*, 569c). The brothel thus offers legitimate refuge from clandestine liaisons with another man's wife, "a fearful union in the dark" (*lechē gar skotia numpheuei lathrai*, 568f):

> [In this city] there are very pretty (*euprepōn*) girls
> in the brothels whom you can see
> basking in the sun, their breasts unclad,
> stripped (*gumnas*) for action and arrayed for battle (*tetagmenas*).
> You can choose from these the girl that pleases,
> thin, plump, compact, tall or withered,
> young, old, middle-aged, over-ripe,
> and not set up a ladder and climb in secretly,
> nor creep in through the chimney below the roof,
> nor be craftily carried inside under husks.
> For the women use force and drag them in,
> calling those who are old men
> "Daddy," and the younger ones, "Little Brother."
> And you can have any one of these without fear, at little
>   cost (*eutelōs*),
> during the day, at evening, and in any sexual position.
>   (Xenarchus, *Pentathlon* F4 KA = 569b–c)

The specification of the sizes and ages of these brothel whores plays up their status as commodities, as does the allusion to their reasonable price (*eutelōs*). Whereas the nakedness of the prostitutes depicted by Eubulus and Xenarchus marks them out as "not wives," it also suggests, at least on a verbal level, the activities of men. The formula *gumnas . . . tetagmenas*, repeated in three different comic fragments, evokes wrestling and military training, respectively, metaphorical language also used by the poets of Attic Old comedy in speaking of sexual intercourse and found in connection with hetaeras in other Second Sophistic texts.[14] Elsewhere a courtesan is likened to an athletic trainer (*paidotribēn*, 584c), another common metaphor for sexual activity, as well as a possible pun on the verb *tribein*. Their presence out of doors, in the sun, also likens them to men: in Aristophanes' *Ecclesiazusae*, one of the female characters states that she has oiled herself and exposed her body to the sun in order to make it darker, like that of a man.[15] As with their raucous laughter, the public nudity of courtesans becomes the tangible sign of their aggressive, even masculine, sexuality, an idea underscored by the description of courtesans bodily dragging their clients off the streets and into the house.[16]

The open nakedness of brothel prostitutes not only advertises their availability, it also signifies, for Cynulcus at least, a lack of deception normally associated with hetaeras. According to a quotation adduced from Philemon's *Adelphoi* (Brothers), Solon, the man who invented the euphemism, also established civic brothels with a view to preventing adultery.[17]

> [Solon], seeing Athens full of young men,
> with both an instinctual compulsion (*tēn anagkaian phusin*),
> and a habit of straying in an inappropriate direction,
> bought women and established them in various places,
> equipped and common to all.
> The women stand naked that you not be deceived.
> Look at everything.
> Maybe you are not feeling well. You have
> some sort of pain. Why? The door is open.
> One obol. Hop in. There is no coyness,
> no idle talk, nor does she snatch herself away.
> But straight away, as you wish, in whatever way you wish.
> You come out. Tell her to go to hell. She is a stranger to you.
> (Philemon, *Adelphoi* F3 KA = 569e–f)

Central to Cynulcus' discourse is the equation of the brothel worker with truth and the hetaera with deception: because their bodies are displayed and only thinly concealed, if covered at all, they offer the onlooker truth in advertising. Their exposure recalls the generic function of comedy in stripping away illusion and revealing vulnerabilities in much the same way as the shameless discourse of the Cynics. Like the courtesan, the brothel prostitute alleviates pain, but in contrast, does not require a long-term relationship.

In contrast, highly paid hetaeras, at least as represented by Myrtilus, do not offer themselves for public display but rather manipulate what men are allowed to see. Theodote shows her visitors "only as much as decency allows" (note the verb *epideiknuein*, Xen. *Mem.* 3. 11. 1), while Phryne is to said to have wrapped her garments closely about her body and to have avoided the public baths (590f); in this respect they imitate legitimate wives. Constant visibility, in contrast, marked out the prostitute's body as readily available and could even signify a change of status from hetaera to common whore: for example, the courtesan Lais in her youth was reputedly more difficult to see than a Persian satrap, but past her prime, she became "easier to see . . . than to spit" (570c–d).

But the appearance of hetaeras are nonetheless quite different from respectable wives, particularly in their use of cosmetics. The young citizen wife of Xenophon's *Oeconomicus* is scolded by her husband for wearing clothing, make up, and shoes that hide her true form and stature (Xen. *Oec.*

10. 2), whereas the hetaera craftily conceals her physical flaws through costume and cosmetics. To underscore this point, Cynulcus quotes from a section of Eubulus' *Stephanopolides* (Wreath Sellers) that contrasts unadorned wives with cosmeticized hetaeras.[18]

> By Zeus, they are not plastered over with white lead,
> nor, like you, do they have their cheeks smeared with
> mulberry dye. And if *you* all go out on a hot day,
> two streams of inky water flow from your eyes,
> and the sweat running from your cheeks
> to your neck makes a streak of chalky rouge (*miltōdē*),
> while the hairs straying about your faces
> look gray, being full of white lead.
> (Eubulus, *Stephanopolides* F97 KA = 557f)

The use of makeup, as Bernheimer argues in his analysis of Baudelaire, "permits a woman to construct herself as a fetish, as a dazzling, shiny surface that covers over and obscures the corrupt sexual nature beneath" (Bernheimer 1993: 63). It also serves to identify the courtesan with theatrical performance and with literary artifice. Eubulus in this passage may even allude to the masks donned by the characters in the play, which signified their status as courtesans by means of facial color, hairstyle, or other ornament.[19] The close association of cosmetics with hetaeras is elsewhere supported by a vision Alcibiades allegedly experienced shortly before his death: he imagined himself dressed in his courtesan's clothing while she adorned his face, like a woman's, with paints and white lead (Plut. *Alc.* 39).

An exhaustive comic list of beauty aids employed by courtesans further identifies them with cosmetic and sartorial artifice: clippers, mirrors, scissors, grease-paint, soda, false hair, purple trimmings, bands, ribbons, lead paint, white lead, myrrh, pumice stone, breast bands, buttock pads, veils, seaweed paint, necklaces, eye paint, soft woolen garments, gold ornaments for hair, hair nets, girdle, mantilla, morning dress, dress purple-hemmed on both sides and with a purple border, dress with a train, shifts, combs, earrings, necklaces, bracelets (Ar. *Thesm.* β F332 KA = Pollux 7. 95). The use of such contrivances had affinities with theatrical performance: the same white lead paint, *psimuthion*, both served as a foundation for lightening the face as well as for the dramatic mask.[20] So fully identified with make up were hetaeras that many took their names from cosmetic substances, such as Milto (a kind of rouge), the original name of Aspasia the Younger. The white paint effectively transformed the face of the individual woman into an impassive mask that both distanced her from her real identity while at the same time fabricating an exaggerated and artificial femininity, in much the same way as their names. And as will be demonstrated below, the painted faces of hetaeras resembled not only theatrical masks, but also the painted portraits for which they served as models.

The numerous allusions to garments in the Aristophanic fragment quoted above further associate hetaeras with theatrical costume. Indeed, Cynulcus cites a lengthy passage from Alexis' *Isostasion* (Equal Measure), to expose the cosmetic contrivances employed by hetaeras to attract customers. The play's title itself could be interpreted as an ellipsis of *isostasion muron*, "perfume of equal weight/value," and most likely refers to a hetaera.[21] Arnott conjectures that the fragment, the longest extant that can be positively assigned to Alexis, is a harangue delivered by a father to his son about the dangers of patronizing courtesans (Arnott 1996: 268).

First for profit and to rob their neighbors,
everything else becomes superfluous to them, for they stitch
plots against all. Whenever they prosper,
they take in new hetaeras, fledglings in the art.
Right away they remodel (*anaplattousi*) them, so that
neither their manners nor their looks resemble who they really are.
One happens to be short—cork is stitched
into her shoes. One is tall—she wears flat heels
and walks with her head tipped to her shoulder.
This reduces her height. One does not have hips.
She dresses her underneath with sown-on haunches, so that
all who see her shout out that the girl has
fine buttocks (*eupugia*). One has a fat stomach.
For her they have breasts made out of those the comic actors use.
Having put attachments just like this on straight . . . .
One has pale eyebrows—they paint them black (*zōgraphousin
    asbolōi*).
Another happens to be too dark—she smears on white lead
    (*psimuthiōi*).
One is too fair-skinned—she rubs on rouge (*paiderōt'*).
A part of one's body is beautiful—she displays this bare.
She has well-formed teeth—she must of course laugh (*gelan*)
so that everyone present might see what a fine mouth she has.
But if she does not like to laugh (*gelōsa*), she spends her day
inside, and like the wares displayed by the butchers,
whenever they offer goats' heads for sale,
she must keep a thin piece of wood straight between her lips,
so that she grins, whether she wants to or not.
By such arts do they manufacture their appearance.

                                    (Alexis, *Isostasion* F103 KA = 568a–d)

The prosperous hetaera described by this passage functions as a procuress who shapes (*anaplattousi*) the manners (*tropous*) and appearance (*opseis*) of her subjects so that they no longer resemble their "real" selves (*mēte . . . ousas eti*, 568a–b). On one level, this creation story recalls that of Pandora, the first woman, whom Hephaestus molds from clay (*sumplasse*, Hes. *Theog.* 571), and reminds us that, for the Greeks, the erotic aesthetic implicit in viewing the female body always involved adornment.[22] Allusions to stitching, sewing, molding, plastering, and painting similarly emphasize the feminine artifice and deception involved in such transformations. But the most prevalent metaphor is that of theatrical performance: at one point, the hetaera is compared to the comic actor (*hoi kōmikoi*, F103. 12–15 KA) in her use of padding, while the word *toiauta* (just like this) suggests some sort of stage gesture on the part of the male actor playing the old hetaera that might have called attention to his costume.[23] Several Aristophanic passages mention the use of rouge and other substances in connection with female characters, particularly old women.[24] Like that of the actor, the hetaera's false exterior creates a theatrical illusion calculated to arouse an emotional response in her viewers. The nickname of Nannion, Proscenion (Stage), aptly encompasses the hetaera's theatricality by alluding first to the actual site of dramatic performance: her fair exterior, described as *prosōpon* (mask), and her fine clothing nonetheless conceal a whorish interior (*tripornos*, 587b).

On the comic stage, as in everyday life, special clothing distinguished courtesans from respectable women. The comic passages adduced by Cynulcus mention a very finely woven, almost transparent drapery worn by brothel workers, and made from linen or silk and of eastern origin that both covered the body and yet evoked the form beneath (*leptopēnois huphesin*, 568e, 569f).[25] It is possible also that the association of courtesans and prostitutes with finely woven garments informs Socrates' analogy of the hetaera as a spider that entraps with its intricate web (*lepta huphēnamenai*, Xen. *Mem.* 3. 11. 6).[26] Garments with purple borders, as described in the Aristophanic fragment quoted above, were also identified with courtesans: according to Athenaeus, Syracusan law stated that a woman was forbidden to wear gold ornaments or colored dresses or garments with purple borders unless she admitted to being a common hetaera (*hetaira . . . koinē*, 12. 521b).[27] Another fashion associated with the hetaera was a simple, short tunic termed *monochitōn*, a garment that ended above the knee and had the sides slit up so high the entire thigh was exposed (Pollux 7. 55), in contrast to the more traditional female *chitōn* of longer length.[28] Since this garment was normally worn next to the body, under the mantle or *himation*, the prefix *mono* may indicate a departure from normal custom, e.g., the hetaera wore the *chitōn* alone, without a covering. In Book 13 of Athenaeus, Myrtilus describes statues of Cleino set up in Alexandria wearing this costume and holding a rhyton (576f). The courtesan Melissa also purportedly donned the *monochitōn* while acting as wine-pourer for the workmen in the fields (589f). Another type of garment, of unknown construction, but identified as a *lēdion*, is attributed to the hetaera Glycerion in Book 13 (582e).

Metaphors of the Body

The comic quotations marshaled by Cynulcus in his invective construct the bodies of brothel workers as inexpensive objects of fleeting lusts and those of hetaeras as risible and even frightening. The passsage from Epicrates' *Anti-Lais* that concludes his speech exemplifies his technique: he takes a courtesan celebrated for her beauty and reveals her as a bibulous, gluttonous old woman, her body grotesquely distorted by age:

> When Lais was a chick (*neottos*) and young,
> she was made wild by golden staters,
> you would have seen Pharnabazus more quickly than her.
> But since she has now run the long course,
> the symmetries of her body have become slack
> (*tas harmonias te diachalai tou sōmatos*),
> and it is easier to see her than to spit.
> She now goes everywhere on the wing,
> and she will accept a stater or three obols,
> she goes with both young and old alike.
> She has become so tamed, my dear friend,
> that she takes the money right out of your hand.
> (Epicrates, *Antilais* F1–2 = 570c–d; trans. adapted from Gulick)

The once elusive Lais, treated extensively in Myrtilus' subsequent encomium, is here rendered visible, and risible, a commodity to be enjoyed by all. By exposing the cosmetic artifice of hetaeras, the philosopher attempts to demystify them and to render them objects of male scorn and derision.

The aging courtesan is a familiar literary trope actively deployed throughout the epigrammatic corpus. One by Claudianus describes an aging courtesan as cloaking her breasts in a "counterfeit splendor" (*aglaiē nothē, Anth. Pal.* 9. 139). No longer the site of sexual pleasure, the body of the aging prostitute evokes mortality and death: it is a funerary urn (*soros,* 580d), a grave monument (Ar. *Eccl.* 1105–111), an owl that "sits upon the tomb."[29] The eroticized crones of Aristophanic comedy are similarly represented: in *Plutus*, the youth likens the seductive crone to a corpse (Ar. *Plut.* 1008, 1033), while at the end of *Ecclesiazusae*, three old women figured as courtesans haggle over sexual access to a young man (Ar. *Eccl.* 877ff.). One epigrammatist speaks of "touching Hades" in the form of a courtesan (*ethigon t' Aida*, Asclepiades, *Anth. Pal.* 5. 162). In another epigram, the narrator describes the physical imperfections of his aging mistress and then compares her to a tomb by which wayfarers pass (*hōs de taphon nun se parerchometha*, Rufinus, *Anth. Pal.* 5. 21. 6). A hetaera in one of Alciphron's letters, complaining about her lover's lack of gifts, compares him to a dirge singer (*thrēnōdon*, Alciphr. 4. 9. 5), who sends flowers and garlands "as to an untimely tomb" (*aōrōi taphōi*, Alciphr. 4. 9. 5). Artemidorus similarly analyzes the dream of being unable to leave a brothel as signifying impending harm because, as a public space, the brothel resembles a cemetery where human seed dies (Artem. 1. 78).[30] The association of courtesans with death has a certain intrinsic cultural logic, as Foucault points out; medical writers such as Galen analogize epilepsy to the sex act because they produce the same type of convulsions, while, in the case of prostitution, sexual activity itself involves wasted expenditure.[31]

The public visibility and sexual availability of the prostitute's body likens it to public structures, conveyances or thoroughfares accessible to all, and underscore its status as a commodity. As early as archaic lyric poetry, her body is compared to a thoroughfare (Anac. *PMG* 346. 12). For Artemidorus, an individual who dreams of becoming a bridge will become a prostitute, a public thoroughfare trampled upon by many (Artem. 4. 66).[32] The metaphor is also active in Roman literature, as Plautus in the *Curculio* refers to a prostitute as the *publica via* (33–38). The courtesan's body resembles a well-traveled ship and a house that has had several occupants in a conventional dialogue cast between the philosophers Aristippus, the lover of Lais, and the Cynic Diogenes, recorded by Athenaeus.

> "Aristippus, you cohabit with a common whore (*koinē . . . pornē*). Therefore either become a Cynic like me," I said, "or stop it." And Aristippus said, "Does it seem strange to you, Diogenes, to live in a house in which other men have lived before?" "Not at all," he replied. "How about sailing in a ship in which many have sailed?" "Not that either," he said. "That being the case, then it isn't strange to consort with a woman whom many have enjoyed." (Diog. Laer. 2. 8. 74 = 588e–f)

Staged between a Cynic philosopher and the Socratic philosopher Aristippus, the anecdote encapsulates the quarrel of Myrtilus and Cynulcus over the virtues and vices of courtesans in Book 13. In Cicero's version of the anecdote, the Socratic has the last word by asserting "*Habeo . . . non habeor a Laide*" ("I have Lais, but I am not had by her," Cic. *Fam.* 9. 26). In Theophrastus' *Characters*, the metaphor is reversed: a house "practically has its legs in the air" (*oikia tis autē ta skelē*, Theophr. *Char.* 28. 3), a sexual position typically associated with courtesans. An epigram from the *Palatine Anthology* compares the body of Timo to a worn-out ship that no longer endures "the strokes of Cypris' rowers" (Meleager, *Anth. Pal.* 5. 204), while in another, two hetaeras adopt the names of ships, Lembion and Kerkyrion (Rufinus, *Anth. Pal.* 5. 44). Using a similar metaphor, Aristophanes in his *Knights* describes a virgin trireme as one that has not gone near men (*hētis andrōn asson ouk elēluthei*, Ar. *Eq.* 1306). The association of female sexuality with ships further underlies the nautical terminology used to describe sexual intercourse in Attic Old comedy (Henderson 1991: 164–5).

Performing the Hetaera

Whereas Cynulcus privileges the "true" bodies of whores over the lying bodies of hetaeras as products of deliberate artifice, Myrtilus downplays their corporeality, focusing instead on artifice of another sort, their ability to perform a kind of respectability. In this sense, the hetaera can also be compared to a dramatic actor: so the description of Phryne's affected displeasure at a lover's joke analogizes her performance to that of an orator or actor (*kath' hupokrisin eskuthrōpasen*, 585f). The grammarian similarly emphasizes the hetaera's ability to behave respectably, even to play the part of a wife; he adduces a fragment of Eubulus' *Kampylion* (Hunchback) to illustrate the table manners of the well-behaved courtesan:

> How modestly (*kosmiōs*) she dined,
> not like other women, who, rolling their leeks into balls,
> stuffed their cheeks and disgracefully bit off
> chunks of meat, but she would taste
> a little of each, just like a virgin from Miletus.
> (Eubulus, *Kampylion* F42 KA = 571f–572a)

At table, the *kosmia* hetaera resembles a well-bred girl; in performing refinement, as in her staged reclusiveness, she is almost closer to the respectable matron than to the brothel worker.[33] Another Second Sophistic text depicts a mother advising her daughter, a hetaera-in-training, not to eat or drink too much or too quickly in the company of men (Lucian *Dial. meret.* 6. 3).

In addition to playing the part of a respectable woman, courtesans are viewed as performing a spurious affection for their clients, as demonstrated by the witticism of Phryne above. In a parody of epic invocation from the fragmentary prologue of Menander's *Thais*, a character complains of these feigned emotions:

> Sing to me, Goddess, of this sort of woman,
> one who is bold, voluptuous, and altogether clever (*pithanēn*),
> who is unjust, who shuts out her lovers, who begs excessively,
> but who loves no one and yet always pretends to (*prospoioumenēn*).[34]
> (Men. *Thais* F163 KA)

This quotation represents the hetaera as continually shifting her persona in response to each situation, much as the actor manipulates voice and gesture. In Book 13, Leonidas explains why the hetaera must perform such affections with a quotation from another comic play: while the wife legitimately remains at home in proud contempt, the courtesan knows that a man must be "bought by her ways" or risk losing him to another (*tois tropois ōnēteos*, Amphis, *Athamas* F1= 559a–b).

For Socrates, the hetaera's body itself practices this deception, performing the part of a welcoming and eager lover: "You persuade not by speech," he remarks in response to Theodote, "but by your actions" (*ou logōi all' ergōi anapeitheis*, Xen. *Mem.* 3. 11. 10). He then enumerates the various ways she plays her part:

> And inside [your body] you have a soul that teaches you what glance will please, what words delight, and tells you that your business is to give warm welcome to an eager suitor, but to slam the door upon a player. And when a friend has fallen sick, to show your anxiety by visiting him; and when he has had a stroke of good fortune, to congratulate him eagerly; and if he is eager in his suit, to put yourself at his service with your whole soul. (Xen. *Mem.* 3. 11. 10; trans. Marchant)

Theodote protests that she acts naturally and genuinely, without contrivance (*ouden mēchanōmai*). Socrates, assuming the role of erotic advisor, instructs her to behave both naturally (*kata phusin*) and properly (*orthōs*, 3. 11. 11). In all of these accounts, the hetaera is represented as inherently theatrical: she is never herself, but always performs the part of someone else.

The Movements of Hetaeras

The spectacle of the hetaera also involved calculated physical display through dance, gait, or participation in sympotic beauty contests. Athenaeus makes no reference to the physical movements of hetaeras, beyond mentioning that some performed as dancers, and yet their motions comprise another important aspect of their public performance that differentiates them from respectable wives.[35]

> Feminine movements and daintiness and wantonness ought to be curtailed. For the delicacy of movement (*habrodiaiton*) as one goes about and the "walking *saula*," as Anacreon says, are altogether like a hetaera.[36]

To walk in a *saula* fashion is to walk with a hip-swaying swagger: only hetaeras and dissolute men move in this manner. In Aristophanes' *Wasps*, the chorus describes "today's young men" as pathics with a swaggering, effeminate walk (*diasalakōnison*, Ar. *Vesp.* 1169). Similarly, a girl in an epigram by Rufinus is said to roll her hips in a lascivious fashion (*saleuomenai*, *Anth. Pal.* 5. 60. 4). Clement takes issue not simply with the fact that this type of walk might brand a proper Christian woman a hetaera, but that it involves artifice and deception. This specialized walk appears in several other places, including an epigram from the mid-first century C.E., to give just one example: "Take off these nets, Lysidice, you tease, / and don't roll your hips on purpose as you walk" (Marcus Argentarius, *Anth. Pal.* 5. 104; trans. Paton). The adverb *epitēdes*, translated as "on purpose," reinforces the idea of artifice; it is not a natural gait, but one contrived. A hetaera's walk might even leave physical traces as she moved around the city: a ceramic sandal that presumably imitates one worn by a hetaera has inscribed on its sole the word *akolouthi* (follow me), thereby making legible her body as she walked.[37] So constructed, the hetaera's body can even become a site of reading: Asclepiades describes a girdle worn by the courtesan Hermione as embroidered with the words, "Love me, but do not be pained if another man has me" (*Anth. Pal.* 5. 158).

In addition to an affected walk, hetaeras were skilled dancers and artful seducers: "O artful movement," exclaims one epigrammatist of an Italian dancer (*ō katatechnotatou kinēmatos*, Philodemus, *Anth. Pal.* 5. 132). The word *kinēma* compares the dancer's movements to physical congress, just as the flute player's musical activities are conflated with fellatio.[38] Indeed, the term for a dance step or figure, *schēma*, also applies to sexual positions, a specialty of courtesans highlighted in Machon's *Chreiae* and other comic sources. Such performers entertained at the male symposium: figures of dancing courtesans, some even being instructed by a procuress, appear on several Attic red figure vases. The character of Euripides at the end of *Thesmophoriazusae* explains that the dancing girl he has brought onstage to entice the Scythian must rehearse her steps for the symposium (Ar. *Thesm.* 1177–8). Even the performance of the auletris involved gestural movement, as she is described as using her body as she plays, an activity designated by the verb *morphazein*, to emphasize her meaning.[39]

As foreigners and exotics, courtesans performed Ionic dances, "notorious for their softness and lasciviousness,"[40] and various figures involving the gyration of the pelvis. Only comic dances, such as the kordax, used the lower body.[41] Dancers of the kordax leaped, kicked, slapped their own bodies, they whirled and turned dizzily, but its essential characteristic was always rotation of the hips and abdomen.[42] Black figure vases from the archaic period feature obscene padded dancers who display their buttocks and genitals, a convention that influenced representations of heterosexual copulation of *kōmoi*, the revels that followed the symposium (Sutton 1992: 9). Other dances associated with courtesans included the *maktēr* or *maktrismos*, from the word for "kneading-trough" and the similar *igdē* or *igdis*, deriving from a word for the pestle in a mortar. A passage in Athenaeus attributes the nickname Theatrotoryne to the courtesan Melissa, a hapax legomenon that appears to be a combination of *theatron* "theater," and *torunē*, "ladle" or "stirring implement" (4. 157a). The name may suggest the actual dances of courtesans in the theater as well as emphasize their status as public performers (Lawler 1978: 135).

Such dancing appears to have been associated with drunkenness and a lower order of prostitute. A mother in Lucian's *Dialogues of the Courtesans* scolds her daughter for her drunken dancing at a symposium:

> Diphilus said you were drunk and got up and danced in the middle of the company (*es to meson anastasan orchēsasthai*), although he attempted to stop you, and then you kissed his friend. (Lucian *Dial. meret.* 3. 1)

Wine also induces her friend, Thais, to dance with her gown pulled up high enough to reveal her ankles (*anastasa ōrchēsato prōtē apogumnousa epi polu ta sphura*, Lucian *Dial. meret.* 3. 2). Meleager similarly describes a drunken courtesan dragging herself home after a night of hard partying, her limbs unsteady with wine (*guia saleuta*, *Anth. Pal.* 5. 175. 6). But here the wayward motions of the hetaera do not arouse passion, as in many of the other epigrams in the *Palatine Anthology*, but disgust, prompting the narrator to condemn her as a common whore (*gunai pangkoine*).

Another public display of the body associated with hetaeras, *kallipygia*, was a commonplace of female seduction as early as Hesiod's *Works and Days* where the narrator cautions, "Don't let a woman who wags her ass at you deceive your mind" (*pugostolos . . . haimula kōtillousa*, Hes. *Op.* 373–375). Similarly, a Lydian girl in a comic play shakes her hips like a water thrush, a type of bird that twitches its tail feathers rapidly (Autocrates, *Tympanistae*, 1. 7–10 KA).[43] The fragment of Alexis' *Isostasion* discussed earlier in this chapter shows how a hetaera with no hips might become *eupygia*. The gesture of *anasyrma*, the raising of the garments to reveal the buttocks, is an erotic *schēma* that figures in impromptu competitions of *kallipygia* at the symposium (Säflund 1963: 45). Among the Second Sophistic writers, it is coupled with dances that call attention to the lower body, namely the gyrations of the *idgis*. Alciphron graphically describes how the hetaera Plangon aroused the lust of the god Pan by wildly gyrating her hips in an erotic dance at an al fresco symposium (*katōrchēsato . . . tēn osphun anekinēsen*, Alciphr. 4. 13. 12). In another letter, a courtesan named Myrrhine unfastens her girdle and begins to shake her hips rapidly with a movement that recalls the hetaera's specialized walk (*tēn osphun anesaleusen*, Alciphr. 4. 14. 4). But here the narrator focalizes the reader on her ass by representing the hetaera as gazing back at this part of her anatomy as she dances, a typical gesture in visual representations of *anasyrma* (*ta kinēmata tēs pugēs*, Alciphr. 4. 14. 4). A competition ensues with another hetaera, Thryallis, who strips as if in a wrestling match (*en gumnikōi*, Alciphr. 4. 14. 5), and wins with the vigorous shaking of her buttocks (*palmon . . . tēs pugēs*, 4. 14. 6).

In Book 12 of the *Deipnosophistae*, Athenaeus adduces a contest of *kallipygia* between two peasant girls as an etiology for the origins of a temple of Aphrodite *Kallipygos* at Syracuse, "so dependent on their sensual pleasures were the men of those days that they actually dedicated a temple to 'Aphrodite of the Beautiful Buttocks.' "[44] The two girls fell to arguing one day about who was the most beautiful and went to the nearby road to settle the dispute. A wealthy passerby fell so violently in love with the elder daughter that he took to bed upon arriving home. His brother, hearing the story, went to see the girls for himself, and chose the younger one, resulting in marriages between the two sibling pairs. Known as "the girls with the beautiful buttocks," they dedicated a temple of Aphrodite *Kallipygos* with their new-found wealth (Ath. 12. 554c). Indeed, one of the anathematic epigrams speaks playfully of a hetaera making a dedication of her *pugē* to Aphrodite, as a specialty of the house (Lucian, *Anth. Pal.* 6. 17).

The display and movement of the female body also have a place in ancient reproductive ideology. A curious account of a pregnant entertainer, probably a singer, but most certainly a prostitute, mentioned both in the Hippocratic corpus and in Soranus, describes a kind of dance maneuver employed as an abortifacient and reminiscent of the comic kordax:

> A kinswoman of mine owned a very valuable singer (*mousourgos*), who used to go with men. It was important that this girl not become pregnant and thereby lose her value. Now this girl had heard the sort of thing women say to each other—that when a woman is going to conceive, the seed remains inside of her and does not fall out. She digested this information and kept a watch. One day she noticed that the seed had not come out again. She told her mistress, and the story came to me. When I heard it, I told her to jump up and down, touching her buttocks with her heels at each leap (*pros pugēn pēdēsai*). After she had done this no more than seven times, there was a noise, the seed fell out on the ground, and the girl looked at it in great surprise." (Hippoc. *Nat. Puer* 13. 1–2, trans. Lonie)[45]

As Lonie remarks, this gymnastic feat resembles a Spartan dance—in which a naked performer kicks her heels to her rump—mentioned by Aristophanes (*gumnaddomai ge kai poti pugan hallomai*, Ar. *Lys.* 82; Lonie 1981: 165) while at the same time recalling the lascivious *schēmata* of prostitute dancers. The term *pugē* has strong erotic connotations, as we have seen; in this passage, however, the motions that seduce ultimately thwart the process of female reproduction. The violent, suggestive motions of hetaeras and other types of prostitutes, as well as their restless movements through the spaces of the city normally occupied only by men, mark them out as bodies for pleasure, not reproduction. Indeed, the unwanted byproducts of prostitution supplied the Hippocratics with fetuses for their studies.[46] In contrast, the inactivity and spatial seclusion of the bodies of wives defines them as repositories for the children of citizen men. In Plutarch, the bodies of courtesans are represented as disrupting even the stillness of men and their quiet repose at the side of their wives (*hēsuchia*, Plut. *Mor.* 125a).

The Hetaera and *Epideixis*

The pervasive associations of the hetaera with public display, theatrical illusion, and aesthetic ornament made her the ideal metaphor for epideictic oratory in classical Athens, as well as in the later rhetorical tradition. The close connection between rhetoric and the body of the hetaera is seen in the Greek word *schēma*, a term that refers to sexual positions associated with prostitutes, their movements in the dance, and to rhetorical figures; taken together, it signifies appearance as opposed to reality.[47] Plato's *Menexenus* directly links epideictic oratory with the courtesan's seductive arts. In the dialogue, itself a puzzling parody of Pericles' funeral oration, Socrates attributes his great speech to Aspasia, the politician's famous concubine (Pl. *Men.* 236a–b). Unlike Socratic dialectic, the epideictic speech involves memorization; it must be rehearsed before delivery and often makes use of pastiche (*sugkollōsa*, 236b). Indeed, Socrates states that he has committed to memory the speech Aspasia herself has memorized and imparted to him (*mnēmoneusais*, 236b). Like the hetaera's painted face, her feigned manners, and her concern for appearance, the epitaphios is a copy of a copy, one that seeks to entertain rather than to reveal the truth, the noble end of Socratic enquiry. It is mere play (*paizein*, 236c), not simply a child's frolic, but "playing around" in the sexual sense. To recite such a speech effectively turns the philosopher into a whore, or so Socrates says, when he threatens to perform a kind of erotic dance as a "favor" to his listener:

> Yes, then, I must surely gratify you (*soi ge dei charizesthai*); for indeed I would almost gratify you if you were to bid me strip and dance (*apodunta orchēsasthai*), now that we two are alone. (Pl. *Men.* 236d)

As we saw above, hetaeras and other types of prostitutes engaged in erotic dancing at the symposium. The image of Socrates doing an intimate striptease for his youthful interlocutor surely provokes the laughter intended to ridicule rather than to arouse (*katagelasei*, 236c). The allusion to *charis* here and elsewhere analogizes the relationship between the philosopher and his pupil as one of prostitutional gift exchange. Even Socrates' final enjoinder to "follow me" (*akolouthei met' emou*, 249d) recalls the advertisement inscribed on the sole of the hetaera's sandal and completes the comic portrait of the philosopher as hetaera. In deploying these metaphors of prostitution, however, Socrates has a more serious aim: that of discrediting Aspasia and all that she stands for, particularly the sophistic movement and its influence on rhetoric and epideictic display (Bloedow 1975: 48). As in Gorgias' encomium for Helen, physical beauty and its seductions become a metaphor for the enchanting, and dangerous, allure of persuasive words.

Another Socratic dialogue with a courtesan, and one mentioned by Athenaeus in Book 13 of the *Deipnosophistae* (588d), similarly situates problems of persuasion, epideixis, and viewing within the context of prostitution. After brief dialogues with a painter, a sculptor, and an arms maker, Socrates turns to the artist's model in his quest for understanding the usefulness of philosophy.[48]

> At one time there was in Athens a beautiful woman by the name of Theodote who kept company with anyone who persuaded her (*suneinai tōi peithonti*). One of those present mentioned her, stating that the beauty of the woman exceeded description and adding that artists visited her to paint her portrait, and she showed them as much as decency as allowed. (*epideiknuein heautēs hosa kalōs echoi*, Xen. *Mem.* 3. 11. 1)

The public notoriety of the hetaera, as evidenced by the presence of her name and the visibility of her body, is countered by her attempts at modesty; as discussed above, hetaeras of the highest level manipulated what their clientele, indeed their public, could see. So, too, the Cnidian Aphrodite with her covering hand gesture performs a kind of modesty while fully exposed to the male gaze (Havelock 1995: 30–1), the visual analogue of this literary tableau, as we will see in the next section. The verb *epideiknuein* connects her activity as a portrait model, available for others to copy, to the kind of rhetorical display critiqued by Socrates in the *Menexenus*.

> Ought we to be more grateful to Theodote for showing us her beauty (*to kallos heautēs epedeixen*), or she to us for looking at it (*etheasametha*)? Does the obligation rest with her, if she profits more by showing it (*epideixis*), or with us, if we profit more by the sight (*thea*)? (Xen. *Mem.* 3. 11. 2)

The word *charis* establishes the relationship between spectacle and viewer as one of exchange, only here it evokes the erotic transactions involved in patronizing hetaeras. Socrates then analogizes the sight of the courtesan's body both to artistic and theatrical viewing (*etheasametha, thea*) as well as to the epideictic display of oratory (*epideiknunein, epideixis*). As the embodiment of epideictic display rather than dialectic, Theodote operates outside of verbal discourse: the very sight of her leaves the male viewers speechless (*hoti kreitton eiē logou to kallos tēs gunaikos*, Xen. *Mem.* 3. 11. 1). In the Socratic view, epideictic genres, whether artistic or rhetorical, do not seek to uncover the truth but to dazzle the spectator with beauty and performative finesse, creating a world of illusion, just as the hetaera woos her clients with her deliberate artifice.

The Courtesan as Model: Phryne and her Statues

Socrates' visit to the salon of Theodote no doubt influenced subsequent literary narratives that depicted courtesans as the models for artistic representations of Aphrodite. These accounts linked the beauty of the hetaera to aesthetic illusion and rhetorical display. By the third century, the fusion of the categories of divine and mortal had become an emergent trend in both art and politics, exemplified by the quasi-deification of the Hellenistic monarchs as well as by the identification of hetaeras with oversize images of Aphrodite (Havelock 1995: 126–7). The popularity of Aphrodite in art coincided not only with the popularity of public spectacle in the Hellenistic world, but also with the development of the female nude in monumental sculpture in the second half of the fourth century B.C.E. In the earlier period, female figures rarely appear nude outside of vase painting, a private medium.[49] About the same time, courtesans became a popular subject of drama and historical and periegetic narratives, prominent sources for Athenaeus, as we have seen. Central to this discourse about the spectacle of the body is the biographical tradition surrounding the fourth-century courtesan, Phryne, that chronicles her public nudity in several venues: at religious festivals, in the law court, and as a famous statue.

Stories of hetaeras as models and mistresses of famous artists probably developed out of a desire to explain the peculiarities of prominent monuments and inscriptions encountered in everyday life. As with actors, the association between artists and courtesans also reflects their similar economic status as part of the class of itinerant, skilled professionals that earned a wage (*misthos*) for their specialized work.[50] When the painter Zeuxis charges money to see his Helen, she can rightly be described as a courtesan (Aelian, *VH* 4. 12; Anderson, G. 1993: 153). Of the four erotic painters mentioned as pornographers by Cynulcus, Pausias, credited with the invention of encaustic painting, is said to have painted a picture of his mistress, Glycera—her name, as well as her profession as a wreath seller potentially identify her as a hetaera (Plin. *HN* 35. 125)—while the Theban painter Aristides the Younger is credited with a famous portrait of Leontion, the courtesan associated with Epicurus (Plin. *HN* 35. 100).

Phryne is one of the most frequently mentioned Athenian courtesans not only in Book 13 of the *Deipnosophistae*, but in the Greek literary tradition more generally (see Appendix III).[51] Her trial, as well as her liaison with Praxiteles, contributed to this notoriety, which is said to have extended from Athens to all of Greece (Alciphr. 4. 4. 1; cf. 590f). Citing prosopographies by Apollodorus and Herodicus, Athenaeus differentiates two women named Phryne (Toad), itself a nickname that apparently referred to the paleness of the courtesan's complexion (*ōchrotēta*, Plut. *Mor.* 401b); one bore the name Clausigelos (Teary Laughter) and the other Saperdion (Little Fish). From Herodicus, we learn further that the orators called one Sestus (Fleecer) and the other the Thespian (591c). However, as Raubitschek argues, it is probable that one woman was incorrectly differentiated into two by these Hellenistic prosopographers. In any case, the chronology supports the view that the Phryne made famous for revealing her naked body in the Attic law courts was the same woman as Praxiteles' mistress and model.[52]

This Phryne was probably born around 371 B.C.E., in Boeotian Thespiae, and was the daughter of Epicles. Her birth name was Mnesarete (591e), but she also went by the names of Phryne and Saperdion. Aphrodite may have been the patron goddess of Thespiae; indeed, she is the only female deity well attested there, while an inscription on a bronze hydria from the fifth century is addressed to Aphrodite *Thespiae*.[53] The prominence of Aphrodite in Thespiae explains the continual conflation of Phryne with the goddess in her two major narratives, or may even represent a later attempt to read this motif back into her history. Phryne escaped her early poverty—the comic poets represent her as picking capers for her keep—to become one of the wealthiest women in the Hellenic world (*eploutei de sphodra*, 591d). She is best known for her impiety trial, in which the orator Hyperides, possibly also one of her lovers, defended her soon after 350 B.C.E. She is said to have served as the model for Praxiteles' Cnidian Aphrodite as well as for Apelles' painting, Aphrodite *Anadyomenē* (Rising from the Sea), during the 340s, and apparently outlived the rebuilding of Thebes after 316.[54]

Phryne's legendary beauty explains her pervasive association with art objects, rhetorical *epideixis*, and stories of voyeurism and display; indeed, it forms the heart of Athenaeus' brief biographical excursus about her (590d–592f).[55] A central trope contrasts her genuine beauty with the spurious attractions of other courtesans: so Athenaeus states that Phryne was in reality more beautiful in her hidden parts (*ēn de ontōs mallon hē Phrunē kalē en tois mē blepomenois*, 590f), the very areas cosmetically enhanced by the artful courtesans of Alexis' *Isostasion* quoted above (F103 KA = 568a–d). A passage from Galen, a contemporary of Athenaeus, similarly distinguishes between the natural attractiveness of Phryne and the cosmeticized beauty of other courtesans. In a sympotic game in which participants took turns ordering each other to perform outlandish feats, Phryne required the women at the table, presumably all hetaeras, to wash the makeup—alkanet, white lead, and red paint—off their faces. Full of blemishes, they all looked like monsters (*mormolukeioi*), while Phryne herself appeared even more beautiful (Gal. *Adhortatio ad artes addiscendas* 10. 43–52).

To judge by Myrtilus' account, Phryne was also considered skillful at witticisms: Machon attributes a *chreia* to her, in which she responds to a client's complaint about her high price by stating that she will accept a lower amount when she, not he, wants to make love (*binētiasō*, 583c). Lynceus in turn makes her the author of a scatalogical joke on the stone that Machon elsewhere associates with Mania (584c–d; cf. 578e). She figures prominently in Aristodemus' *Geloia Hypomnemoneumata*, which identifies several other jokes with Phryne concerning various subjects, such as a man who smelled like a goat, the stinting amount of wine sent by an admirer, sympotic wreaths, and the mockery and flattery of her lovers (585e–f). Sources outside Athenaeus also allude to her witticisms: a very late text attributes to her the following quip: "The hetaera Phryne said of a young man who had lost his field and was pale on account of sickness, 'Boy, why are you pale? You've not eaten your land?' " (*Gnom.* 577. 1). A popular story about her unsuccessful attempt to seduce the celibate philosopher Xenocrates gives the hetaera the last laugh as well as underscores her strong identification with statuary. Although the philosopher had offered to share his only couch with her when she sought refuge inside his house, he refused to have intercourse with her. Upon her departure, she joked that she had left not a man (*andros*) but a statue (*andria*, Diog. Laer. 4. 7. 2).[56]

The joke on the man and the statue possibly has its origins in her notorious portrait statue at Delphi (591b), which will be more fully examined in the next chapter, as well as the tradition that she served as a model for Praxiteles' Cnidian Aphrodite. The connection between Phryne and art objects probably influenced later accounts of her notorious trial in which her naked breasts were displayed, statue-like, to the jurors. Other stories similarly emphasize the public spectacle of her body, although the sources are characteristically equivocal about the extent of her nudity. At the Eleusinia and a festival of Poseidon, Phryne is said to have set aside her cloak (*apothemenē thoimation*) in sight of all the Greeks, and after letting down her hair (*lusasa tas komas*), to have stepped into the sea (590f). At Eleusis, her immersion in the sea may have signified rites of purification and initiation to promote fertility, while the Poseidonia at Aegina had close associations with Aphrodite and courtesans.[57] The gesture, according to Athenaeus, inspired Apelles' *Anadyomenē*, although Pliny makes Pancaspe, an erstwhile mistress of Alexander, the model for this painting (Plin. *HN* 35. 36. 86–86).[58] But the story coyly does not allow the reader to view the courtesan's nakedness, following, as it does, upon the narrator's statement that one could not easily see Phryne naked as she always wore a little *chitōn* fitted close to the flesh (*echesarkon*) and did not frequent the public baths. These stories probably did not precede or influence the art works to which they are linked, as the authors suggest; rather, the art itself, publicly displayed and viewed by thousands of citizens and tourists alike, probably engendered numerous stories about its creation (Keesling 2002).

Let us turn now to the most famous accounts of Phryne's public nudity, her transformation into a statue in the popular tradition surrounding Praxiteles' Cnidian Aphrodite, and the related story of her public disrobing when tried for impiety at Athens. To understand the story of Praxiteles and Phryne, it is necessary to consider, however briefly, the role of female nudity in ancient Greek art, particularly in connection with Aphrodite. Influenced by Near Eastern artistic conventions, female nudity made a brief appearance in archaic Greek art, especially in the representation of fertility figures; but in most cases it occurred only in scenes of pathetic or erotic appeal, or served an apotropaic function.[59] The Greek tradition of depicting the nude Aphrodite probably conformed to Near Eastern visual conventions surrounding the fertility goddess Inanna/Ishtar.[60] Because nakedness in the earliest times could also signify vulnerability and subservience, worshipers and attendants of the gods could also be represented without clothes. The male *kouros* figure, a monumental work of sculpture that functioned as a grave marker or votive offering in archaic Greece, also represents an example of sacred nudity (Bonfante 1989: 551). From the standpoint of cult, the naked body of the courtesan incarnated the erotic power of Aphrodite, while gazing on the naked female body in Greek myth, as if on the goddess herself, typically aroused feelings of fear and vulnerability in the male spectator. Even as late as Alciphron, the nude statue of Aphrodite cautions her creator, the sculptor Praxiteles, not to be afraid.[61] The stories of surprised bathing in Greek myth further reinforce the notion of danger attendant upon male voyeurism (Osborne 1994: 83).

In monumental sculpture, the naked male *kouros* figure appears as a "public actor" without reference to the viewer; the female *korē*, on the other hand, always enacts a role in a "drama scripted by men," reminding the spectators of her status as symbolic capital.[62] Archaic conventions thus naturalized male nakedness while encouraging viewers to understand the clothed female as constructed.[63] In Andrew Stewart's words, "clothing is the index of the socialized, acculturated woman, the woman brought back under control"; in contrast, male nakedness reinforces the notion of his bounded subjectivity, his ability to act freely in the real world (Stewart, A. 1997: 41). In contrast, courtesans and other types of prostitutes are commonly depicted as cavorting naked with men on sympotic vases.[64] Although they appear as performers in a male space, these women, a large number of whom are flute players, do not resemble the idealized male subjects of monumental Greek sculpture, but rather serve as pornographic objects of male pleasure. The puzzling depictions of hetaeras engaged in wool working and situated in restrained domestic surroundings apart from men perhaps represent an attempt to imbue these figures with the refinement and decorum of well-born wives, reflecting the tendency toward euphemism found in the literary tradition. However, the theory that these brothels functioned simultaneously as textile factories should not be discounted; this arrangement probably underlies the witticism of Strabo's hetaera that serves as the epigraph in Chapter 3.[65]

The tradition of the monumental female nude commences with Praxiteles' creation of a cult statue of Aphrodite in the middle of the fourth century B.C.E that established a canon for the female body in Western art.[66] Fictive accounts of the romance of Phryne and Praxiteles appear to have proliferated around 100 B.C.E., particularly among the epigrammatists (Havelock 1995: 2). Athenaeus follows the tradition in making Phryne the model for this work (591a), although Clement of Alexandria names Cratina, another of Praxiteles' alleged mistresses.[67] The conflation of divine and mortal categories found in stories about this work may reflect the fact that the city of Thespiae housed two statues by Praxitiles, one of Phryne and the other of Aphrodite.[68] Elsewhere we learn that she posed for a statue of the Smiling Courtesan (*meretricis gaudentis*) by Praxiteles, in which the viewer could detect "the love of the artist and the reward (*mercedem*) revealed in the face of the courtesan" (Plin. *HN* 34. 70; Havelock 1995: 46). This passage from Pliny clearly alludes to the epigram purportedly inscribed on the base of Praxiteles' statue of Eros that stood near the theater of Dionysus at Athens and quoted by Athenaeus in Book 13:[69]

> Praxiteles made his Eros show that which he suffered,
> drawing his model from his own heart,
> dedicating me to Phryne as the price (*misthon*) of me.
> The love spell I cast comes no longer from my arrow,
> but from gazing upon me.
>
> (*Anth. Pal.* 16. 204 = 591a)

The emphasis on the price or reward in this epigram equates the professions of artist and courtesan by emphasizing their commercial aspect. Several other stories revolve around this statue and its dedication to Phryne: in Book 13, Athenaeus remarks that when the sculptor offered Phryne one of his statues, she chose the Eros and dedicated it to the Thespians (591b). In another version, the hetaera demanded to know from the sculptor his favorite statue; when he refused to name it, she tricked him into confessing his preference for his Satyr and Eros by pretending his studio had caught fire. Phryne confessed the ruse, choosing the latter (Paus. 1. 20. 1). Both versions of these stories, and subsequent allusions among the epigrammatists, were probably fanciful conjectures about the origins of the inscription on the base of the statue itself. From a broader perspective, the sculptor's love for the model, with its similarities to the Pygmalion story, appealed to the romantic sensibilities of a late Hellenistic audience and was frequently elaborated, especially by the epigrammatists.

The Cnidian Aphrodite, shown as a bather, evolved from bathing scenes on Attic vases that first appeared on the tondos of wine cups and then on the exterior, a move that reflects a shift from pornographic titillation to a more generalized or euphemistic expression of female sexuality.[70] The act of bathing itself provides a pretext for her nudity, while the cast off clothing placed alongside renders it more respectable (Havelock 1995: 23–24). According to tradition, the Cnidian Aphrodite was one of the most viewed statues in all antiquity. Pliny records that Praxiteles originally created two statues of the goddess, one modestly draped and the other naked. Rejected by the people of Cos, who chose the clothed version, the naked Aphrodite went to Cnidos where it was displayed in the round to an admiring public:

> The shrine in which it stands is entirely open so as to allow the image of the goddess to be viewed from every side, and it is believed to have been made this way with the blessing of the goddess herself. The statue is equally admirable from every angle. (Plin. *HN* 36. 4. 20–21; trans. Eichholz)

Its pornographic effect on the male viewer was the subject of numerous anecdotes, including a series of epigrams in the *Palatine Anthology* (*Anth. Pal.* 16. 159–63 and 165–70).[71] One, attributed to the philosopher Plato, imagines the reaction of the goddess to her image:

> Paphian Cytherea came through the waves to Cnidos, wishing to see her own image, and having viewed it from all sides in its open shrine, she cried, "Where did Praxiteles see me naked?" (Plato, *Anth. Pal.* 16. 160; trans. Paton)

The first letter of Alciphron's *Letters of Courtesans* similarly inverts the tradition of male gazing at erotic artwork.[72] In this letter, the model assumes the role of the goddess in addressing her creator. Her opening command, "have no fear," evokes the dangers of viewing female nudity but then answers the questions posed by the authors of the *Palatine Anthology* by allowing the spectators to imagine the naked body of the courtesan behind the sculpted goddess:

> For you have wrought a very beautiful work of art, such as nobody in fact has ever seen before among all things fashioned by men's hands: you have set up a

statue of your own mistress in the sacred precinct. (Alciphr. 4. 1. 2–5; trans. Benner and Fobes)

By attesting to the artist's skill at verisimilitude, these scenes draw attention both to the statue and the hetaera as constructed bodies, figures of artifice and performers in a drama cast and created by men. In these Cnidian vignettes, the voice of the goddess and the hetaera disrupt the process of artistic illusion by reminding the spectators that what they behold is not real.[73]

The story of Phryne as the model for Praxiteles' Cnidian Aphrodite not only becomes a popular motif in the literary tradition, it also serves as a stock theme in later rhetorical works. A very late writer, Choricius, a Greek sophist and rhetorician living in Egypt in the late fifth century C.E., moralizes about the statue's fusion of mortal and divine. He states that Praxiteles created the statue of Aphrodite at Delphi in imitation of Phryne (*pros mimēsin*) the hetaera, since she was his lover, to relieve the Spartans of a plague sent by the goddess (Choricius, *Opera* 29). In his account, the statue remains that of his lover, only he gives it the name of Aphrodite "as one would ornament a mistress with an epigram" (29). But then he questions, "shall we pray and shall we sacrifice to Phryne, and shall we sing songs to her?" Christian writers such as Gregory of Nazareth similarly pondered the problem of honoring hetaeras with temples and statues (*Carmina Moralia* 743. 3), while Clement of Alexandria derides sculptors for idolatry and the worship of hetaeras (Clem. Al. *Protr.* 47).

The Rhetoric of the Body: Phryne's Trial

Phryne was once the most illustrious of us courtesans by far.
And even though you, girl, are too young
to remember that time, you must at least have heard of her trial.

Posidippus, Ephesia F13 KA

The most famous account of the spectacular display of Phryne's body comes not from the annals of art history, but from Attic oratory. By the late second century C.E., Phryne and her notorious trial had become a staple of rhetorical works. Although there is no contemporary account of the trial, which occurred shortly after 350, two Second Sophistic texts offer the fullest descriptions of the disrobing, Athenaeus' *Deipnosophistae* (13. 590d–591e), and Plutarch's *Vitae Decem Oratorum* (849d–e; Cooper 1995: 307 n. 10). Both versions derive from the same third century biographer, Hermippus (c. 200 B.C.E.), who in turn relies on Idomeneus of Lampsacus' lost polemic against the Athenian demagogues (c. 270 B.C.E.).[74] According to Athenaeus, Euthias accused Phryne of impiety, a charge that carried the death penalty (590d), and hired the fourth-century rhetorician, Anaximenes of Lampsacus, to write the speech (Hermippus F67 Wehrli). Hyperides, in contrast, alleges at the beginning of his lost speech that he defended Phryne because of his love for her (*homologōn eran tēs gunaikos*, F171 Jensen = 590d). In both accounts, Hyperides' affair with Phryne forms a major part of a discourse about the orator's licentious lifestyle, supported by his numerous liaisons with other named courtesans; his habit of frequenting the fish market is adduced by Plutarch as further evidence of his tendency toward excess (Plut. *Mor.* 849d).

As in most cases, charges of impiety—the central focus of scholarship on the speech—were frequently politically motivated, and, as in most references to hetaeras in oratory, usually attempted to defame an opponent.[75] An anonymous rhetorical work that preserves the end of Euthias' speech defines the charges as reveling shamelessly (*kōmasasan*), introducing a new god, and bringing together unlawful companies (*thiasous*) of men and women (1. 390 Spengel). All three charges are related in that they allege that Phryne engaged in illicit activities under the pretext of religion (Cooper 1995: 306 n. 9). The fact that Euthias, and another writer credited with composing a speech against Phryne, Aristogeiton (F176 Jensen = 591e), were known political enemies of Hyperides supports the view that the allegations were specious. The later biographical tradition, however, turns the trial into a lovers' quarrel over a hetaera: "on the one hand, Euthias is presented by biographers as the scorned and rejected lover, who gets his revenge by defending her in court. On the other hand, Hyperides is presented as a philanderer" (Cooper 1995: 305). Certainly, this view informs some of Alciphron's letters: the hetaera Bacchis, for instance, portrays Euthias as a jilted lover who seeks revenge by prosecuting his mistress, while Hyperides appears as her new lover and champion (Alciphr. 4. 3; cf. 4. 4).

Myrtilus uses this famous trial to frame his biography of the courtesan, beginning with Hermippus' account of her disrobing and ending with the earliest known version of it, a fragment of Posidippus' *Ephesia* (c. 300 B.C.E.). While the latter does not mention the disrobing, it does depict a scene of supplication:

> Phryne was once the most illustrious of us courtesans by far.
> And even though you (female) are too young
> to remember that time, you must at least have heard of her trial.
> Although seeming to have wrought too great injury to men's lives,
> she nevertheless conquered the court with regard to her life,
> and clasping the hands of the jurors one by one
> with tears she saved her life at last.
>
> (Posidippus, *Ephesia* F13 KA = 591e–f)

Posidippus appears to have borrowed from the tragic stage this conventional act of supplication, in which a socially subordinate figure, normally a woman, petitions a powerful male by weeping and clasping part of his body.[76] And yet his omission of the disrobing incident leads to the conclusion that it was a later invention, possibly current during the time of Idomeneus (Cooper 1995: 314). The new version of the trial seems to incorporate the art historical tradition by fashioning the courtesan into an image of Aphrodite:

> When his speech was accomplishing nothing and it became apparent that the judges were about to condemn her, Hyperides led her into the sight of all (*paragagōn autēn eis toumphanes*) and, ripping off her garments (*perirrhēxas tous chitōniskous*), made bare her chest (*gumna te ta sterna poiēsas*). He delivered an epilogue made piteous at the sight of her and caused the jurors to fear as a deity (*deisidaimonēsai*) this prophetess (*hupophētin*) and servant of Aphrodite (*zakoron Aphroditēs*), and indulging in pity, they did not put her to death. (Hermippus F68 = 590d–e)

The remarkable homogeneity of language among Second Sophistic accounts of Phryne's disrobing indicates a single source, whether the original of Hyperides or a later biographical account (Cooper 1995: 313). So we find in Plutarch's version:

> When [the orator] saw that she was about to be condemned, he led her into the middle of the room (*paragagōn eis meson*) and ripping off her clothing (*perirrhēxas tēn esthēta*), displayed the chest of the woman (*epideixe ta sterna tēs gunaikos*). And when the jurors saw her beauty (*kallos*), they acquitted her. (Plut. *Mor.* 849e)

Both versions emphasize her public visibility, the orator's act of tearing off her clothing, and the nakedness of her breasts. Phryne's public nudity simultaneously signifies an act of supplication while evoking her status as an art object. The verb, *perirrhēxas*, which occurs in almost all of the later accounts of the disrobing, suggests debasement and supplication rather than erotic titillation. Dio Chrysostom uses it to describe supplicating women with their torn garments (*perirrhēgmenas*, Dio Chrys. *Or.* 46. 12; cf. 35. 9). It is possible, however, that Hermippus borrowed some of his language from a famous Euripidean scene, the disrobing of the Trojan princess Polyxena before her sacrificial death:

> Taking her garments from the upper part of her shoulder,
> she ripped them (*errhēxe*) down to the middle of her belly,
> and revealed her breasts, as lovely as a statue
> (*mastous t' edeixe sterna hōs agalmatos/kallista*).
>
> (E. *Hec.* 558–60)

In both instances, the nakedness of the women likens them to statues. The baring of the breasts, a gesture that accompanied female supplication as early as Homer (Hom. *Il.* 22. 79–81), can also have an erotic dimension, as in the case of Helen's seduction of Menelaus after the fall of Troy (E. *Andr.* 629). In Hermippus' version of the Phryne story, however, the disrobing not only inspires pity, it instills fear, converting the nude hetaera into an embodiment of Aphrodite. The unusual words *hupophētis* and *zakoros* effectively blur the boundary between divine and mortal, turning the hetaera into a medium for the divinity. Viewed in the context of the Cnidian Aphrodite, Semenov's conjecture that the jurors believed they were seeing Aphrodite herself does not seem so far fetched (Semenov 1935: 278–79).

The remarkable afterlife of this story is largely due to its popularity among the late rhetorical writers and commentators, for whom it served as the supreme example of the pity *schēma*, in addition to being a fine example of oratory (Longin. *De subl.* 34. 203; Cooper 1995: 305 n. 8). For Quintilian, it demonstrates the problem of defining rhetoric as a power of speech, because many other things, such as money, influence, authority, and the rank of the speaker, or even sight (*aspectus*), may persuade the listener (Quintil. 2. 15. 6). Antonius, for example, tore open his client's robe and revealed his battle scars while Servius Galba won acquittal by bringing his own young children into the courtroom (2. 15. 8). So, too, he argues, Phryne was saved not only by the *actio* of Hyperides, but also by the sight of her body (*conspectu corporis*), which she exposed most spectacularly by pulling aside her tunic (*speciosissimum*, 2. 15. 9). In this account, as in other later accounts, however, the hetaera herself, not the orator, tears off her garments, as if to emphasize its status as a feminine ruse (cf. Phld. 1. 20. 4).

Similarly Sextus Empiricus, whose works probably date to the end of the second century C.E., states that Plato defined rhetoric as a means of persuasion by words (Pl. *Grg.* 453a) because many other things persuade, notably the sight of Helen before the Trojan Elders (Hom. *Il.* 3. 156–57) and Phryne in Hyperides' pleading. When on the point of being condemned, she tore apart her garments (*katarrēxamenē tous chitōniskous*) and with her bared breasts prostrated herself before the jurors, "because her beauty had more power to persuade her judges than the rhetoric of her advocate" (Sext. Emp. *Math.* 2. 4. 1). A popular Roman rhetorical exercise appears to have been the translation of Hyperides' defense speech from Greek into Latin (Quintil. 10. 5. 2).

In disrobing the body of Phryne, the orator turns the hetaera into a rhetorical *schēma* infused with the language of supplication and religious cult: through her mute body, the male orator speaks and the jury is persuaded. As a kind of *epideixis* made flesh, the story of Phryne's public nudity demonstrates the strong association between the courtesan and rhetors and sophists in classical antiquity. Indeed, the reliance of these professions on coinage explains their absence in archaic Sparta: "no speechifying sophist set foot in Sparta, no begging prophet, no purveyor of hetaeras" (Plut. *Lyc.* 9. 5). The widespread circulation of the story of Phryne's disrobing among rhetorical writers of the late Roman Empire shows the strong presence of courtesans in the rhetorical tradition and may explain, at least in part, their attraction for writers such as Athenaeus. As a rhetorical figure and the subject of a school exercise, Phryne is made to disseminate Attic culture across genres and periods, much like the witty Gnathaena in Chapter 3.

Conclusion

This chapter has shown how the Greek literary tradition, from Attic Old comedy to the Second Sophistic period, constructs the body of the courtesan around ideas of performance and display. Through the speeches of Cynulcus and Myrtilus, Book 13 of the *Deipnosophistae* distinguishes the truthful body of the brothel whore, readily available and without guile, from the elusive body of the courtesan, constructed by artifice and difficult to see. As figures of comedy, whether performed by male actors or actual prostitutes, their bodies serve as a metaphor for theatrical spectacle, while their use of clothing and cosmetics affiliates them with theatrical illusion. The bodies of courtesans are thus never natural, but always constructed: their manners, their movements, and even their public nudity are viewed as the deliberate product of artifice, all calculated to seduce the viewer. For this reason, the literary tradition affiliates them with rhetorical *epideixis* and aesthetic verisimilitude, representational modes that seek to persuade the spectator that what they see is real rather than illusory. The increased importance of orchestrating self-representation through clothing, gesture, and manner in classical Athens, as well as in the Second Sophistic period, invites a comparison between courtesans and the sophists of Athenaeus' table. Just as hetaeras embody notions of epideictic display and aesthetic artifice, so, too, the symposiasts of the *Deipnosophistae* do not engage in authentic dialogue, but rather put on display a rote knowledge of the classical past, a copy of a copy.

CHAPTER 5

Temples and Mirrors:
The Dedications of Hetaeras

Let us go to the temple to see the statue of Aphrodite,
how cunningly wrought it is of gold.
Polyarchis erected it, having gained much substance
from the glory of her own body.[1]

Sanctuaries, monuments, and dedications of courtesans, whether fi-
nanced by their revenues or established by their admirers, served as yet
another form of spectacle that placed them in the public eye and simultaneously engendered a narrative tradition of critical importance for
Book 13 of the *Deipnosophistae*. From as early as Herodotus, the monuments of courtesans figured prominently in ancient ethnographic narratives of the exotic, from Rhodopis' tithe of iron spits to the temple of
Cheops' daughter, constructed, stone by stone, from the wages of her
prostitution (Hdt. 2. 134–35 and 2. 126).[2] The sanctuaries (*hiera*) and
large-scale monuments (*mnēmata*) mentioned by Athenaeus are largely
situated in exotic locales such as Babylon, Abydus, and Ephesus, with the
exception of the precinct of Aphrodite *Pandēmos* at Athens said to have
been founded from the revenues of the women in the brothels (569d–e),
as well as the funerary monument of Pythionice that stood on the Sacred
Way.[3] Dedicatory offerings (*anathēmata*) such as Rhodopis' spits or the
portrait statue of Phryne, usually have a Hellenic context. By the time of
Athenaeus, however, the physical remains of most of these sites and artifacts had disappeared; instead they survived largely through the historiographic and periegetic narrative tradition. Within Book 13, allusions to

these monuments and dedications occur exclusively in Myrtilus' encomium, where they are deployed to show the importance of hetaeras and their commemoration in the transmission of Hellenic heritage. Monuments and dedications put hetaeras on public display and yet often situated this spectacle in a context of religious viewing, conflating them with the goddess Aphrodite, while simultaneously stressing their commodity status. Indeed, the revenues of courtesans' bodies are frequently mentioned as the primary means of financing their monumental buildings and extravagant dedications.

Although the public commemoration of important women, such as queens, with spectacular monuments was a common feature of the Hellenistic landscape, their association with courtesans almost always involves transgression, even in the context of Myrtilus' encomium. The narratives utilized by Athenaeus often contain an element of travesty, or even subversion, as if parodying normative conventions of gender, display, and religious dedication, in a manner similar to the jokes of courtesans discussed in Chapter 3.[4] A comic fragment illustrates how the intrusion of a hetaera into a sanctuary of Athena profanes a sacred space by transforming it into a brothel: "He [Demetrius Poliorcetes] took over the Acropolis as his inn, introducing his hetaeras to the virgin goddess" (Philippides, F25 KA= Plut. *Demetr.* 26. 1. 3). Outrageous dedications of public buildings or gilded statuary put the names of courtesans into circulation even as they transgressed religious norms. In contrast, artifacts commemorating the collective actions of unnamed groups of courtesans are represented as preserving the community, and even democratic ideology. In all of these cases, physical objects engendered a range of narratives to explain their origins, many of which made use of stock motifs and conventions. In formulating Myrtilus' encomium, Athenaeus drew on historiographic sources, such as those of Theopompus and Phylarchus for his accounts of sanctuaries and *mnēmata*, and works on dedicatory offerings, such as those by Polemon and Alcetas (on these authors, see Appendix I). For Second Sophistic readers, these monuments and the hetaeras they celebrated conjured simultaneously both the exotic and the familiar, "the irreducibility of strangeness, a feature of tourist discourse more generally, inscribes on the geography of the exotic a history of receding thresholds of wonder."[5] In the fourth and third centuries, Phryne's statue in the sanctuary of Delphi or Pythionice's memorial on the Sacred Way could be rhetorically deployed to evoke shame and outrage or to deride the incontinence of foreign kings and Macedonian monarchs. By the time of Athenaeus, however, the same monuments had become familiar elements of the literary landscape, continually displayed and re-exhibited by narrative re-constructions of the classical past.

Hetaeras and the Worship of Aphrodite

> For good reason is a shrine (*hieron*) of the Hetaera found everywhere,
> while nowhere in Greece is there a shrine to the Wife.
>
> (Philetaerus, *Corinthiastē* F5 KA = 559a, 572d)

The comic quotation above appears twice in Book 13, initially to support Leonides' invective against wives, and later to prove the respectability of hetaeras in Myrtilus' encomium.[6] In the latter case, the passage introduces a discourse on their religious role, one that assimilates, as did the stories of Praxiteles' Cnidian Aphrodite discussed in the previous chapter, the goddess to her mortal embodiments. In the first part of his speech, the grammarian argues along semantic lines that the term hetaera originated as an epithet of Aphrodite and did not at first imply an erotic attachment. His argument shows the close connection between the hetaera and the goddess:

> They are the only women addressed by the name of "friendly" (*philias*), or who are called by the Athenians after *Hetaira* Aphrodite. Concerning this Apollodorus states in his work *On the Gods*, "*Hetaira* Aphrodite is she who brings together companions, both male (*tous hetairous*) and female (*tas hetairas*), that is, female friends (*philas*). (Apollodorus *FGrH* 244 F112 = 571c)

Mytrilus identifies the hetaera with her patron deity, but attempts at first to cleanse the epithet of its negative implications by defining it as a form of non-erotic fellowship.[7] Nor, he argues, does a cognate term, the Hetairideia, a festival celebrated by the Magnesians as well as the Macedonian kings, have any connection with courtesans.[8] At the same time, cult epithets such as *Hetaira* at Athens and Ephesus (573a), and *Pornē* at Abydus on the Hellespont (572e–f), explicitly affiliate Aphrodite and her sanctuaries with prostitution.[9] These references are evoked to support Myrtilus' initial claim, that the term hetaera, given its religious significance, properly invites respect rather than vilification. The monuments and dedicatory offerings of hetaeras must be viewed in the same light, as part of the encomium geared to counteract the invective of the philosopher Cynulcus.

Most of the accounts of dedications and monuments in Book 13 of the *Deipnosophistae* link courtesans to Aphrodite and her worship. The deity was celebrated both by citizen wives in her capacity as a goddess of sexuality and procreation, as well as by courtesans and other types of prostitutes for her powers of seduction. Such women had a special reason to worship Aphrodite because of their need to perpetuate the desirable qualities of youth and beauty that would attract their clientele, exemplified by the statue of Aphrodite *Ambologēras* (She Who Turns Away Old Age) said to stand in ancient Sparta.[10] They required her protection and patronage in transacting the business of *aphrodisia* and in turn came to embody her sacred power of sexuality.[11] To the courtesan Lais II, Myrtilus tells us, the deity in her capacity as Aphrodite *Melainis* (Of the Dark) appeared at night (*nuktos epiphainomenē*) with premonitions of wealthy lovers (Polemon F44 Preller = 588c).[12]

Although courtesans and other types of prostitutes had a close association with Aphrodite, there is no solid evidence for the practice of sacred prostitution in ancient Greece. Myrtilus' account of Corinthian hetaeras in Book 13 of the *Deipnosophistae* provides one of the most extensive discussions of this custom in the Greek literary tradition. Prenuptial traffic in daughters is alluded to by Herodotus in his Babylonian narrative (Hdt. 1. 196). The custom is also attributed to the Lydians, the Locrians, known for the licentiousness of their women, as we saw in Chapter 3, and the inhabitants of Cypris (*tōn hetairismōi tas heautōn koras aphosiountōn*, Clearchus F43a Wehrli = 516a–b).[13] In this type of prostitution, the offering of virginity serves to propitiate the deity and symbolically opens the closed circle of the family to outsiders. Another predominant form of sacred prostitution involved a priestess class attached to a specific temple whose actions not only facilitated the fertility of the community, but also enhanced the wealth of the sanctuary. Sacred prostitution at Corinth, if it happened at all, would have belonged to this latter category.

Arguments for temple prostitution at Corinth have largely relied on Athenaeus' misreading of classical sources, particularly Pindar.[14] Indeed, the lateness of all of the references to this practice makes them of questionable value. In Book 13 of the *Deipnosophistae*, the evidence for this type of prostitution is found in Myrtilus' "Ionian discourse," in which he begins by mentioning his special regard for the city. The grammarian deduces the practice of sacred prostitution at Corinth first from the story of supplicating courtesans commemorated on a pinax in the temple of Aphrodite, and second, from an ambiguous passage of Pindar as filtered through the biographer Chamaeleon.

> It is an ancient custom in Corinth, as Chamaeleon of Heracleia records in his book *On Pindar*, whenever the city prays to Aphrodite in important matters, to invite as many hetaeras as possible to join in their supplication, and these women add their prayers to the goddess and join in the sacrifices (*hierois*) afterwards. (Chamaeleon F16 Koepke = 573c)

Nothing in this passage associates the courtesans with ritual prostitution, only with ritual activity—supplication and divine petition—alongside citizen women. The inclusion of hetaeras in such religious rituals must have been exceptional, reserved only for times of crisis, thus prompting comment from later authors. The function of these prayers as an example of a salvific action worthy of commemoration, a common motif in stories of monuments connected with courtesans, is discussed more fully below.

Somewhat more difficult to interpret, however, is Athenaeus' quotation of Pindar. He states that it was the custom at Corinth for individuals to vow to consecrate (*apaxein* or *epaxein*) hetaeras to Aphrodite in exchange for the fulfillment of their prayers (573e), as did a certain Xenophon of Corinth for his victory in the Olympian games. A drinking song of Pindar (F122) is adduced as evidence of this promise, although the fragment says very little about Xenophon himself. And despite the fact that Athenaeus frames the quotation with several references to the women as hetaeras, the poet almost completely avoids explicit prostitution terminology in this passage:

> Young girls, hospitable servants (*poluxenai neanides amphipoloi*)
> of Peitho in wealthy Corinth,
> you who burn the amber tears of fresh frankincense . . .
> without blame it is granted to you,
> o children, to pluck the fruit of soft beauty
> in your lovely beds. . . .
> But I wonder what the masters of the Isthmus
> will say of me, devising such a beginning
> to my honeyed song,
> consorting with common women (*xunais gunaixi*).
>
> (Pindar F122 = 574a–b)

The adjective *poluxenos* normally refers to places, or men, not to women; in this context, it suggests a euphemism for sexual availability. Similarly, the term *amphipolos* (servant) recalls the religious terminology deployed in Athenaeus' description of Phryne's disrobing (*hupophētin kai zakoron Aphroditēs*) and identifies the women with Aphrodite, but not necessarily with sacred prostitution.[15] The allusion to "common women" also suggests prostitutes; a brothel keeper in one of the Hellenistic epigrams is described as maintaining such women (*koinas*, M. Argentarius, *Anth. Pal.* 7. 403). While the poet may in fact address hetaeras—according to Athenaeus, the *skolion* was performed at the sacrifice to Aphrodite in which the courtesans participated—nothing in the quotation suggests that they were *hierodouloi*, temple slaves dedicated to prostitution. For that idea, one must turn to Strabo:

> The temple of Aphrodite was so rich that it possessed more than a thousand slave courtesans (*hierodoulous . . . hetairas*), whom both men and women had dedicated to the goddess. And therefore it was on account of these women that

the city was crowded with people and grew rich; for instance, ship captains readily squandered their money and hence the maxim, "Not for every man is the voyage to Corinth." (Strabo 8. 6. 20)

The notoriety of Corinth for its prostitution, a topos fully developed in
Middle comedy, as well as its wealth, probably had more to do with its
function as a port city than with the sacredness of its courtesans.[16] Similarly, the proverbial "voyage to Corinth," a saying that seems to have originated in comic discourse, turns on a commonplace about the economic
perils of frequenting prostitutes.[17] Interestingly, very few of the famous
courtesans discussed by Athenaeus had any association with Corinth; three
are early, from the late sixth and fifth centuries, including Lais I, Damasandra, and Scione. From the later period come Ocimon (probably a generic
nickname) and Lais II, the reputed daughter of Damasandra (see Appendix III). Neaera allegedly spent her early career in Corinth, but soon left
([Dem.] 59. 26). Instead, the hetaeras of Corinth in these accounts appear
only as a collective body that supplicates on behalf of the city, or as nameless and faceless brothel workers contributing to the city's coffers.

Certainly, Athenaeus and his sources depict hetaeras not only as visiting
temples of Aphrodite and participating in her festivals, but also as celebrants
in a variety of religious contexts that honored the goddess, particularly festivals of license, with their emphasis on drinking and the suspension of
hierarchical rank.[18] Indeed, they were closely linked to the Adonia, a festival that honored the untimely death of Aphrodite's mortal consort with
lamentations and drinking.[19] The Aphrodisia, perhaps not much more
than a special symposium, celebrated the pleasures of love; to such a banquet the hetaera Gnathaena invites the comic poet Diphilus in Machon's
Chreiae (Machon 263 = 579e).

> The city celebrates a festival of Aphrodite for the hetaeras,
> but it is different from the one held separately for freeborn women.
> On these days it is the habit of those women to revel (*kōmazein*),
> and it is customary for the hetaeras to get drunk here with us.
> (Alexis, *Philousa* F255 KA = 574b–c)

Whether a civic festival of Aphrodite or a private symposium, the occasion
allowed a moment of temporary license, with its potential for political and
social subversion. Indeed, drinking and carousing with courtesans fur-
nished the ideal opportunity to stage a political coup at Thebes.[20] On the
pretext of celebrating the Aphrodisia, a festival that always marked the end
of the polemarch's term in office, Phillidas invited the polemarchs to a
symposium in which he got them drunk, and then brought in the hetaeras,
who were actually men disguised as women (Xen. *Hell.* 5. 4. 4). The motif
of courtesans exploiting the vulnerability of drunken symposiasts to effect

political change is a commonplace among the later historians preserved by Athenaeus, as we shall see below, and sometimes provides an aetiology for material commemoration.

Narratives of Transgression

No woman who has been a slave (*douleusasa*) should be a queen (*despoina*).[21]

Although commonly associated with Aphrodite and her worship, the public commemoration of individual hetaeras, whether a temple (*naos*), sanctuary (*hieron*), funerary monument (*mnēma*), or prominent dedication (*anathēma*), almost always constitutes a form of religious transgression. Some of these monuments may have originated in the Aphrodite-cults associated with the Hellenistic queens and the general trend towards ruler cults of the period. The increasing freedom of women in the post-classical period, combined with the quasi-deification of the Hellenistic monarchs, changed the nature and function not only of commemorative temples and shrines, but also of honorific portraits. Ptolemy II Philadelphus is known to have established a ruler cult for his wife and himself while still living; in the subsequent reigns, each Ptolemaic king and queen were honored with such a cult after their succession to the throne.[22] The Seleucids, for instance, were worshipped as gods by the Milesians (Ridgway 1987: 408). Stratonice, the daughter of Demetrius Poliorcetes, and first wife of Seleucus I, had a temple of Stratonice-Aphrodite dedicated to her by her grandson, King Seleucus II; she was even addressed as thea Stratonice (Stratonice the goddess).[23] Moreover, the attribution of Aphrodite cults and divine honors to women had a strong association with the Ptolemaic queens in the Hellenistic period. Arsinoe II, the sister-wife of Philadelphus and former wife of Lysimachus, the subject of a joke discussed in Chapter 3, was honored by an Arsinoeion (Temple of Arsinoe) in Alexandria together with a special priestess and a sanctuary of Arsinoe-Aphrodite.[24] Given their connection with the Hellenistic monarchs, it is not surprising that the Aphrodite cults associated with named courtesans have affinities with those honoring the Hellenistic queens.

Indeed, a common narrative motif in the literary tradition, as represented by Book 13 of the *Deipnosophistae*, describes the transformation of lowly brothel slaves into queens by paramours besotted with passion. So Plutarch describes the ascent of the Syrian slave Semiramis from concubinage to the throne as the wife of king Ninus the Great. The woman purportedly grew so powerful that she seized the throne, putting the king to death, and henceforth "ruled gloriously over Asia for many years" (Plut. *Mor.* 753d–e). Such stories often involve Asiatic settings and gender role inversions: prostitutes of low status such as musicians or the "slaves of slaves" exploit weak and effeminate men (*di' astheneian heautōn kai malakian*, Plut. *Mor.* 753f). Similar narratives often involve the Hellenistic monarchs, some of whom encouraged their subjects to view them and their queens as divine, and who liberally incorporated courtesans and their children into their dynasties. Ptolemy II Philadelphus fell in love with Belestiche, "a barbarian bought in the marketplace" (*barbaron ex agoras gunaion*), to whom the Alexandrians were encouraged to maintain shrines (*hiera*) and temples in honor of Belestiche-Aphrodite (*naous*, Plut. *Mor.* 753f).[25] Athenaeus mentions Peitho, a woman who "stood at the brothel door" and eventually became the wife of a Syracusan tyrant, Hieronymous (Eumachus of Neapolis, *FGrH* 178 F1 = 577a). The hetaera Agathocleia reputedly ruled over Ptolemy IV Philopater after their marriage, turning the whole monarchy upside down (*hē kai pasan anatrepsasa tēn basileian*, 577a); her influence over the king was allegedly so extreme that Strabo refers to her as his mother.[26] And we are told that Lamia, the flute-playing lover of Demetrius, likewise had complete control over her man (*kratousēs*, Plut. *Demetr.* 19. 4). The monuments of courtesans in Book 13 of the *Deipnosophistae* often play a prominent role in narratives of this type, exemplifying the excesses of famous rulers, particularly those of foreign or non-Attic birth.

Myrtilus alludes to a "porne's famous temple" (*pornēs ho kleinos naos*, 595f) commissioned by Harpalus in honor of his mistress, Glycera, and built on the Indus River at Babylon during his satrapy, as found in a fragment of the satyr play *Agen*.[27] That this temple represented a distinctly Eastern form of death cult is evidenced by the claim of barbarian *magi* to be able to lure the soul of Pythionice, his prior mistress, to the upper world (*hōs axiousi tēn psuchēn anō*). Similarly, the Athenians and the Thebans were said to have deified Leaena II and the auletris Lamia by founding temples (*hiera . . . hidrusanto naon*) in their honor to flatter Demetrius Poliorcetes (Demochares *FGrH* 75 F1 = 253a–b). Another set of flatterers, those affiliated with Adeimantus of Lampasus, also attempted to curry favor with Demetrius by establishing temples and setting up statues (*agalmata hidrusamenoi*) of Aphrodite Phila, his daughter with Lamia (6. 255c; cf. Diog. Laert. 5. 76). These stories may have had some basis in reality, since it has been proposed that after Alexander the Great partially destroyed Thebes in 335 B.C.E., Demetrius restored the sacred sanctuary of Aphrodite and gave it the name of his mistress.[28] In any case, such shrines bordered on sacrilege as they applied the name of a mortal woman to a divinity as a cult epithet, and that of a courtesan no less; this is far different from celebrating Aphrodite in her general capacity as a patron of prostitution. Even Demeterius, we are told, considered the temples (*hiera*) that honored Lamia and Leaena II, and the flattery they embodied, altogether offensive and demeaning to himself (*pantelōs aischra kai tapeina*, 6. 253a).

Funerary Monuments

In addition to temples, Myrtilus mentions funerary monuments (*mnēmata*) as examples of the extravagant and transgressive public commemoration of famous hetaeras. Tombs and funerary sculpture, whether located within or outside of an established cemetery, were some of the most visible monuments in the ancient world, in part because they tended to be positioned along the busiest thoroughfares of Greek cities (Boardman 1995: 115). From the archaic period onward, the use of sculpture to mark the tombs of the dead guaranteed that the individual, normally male, would be remembered by future generations.[29] Funerary monuments that honored dead courtesans and prostitutes, in contrast, were an innovation of the late fourth century and may reflect the peculiarly Hellenistic emphasis on the fusion of mortal and divine.[30] Most of those described by Athenaeus are seriously over-the-top, even verging on poor taste, in their attempts to raise women of servile origins to divine heights. Their gigantic size and broad visibility reflect the excesses of the Macedonian dynasts and Asiatic despots, and their interest in self-glorification and deification. For example, the hetaera Stratonice, one of Ptolemy II Philadelphus' mistresses (not the same as the daughter of Demetrius), was said to have been honored by a large funerary monument (*mega mnēmeion*, 576f) located near the sea at Eleusis, although we know nothing of its design.

Just as temples and sanctuaries honored courtesans in the name of Aphrodite, so, too, their funerary monuments could recognize the goddess. Indeed, Myrtilus mentions a tomb monument dedicated to Aphrodite the Hetaera at Ephesus that simultaneously honored the unnamed mistress of the Lydian king, Gyges:

> Gyges, the king of Lydia, became notorious (*periboētos*) for his mistress (*erōmenē*), not only while she lived, handing over his whole self and his entire empire to her, but also even after her death. He gathered all of the Lydians of the country together and created a monument (*mnēma*) to the Hetaera, still so called even to this day. He raised it up high so that when he traveled within the region of Mt. Tmolus, wherever he happened to turn, he could see the monument (*kathorān mnēma*) and it was visible (*apopton*) to all of the inhabitants of Lydia. (Eualces *FGrH* 418 F2 = 573a)

The visibility of this monument reflects the general principle of funerary sculpture: tourists and pedestrians would have probably had more access to statues placed in a funerary context than those found in sanctuaries. But the panoptic presence of this *mnēma* as that which can be seen throughout the land combined with the number of men involved in its production suggest a scale far surpassing that of most funerary monuments. By converting the tomb of an unnamed but notorious woman into a shrine of Aphrodite, the courtesan is effectively deified as a goddess. From a narrative perspective, the public visibility, the size, and the fusion of divine and mortal exemplified by this monument emphasize the complete subjugation of the king to his hetaera mistress.

Probably the most famous of the *mnēmata* constructed in honor of hetaeras is that of Pythionice, mistress of Harpalus. Not much is known of this courtesan outside of her association with the Macedonian official. She appears in numerous comic passages, as one of the aging hetaeras figured as an Erinys in a play by Timocles, and in a series of others that equate her clientele with different types of fish, and allude to her insatiable appetite for the delicacy.[31] Myrtilus gives a brief biography of Pythionice, and her successor, Glycera, from 594e to 596b. Quoting from Theopompus' *Letter to Alexander*, a work that chronicled the activities of Harpalus during the king's absence in India, the grammarian reports that he founded not one but two *mnēmata* in honor of Pythionice, the first on the Sacred Way between Athens and Eleusis, and the second in Babylon. Theopompus predictably plays up the servile origins of Pythionice in order to enhance his invective against Harpalus:

> Indeed, she was the slave of the flute-player Bacchis. That woman, in turn, was the slave of the Thracian woman, Sinope, who had transferred her brothel business from Aegina to Athens; hence Pythionice is not only triply a slave (*tridoulon*) but also triply a porne (*tripornon*). (Theopomp. *FGrH* 115 F253 = 595a–b)

Like Semiramis, Pythionice is said to be the slave of a slave, a legal impossibility in ancient Greece, as we saw in Chapter 2. Rather, the allegation that Pythionice was thrice a slave serves a rhetorical purpose: by exaggerating the distance between her lowly origins as a slave porne and her lavish public commemoration, the author plays up the weakness and extravagance of Harpalus. A comic fragment also quoted by Myrtilus similarly lampoons Pythionice's precipitous ascent from brothel prostitute to queen of Babylon, "You will be queen (*basilissa*) of Babylon, if you are lucky./ For you have heard of Pythionice and Harpalus" (Philemon, *Babulonios* F15 KA = 595c).[32] To the trope of status inversion, this passage adds an Asiatic setting, a conventional element in this type of narrative motif.

Pythionice's Attic monument stood in one of the most conspicuous and important sites in ancient Greece, on the Sacred Way between Athens and Eleusis. The large number of ancient references to this *mnēma* can be explained not only by its prominent location, but also by its longevity; indeed, part of the foundation can still be seen today.[33] As with so many narratives of monuments connected with courtesans, Pythionice's *mnēma* exemplifies the moral deficits of her paramour, and raises the possibility that he may even have squandered public funds on the hetaera.[34]

> Harpalus, the Macedonian who plundered large sums of money from Alexander's funds and then fled to Athens, fell in love with the hetaera Pythionice. He

spent an enormous amount of money on her, even though she was a hetaera. And when she died, he erected a lavish monument (*polutalanton mnēmeion*). "And bringing her to her burial place," as Posidonius says in Book 22 of his *Histories*, "he escorted the body with a large chorus of the most distinguished artists, with all kinds of instruments and sweet tones." (Posidonius *FGrH* 87 F14 = 594e)

Pausanius describes the monument as the most worthy of viewing of all the Hellenic tombs (*theas malista axion*, Paus. 1. 37. 5). Myrtilus reinforces this opinion in his quotation of Dicaearchus, who states that its large size distinguished it from the other monuments viewed as one traveled toward Athens along the Sacred Way:

> For there, positioning himself at the point from which the temple of Athena and the city are first seen in the distance, he will see built right by the road a monument (*mnēma*) such as no other can approach in size. One would say at first that it was quite certainly a monument of Miltiades, or Pericles, or Cimon, or some other man of good character (*agathōn andrōn*), and that it had been erected by the city, or failing that, that permission to construct it had been given by the city. But when, on looking again, one discovers that it is a monument to Pythionice, the hetaera, what must one be led to expect? (Dicaearchus *FGrH* 2. 266 = 594f–595a)

The exceptional visibility of this object, especially its placement along the line of sight leading to the Parthenon, indicates a type of honor accorded only to important political figures of the past, not to women, and especially not to hetaeras. It thus reflects a transgression of gender categories typically associated with hetaeras, elsewhere exemplified by their crude jesting and public nudity. Moreover, the monument inverts norms of public display: its presence on a major thoroughfare betokens civic wealth, prompting the bystander to conclude that only a city could fund such a monument, not a private citizen motivated by personal passion. Similarly, as Theopompus reminds us, while Harpalus neglected to "ornament the graves" (*kekosmēke ton taphon*) of Alexander's freedom fighters killed in Cilicia, he lost no time in disbursing 200 talents for the two monuments of Pythionice (595b). The expense lavished on the monument by Harpalus recalls the role of prostitutes in charges of prodigality among the Attic orators, where the patronage of hetaeras and the squandering of patrimony are often rhetorical bedfellows.

The other monument that honored Pythionice purportedly consisted of a sanctuary of Aphrodite, complete with temple and altar, built in Babylon:

> For the hetaera Pythionice, the monument at Athens and the other in Babylon (*to d' en Babulōni mnēma*) have already stood completed a long time. Here was a woman who, as everybody knew, had been commonly shared by all who desired her (*koinēn tois boulomenois gignomenēn*) at the same expense for all (*koinēs dapanēs*), and yet your [Alexander's] alleged friend dared to set up a shrine and a

sacred enclosure (*hieron kai temenos hidrusasthai*) and to call the temple (*naon*) and the altar (*bōmon*) Aphrodite Pythionice, thereby showing his contempt for the vengeance of the gods and attempting to insult your honor. (Theopomp. *FGrH* 115 F254 = 595b–c)

This passage gives a clear indication that the deification of the hetaera as the embodiment of Aphrodite and the use of her name as a cult epithet constituted a significant form of sacrilege in the fourth century B.C.E. For this reason, the sanctuary is situated in exotic Babylon where such practices, in the Athenian imaginary, rightfully belonged. From a rhetorical perspective, Theopompus' account of a lavish temple set in its Asiatic precinct fully exposes Harpalus as a prodigal and treacherous enemy of Alexander, the letter's addressee. The repetition of the word *koinē* (common) reminds us that the mortal woman accorded divine status is no more than a common whore, available to all.

In contrast, a more austere monument commemorates the burial site of Lais II, the daughter of Damasandra/Timandra, for whom Athenaeus formulates a brief biography at 588c to 589b. According to Athenaeus, her grave was located near a shrine of Aphrodite *Anosia* (Unholy) on the Peneius river in Thessaly.[35] A stone hydria engraved with an epigram purportedly marked (*sēmeion*) the grave:

> Braggart Hellas, invincible in its strength, was once
> enslaved by the divine beauty of this woman here,
> Lais. Eros begot her; Corinth reared her.
> Now she lies on the famous plains of Thessaly. (589b)

The personification of Greece as a lover subjugated by the hetaera comprises a common motif among the epigrammatists (*Anth. Pal.* 6. 1, 18–20, 71); one poem actually describes her as laughing derisively at Hellas (*sobaron gelasasa*, 6. 1.1), much like the mocking hetaeras of Machon and Theocritus' *Idyll* 20. Pausanias places her tomb in a cypress grove called the Craneum at Corinth, near the sanctuary of Aphrodite *Melainis*, said to counsel her in dreams. Instead of a hydria, however, this monument took the form of a lioness holding a ram in her fore-paws, an image also associated with a commemorative statue of Leaena I on the Athenian acropolis (Paus. 2. 2. 4–5).

Clearly, the epigram engendered narratives that attempted to account for Lais' puzzling translation to Thessaly. Citing the historian Timaeus, Athenaeus explains that Lais, in love with a Thessalian man, was murdered by a band of jealous Thessalian women who beat her to death with footstools in the temple of Aphrodite. Thereafter, it became known as the temple of Aphrodite *Anosia* (589a). Plutarch's account portrays the hetaera as fleeing to Thessaly to escape the multitude of her lovers and a vast "army of hetaeras" (*megan straton hetairōn*, Plut. *Mor.* 567f). Incurring the jealously of the Thessalian women, she was stoned to death in the temple of Aphrodite; subsequently the goddess became known as *Androphonos* (Murderous). In both versions, the temple setting, the maenad-like band of women, the preposterous form of her murder, and the combination of sacred and profane, have all the earmarks of tragic history. These conflicting accounts probably arose from a desire to explain how a Corinthian courtesan came to be buried at Thessaly and were based not on a factual knowledge of Lais but on the epigram that survived her. The fanciful nature of the courtesan's biography becomes even more transparent if we look to the stage: one comic version of her death has her expiring from too much sex (*teleutōs' apethanen binoumenē*, Philetaerus, *Cynagis* F6 KA = 587e).

A similarly gruesome and transgressive death, although one not publicly commemorated, befalls the Thessalian orchestris, Pharsalia, to whom Philomelus gave a golden crown of laurel leaves, a votive offering of the Lampascenes.[36] Athenaeus devotes a small portion of Book 13 to the dedicatory objects stolen from Delphi in the Sacred War of 355 B.C.E. and recorded by Theopompus. The fact that these artifacts were inscribed with the names of their original dedicators before being given to others did not seem to bother either the looters or their recipients. To the auletris Bromias, Phaÿllus, tyrant of Phocis, gave a silver karchesion (goblet), a votive offering of the Phocaeans, and an ivy wreath of gold, dedicated by the Peparethians (605b). The transgressive nature of both the gift and the girl is seen in Theopompus' subsequent comment that Bromias would have played the flute at the Pythian games had she not been forbidden by the masses (*ei mē hupo tou plēthous ekōluthē*, Theopompus *FGrH* 115 F248 = 605b). Philomelus' gift, impiously offered to a mortal woman of humble status, attracted divine wrath. As a consequence, the dancer lost her life in Metapontium at the hands of crazed prophets who tore her to pieces as she stepped into the market place, much like the Thessalian women who murdered Lais. Later, people concluded that she had been killed because of her sacrilege in possessing the wreath of a god (*dia ton tou theou stephanon anēreimenē*, Theopompus *FGrH* 115 F248 = 605c–d). Although these accounts of the deaths of courtesans and the ways in which they were commemorated differ in some of their particulars, all of them involve the intrusion of the profane into the sacred: the panoptic funerary monuments of courtesans dared to elevate individual women of low status to the level of the divine, while their brutal murders stained sacred spaces and objects with the pollution of their blood. From a political perspective, lavish tombs are viewed as encouraging or legitimating Eastern despotism and corruption, while the hetaera "out of place," the Corinthian Lais in Thessaly or Pharsalia in the Phocian marketplace, transgresses religious norms, inciting madness and violence.

Dedications

The public dedications (*anathēmata*) of hetaeras, whether ritual objects, like Rhodopis' spits, or an honorific portrait statue (*eikōn*), such as that of Phryne, not only signified the economic agency of the women, but often violated normative dedicatory conventions. This is especially true in the case of grandiose offerings meant to glorify an individual, named courtesan. According to Keesling, women in ancient Greece did not tend to dedicate votive objects with anywhere near the frequency of men, particularly not votive statues. A total of only seventeen names of women dedicators appear in the votive inscriptions on stone from the Athenian Acropolis, less than ten percent of the approximately 200 dedicators whose names have been fully or partially preserved. Of these, only thirteen women dedicated statues rather than votive reliefs and all but one belong to the period between 510–480 B.C.E.[37] By the fourth century, however, there was an unprecedented increase in female patronage in Greece, in the form of architectural sponsorship, the erection of buildings and structures as civic projects (Ridgway 1987: 406).

As with sanctuaries and *mnēmata*, the more lavish the offering, the more it bordered upon sacrilege. The idea of transgression seems especially pronounced when the hetaera makes the dedication to commemorate herself, conflating the categories of religious offering (*anathēma*) and *mnēma*. The prototype for such dedications is found in Herodotus' account of the spits of Rhodopis, to which Athenaeus also alludes in Book 13 of the *Deipnosophistae*. Through Myrtilus, the author argues that Herodotus mistakenly referred to the hetaera as Rhodopis, instead of Doriche, and that she dedicated at Delphi not *obeloi*, but *obeliskoi* (*tous periboētous obeliskous*, 596c), an offering that earned her notoriety because of its extravagance:

> Rhodopis remained in Egypt, and, with her beauty (*epaphroditos*) becoming well-known, she made a lot of money, enough for a Rhodopis, but not enough for any sort of pyramid. . . . For Rhodopis desired to leave a memorial of herself in Greece, by having something made which no one else had contrived and dedicated in a temple, and presenting this at Delphi to preserve her memory. So she spent the tenth part of her wealth on the making of a great number of iron ox-spits (*obeloi*), as many as the tithe would finance, and she sent them to Delphi. (Hdt. 2. 135)

The reference to the pyramid serves as a clarification of a point made earlier by the narrator, that some people wrongly attribute the pyramid of Mycerinus to the courtesan. But in making the correction, he imputes to Rhodopis the ambition of building a very conspicuous public monument, far grander than that of Pythionice. In fact, Herodotus has just told us that the nameless daughter of the pharoah Cheops ingeniously managed to finance her own pyramid through prostitution, by collecting a stone from each of her partners (Hdt. 2. 134).

But Rhodopis had to make do with a more common type of votive offering, a tithe paid in money or precious metals customary from the earliest period of ancient Greek society.[38] Such tithes were typical of merchants, artisans, and other professionals engaged in trade and acknowledged the role of the deity in their profits; in this respect, they blatantly advertised the economic status of the dedicator.[39] This practice explains the frequent allusions to the revenues of hetaeras and their role in financing dedications in the literary tradition. It has even been argued that *obeloi*, such as those dedicated by Rhodopis, may have served as a proto-monetary form.[40] But while Rhodopis' offering, as a tithe, was conventional, its lavishness as well as its visibility made it a form of self-advertisement; although resident in Egypt, Rhodopis sent the offering to Delphi, where it would attract the most attention. Von Reden interprets it as a sign of her "hilarious ignorance" of dedicatory customs (von Reden 1995: 173), that is, she fails to recognize normative Hellenic conventions with respect to size and number. By asserting that Rhodopis intended her dedicatory offering at Delphi to serve as a memorial to herself (*mnēmēion heōutēs*, and *mnēmosunon heōutēs*, Hdt. 2. 134), Herodotus calls attention to her dedication as a form of hybristic self-glorification.

Dedications of hetaeras could also take the form of a portrait statue (*eikōn*) placed in a sanctuary. Such images carried connotations of transgression to the ancient Greeks, a view consonant with the many stories ascribing the practice to the Hellenistic monarchs and their courtesans. On the one hand, they exemplified the Hellenistic practice of honoring female benefactors; on the other, they potentially transgressed religious norms, if we consider that honorific images of women typically celebrated priestesses, not hetaeras. The idea of honoring courtesans and concubines with graven images has a parallel in a foreign death cult described by Herodotus: following the story of the incestuous Egyptian king Mycerinus and his daughter's macabre burial in a hollow cow, the narrator states he had statues of his concubines (*pallakeōn*) placed in a chamber of his palace at Sais, "Indeed there are about twenty colossal wooden figures (*hestasi . . . xulinai kolossoi*) there, made like naked prostitutes" (*gumnai ergasmenai*, Hdt. 2. 130).

In Greece, however, the portrait statues of courtesans coincided with an increasing interest in realistic portraiture that emerged during the fourth-century B.C.E.: according to Lucian, the early-fourth century Athenian sculptor Demetrius created lifelike images (Lucian *Philops.* 18; Steiner 2001: 61–2). Realistic portraiture also had a widespread appeal among the Macedonian dynasts; for example, faience wine jugs bearing relief portraits of the Hellenistic queens were widely manufactured for use at civic festivals (Pollitt 1986: 273 and 254, plate 274). Prior to this period, there was a marked distaste for honorific images among the Greeks; the mortal arrogance implicit in such images was thought to invite divine retaliation. Lysander's dedication of an oversize bronze portrait statue of himself at Delphi after his defeat of the Athenians in 405 confirmed the Spartan's sense of his excessive ambition and ultimately facilitated his political demise.[41] But honorific portrait statues, along with honorific monuments, increased enormously by the Hellenistic period (Kron 1996: 142). Most of these celebrated men, such as the Athenian general Conon, who was awarded an honorific statue that stood in the Agora for his success against the Spartans in 394.[42]

In the archaic and classical periods, portrait statues of women and dedicatory inscriptions by women were much less in evidence than those of men; most honored priestesses, such as those of Athena Polias on the Acropolis, and were dedicated either by the civic community or by the family.[43] Not until the beginning of the fourth century do we find statues dedicated by the priestesses themselves: one example, the heavily draped form of Niceso, priestess of Demeter, from Priene (c. 300–350), stood at the entrance of the sanctuary. Sacerdotal votives such as these mingled self-confidence and pride with piety, as well as indicated women's economic independence.[44] Non-sacerdotal votive statues of women were even more rare; but even these appear to have had a religious dimension. The image of Nicandre found in the sanctuary of Artemis at Delos, a monumental kore of the daedalic type, represents the earliest known example (Kron 1996: 154–6); however, the statue could represent Artemis and not a mortal woman. By the end of the fourth century private individuals, usually male, as well as cities, commonly placed honorific portrait statues in sanctuaries or in the agora; indeed, Alexander the Great made the honor commonplace.[45] By the mid-fourth century, most Attic funerary reliefs included at least one or more female figures, who were placed in a visually prominent position (Ridgway 1987: 405). The physical presence of women in the form of statues and monuments became even more conspicuous in the Hellenistic period as an increasing number of women, especially royalty, assumed the role of benefactors in public life, "doling out largesses, financing festivals and banquets or founding civic, religious buildings" (Kron 1996: 178–9). This development also stems from the newfound willingness of Greeks after Alexander's conquests of Asia to put the names of dedicators on building facades, a gesture encouraged by the atmosphere of the Hellenistic courts (Ridgway 1987: 407).

Nonetheless, the dedication of a portrait statue of one's self, especially by a woman, or worse, a hetaera, would have been anomalous in ancient Greece, even by the end of the fourth century, appropriate only for civic benefactors such as priestesses, female victors in the Panhellenic contexts, and the Hellenistic queens.[46] Book 13 of the *Deipnosophistae* mentions four such portrait statues in connection with courtesans and other types of prostitutes. After the death of Pythionice, Harpalus allegedly set up (*anatithenai*) a bronze image (*estēsen te eikona*) of his new mistress, Glycera, in Rhossus, Syria, near where he planned to set figures of Alexander and himself (595d). The placement of the statue not only challenged social hierarchy by equating the hetaera's political status with that of Alexander the Great, its establishment outside Greece identified it with the exotic Near East. The erosion of gender and status hierarchies, again facilitated by the Asiatic setting, is further seen in Theopompus' claim that Harpalus forbade his subjects from offering him a crown unless they also offered one to his porne:

> Moreover, he has given to her the right to reside in the royal palace at Tarsus and tolerates her to be worshipped by the people (*proskunoumenēn*) and to be addressed as queen (*basilissa*) and to be honored by other gifts more appropriately bestowed upon your mother and your wife (*sunoikousan*). (Theopompus *FGrH* 115 F253 = 595d)

Given the anti-Macedonian bias of Theopompus, this passage clearly exaggerates details of the hetaera's life at Tarsus to portray Harpalus in the least flattering light possible. In so doing, it makes use of a conventional rhetorical topos, the erotic enslavement of a powerful political figure by a lowly prostitute and her elevation to the status of a divinity which the local populace is forced to worship.[47] It also involves an Asiatic setting, as in so many of the examples discussed above. The moralizing allusion to the mother and daughter of Alexander the Great reminds the reader that the honor of public commemoration properly belongs only to legitimate family members within the Macedonian dynasty. Similarly, the portrait statues of Cleino, a wine-pourer to Ptolemy II Philadelphus alluded to by Athenaeus, reflect the sexual incontinence of the ruler-dedicator as well as the foreign tolerance for blasphemous images: "Many images (*eikonas*) of Cleino, the girl who was his cup bearer, are set up (*anakeisthai*) in Alexandria, wearing a *monochitōn* and holding a rhyton in her hands" (Polyb. 14. 11 = 576f).[48] The language of this passage, particularly the omission of *anatithenai*, suggests that these statues had a civic rather than religious viewing context.

The sacrilegious aspects of portrait statues honoring courtesans are perhaps most famously exemplified, both in Book 13 of the *Deipnosophistae* and elsewhere, by Praxiteles' statue of Phryne at Delphi. The fabrication of the statue out of gold is viewed as conflating divine and mortal categories while its placement within the sanctuary disturbs social hierarchies:

> And that woman down there who shares a temple and worship with Eros, whose gilded statue stands at Delphi with those of kings and queens, what dowry had she to subjugate her lovers? (Plut. *Mor.* 753e–f)

As in the case of the monuments and shrines that equated hetaeras with the goddess Aphrodite, so, too, Phryne's portrait statue implicitly likens her to a deity, since gilding was normally reserved for portraits of the gods (Keesling 2002). Like the *mnēma* of Pythionice, the placement of this statue near the monuments of famous men in the most visually prominent part of the sanctuary ultimately renders it transgressive.[49]

> The neighbors of Thespiae set up a golden statue (*andrianta*) of Phryne in Delphi, on a pillar of Pentelic marble; upon seeing it, the Cynic philosopher Crates called it a monument (*anathēma*) of Hellenic indulgence (*akrasia*). This image (*eikōn*) stands midway between that of Archidamus, king of Lacedaemon, and that of Philip, the son of Amyntas, and bears a label, "Phryne, daughter of Epicles, of Thespiae"; so says Alcetas in the second book of his work *On the Dedicatory Offerings at Delphi.* (591b–c)

This account situates the statue near portraits of Archidamus III of Sparta and of Philip II, while Pausanias places it near statues of Apollo dedicated by the Epidaurians and the Megarians. Plutarch, on the other hand, conveniently locates the statue near the legendary spits of Rhodopis (Plut. *Mor* 401a–b; cf. 596c). Accounts also vary as to whether Phryne herself, or the sculptor Praxiteles, dedicated the statue. Athenaeus vaguely alludes to "neighbors" (*hoi periktiones*, 591b), probably the Thespians.

The subversive nature of the statue is further seen in Crates' condemnation of it as a monument to Greek *akrasia.* In the passage above, the philosopher reacts not only to the effrontery of dedicating such an expensive statue to a deity and its conspicuous placement within the sanctuary, but also to the sexual incontinence it embodies. This story is recounted numerous times in antiquity, especially among Second Sophistic writers. Diogenes Laertius makes Diogenes himself the author of the remark, alleging that the philosopher inscribed upon the statue, dedicated by Phryne herself, "from the *akrasia* of the Greeks" (Diog. Laer. 6. 60. 5). Aelian attempts to salvage Hellenic reputation by alleging that not all the Greeks, but only the immoral ones, dedicated the statue at Delphi (*akratesterous,* *VH* 9. 32. 1). By late antiquity, Phryne herself had become a byword for sexual incontinence: the ability to abstain from a Lais or a Phryne came to signify a man's sexual self-control (Sext. Emp. *Math.* 9. 153. 5–6; Plut. *Mor.* 125a). So, too, in the context of Book 13, the discourse on hetaeras, in the view of the philosopher Cynulcus, encapsulates the incontinence of the grammarian.

Athenaeus mentions one last portrait statue in connection with courtesans, a small figurine (*eikonion*) of the hetaera Cottina recorded by Polemon in his work on the dedicatory offerings at Sparta.

> And further, there is a small statue (*eikonion*) of the hetaera Cottina, who was such a sensation (*epiphaneian*) that even today there is a brothel (*oikēma*)

named after her, very near Colone, where the temple of Dionysus is. The house is conspicuous and well known to all of the inhabitants of the city. Her votive offering, beyond the statue of Athena of the Bronze House, consists of a small bronze cow and the small image of herself previously mentioned. (Polemon F18 = 574c–d)

As in the case of Phryne, the honorific portrait statue of Cottina contributes to her notoriety (*diaboētou*) as a shameless encomium to herself. Her other votive offering, a bronze cow (*boun anatheinai chalkēn* and *boidion ti chalkoun*), represents a common form of dedication in ancient Greece, discussed more fully below, that usually had a sacrificial significance (Rouse 1975: 296–301). At the very least, the dedications of these objects indicate that courtesans such as Cottina and possibly Phryne, because of their considerable wealth, had the means to finance expensive votive offerings in their own names.

Narratives of Benefaction

The public commemoration of courtesans, whether it assumed the form of a sanctuary, funerary monument, or religious dedication, did not always have negative or transgressive implications. In some cases, public dedications or the establishment of sanctuaries recognized the heroic actions of hetaeras and their role in preserving the community. From a literary perspective, these artifacts and sites engendered a host of narratives that borrowed their techniques of characterization and plot from tragic drama and the later historians. Indeed, the self-sacrificing courtesan appears to have been an invention of tragic history as exemplified by Phylarchus' oeuvre. Like Euripides' Alcestis, these heroines put their men first, at the expense of their own lives; in so doing, they become more like wives than courtesans. An extended quotation in Book 13 of the *Deipnosophistae*, for instance, details the heroic actions of Danae, the daughter of the hetaera Leontion, the follower of Epicurus. Like her mother before her, this courtesan also served as the eromene of the Ephesian commander Sophron, whose murder was plotted by a hetaera named Laodice.

> Understanding that Laodice wished to kill Sophron, she beckoned (*dianeuei*) to him, communicating the plot. And he, comprehending her meaning, pretended to agree to Laodice's proposals, but requested two days in which to consider them. And when she agreed, he fled that night to Ephesus. Upon learning what Danae had done, Laodice threw the creature from a precipice, with no concern for past acts of kindness. And they say that Danae, when she perceived her imminent danger, did not deign to answer the questions Laodice put to her. As she was led away to the precipice, she said that rightly did men hold the divine in contempt, since,

"I, having saved him who was my man (*moi andra sōsasa*), take this sort of reward from the deity, while Laodice, after killing her own man (*ton idion*), is deemed worthy of honor (*timēs*)." (Phylarchus *FGrH* 81 F24 = 593c–d)

Tragic drama clearly influences this narrative: the request for a fixed period of time before taking action recalls Medea's supplication of King Creon for an additional day in which she can work her revenge (Eur. *Med.* 340–47). Death from a precipice is a recurrent motif in Athenian mythology as deployed by the tragedians: the daughters of Cecrops plunge to their deaths after spying upon baby Erichthonius, while their descendants Aegeus and Theseus also endure similar deaths. The emphasis on *sōtēria* (salvation) evokes the numerous sacrificial deaths found in Attic tragedy, from virgins such as Macaria and Iphigeneia to wives like Alcestis and Evadne. Even the direct quotation of Danae's final words recall tragic conventions, in which the sacrificial heroine guarantees her enduring fame through a final speech. So Evadne proclaims "It is sweetest to die together with one's family" (Eur. *Suppl.* 1006–7), while Alcestis reminds her husband of her ultimate sacrifice, "In dying, I have put your life first and I allowed you to look upon the light instead of me" (Eur. *Alc.* 281–4). Danae similarly emphasizes the magnitude of her sacrifice, contrasting her actions as a savior (*sōsasa*) with the murderous intentions of her rival.

Two other stories of heroic hetaeras involve political crises in which their lovers are deposed. Eirene, mistress of Ptolemy, a son of Ptolemy II Philadelphus, who commanded a guard at Ephesus, took refuge with her lover in a temple of Artemis to escape murder at the hands of the Thracians. After they had killed him, she clung to the knockers of the temple doors and sprinkled the altar with her blood until they sacrificed her, too (*katesphaxan*, 593b). The graphic depiction of Eirene's murder borrows from tragedy the motif of the perverted sacrifice; instead of an animal, the girl is sacrificed on the altar, just like Iphigeneia in Aeschylus' *Agamemnon* (Aesch. *Ag.* 226–49). Like Lais, she dies in a temple and thus profanes a sacred space; but in contrast, her death is motivated by a political crisis. Phylarchus gives another heroic narrative of a courtesan in the story of Mysta, the eromene of King Seleucus. After the king's defeat by the people of Galatia and his safe escape, Mysta removed her royal garments (*basilikēn esthēta*) and donned the rags of a servant (*rhakia . . . therapainidos*). At Rhodes, she was captured and sold into slavery, along with her own maidservants; once she revealed her true identity, Mysta was sent back to the king, in an example of virtue rewarded (Phylarchus *FGrH* 81 F30 = 593e). These narratives reverse conventional views of hetaeras: in times of crisis, they protect their lovers instead of betraying them; they humble themselves with servile clothing instead of demanding to be crowned; they share in the fate of their men instead of protecting their own interests. The structure and content of these stories, as I have argued, owe much to tragic drama and its representation of sacrificial death, as well as to the sensationalist narratives of Phylarchus.

One final account of a heroic courtesan mentioned in Book 13 of the *Deipnosophistae*, and arguably the most famous in the literary tradition, involves not the construction of monuments in her honor but her destruction of them as a means of protecting or ennobling Hellenic ideology. Thais, the courtesan of Alexander, purportedly set Persepolis on fire in revenge for Persia's earlier destruction of Athens and its monuments. Athenaeus, citing Cleitarchus, mentions the incident, but does not develop it at any length; from him we learn only that she married Ptolemy I Soter, the first king of Egypt, after the death of Alexander, and bore to him three children, Leontiscus, Lagus, and a girl, Eirene (576e). To celebrate his recent victory at Persepolis, Alexander the Great and his compatriots spent the evening drinking and whoring when a kind of madness (*lussa*) possessed them to see the city in flames. As we saw above, the temporary license afforded by the symposium and its potential for engendering political revolt is a conventional narrative motif among the historians and one that often makes use of courtesans.[50] In all of these stories, gender roles become inverted to the extent that the courtesan, not the drunken men, initiates the action:

> At this point, one of the women present, by the name of Thais, and Attic by birth (*Attikē de to genos*), said that for Alexander it would be the finest of all his deeds in Asia if he joined them in a drunken procession (*kōmasas*), set fire to the palaces (*ta basilea*), and permitted women's hands to extinguish the famous works of the Persians (*ta Persōn periboēta*) in a minute. This was said to men who were still young and giddy with wine (*eis andras neous kai dia tēn methēn alogōs meteōrizomenous*), and so, as would be expected, someone shouted out to lead the way and to light torches, and encouraged all to take vengeance for the destruction of the Greek temples. (Diod. Sic. 17. 72. 2–4)

Thais not only dreams up the idea of setting fire to the city, she leads the whole action (*kathēgoumenēs tēs praxeōs Thaïdos tēs hetairas*, Diod. Sic. 17. 72. 5–6), hurling the first torch into the palace; she acts as the agent of transgression and reversal. By calling attention to her Attic origins, the narrator gives a political meaning to an otherwise idle act of vandalism. As Xerxes invaded Greece and burned the Athenian Acropolis over one hundred years prior, so Thais "conquers" Persia and its central city:

> It was most inexplicable (*paradoxotaton*) that the impious act of Xerxes, king of the Persians, against the acropolis at Athens should have been repaid in kind after many years by one woman (*mia gunē politis*), a citizen of the land which had suffered it, and in sport (*en paidia*). (Diod. Sic. 17. 72)

In contrast to the other stories of heroic courtesans, Thais encounters little threat of danger; in fact, she acts on a whim (*en paidia*) rather than out of a sense of political mission. Nonetheless, the hetaera and her drunken capriciousness make a mockery of Persian power while at the same time affirming Hellenic hegemony.

Narratives such as these similarly inform Athenaeus' accounts of sanctuaries and dedications that commemorate the heroic actions of hetaeras. These contrast the transgressive monuments and dedications in the first part of this chapter in several significant respects: they are established by an entire community, not by an individual hetaera or her lover; they mark the preservation of the political order; and they are not portraits. For example, the bronze image of a lioness placed in honor of Leaena I at the entrance to the Athenian acropolis, near a statue of Aphrodite, commemorated the courtesan's act of silence that reputedly facilitated the establishment of democracy at Athens:

> Of high repute (*endoxos*) also is the hetaera Leaena, mistress of Harmodius the tyrannicide. When tormented by the agents of the tyrant Hippias, she refused to speak and died under torture. (596f)

Because the lion had long been used to personify martial valor and often marked the graves of warriors, this dedicatory object encouraged viewers to see the hetaera as the embodiment of masculine virtue.[51] Although Athenaeus does not mention the actual statue, only the act it commemorated, many other ancient authors appear to have been familiar with it. Pausanias discusses Leaena in connection with Hippias, stating that no one had yet committed the story of her torture to writing; to commemorate her (*mnēmē tēs gunaikos*), the Athenians erected a statue (*agalma*) of a bronze lioness (Paus. 1. 23. 1–2). Pliny gives a similar version of the story, explaining that because the Athenians did not want to honor a whore (*scortum*), they had the statue made into the form of a lioness, the embodiment of her name, and specified that she have no tongue (Plin. *HN* 34. 72). Plutarch further elaborates the meaning of the statue, "representing by the spirited courage of the creature the invincible nature of the hetaera and by its lack of a tongue, her absolute silence" (Plut. *Mor.* 505e). The complete obscurity of this hetaera, in contrast to Leaena II, the woman associated with Demetrius Poliorcetes, until the first and second centuries C.E. may indicate the circulation of an oral tradition—indeed, Pansanias states that he is the first to commit the story to writing—surrounding the actual statue that sought a fanciful explanation for its mutilated condition.[52]

Positive dedications in Book 13 of the *Deipnosophistae* commonly recognize the collective actions of a group of unnamed women rather than a named individual. The temple of Aphrodite *Porne* at Abydus is said to commemorate the salvific efforts of a group of unnamed courtesans during a time of civic unrest as well as to celebrate the restoration of a more democratic political order.[53] As in the account of Thais and Persepolis, the hetaeras exploit a moment of temporary license, the drunkenness of their captors, to save the city:

> For when that city (Abydus) was checked by slavery (*douleia*), the guards in it once made a sacrifice, as recorded by Neanthes in his *Legends*. When they had gotten drunk, they had their way with a number of hetaeras, one of whom, seeing that the guards were asleep, took the keys, and climbing over the wall, delivered a message to the people of Abydus. They immediately came with weapons, and after killing the guards, took possession of the walls, and having recovered their freedom (*eleutheria*), they set up a temple (*naon hidrusasthai*) of Aphrodite Porne in gratitude to the porne. (Neanthes *FGrH* 84 F9 = 572e–f)

The low social status of the women identifies them with democratic principles, with commoners such as artisans and athletes, as we also saw in some of Machon's anecdotes in Chapter 3, as does the cult epithet, which honors the porne, not the hetaera. Yet here, the subversion associated with courtesans and other types of prostitutes works the opposite effect, defending, rather than disrupting, the status quo.

The collective heroic actions of Corinthian courtesans during the Persian war leads to another kind of commemoration: the inscription of their names on a tablet, a dedicatory form, like that of Leaena I discussed above, that probably did not actually depict the image of a living person. According to accounts of Theopompus and Timaeus, when the Persians invaded Greece, the Corinthian prostitutes prayed for the deliverance of the Greeks, having taken refuge in the temple of Aphrodite. Out of gratitude, the Corinthians dedicated a votive plaque (*pinax*) on which they recorded the names of the hetaeras who had supplicated on that occasion.[54] Although Athenaeus states that the plaque listed separately the names of hetaeras involved in this communal supplication (*tas hetairas idiai grapsantōn*, 573d), the epigram of Simonides that he also quotes does not[55]:

> These women here were dedicated to pray to the goddess Cypris
> for the Greeks and their fair fighting fellow citizens.
> For the divine Aphrodite did not plan that the citadel of the Greeks
> be betrayed into the hands of the Persian bowman.
> <div align="right">(Plut. <i>Mor.</i> 871b = 573d–e)</div>

Plutarch approvingly cites this story even as he censures Herodotus for omitting it; but in his version, the prayers of Corinthian wives, not courtesans, instills an eros for combat in their husbands. This salvific act of supplication earns the women commemoration in the form of honorific statues made of bronze and set up in the temple of Aphrodite (*chalkōn eikonōn*, Plut. *Mor.* 871a–b).[56] The stories of the supplicating courtesans of Corinth and of the heroic silence of Leaena I at Athens share similarities with the martyred mistresses Eirene and Mysta, and with the pornae who aided in the coup at Abydus that resulted in the establishment of a temple of Aphrodite *Porne*. Through their loyalty and self-sacrifice, such women are represented as contributing to the preservation of the community, and even democratic ideology.

Groups of hetaeras could also finance large-scale dedications in honor of the goddess Aphrodite from the wages of their work, as evidenced by Myrtilus' reference to the sanctuary Aphrodite *Pandēmos* at Athens (569d–e). This type of offering also appears in the account of the hetaeras said to have accompanied Pericles to Samos during the Athenian siege of the city in 440 B.C.E. According to Plutarch, the Athenian leader undertook the expedition to gratify Aspasia, thereby showing her power over him (*technēn ē dunamin*, Plut. *Per.* 24. 1–2). These women were said to have pooled the profits of their bodies to finance a major statue of Aphrodite:

> The Aphrodite of Samos, whom some call "In the Reeds" (*en kalamois*), others, "In the Swamp" (*en helei*), was dedicated (*hidrusanto*) by the Attic hetaeras who accompanied Pericles when he sacked Samos, having made enough money from their youthful beauty (*apo tēs hōras*). (Alexis of Samos *FGrH* 539 F1 = 572f)

Established in honor of a deity rather than a mortal woman, this statue represents a collective, and therefore positive, form of dedication that commemorated the political victory of the Athenians over Samian tyranny.

Monuments dedicated by hetaeras could also serve as public benefactions that contributed to the cultural and political life of the city while at the same time glorifying the name of the benefactor. Lamia, the auletris associated with Demetrius Poliorcetes and for whom the Athenians dedicated a temple, gave to Sicyon a painted porch (*stoa poikilē*):

> Of Lamia, Polemon says, in his book *On the Painted Porch in Sicyon*, that she was the daughter of Cleanor of Athens, and that she built (*kataskeuasai*) for the Sicyonians the Porch in question. (Polemon F45–46 Preller = 577c)

The Painted Porch was actually an art gallery that contained famous works of fourth-century masters. Most of these were sold in 56 B.C.E. to pay off the Sicyonian national debt and some may have ended up in Rome, where Pliny saw them (Griffin 1982: 152). The striking reference to Lamia's father, Cleanor of Athens, emphasizes her Attic origins as well as her respectability, just as the inscription on the base of Phryne's famous Delphic statue referred to her as the daughter of Epicles of Thespiae (591c). This civic benefaction, whether it actually took place or not, shows that courtesans could perform acts of *euergasia* from the profits of their professions. Similarly, Phryne is said to have dedicated Praxiteles' Eros, the statue that she won with her ruse of fire, to her fellow Thespians (591b). Much later in her life, she vowed to rebuild the walls of Thebes, but only if the inhabitants would inscribe on it the following: "Alexander destroyed them, but Phryne the hetaera restored (*anestēsen*) them" (Callistratus *FGrH* 348 F1 = 591d). The inscription juxtaposes the name of Alexander at the beginning of the line with Phryne at the end, suggesting an equivalence between the Macedonian king and the wealthy hetaera, in much the same way as the anecdote about the destruction of Persepolis equates Thais with Xerxes. This boast, and its conceit, that a hetaera could be the equal of a king, challenged boundaries of gender and political status, ultimately stigmatizing the benefaction as transgressive.

Tools of the Trade: Anathematic Epigrams

Although not mentioned by Athenaeus, the collection of late epigrams known as the *Palatine Anthology*, particularly Book 6, is rich in descriptions of personal votive offerings made by hetaeras. The epigram of Nossis that opens this chapter depicts the hetaera Polyarchis as dedicating a gilded statue of Aphrodite to the goddess from the profits of her work. It is one of a collection of epigrams focused on works of art, either the painted representations of women or their dedications to female deities.[57] Not all of the promiscuous women in anthology are prostitutes, and in fact, clear prostitution terminology rarely appears; most may have been independent women of means celebrated during the Hellenistic period for their learning and beauty. Aeschra, the perfume seller of *Anth. Pal.* 5. 181, according to Gutzwiller, "is probably typical of the women known to the poet-lover of the collection—not a professional hetaera nor a protected maiden, but an independent woman who may sometimes confuse business and love."[58]

But other epigrams do allude directly to prostitutes as hetaeras, pornae, or female entertainers, such as the musicians Melo and Satyra (Leonidas, *Anth. Pal.* 5. 206). The anathematic epigrams discussed in this section deal specifically with hetaeras, recognizable by references to their names and to their profession. Almost all of these conform to one ritual type, the dedication of tools upon retirement from a profession; in the case of hetaeras, this occurred at the onset of old age, when the charms of Aphrodite have faded.[59] Typical feminine votive offerings for women of all periods were items of personal adornment such as belts, pins, bracelets, necklaces, and mirrors; these were dedicated not only to Aphrodite, but also to Eilithyia and Brauronian Artemis, both goddesses associated with childbirth.[60] Keesling argues that offerings depicted by the epigrammatists represent "a parodic twist on the ubiquitous genre of the modest votive offering."⁶¹ Because Athenaeus is concerned with larger cultural discourses, he does not mention this type of dedication, only public monuments that would have been widely viewed, and described, by earlier authors, or attested by extant inscriptions. Nonetheless, a consideration of a representative sample shows how they play off the tradition of hetaeras as civic and religious benefactors and their close association with Aphrodite.

The epigrams frequently allude to the tithes of courtesans as an economic transaction in which the profits of the couch are applied to the goddess upon retirement or in gratitude for the fulfillment of a request. In one epigram, the courtesan Parmenis offers to Aphrodite Ourania (Heavenly) her fan, as the tithe of her bed (*ex eunēs dekateuma, Anth. Pal.* 6. 290). In some cases, the offering marks the beginning of a career in prostitution; so Bitto, a weaver, dedicates her shuttle to Athena, finding Aphrodite's profession more profitable.⁶²

> Bitto dedicated to Athena her song-loving shuttle,
> implement of her unprofitable work (*ergasia*),
> saying, "Farewell, goddess, and take this. For I, a widow
> upon entering my fortieth year,
> renounce your gifts. I undertake instead
> the work of Cypris; for I see desire is stronger than youth."
> (Antipater of Sidon, *Anth. Pal.* 6. 47)

This epigram, similar to the one that follows (6. 48), clearly plays on the tradition associating textile production with prostitution as one of the few livelihoods available to women with no other means of support. Indeed, the joke of Strabo's hetaera that serves as the epigraph in Chapter 3 conflates wool-working and sexual activities. The term *ergasia* and its cognates apply not only to brothels but also to the professional activities of prostitutes, even to their sexual specialties (for which, see *Anth. Pal.* 6. 17). Moreover, the acknowledgement of the dedicator's age in line four turns the whole epigram into a joke, as she claims to embark on her career at the very point when the thoughts of most hetaeras turn to retirement. The whole epigram plays on an antithesis between the virginal Athena and the sluttish Aphrodite, and the stages of female life each governs.

A large number of the dedicatory epigrams focus on mirrors: once the supreme symbol of youth and beauty, they are now a reminder of old age. Mirror dedications exemplify the importance of the body, and physical beauty, for all women in ancient Greece, but especially for courtesans (Pirenne-Delforge 1994: 429). They are the physical equivalent of the cosmetic arts practiced by hetaeras in Attic comedy that speak to her function as a fetish. Andrew Stewart has even argued that one particular bronze case mirror from Corinth c. 330–320 B.C.E. may have belonged to the famous courtesan Leaena II, featuring her specialty, the notorious lioness *schēma*, a position featured in the Machon anecdote discussed in Chapter 3. Many of the mirror dedications feature the hetaera Lais, fully elaborated as a fictional character. She epitomizes for the epigrammatists from a diverse range of periods the painful loss of youth and beauty. In the first, she offers her mirror to Aphrodite, since she cannot bear to see herself as she really is, nor can she look at who she once was (*epei toiē men horasthai/ ouk ethelō, hoiē d' ēn paros ou dunamai*, Plato, *Anth. Pal.* 6. 1). In another, one of a series by Julianus, the ruined beauty of the hetaera is contrasted with the immortal beauty of the goddess Aphrodite through the repetition of the word *morphē* (form, beauty) in the first and last lines:

> Lais, her beauty demolished by time,
> hates the witness of her wrinkles, signs of aging;
> detesting the bitter reproach of her mirror,
> she dedicates it to the queen (*despoinē*) of her former splendor,
> "Receive from me, Cytherea, this disk,
> companion of my youth, since your beauty does not fear time."
>   (Julianus, *Anth. Pal.* 6. 18; cf. 19–20)

In a reversal of the standard trope, the mirror forces a disjunction between the hetaera and Aphrodite.

In addition to mirrors, courtesans dedicated articles of clothing and jewelry to Aphrodite upon their retirement: the amorous Nicias, beyond her 50th year, offers her sandals, locks of her uncoiled hair, a bronze mirror "not wanting in accuracy," a costly *zōnē* or hip band, and "things of which a man may not speak" (*ha t' ou phōnēta pros andros*, Philetas of Samos, *Anth. Pal.* 6. 210). Two other epigrams describe the collective gifts of a group of possible courtesans, all of the same age, to Aphrodite Ourania: sandals, a hair band, a fan, a veil "fine as a spider's web," and a golden ankle bracelet in the shape of a serpent (Antipater of Sidon, *Anth. Pal.* 6. 206). In the subsequent epigram, they are said to be from Naucratis (Archias, *Anth. Pal.* 6. 207), but the reference to one of the women as the "daughter of Aristotle" in both epigrams may indicate that they are not in fact courtesans. Another speaks of Calliclea as dedicating to the "legitimate" Aphrodite (*gnēsia*) a silver Eros, an ankle bracelet, a purple coil of her Lesbian hair, a pale-blue breastband, a bronze mirror, and a wooden comb, in exchange for fulfilling her wishes (Leonidas of Tarentum, *Anth. Pal.* 6. 211).

In some cases, the dedication marks a transition from hetaera to lawful marriage although the occasion is not always stated.[63] We hear of Alcibië, perhaps the well-known courtesan, dedicating her hair net to Hera upon obtaining lawful marriage (Archilochus, *Anth. Pal.* 6. 133). It is also possible that epigrams 206 and 207 in Book 6 signify such a transition; in any case, the point is made explicit in 208. In the latter, an epigram by Antipater, a visual representation of three women bringing their offerings to the temple of Aphrodite is addressed:

> She who brings the shoes is Menecratis,
> she with the cloak is Phemonoe, and Praxo she who holds the cup.
> The temple and statue belong to the Paphian.
> They make their offering in common.
> It is the work of Aristomachus, the Strymonian.
> They were all citizen hetaeras; but now they meet with
> a more temperate love, now each one belongs to one man.
> (Antipater, Anth. Pal. 6. 208)

This portrait dedication, in contrast to the portraits of Phryne and Cottina discussed above, has no subversive implications, perhaps because the women have relinquished their profession for legitimate unions. These tools-of-the-trade epigrams borrow famous courtesans from the literary tradition and develop fictive situations around them. The dedications they describe reflect the types of offerings that Greek hetaeras might have actually made to Aphrodite. But because they are private, they are not represented as transgressing religious or social boundaries in the same way as the large-scale public monuments and honorific portrait statues discussed above.

Conclusion

The various artifacts connected with hetaeras in Book 13 of the *Deipnosophistae* and its sources span a broad range, from temples and sanctuaries that honored Aphrodite, to hand mirrors and ribbons that marked their retirement from the profession. With the exception of the personal votives celebrated in the anathematic epigrams, most accounts of the dedicatory offerings of hetaeras preserved by Athenaeus are drawn from historiographic sources, with Herodotus' *Histories* serving as the prototype. According to these ancient accounts, the monuments of hetaeras dotted the exotic landscapes of Babylon, Egypt, and Persia; the stories that attached to them sought to explain not only local customs, but also the origins of the actual landmarks and the character of the men who established them. The need to account for the peculiarities of physical evidence, such as the missing tongue of Leaena's lion statue, or conflicting literary accounts, like the two burial sites of the Corinthian Lais, probably generated many of these fanciful stories.

While public monuments and dedications put the hetaera on display and inserted her name into public discourse, they frequently carried negative connotations by suggesting that an individual woman of humble birth could approach the status of powerful men, and even of deities. Temples that honored a mortal woman in connection with Aphrodite represented a powerful form of sacrilege and were thus associated with Asia, Egypt, and the Near East as well as with political corruption and despotism closer to home. Even the temples of Lamia and Leaena in Greece are represented as violating religious norms and functioned, according to Athenaeus, as a political tool meant to flatter a Macedonian monarch. Tomb monuments, especially those of Pythionice, but also that of Gyges' unnamed mistress, conveyed an exotic weakness for lavish display and mortal arrogance. Their panoptic presence in Lydia and even Athens challenged the boundaries of male and female, divine and mortal, public and private.

These narratives of excess promulgated by Theopompus and the other historians portray the complete subversion of social categories brought about by the elevation of the courtesan to near-royal status. The accounts of locals bowing down to royal mistresses such as Glycera at Tarsus exposed Harpalus' masculine lack of self-control and his subordination to a slave. Even the public dedications and civic benefactions of individual hetaeras could challenge normative religious and social categories. Instead of glorifying herself with a pyramid, Rhodopis sent a set of enormous spits to Delphi to immortalize herself among the tourists of the Hellenic world. Phryne's offer to rebuild the ravaged walls of Thebes arrogantly equated her status with that of Alexander the Great. The hetaeras in these stories, and the men with whom they consorted, are depicted as subverting the divine and political order through their acts of self-glorification.

Whereas many of the memorials made by or on behalf of individual, named courtesans are affiliated with despotism and corrupt political regimes, those commemorating the salvific actions of a group of prostitutes are seen as preserving the community, and even as reinforcing democratic ideology. So the tongueless lion of Leaena I commemorated the silence that facilitated the democratic revolution at Athens, while the shrine of Aphrodite *Porne* at Abydus recalled the role of prostitutes in overthrowing an oppressive political regime. Similarly, the devout prayers of courtesans are said to have saved the city of Corinth from Persian domination. Almost two centuries later, Thais' capricious act of pyromania inverted and repaid in kind the Persian destruction of the Athenian Acropolis. In these instances, the hetaera functions as a defender of public welfare, rather than as an agent of its subversion, by freeing the community from the bonds of monarchy and despotism.

CHAPTER **6**

Conclusion

The teacher of rhetoric would speak to you somewhat in this way, drawing away whatever remained of his hair and smiling in that refined and tender way so typical of him, imitating Thais herself of comic fame, or Malthace or Glycera, in the gentleness of his voice. For masculinity is crude and not appropriate to a delicate and lovely sophist.[1]

This book has examined some of the predominant aspects of the representation of hetaeras in the Greek literary tradition, and the genres and discourses that constructed them, from the perspective of Book 13 of Athenaeus' *Deipnosophistae.* It looked first at the cultural forces that shaped this late second-century discourse on hetaeras, particularly the widespread nostalgia for a unified Hellenic past realized through the sophistic pursuit of classical *paideia.* In Athenaeus, this longing is expressed through the genre of the literary quotation, which simultaneously evokes a unity of origins and its subsequent loss; at the same time, it is a derivative and inauthentic discourse that replicates rather than originates. The concept of the fetish also helps to explain the fragmentation of the courtesan as a literary figure into a series of narratives about names, witticisms, and public spectacles, not only in Athenaeus, but also in his major sources, particularly the Alexandrian courtesan treatises. By embedding these quotations in a rhetorical structure that makes use of antithesis and stock characters, Athenaeus slants their original meanings in significant ways. For example, although Neaera is mentioned numerous times in Myrtilus' discourse, there are no references to the derogatory content of the original oration. In insisting on the respectability of hetaeras, even in the face of textual contradiction, Myrtilus fashions a hetaera quite distinct from that of Cynulcus, a glamorous sophisticate and witty purveyor of Attic heritage immortalized by public monuments and literary texts.

But there is another side to Myrtilus' encomium. The passage from Lucian's *Teacher of Rhetoric* that serves as the epigraph for this chapter reminds us that the hetaera as a cultural sign often appeared in contexts of parody and defamation. Composed just a couple of decades before the *Deipnosophistae*, it satirizes the new trend in oratory that privileged entertainment and performative display over serious political persuasion. According to the scholiast, the treatise may have been aimed at Lucian's contemporary, the lexicogapher Pollux, who, like Athenaeus, hailed from Naucratis. In the dialogue, the narrator advises a youth as to how he might win the sublime and prestigious name of "sophist." To do so, he must reject the hairy, masculine rhetoric of the past and embrace the clever and effeminate art of the present (Lucian *Rhet. praeceptor* 10–11). Like the passage from Dionysius of Halicarnassus that compares the decadence of the Asiatic style to a ruinous hetaera, so, too, Lucian portrays the new rhetoric as a male whore, with his swaggering walk (*diasesaleumenon*), feminine glance (*gunaikeion to blemma*), honeyed voice (*melichron to phōnēma*) and carefully coifed hair. [2] To succeed at this type of oratory, the pupil is advised to pay special attention to his appearance, wear transparent Tarantine clothing, and speak Attic Greek, just like a hetaera. Both the sophist and the hetaera are represented as actors in a public space, both construct a false exterior intended to seduce their interlocutors, both exemplify a decadent aesthetic that privileges artifice and ornament over a natural, unadorned style. And yet the hetaera in this passage is marshaled in critique of the corrupting power of rhetoric and as a parody of the affected manner and vain pretensions of the sophist.

The discourse on hetaeras in Book 13 of the *Deipnosophistae* serves a similar purpose: it pokes fun at the grammarian even as his encomium exposes the hypocrisy of his discursive opponent. With his whorish discourse and pedantic proclivities, Myrtilus exemplifies some of the worst attributes of the contemporary sophist in Cynulcus' view. Like the putative object of Lucian's satire, he is a lexicographer and grammarian, concerned with superfluous names and debased genres. His humble origins as the son of a cobbler recall the lower-class background of Lucian's teacher of rhetoric, himself the son of a slave and seamstress (Lucian *Rhet. praeceptor* 24). Myrtilus once resided in Corinth, a place legendary for its prostitution (573c), and like the pallake Aspasia (5. 219d), is called an *erōtodidaskalos*, a teacher of eros (567b). His fine erudition (*kalēs . . . polumathias*, 567b, 610b) is analogized both to the fine sayings of hetaeras (*kala*, 588a) as well as to the fine sayings of his fellow sophists at table (*tōn kallistōn*, 1. 1a–b). Lastly, the dialogue between Stilpo and the Glycera quoted by Myrtilus, and the Socratic tradition that informs it, equates the teachings of the sophist with that of the hetaera (596e); both have a deleterious effect on the pupil, corrupting (*diaphtheirein*) rather than improving him. By making the courtesan into a symbol of Greek literary culture, Athenaeus deploys a conventional rhetorical form, that of the paradoxical encomium, which aims to praise subjects that normally incur abuse. In this respect, Myrtilus' speech is perhaps intended as a parody of itself, a comic burlesque of the scholarly tradition of sophistic learning and its love of Attic obscurities.

By the time of Athenaeus, the Greek hetaera had become a kind of historical relic, a literary figure associated with an outmoded social and political milieu, not to mention bygone literary genres and vanished monuments. And yet as a literary fiction that continued to be deployed in new ways, she transmitted, even as she parodied, a cultural heritage threatened by the political and social challenges of Greeks living in the Roman Empire.[3] As an urban creature figured both as Asiatic and Attic and continuously represented throughout the Greek literary tradition, the figure of the hetaera was uniquely suited to conveying contemporary concerns with cultural identity, rhetorical display, literary production, and the transmission of Greek *paideia*. In Athenaeus' *Deipnosophistae*, the hetaera must be viewed as part of a larger cultural project, the reification of the classical past through a continual process of exhibition as literary knowledge. And yet even as this character enjoyed an unprecedented literary resurgence in the Second Sophistic period, she was nonetheless an anachronism, an icon of an irrecoverable and rapidly vanishing past.

List of Authors and Titles in Book 13 of Athenaeus' *Deipnosophistae*

Adaeus of Mytilene, *On Sculptors* (606a)

Aeschines, *Against Timarchus* (572d)

Aeschylus, *Agamemnon* (556c; 573c); *Danaids* (600b); *Myrmidons* (601b, 602e)

Aeschylus of Alexandria, *Amphitryo* (599e); *Epic of Messenia* (599e)

Alcetas, *On the Dedicatory Offerings at Delphi* (591c)

Alcidamas, pupil of Gorgias, *Nais* (592c)

Alcman (600f–601a)

Alexander or Python of Catana, *Agen* (586d, 595e–596b)

Alexis, *Apokoptomenos/-e* (Shorn man/woman, 562d); *Cleobouline* (586a); *Graphe* (Portrait, 606a); *Helen* (563d); *Hippeus* (Knight, 610e); *Isostasion* (Equal Measure, 568a–d); *Lykiskos* (595c); *Manteis* (Prophets, 558f); *Opora* (Harvest, 567c); *Phaedrus* (562a–c); *Philousa* (Girl in Love, 574c); *Pyraunos* (Fire Lighter, 590b); *Tarentinoi* (587b); other (565b)

Alexis or Antiphanes, *Hypnos* (Sleep, 572c)

Alexis of Samos, *Samian Annals* (572f)

Ammonius, *On Athenian Courtesans* (567a)

Amphicrates, *Endoxoi* (On Famous Men, 576c)

Amphis, *Athamas* (559a–b); *Dithyrambos* (563c); *Kouris* (Tirewoman, 567f, 591d)

Anacreon (564d, 600d–e)

Anaxandrides, *Gerontomania* (Madness of Old Men, 570d–e)

Anaxilas, *Neottis* (Chick, 558a–e, 572b)

Anaximenes or Euthias, *Against Phryne* (591e)

Anaxippus, *Keraunoumenos* (Thunder Struck, 610f)

Anticlides, *Nostoi* (Returns, 609d)

Antigonus of Carystus, *Biography of Zeno* (563e, 565e, 603e, 607e–f)

Antimachus, *Lyde* (597a)

Antiphanes, *Agroikos* (Rustic, 567d); *Akestria* (Seamstress, 586a); *Arka-dia* (586a); *Halieuomene* (Female Fish Monger, 586a); *Hydria* (572a); *Hypnos* (or Alexis, 572c); *Kepouros* (Gardener, 586a); *Neottis* (586a); *Philopator* (Fond of his Father, 559d); other (555a, 565f)

Antiphanes, *On Athenian Courtesans* (567a, 586b, 587b)

Antisthenes the Socratic(589e)

Apollodorus, *On Athenian Courtesans* (567a, 583d, 586a–b, 591c); *On the Gods* (571c–d)

Apollonius Rhodius (555b)

Araros or Eubulus, *Kampylion* (Hunchback, 562c–d; cf. 571f)

Archilochus (594d)

Archytas (600f)

Aristagoras, *Mammakuthos* (Blockhead, 571b)

Aristarchus (612f)

Aristippus (565d)

Aristo of Ceos, *Erotika Homoia* (Erotic Resemblances, 563f, 564a)

Aristodemus, *Geloia Apomnemoneumata* (Amusing Memorabilia, 585a)

Aristogiton, *Against Phryne* (591e)

Aristophanes, *Acharnians* (570a); *Gerytades* (592d); *Plutus* (592d)

Aristophanes of Byzantium, *On Courtesans* (567a, 583d, 586f)

Aristophon, *Callonides* (559d); *Disciple of Pythagoras* (563b); other (577c)

Aristotle, *On Noble Birth* (556a); *Constitution of Massilia* (576a–b); other (556d–e, 564b, 566e)

Aristoxenus (556a)

Asclepiades, son of Areius, *History of Demetrius of Phalerum* (567d)

Bion, *Aethiopika* (566c)

Calliades or Callias, *Choregis* (577c)

Callias or Calliades, *Choregis* (577c)

Callicrates, *Moschion* (586a)

Callimachus, *Pinax ton Nomon* (Tablet of Rules, 585b); other (571a)

Callisthenes, *On the Sacred War* (560c); other (556a)

Callistratus, *On Courtesans* (591d)

Carcinus, *Semele* (559f)

Carystius of Pergamum, *Historika Hypomnemata* (Historical Notes, 577b–c, 603b, 610e)

Cephalus, *Lagis* (592c)

Chamaeleon of Heracleia, *On Pindar* (573c); *On Sappho* (599c–d); *On Simonides* (611a); other (600f)

Chaeremon, *Alphesiboea* (608d); *Centaur* (608e); *Dionysus* (608e); *Io* (608e); *Minyae* (608f); *Odysseus* (608e); *Oeneus* (608b–c); *Thyestes* (608f); other (562e)

Chares of Mytilene, *Histories of Alexander* (575a–f)

Chrysippus, *On Pleasure and the Good* (565a, 565d)

Clearchus of Soli, *Erotika* (Erotic Matters, 564a–b, 573a, 589d, 597a, 605e, 606c); *On Proverbs* (555c–d); other (590c, 611b)

Cleitarchus, *Histories of Alexander* (576e, 586c)

Cratinus (566e, 596c)

Critias (600d–e)

Ctesias (560d)

Demetrius of Magnesia, *Homonymoi* (Like-named People, 611b)

Demetrius of Phalerum (556a)

Demochares, *In Defense of Sophocles* (?) (610f)

Demosthenes, *Against Androtion* (585f); *Against Medon* (586e); *Against Neaera* (573b, 586e, 592c, 594a–b); *Against Philonides* (586e); *On the Bribe of Gold* (592e)

Dicaearchus, *On the Descent into the Cave of Trophonius* (594f); *History of Greece* (557b); *On the Sacrifice at Ilium* (603b)

Dinon, *Persian History* (556b, 560f, 609a)

Diocles, *Thalatta* (567c)

Diogenes (565c)

Dionysius of Athens, *Elegies* (602c)

Dionysius of Leuctra (609f)

Diotimus, *Epic of Heracles* (603d); other (611b)

Diphilus, *Sappho* (599d)

Diyllus (593f)

Duris of Samos, *Histories* (560b); *History of Agathocles and his Times* (605e); other (560f, 606c–d)

Echemenes, *History of Crete* (601f)

Ephippus, *Empole* (Traffic, 571e–f); *Philyra* (571b); *Sappho* (572c)

Epicrates, *Antilais* (570b–d, 605e)

Epicurus, *Letters to Hermarchus* (588b); other (588a)

Erxias, *History of Colophon* (562a)

Eualces, *Ephesian Chronicles* (573a)

Eubulus, *Cercopes* (567c); *Chrysilla* (559b–c); *Clepsydra* (567c); *Kampylion* (Hunchback, 571f; cf. 562c–d); *Pannychis* (Vigil, 568e); *Stephanopolides* (Wreath Sellers, 557f)

Eubulus or Araros, *Kampylion* (Hunchback, 562c–d; cf. 571f)
Eubulus or Philip, *Nannion* (568f)
Eumachus of Neapolis, *Histories of Hannibal* (577a)
Eunicus or Philyllius, *Anteia* (567c, 586e)
Euripides, *Auge* (600d); *Heracles* (608f); *Hippolytus* (600c); *Medea*
   (556c, 582c–d); other (561a–c, 566b, 599f–600a, 608f)
Euthias or Anaximenes, *Against Phryne* (591e)
Gnathaena, *Nomos Syssitikos* (Table Manners, 585b)
Gorgias of Athens, *On Courtesans* (567a, 583d, 596f)
Hagnon the Academic (602e)
Hegesander, *Hypomnemata* (Commentaries, 564a, 572e, 584f, 592b)
Heraclides Lembus, *Histories* (566a, 578a)
Heraclides of Pontus, *Peri Erotikon* (On Erotic Matters, 602b)
Heraclitus (610b)
Hermeias of Curium, *Iambics* (563e–f)
Hermippus, *On Isocrates* (592d); *On Aristotle* (589c); *On Lawgivers*
   (555c)
Hermesianax, *Leontion* (597b–599b)
Herodicus the Cratean, *Komoidoumenoi* (Persons Mentioned in Com-
   edy, 586a, 591c)
Herodorus (556f)
Herodotus (596c–d, 603a)
Hesiod, *Epic of Melampus* (609d); other (557a)
Hieronymus of Rhodes, *Historical Notes* (556b, 557e, 604d); other
   (602a–b)
Hippias the Sophist, *Synagoge* (A Collection, 609a)
Hippon (610b)
Homer, *Iliad* (556b–c, 556e, 563f, 566b–d); other (592a–b)
Hyperides, *Against Aristagora* (586a, 587d, 588c); *Against Mantitheus*
   (586b); *Against Patrocles* (566f, 587a, 587c); *In Defense of Phryne*
   (590d)
Ibycus (564f, 601b–c, 603d)
Idomeneus (576c, 590d, 592f, 611e)
Ion, *Epidemiai* (Sojournings, 603f)
Isocrates, *Areopagiticus* (566f)
Istrus, *History of Attica* (557a)
Lamynthius, *Lyde* (597a)
Lyceas of Naucratis, *Egyptian History* (560f)
Lycimnius of Chios (564c–d, 603d)
Lycophron of Chalchis, *On Comedy* (555a)
Lycophronides (564a–b)

Lycurgus, *Against Leocrates* (587a)

Lynceus of Samos, *Apomnemoneumata* (Memorabilia, 583f, 584b, 584f)

Lysias, *Against Alcibiades* (574e); *Against Lais* (586e, 592e); *Against Medon* (586e); *Against Philonides* (592c); *Letters* (592b); *On Contracts* (611d); other (612c–f)

Machon, *Chreiae* (577d–f; 578b–583d)

Menander, *Auletris* or *Arrephoros* (Icon-bearer, 559e); *Epimpramene* (She Set Herself on Fire, 559f); *Kolax* (Flatterer, 587e); *Parakatatheke* (Deposit, 571e); *Phanion* (567c); *Pseudo-Heracles* (587b); *Thais* (567c); other (594d)

Menetor, *On Votive Offerings* (594c)

Metagenes, *Aurai* (Breezes, 571b)

Myrsilus, *Historical Paradoxes* (610a)

Neanthes of Cyzicus, *History of Greece* (576d); *Mythikoi* (Legends, 572e); *On the Rituals of Initiation* (602d)

Nicaenetus, *Catalogue of Women* (590b)

Nicander of Colophon, *History of Colophon* (569d); *Peripateiai* (Reversals, 606c)

Nicias of Nicaea, *Diodochoi* (Succession, 591f); *History of Arcadia* (609e)

Nicolaüs of Damascus (593a)

Nicostratus, *Pandrosus* (587d)

Nymphodorus of Syracuse, *Voyage around Asia* (596e, 609e); *Wonders of Sicily* (588f)

Pamphilus (572e)

Panaetius of Rhodes (556b)

Parmenio, *Letter to Alexander* (607f)

Persaeus of Citium, *Sympotikoi Hypomnemata* (Sympotic Notes, 607b–e)

Pherecrates, *Corianno* (567c); *Ipnos* (Oven, 612a); *Pannychis* (Vigil, 612a)

Pherecydes (557b)

Philemon, *Adelphoi* (569d–f); *Babylonian* (595c); *Neaera* (590a); other (594d, 606a)

Philetaerus, *Corinthiastes* (559a); *Cynagis* (570f, 572d, 587e)

Philon, *Against Sophocles* (610f)

Philip or Eubulus, *Nannion* (568f)

Philoxenus of Cythera, *Cyclops* (564e)

Philyllius or Eunicus, *Anteia* (567c, 586e)

Phrynichus (564f, 604a)

Phylarchus, *Histories* (593c–e, 606d–607a, 609c, 610d)

Pindar (56ab, 564e, 573f–574b, 601c, d–e)

Plato, *Symposium* (566e); other (589c–d)

Polemon, *Of Hellas* (possibly by another author, 606b); *On the Acropolis* (587c); *On Spartan Dedications* (574c); *On the Painted Porch in Sicyon* (577c); *On the Painted Tablets of Sicyon* (567b); *Replies to Neanthes* (602e); *Reply to Timaeus* (588c); other (589a)

Polybius, *Histories* (576f)

Posidippus, *Aesopeia* (596c); *Ephesia* (591e)

Posidonius, *Histories* (594e)

Praxilla (603a)

Praxiteles (591a)

Ptolemy Euergetes, *Notes* (576e)

Ptolemy Megalopolis, son of Agesarchus, *Histories of Philopater* (578a)

Pythaenetus, *On Aegina* (589f)

Python of Catana or Alexander, *Agen* (586d, 595e–596b)

Sacadas of Argos, *Ilioupersis* (610c)

Sappho (564d, 571d)

Satyrus, *Lives* (556a, 557c–e, 584a)

Simonides (573d–e, 604b)

Solon (602e)

Sophocles, *Colchian Women* (602e); *Niobe* (601a); *Sheperds* (587a); other (564c, 601a–b, 604f)

Sosicrates/Sostratus of Phanagoreia, *Eoioi* (Such Men As, 561f, 590b)

Stesichorus (601a, 610c)

Stesimbrotus of Thasos, *On Themistocles, Thucydides, and Pericles* (589e)

Strattis, *Macedonians* or *Pausanias* (589a); other (592d)

Theodectas of Phaselis (566e)

Theognis (560a)

Theomander of Cyrene, *On Happiness* (567b)

Theophilus, *Neoptolemus* (560a); *Philaulos* (Flute Lover, 563a, 587f)

Theophrastus, *Erotikos* (562e, 567b, 606c, 609f, 610a); *On Happiness* (567b)

Theopompus, *Histories* (609b); *Letter to Alexander* (595a–c); *On the Chian Letter* (586c); *On the Funds Plundered from Delphi* (605a–d); other (573d, 595d)

Timaeus, *Histories* (573d, 589a)

Timocles, *Marathonians* (570f–571a); *Neaera* (567d, 591d); *Orestautocleides* (567e)

Timon, *Satires* (601c); other: 588b, 610b

Xenarchus, *Pentathlon* (569a–d); *Sleep* (559a)

Xenophon, *Memorabilia* (588d)
Zeneus of Chios or Zenis, *History* (601f)
Zenis or Zeneus of Chios, *History* (601f)
Zeno, *Republic* (561c, 565d)
Zenophanes (576d)
Author unknown, *Against Aeschines the Socratic* (611e–612f)

Narrative Structure of Book 13 of Athenaeus' *Deipnosophistae*

Subject	Speaker	Reference
Invocation	Narrator	555a–b
Encomium of wives	Larensis	555c–557f
Invective against hetaeras		557f–558e
Anaxilas, *Neottis*		558a–e
Invective against wives	Leonidas	558e–560f
Wars waged on account of women		560b–f
Encomium of hetaeras		559b
Encomium of eros	Philosophers	561a–c
	Pontianus	561c–562a
	Plutarch	562a–563c (?)
Invective against philosophers, pederasty	Myrtilus	563d–565f
Beauty of boys		563e–564f
Shaving and *erōmenoi*		564f–565f
Encomium of beauty, male and female		565f–566e
Invective against hetaeras	Cynulcus	565–571a
Invective against Myrtilus		566f–567d
as patron of hetaeras and pornography		566f–567d
Encomium of brothels		568d–569f
Alexis, *Isostasion*		568a–d
Xenarchus, *Pentathlum*		569a–d
Philemon, *Adelphoi*		569c–f
Lais in old age (Epicrates, *Anti-Lais*)		570b–d
Encomium of hetaeras	Myrtilus	571a–610a

APPENDIX III

Named Courtesans and Prostitutes in Book 13 of Athenaeus' *Deipnosophistae*

Name	Other Names	Date	Place	Lovers & Others	Passage	Literary Sources & Notes
Aerope		iv	Athens		587d	Nicostratus F20 KA
Agallis		iv-iii	Athens		583e	Apollodorus *FGrH* 244 F208; Ar. Byz. *FGrH* 234 F 4
Agathocleia[1]		iv	Samos/Athens	Ptolemy II Philadelphus and Ptolemy IV Philopater	576f 577a	Ptolemy Euergetes, *FGrH* 234 F4
Anteia[2]		iv	Athens		567c 570e 593f	Play title, Philyllius or Eunicus Anaxandrides, F9 KA [Dem.] 59. 19
Antheia	Anteia	iv	Athens		586e = 592e	Lys. *Against Lais* F59 Thalheim (confusion of Antheia/Anteia)
Anthis	Aphye	iv	Athens		586b	Apollodorus *FGrH* 244 F 210
Anticyra[3]	Oia	iv	Athens	Nicostratus, a doctor	586f	Lys. *Against Medon* Thalheim p. 366; Ar. Byz. *FGrH* 347 F1 (on nickname); Men. *Kolax* F4
Archaenassa		v-iv	Colophon	Plato	589c	Asclepiades, *Anth. Pal.* 7. 217
Archedice[4]		iv	Naucratis		596d	Hdt. 2. 135
Archippe		v	Athens	Sophocles	592b	Hegesander

Name	Other Names	Date	Place	Lovers & Others	Passage	Literary Sources & Notes
Aristagora[5]		iv	Athens	Hyperides	586a, 587c, 588c	Hyp. *Against Aristagora* F13–31 Jensen
					590d	Idomeneus *FGrH* 338 F14 (on affair with Hyperides)
Aristocleia		c. 340	Athens		592e	Lys. *Against Lais* F59 Thalheim [Dem.] 59. 19
					593f	
Aspasia I[6]		v	Miletus	Pericles	569f–570a	Ar. *Ach.* 524–29
					589d–e	Clearchus, *Erotika* (Pericles' love for her)
					599a–b	Hermesianax (Socrate's passion for her)
Aspasia II[7]	Milto	v-iv	Phocaea	Cyrus	576d	Zenophanes
					589d	Clearchus, *Erotika*
Astra		iv-iii	Athens		583e	Apollodorus *FGrH* 244 F208; Ar. Byz. *FGrH* 347 T2
Bacchis[8] (Auletris)		iv	Samos	Colophonian youth	594b–c	Menetor
					595a	Theopompus *FGrH* 115 F253
Barathron[9] (Auletris)		iv	Athens		587f	Theophilus F11 KA
Bilistiche[10]		c. 260	Argos	Ptolemy II Philadelphus	576f	Ptolemy Euergetes *FGrH* 234 F4 (descent from the Atreids)
					596e	Carystius
Boa (Auletris)		iv	Paphlagonia	Mother of Philetaerus, King of Pergamum	577b	Carystius
Bromias[11] (Auletris)		iv		Daughter of Deiniades; Mistress of Phaÿllus	605b	Theopompus *FGrH* 115 F248
Callistion[12]	Hys (Sow) Ptochelene (Begging Helen)	iv	Athens		583a	Machon 433–38
					585b	Lynceus
Cercope		iv	Athens		587e	Philetaerus F9 KA
Chimaera		iv	Athens		583e	Apollodorus *FGrH* 244 F208; Ar. Byz. *FGrH* 347 T2
Choregis		v-iv	Athens	Aristophon, the orator	577c	Play title, Calliades or Callias; Carystius
Chrysilla[13]		iv-iii	Athens		559b	Play title, Eubulus F115 KA
Chrysis[14]		iv	Athens		567f	Timocles F27 KA
					587e	Philetaerus F9. 3 KA

Name	Other Names	Date	Place	Lovers & Others	Passage	Literary Sources & Notes
Cleino (Oenochoousa)		iii		Ptolemy II Philodelphus	576f, cf. 425e	Polyb. 14. 11. 2
Cleoboline		iv-iii	Athens		586a	Play title, Alexis F109 KA
Clepsydra	Metiche	iv	Athens		567c–d	Play title, Eubulus F54 KA; Asclepiades *FGrH* 157 F1
Conalis[15]		iv	Athens		567f	Timocles F27 KA
Corianno		v	Athens		567c	Play title, Pherecrates F43 KA
Corone I[16]	Theocleia	iv	Athens	Mother of Callistion	583a	Machon 435
					583e	Apollodorus *FGrH* 244 F208; Ar. Byz. *FGrH* 347 T2
Corone II	Tethe (Grandmother)	iv	Athens	Daughter of Nannion	587b	Men. *Kolax* F4
Corone III		iv	Athens		587e; cf. 359e	Philetaerus F9. 6 KA (generic name)
Cossyphe[17]		iv	Athens		587f	Philetaerus F9. 6 KA (generic name)
Cottina			Sparta/Colone		574c–d	Polemon F48 Preller
Cynagis		iv-iii			587e–f	Play title, Philetaerus FF6–9 KA
Damasandra[18]	Timandra	v	Sicily/Corinth	Mother of Lais II and Theodote; mistress of Alcibiades	574e	
Danaë		iii		Daughter of Leontion I; mistress of Sophron of Ephesus	593b–d	Phylarchus *FGrH* 81 F24 (heroic death)
Demo[19]		iv-iii		Antigonus the One-Eyed; Demetrius Poliorcetes (his son)	578a–b	Ptolemy Megalopolis *FGrH* 161 F4 Heraclides Lembus *FHG* 3. 168
Dexithea		iv	Athens		580b	Machon 295–99
Didyme[20]		iii	Egypt	Ptolemy II Philadelphus	576e	Ptolemy Euergetes *FGrH* 234 F4
Doriche[21]		vii-vi	Naucratis	Sappho's brother, Charaxus	596b–d	Sappho F15b 11; Rhodopis at Hdt. 2. 135–36; Posidippus, *Aesopeia* & epigram; Cratinus (lost)
Eirene[22]		iv-iii		Ptolemy, son of Ptolemy II Philadelphus	593b	Phylarchus *FGrH* 81 F30 (heroic death)

Name	Other Names	Date	Place	Lovers & Others	Passage	Literary Sources & Notes
Eirenis		iv	Athens	Leocrates	586f	Lycurg. *Leocr.* 17
Erigone		v	Athens	Sophocles	598d	Hermesianax
Euardis		iv	Athens	Python	583c	Machon 456–62
Eucleia		iv-iii	Athens		583e	Apollodorus *FGrH* 244 F208; Ar. Byz. *FGrH* 347 T2
Euphrosyne		iv-iii	Athens		583e	Apollodorus *FGrH* 244 F208; Ar. Byz. *FGrH* 347 T2
Galene[23]		iv	Athens		587f	Philetaerus F9. 6 'generic name'
Glycera[24]		iv	Athens	Stilpo	584a	Satyrus (dialogue Stilpon)
				Menander	585c–d	Lynceus (milk joke)
				Daughter of Thalassis	586b	Hyp. F21 Jensen
				Harpalus	586c	Theopompus *FGrH* 115 F254 Cleitarchus *FGrH* 137 F30
					586d, 595d–596b	Python, *Agen* = 91 F 1 *TrGF*; Theopompus *FGrH* 115 F253
					605d	Clearchus, *Erotika* (witticism)
Glycerion		iv-iii	Athens		582d–e	Machon 411–21
Gnathaena[25]		iv-iii	Athens	Diphilus; mother or Grandmother of Gnathaenion	558b	Anaxilas F22, 13 KA
					567f	Timocles F27 KA
					578e	Machon 211–17 (stone joke)
					579e–580a	Machon 258–84 (Diphilus' frigid plays)
					580a–581a	Machon 285–332 (various jokes)
					581a–c	Machon 333–48 (procuring Gnathaenion)
					582a	Machon 376–86 (advice to Gnathaenion)
					583a	Machon 432–38 (quarreling hetaeras)
					583e	Apollodorus *FGrH* 244 F208; Ar. Byz. *FGrH* 347 T2
					583f	Lynceus (Diphilus' love)
					584b–f	Lynceus (more jokes)
					585a	Aristodemus (more jokes)
					585b	Author, *Nomos Syssitikos*

Name	Other Names	Date	Place	Lovers & Others	Passage	Literary Sources & Notes
Gnathenion[26]		iv-iii	Athens	Andronicus, the coppersmith	581a–582c	Machon 333–401 (various jokes)
				Granddaughter of Gnathaena	583e	Apollodorus *FGrH* 244 F208; Ar. Byz. *FGrH* 347 T2
Grymea		iv-iii	Athens		583e	Apollodorus *FGrH* 244 F208; Ar. Byz. *FGrH* 347 T2
Habrotonon[27]		iv-v	Thrace	Mother of Themistocles	576c	Neanthes *FGrH* 84 F2; Amphicrates *FHG* 4. 300
Heirocleia		iv	Athens		567f	Timocles F27 KA
Herpyllis[28]		iv	Athens	Mistress of Aristotle; mother of Nichomachus	589c	Hermippus *FHG* 3. 46
Hippaphesis		iv	Athens		586e = 592e	Lys. *Against Lais* F59 Thalheim
Hippe		iv-iii	Alexandria	Theodotus, *epi tou chortou*	583a–b	Machon 439–49 (joke on provender)
Ischas		iv-iii	Athens		587; cf. 166c	Men. *Kolax* F4
Isthmias		iv	Athens		587; cf. 666e	Philetaerus F9 KA
					593f	[Dem.] 59. 19 (doule of Casius of Elis)
Lagis		v-iv	Athens	Lysias	592c	Title of encomium by orator Cephalus
Lagisca,		iv	Athens	Isocrates; had daughter	570e	Anaxandrides F9 KA
Lagisce[29]				w/ him	586e	Lys. *Against Lais* F59 Thalheim
					592b	Lys. *Letters*
					592d	Hermippus F67 Wehrli; Strattis F3. 1 KA (pallake)
Lais I[30]	Axine (Ax)	d. 392?	Hyccara/ Corinth		570b–d	Play title, Epicrates F3 KA
					570d–e	Anaxandrides F9.
					582c–d	Machon 402–410 (joke on Euripides)
					585e	Aristodemus (joke)
					586e	Lys. *Against Lais* F59 Thalheim
					587d	Hyp. *Against Aristagora* F13 Jensen
					587e–f	Philetaerus F9. 4
					592d	Ar. *Plut.* 179
					588c	Polemon F75 Preller

Name	Other Names	Date	Place	Lovers & Others	Passage	Literary Sources & Notes
Lais I (*cont.*)					588c	(Apparition of Aphrodite Melainis); Hyp. *Against Aristagora* 5–6 Jensen
					588c–e	(Liaison with Apelles; painters' model)
					588e–f	(Dialogue betw. Diogenes & Aristippus)
					588f	Nymphodorus *FGrH* 572 F1
					589a–c	Strattis, F27 KA (father unknown); Timaeus *FGrH* 566 F10 (her murder)
					599b	Hermesianax
Lais II		b. 420		Daughter of Damasandra	574e; cf. 535c	Idomeneus *FGrH* 338 F4
Lamia I		vi–v	Athens		576c; cf. 533d	(Themistocles' cart)
Lamia II[31] (Auletris)		iv–iii	Athens	Daughter of Cleanor of Athens	577c	Polemon 45–46 Preller
					577d–f	Machon 168–187 (various jokes)
Lampas			Athens	Demetrius Poliorcetes	583e	Apollodorus *FGrH* 244 F208; Ar. Byz. *FGrH* 347 T2
Lampito		iv	Samia	Demetrius of Phaelerum	593f	Diyllus *FGrH* 73 F4
Lampyris		iv–iii	Athens		583e	Apollodorus *FGrH* 244 F208; Ar. Byz. *FGrH* 347 T2
Laodice[32]				Sophron of Ephesus	593c–e	Phylarchus *FGrH* 81 F24
Leaena I[33]		vi	Athens	Harmodius or Aristogeiton	596f	(Heroic silence under torture)
Leaena II[34]		iv–iii	Athens	Demetrius Poliorcetes	577c–d	Machon 168–173 (joke on schemata)
Leme	Phylacion Paraorama Didrachmon	iv	Athens	Stratocles	596f	Gorgias *FGrH* 351 F1
Lenaetocystus[35]		iv–iii	Athens		583e	Apollodorus *FGrH* 244 F208; Ar. Byz. *FGrH* 347 T2
Leontion I[35]		iv–iii	Colophon	Epicurus	588b	Epicurus
				Mother of Danae	593b	Phylarchus *FGrH* 81 F24
Leontion II		iv–iii		Hermesianax	597a, 593b	Hermesianax
Leontion III		iv–iii			585d	Lynceus (with Glycera at symposium)
Lopadion			Athens		567f	Timocles F27 KA

Name	Other Names	Date	Place	Lovers & Others	Passage	Literary Sources & Notes
Lyca		iv-iii	Athens		567e-f	Timocles F27 KA; Amphis F23 KA
Lyde I		iv		Antimachus	597a	Poem by Antimachus, acc. to Clearchus
Lyde II		iii?		Lamynthius	597a	Poem by Lamynthius, acc. to Clearchus
Malthace		iv			587f	Theophilus F11 KA
Mania[37]	Melissa	iv	Athens/	Demetrius Poliorcetes	578a	Ptolemy Megalopolis *FGrH* 161 F4
			Attike	Leontiscus, pancratiast	578b-e	Machon 188-210 (origin of nickname)
					578e-579d	Machon 211-257 (various jokes)
Meconis					587f	Theophilus F11. 2 KA
Medontis		v	Abydus	Alcibiades; Axiochus	574e, cf. 534f	Lysias F4 Thalheim
Megalostrate		vii-vi		Alcman	600f, 601a	Chamaeleon (a *poëtria* who attracted *erastai* by her *homilia*, also a hetaera?)
Megiste		iv-iii	Athens		583e	Apollodorus *FGrH* 244 F208; Ar. Byz. *FGrH* 347 T2
Metanira[38]		iv	Athens	Isocrates; Lysias	584f	Hegesander (joke about parasite)
					587d	Hyp. *Against Aristagora*; F13 Jensen
					592b-c	Lys. F ep. 3 Thalheim
					593f	(mistress of Lysias)
Mnesis (Auletris)				Ptolemy II Philadelphus	576f	Polyb. 14. 11. 2
Myrrhine[39]		iv-iii	Samos	Demetrius Poliorcetes	567f	Timocles F27 KA
				Hyperides	590c-d	Idomeneus *FGrH* 338 F14
					593a	Nicolaus *FGrH* 90 F90 (sovereignty)
Myrtion[40]		iii		Ptolemy II Philadelphus	576f	Polyb. 14. 11. 2; Ptolemy Euergetes *FGrH* 234 F4
Mysta		iii-ii?		Seleucus II Callinicus	578a	Ptolemy Megalopolis *FGrH* 161 F4
					593e	Phylarchus *FGrH* 81 F30 (heroic loyalty to Seleucus)
Nais[41]		v-iv	Athens	Philonides; Hymenaeus	586e	Lys. F82 Thalheim
				Under guardianship of Archias	587e	Philetaerus F9 KA

Name	Other Names	Date	Place	Lovers & Others	Passage	Literary Sources & Notes
Nais (cont.)					592c–d	Title of encomium by Alcidamas; Ar. Gerytades FF156–190; Ar. Plut. 179
Nannarion		iv–iii			587e	Men. Kolax F4 (Dimin. of Nannion?)
Nannion I		iv	Athens		576c	Idomeneus FGrH 338 F4 (Themistocles' cart)
Nannion II[42]	Aix (Goat) Proscenion	fl. 350 to 320	Athens		558c	Anaxilas F22. 15 KA (as Scylla)
					567e–f	Timocles F27 KA; Amphis F23 KA
					568f	Play title, Eubulus or Philip F67 KA
					587a	Hyp. 44 F141 (on her nickname Aix)
					587b	Alexis FKA (drunkenness); Men. Pseud. F456 Körte; Antiphanes FGrH 349 F2a (nickname Proscenium)
Nanno (Auletris)		vii		Mimnermus	597a, 598a	Hermesianax
Nausion[43]		iv–iii	Athens		587f	Theophilus F11 KA
Neaera		390–40	Athens	Phrynion, Stephanus, Hipparchus, the actor; Xenocleides, the poet; mother of Phano	586e	Title only, [Dem.] Against Neaera
					587e	Philetaerus F9 KA
					590a	Play title, Philemon Neaera F49 KA
					591d	Play title, Timocles Neaera F25–26 KA
					592c	Title only, [Dem.] Against Neaera
					593f, 594a	[Dem.] 59. 19 (slave of Casius)
Neitetis		iv	Egypt	pallake of Cambyses or Cyrus	560e–f	Ctesias FGrH 688 F139; Dinon FGrH 613 F1; Lyceas FGrH 690 F1
Nemeas (Auletris)		iv	Athens		587c	Hyp. 44 F142 Jensen; Polemon F38 Preller (naming taboo)
Neottis		iv	Athens		558c, 572b	Play title, Anaxilas F22. KA
Nicarete[44]		c. 340	Athens/ Megara	Stephanus	593f	[Dem.] 59. 18
					596e	(noble lineage; student of Stilpo)
Nico[45]	Aix (Goat)	v–iv	Samos/Athens	Sophocles; Python; Demophon	582e–f	Machon 421–32 (pugē joke)
					583c–d	Machon 456–62 (joke on Euardis)
					584f	Lynceus (joke on parasite)

Name	Other Names	Date	Place	Lovers & Others	Passage	Literary Sources & Notes
Nicostratis[46]	Aphye (Anchovy)	iv-iii	Athens		586b	Antiphanes *FGrH* 349 F1 (nickname)
Nysa		ii-iv		Seleucus II Callinicus	578a	Ptolemy Megalopolis *FGrH* 161 F4
Ocimon		iv	Corinth		567c	Eubulus F53 KA
					570e	Anaxandrides F9. 6 KA
					587c–d	Hyp. *Against Aristagora* F13 Jensen; Nicostratus F20 KA
Olympia		iv-iii	Sparta	Mother of Bion	591f	Nicias
Opora[47]		iv-iii	Athens		567c	Play title, Alexis FF169–70
Pamphila		iv		Satyrus, the actor	591e	
Pannychis[48]		iv-iii			568e	Title of play by Eubulus, F82 KA
Paroinos		iv-iii	Athens		583e	Apollodorus *FGrH* 244 F208; Ar. Byz. *FGrH* 347 T2
Pasiphile		vii			594c	Archil. F331. 2 West
Peitho		iv-iii	Athens	Hieronymus, tyrant of Syracuse	577a	Eumachus *FGrH* 178 F1
Phanion		iv-iii	Athens		567c; cf. 171a, 314b	Play title, Men. FF388–93 KA
Phanostrate	Phtheiropyle (Louse-gate)	iv	Athens		586a	Dem. 22.56; Apollodorus *FGrH* 244 F209 (nickname)
Pharsalia (Orchestris)			Thessaly		605c–d	Theopompus *FGrH* 115 F248 (murder)
Phila[49]		iv	Athens	Hyperides	587e	Philetaerus F9. 5 KA
					590d	Idomeneus *FGrH* 338 F14
					593f	[Dem.] 59. 19 (slave of Casius)
Philinna[50] (Orchestris)		iv-iii	Athens	Philip; mother of Arrhidaeus	578a	Ptolemy Megalopolis *FGrH* 161 F4
Philyra[51]		iv	Athens		586e = 592e	Lys. *Against Lais* F59 Thalheim
Phryne[52]	Mnesarete Saperdion (Little Fish)	iv	Athens	Apelles; Praxiteles; Moerichus	558c	Anaxilas F22 KA (Charybdis)
					567e	Timocles F25 KA (her early poverty)

Name	Other Names	Date	Place	Lovers & Others	Passage	Literary Sources & Notes
Phryne (cont.)					567f	Timocles F27 KA
	Clausigelos (Teary Laughter)				583c	Machon 450–55 (joke on her price)
	Sestus (Fleecer)				584c	Lynceus (stone joke)
					585e–f	Aristodemus (various jokes)
					588e	(rivalry with Lais)
					590e	Hermippus F68 Wehrli (impiety trial)
					591a	(as model for Apelles and Praxiteles)
					591b–c	Alcetas FGrH 405 F1 (statue at Delphi)
					591c	Apollodorus FGrH 244 F212 (nickname)
					591d	Callistratus FGrH 348 F1 (rebuilding of Theban walls)
					591d	Timocles F25 KA; Amphis F23–24 KA
					591e	Aristogeiton, Against Phryne; Euthias or Anaximenes FGrH 72 F17
					591e–f	Poseidippus F13 KA (impiety trial)
Plangon[53]	Pasiphile	350–330	Miletus	Colophonian youth	558b	Anaxilas F 22 KA (as Chimaera)
					567f	Timocles F27KA
					594b–c	Menetor (rivalry with Bacchis)
Potheine (Auletris)		iv–iii?		Ptolemy II Philadelphus	576f	Polyb. 14. 11. 2
Psamathe		iv			586e = 592e	Lys. Against Lais F59 Thalheim
Pythionice[54]		iv	Athens	Harpalus	567f	Timocles F27 KA
					586c	Theopompus FGrH 115 F254
					594e	Poseidonius FGrH 87 F14 (funeral)
					594df	Dicaearchus, Descent (mnema)
					595a–c	Theopompus FGrH 115 F253 (mnema)
					595c	Philemon F15 KA; Alexis F143 KA
					595e–f	Python Agen 91 F 1 TrGF
Rhodopis[55]	Doriche	vi	Naucratis		596c	Hdt. 2. 135–136
Sappho[56]			Lesbos	Phaon	596e	Nymphodorus FGrH 572 F6

Name	Other Names	Date	Place	Lovers & Others	Passage	Literary Sources & Notes
Satyra[57]		v-iv	Athens		576c	Idomenaeus FGrH 338 F 4 (Themistocles' cart)
Scione		v-iv	Corinth		576c	Idomenaeus FGrH 338 F 4 (Themistocles' cart)
Sige		iv-iii	Athens		583e	Apollodorus FGrH 244 F208; Ar. Byz. FGrH 347 T2
Simaetha		v	Megara		570a	Ar. Ach. 524–525
Sinope I[58]	Abydus	iv			558b	Anaxilas F22 (as Hydra)
					567f	Amphis F23 KA
					585f	Dem. 22. 56
					585f–586a	Herodicus (her nickname); referred to in Antiphanes, Akestria, Arkadian, Halieuomene, Kepouros; Alexis, Cleabouline; and Callicrates, Moschion
Sinope II		iv	Thrace		594b	[Dem.] 59. 19
					595a	Theopompus FGrH 115 F253 (procuress)
Sisymbrion	Aphye (Anchovy)	iv	Athens		587f	Theophilus F11 KA
Stagonion		iv	Athens		586b	Apollodorus FGrH 244 F210 (nickname)
Stratola		c. 340	Athens		593f	[Dem.] 59. 19 (slave of Casius)
Stratonice[59]		iv-iii	Athens	Ptolemy II Philadelphus	576f	Ptolemy Euergetes = FGrH 254 F4
Synoris[60]	Lychnos (Lamp)	iv	Athens		583e	Apollodorus FGrH 244 F208; Ar. Byz. FGrH 347 T2
Telesis or Telesilla[61]		iv	Athens		587e	Philetaerus F9. 2 KA
Thais[62]		iv	Athens/Attike	Alexander the Great	567c	Play title, Men. FF163–69 KA
				Ptolemy I Soter	576e	Cleitarchus FGrH 137 F11; Ptolemy Euergetes FGrH 234 F4
Thalassa		iv-iii			585c	Aristodemus (goat joke)
					567c	Play title, Diocles F6 KA

Name	Other Names	Date	Place	Lovers & Others	Passage	Literary Sources & Notes
Thallousa		iv			587f	Theophilus F11 KA
Thargelia		v	Miletus		608f	Hippias, *Synagoge* (teacher of Aspasia)
Thaumarion		iv-iii	Athens		583e	Apollodorus *FGrH* 244 F208; Ar. Byz. *FGrH* 347 T2
Theano[63]		iv	Athens	Pythagoras	558c	Anaxilas F22 KA (as Siren)
					599a	Hermesianax
Theocleia	Corone	iv		mother of Callistion	583e	Apollodorus *FGrH* 244 F208; Ar. Byz. *FGrH* 347 T2
					586e = 592e	Lys. *Against Lais* F59 Thalheim
Theodote[64]		v-iv	Athens/Attikē	Alcibiades	574e	Xen. *Mem.* 3. 11. 1 (visit by Socrates)
					588d	Anaxandrides F9. 5 KA
Theolyte[65]		iv	Athens		570e	Philetaerus F9. 3 KA
					587e	Hermesianax
Theoris[66]		v	Athens	Sophocles	592b, 598d	
Thryallis[67]		iv-iii	Athens		583e	Apollodorus *FGrH* 244 F208; Ar. Byz. *FGrH* 347 T2
Tigris		iv-iii	Ionia/Leucadia	pallake of Pyrrhus	589f-590a	Pythaenetus? (death by poisoning)
Timosa		v	Persia	pallakis of Oxyartes	609a	Phylarchus *FGrH* 81 F34

1. This Agathocleia may have been two different figures, a mistress of Ptolemy II Philadelphus, who died in 246 BCE, and the other connected with Ptolemy IV Philopater (c. 244–205 BCE); the latter liaison is more widely mentioned, for which see Plut. *Mor.* 753d; *Cleom.* 33. 2; Polyb. 14. 11. 5; on her death at the hands of the mob, cf. Polyb. 15. 33, and 15. 31. Strabo 17. 1. 11 refers to Agathocleia as the mother of Ptolemy IV Philopater.

2. Cf. play title by Antiphanes, F36 KA.

3. Cf. Plut. *Demetr.* 24. 1 (filled Acropolis with prostitutes).

4. Cf. Red figure lekythos NY 26. 60. 78 by the Sabouroff Painter.

5. Cf. 4. 167d–e (lover of Demetrius Poliorcetes, an example of his prodigality); Plut. *Mor.* 849d (mistress of Hyperides).

6. On Aspasia I, see von Rohden *RE* 2: 1716–22; cf. Ath. 5. 219c (author of poem); 220e (erotic teacher of Socrates); 12. 533c (Pericles' passion for her); Plut. *Per.* 24 (daughter of Axiochus, influence over Pericles); 32 (impiety trial); Diog. Laert. 6. 16 (title only); Xen. *Mem.* 2. 6. 36 (advice on matchmaking); *Oec.* 3. 14 (advice on training wives); Pl. *Men.* (author epitaphios); schol. Ar. *Ach.* 526; Harpocr., s. v. *Aspasia*; Clem. Alex. *Strom.* 124; Heracleides Ponticus *Peri Hedones* 11. 533d; Lucian *Imag.* 17, *de salt.* 25; *Amor.* 30; Aristeid. 44. 131; Alciphr. 4. 7. 7. For the name, see *LGPN* 2. 76.

7. Cf. Xen. *Anab.* 1. 10. 3 refers to an unnamed pallake of Cyrus; cf. Ael. *VH* 12. 1 (lengthy bios); Plut. *Artax.* 26.

8. Lucian *Dial. Meret.* 4; Plut. *Mor.* 753d; Plaut. *Bacchid.* 199–200; Ter. *Haut.* and *Hec.*; Epigenes F1–3 KA.

9. Name of place outside Athens where corpses of executed criminals were thrown.

10. For Bilistiche as the pallakis of Ptolemy II Philadelphus, cf. Clem. Al. *Protr.* 4. 42; for the name Belestiche, cf. Plut. *Mor.* 753e (*barbaran ex agorās gunaiōn*).

11. Bromia is the name of a servant in Plaut. *Amph.*; a nymph is named Bromie or Brome, cf. Hygin. *fab.* 182. 3; Serv. *Ecl.* 6. 15.

12. Cf. 11. 486a (epigram of Hedylus); an orchestris is named Callisto on an Attic red figure cup (London E 68); cf. *Anth. Pal.* 5. 123, 192.

13. For the name, cf. *Anth. Pal.* 5. 3.

14. For the name, cf. Lucian *Dial. meret.* 8; *Philops.* 14f.; Men. *Kolax* F4; Plut. *Demetr.* 24. 1 (referred to as a porne); play title by Antiphanes, F223–224 KA; Plaut. *Pseud.* 659.

15. This name is probably corrupt: ms. A contains χριστοσκονσλιστ. Other conjectures include: Κοβαλίς (Meineke); Κουναλίς (Kaibel); Κουναλλίς (Kock); however the editors of LGPN retain the name Κουναλίς.

16. A hetaera on a red figure phiale is called Corone (Berlin inv. 3251). All of the references at *LGPN* 2. 271 refer to visual evidence or comedy.

17. The text is uncertain: Κοστιόδους Schweighäuser; ms. A has πιλακοστ, συσβαστ; the name Κοστιόδαι is attested as that of a Delphic slave.

18. On this courtesan, cf. schol. Ar. *Plut.* 179 (Epimandra); Plut. *Alc.* 39; title of lost oration by Hyperides, *Against Timandra* F54. 165 Jensen.

19. On Demo, cf. Plut. *Demetr.* 24. 1 (Demetrius' desecration of Acropolis with hetaeras); 27.4 (Demo = Mania); *Anth. Pal.* 5. 115 (generic name), 160, 172, 173, 197, 244.

20. For the name Didyme, cf. *Anth. Pal.* 5. 210.

21. Athenaeus maintains *pace* Herodotus that Rhodopis is not the same person as Doriche.

22. For the name Eirene, although not a courtesan, cf. Plut. *Mor.* 243d.

23. For the name Galene, cf. 7. 301d, 318b; *Anth. Pal.* 5. 156; 7. 668.

24. For literary characters with the name of Glycera, cf. Men. *Pk.* and *Epit.*; Alciphr. 4. 1; 4. 14. 1; 4. 18; 4. 19; for the name, cf. Philemon F198 KA and Pliny *HN* 35. 125. See also *LGPN* 2. 94–95, where the name is quite common in inscriptions.

25. For Gnathaena, cf. Ath. 9. 384e (joke on testicles); as a character, cf. Alciphr. 4. 16. 2. See also *LGPN* 2. 95; the name appears in comedy only.

26. Also mentioned at Ath. 9. 371f.

27. For Glycera as a character, cf. Men. *Pk.* and *Epit.*; Lucian *Dial. meret.* 1. 1.

28. All of the mss. have σστπυρστης (actor in a satyr play) for Σπιγυρίστης. For her liaison with Aristotle, cf. Diog. Laert. 5. 12; Alciphr. 4. 7. 3; 4. 10. 2.

29. Athenaeus mentions a Lagisce, one time only, at 570e, where the text has the elided form of a nominative feminine singular name: Λαγίσκ᾽; ἤρθει; however, the missing vowel could be an α or rather than η making her the same woman who appears at 586e, 592b–d. Cf. Plut. *Mor.* 839b (lover of Isocrates); Harpocr. s.v. Λαγίσκα; Suda s.v. φιλίσκος.

30. The name possibly derives from Hebrew K*L*SH. Although Athenaeus does not differentiate the two courtesans, I have followed Geyer *RE* 12: 513–516 in maintaining that there were two different courtesans named Lais, but they are often impossible to distinguish. For the confusion of Nais (mistress of Philonides) and Lais, cf. 592d. Cf. schol. Ar. *Plut.* 179 (Epimandra); Hyp. F13 Jensen; Ael. *VH* 10. 2 (anecdote about Eubatas of Cyrene); 12. 5 (on the nickname Axine mentioned by Aristophanes of Byzantium, FGrH 347 F 2); 14. 35 (on her nickname); Lucian *Ver. Hist.* 2. 18; Diog. Laert. 2. 74–75 (affair with Aristippus); 84–85 (title of lost works); Cic. *Epist.* 9. 26. 2–3 (anecdote about Lais and Aristippus); Plut. *Alc.* 30 (daughter of Timandra); *Nic.* 15 (origins in Hyccara); *Mor.* 750d (love of Aristippus); 759e; *Mor.* 767f (her murder in Thessaly); Paus. 2. 2. 4–5 (tomb at Corinth); Clem. Alex. *Strom.* 3. 6. 5a; Suidas s.v. ἑταίραι (from Corinth). Cf. Alciphr. F5. 4; *Anth. Pal.* 5. 301; 7. 218–220; 9. 260; cf. 5. 20; 6. 18; Prop. 2. 6. 3. *LGPN* 2. 278 gives only three inscriptional entries.

31. On Lamia II, see Geyer *RE* 12. 544–47; cf. Ath. 3. 101e (Attic deipnon for Demetrius); 4. 128b(Attic deipnon for Demetrius); 6. 255c (flattery of Demetrius); 14. 614f (Lysimachus' joke about Demetrius' court as a comic stage); Crates F20–25 KA (play title); Plut. *Demetr.* 16 (spoils of Ptolemy I Soter); 19 (her control over Demetrius); 24 (Lysimachus' joke about Demetrius' court as a comic stage); 27 (taxes collected by Demetrius from the Athenians used to buy soap for Lamia and other courtesans); Demochares F3 = FGrH 2. 419; Ael. *VH* 13. 9 (witticism about Spartan living in Ionia); Clem. Al. *Protr.* 4. 55. 1 (coupled with Demetrius in Parthenon); Diog. Laert. 5. 76 (her noble birth, *eugenēs*); Alciphr. 4. 16. 17. One inscription is given in *LGPN* 2. 279.

32. For Laodice, the model of the painter Polygnotus and possibly a hetaera, cf. Plut. *Cim.* 4. 5.

33. For the story, cf. Paus. 1. 23. 1–2; Plut. *Mor.* 505e; Plin. *HN* 7. 21. 87 (ability to tolerate pain); 34. 19. 72 (described as a harpist); Cic. *de gloria* F12; Euseb. *Hieron. chron.* p. 106. 3; Ar. *Lys.* 231f–32. According to *LGPN* 2. 280 Leaena was not a common Attic name.

34. Alciphr. 4. 12; Lucian *Dial. Meretr.* 5; Suidas s.v. ἑταίραι.

35. Cf. Meineke's emendation, Ἀπγαιὁκοσθϑος.

36. See Geyer *RE* 12. 2047–48; cf. Diog. Laert. 10. 4–7 (Epicurus consorted with her); 23 (pallake of Metrodorus); Epicurus F121; Phylarchus *FGrH* 81; as one of the courtesans, including Boidion, Hedeia, and Nicidion, that visited Epicurus' gardens, Plut. *Mor.* 1089c, 1097d; 1129b; Cic. *de Nat. De.* 1. 33 (author of a book disputing Theophrastus); Plin. *HN* 35. 36. 99 (portrait by the painter Aristides); 35. 40. 144; (portrait of pensive Leontion by Theorus); Alciphr. 4. 7. *LGPN* 2. 280 shows three inscriptions with the name.

37. At Ath. 4. 157a she is called *theatrotorunē* (stage pounder); at Plut. *Demetr.* 27. 3–5, where the hetaera Demo is nicknamed Mania. For the name Melissa, cf. Lucian *Dial. meret.* 4; Alciphr. 4. 13. 6; title of play by Antiphanes F149 KA: *Anth. Pal.* 5. 27. 32; cf. red figure pyxis by Makron, Athens Acr. 560. Melissa is also the name of the daughter of Procles who acted as oenochoousa wearing only a *monochiton*, cf. Ath. 13. 589f. *LGPN* 2. 297 shows seven inscriptions with the name.

38. For her joke on a lung and prophecy, cf. 3. 107e = F91 *TrGF*; cf. [Dem.] 59. 21.

39. See also Plut. *Mor.* 849d (the most expensive prostitute, kept by Hyperides); cf. Μυρρίνα schol. Ar. *Nu.* 109, and the character Μυρρίνη in Ar. *Lys.* passim, possibly the same person as v/iv IG 1³ 1330, 8f., 15 (d. Καλλιμάχος); see *LGPN*² s.v. Μυρρίνη, nos. 7 and 9. Cf. Alciphr. 4. 5, 10, 14. 2.

40. Cf. Lucian *Dial. meret.* 2.

41. According to Ath. 592d, ancient authors frequently confused Nais with Lais.

42. For Nannion, cf. Alexis F225 KA; Amphis F23 KA; and *Anth. Pal.* 5. 207. *LGPN* 2. 325 shows four inscriptions with this name.

43. Proposed emendations: Νάνιον Musurus, Ἡλντριον (?) Kaibel, ἡ Νανιάριον Corbet.

44. For the name, cf. *Anth. Pal.* 5. 153.

45. On the confusion of Nico with Nannion, both nicknamed "Goat," see Ath. 587a; she is also mentioned at Ath. 5. 220f as the "Samian beauty"; for the name, cf. *Anth. Pal.* 5. 205, 209.

46. Athenaeus mentions another courtesan with a similar name, Nicostrata, nicknamed Scotodine (Vertigo), at 11. 467e.

47. For another hetaera named Opora, cf. Ael. *Ep.* 7 and 8; cf. also Ar. *Pax* 706–880. *LGPN* 2. 354 lists one inscription with the name.

48. Possibly also a title by Alexis, F177 = 82 KA; cf. also Ath. 3. 96a and 12. 516d; Lucian *Dial. meret.* 9; Poll. 10. 107.

49. For the hetaera named Phila associated with Hyperides, cf. also Plut. *Mor.* 849d; as the name of the daughter of Lamia and Demetrius Poliorcetes, cf. 13. 577c; on the temple of Phila Aphrodite, cf. 6. 254a.

50. Title of plays by Axionicus F5 KA and Hegemon F1 KA; as a character, cf. Men. *Georg.*; Lucian *Dial. meret.* 3; for the name, cf. Ar. *Nub.* 684 and scholion; *Anth. Pal.* 5. 258, 280.

51. Athenaeus mentions Philyra as the title of the play by Ephippus and states explicitly that it is the name of a hetaera; cf. Ath. 7. 286e; Ephippus FF21–23 KA.

52. Relying on prosopographies of Apollodorus and Herodicus, Athenaeus distinguishes two Phrynes, one from Thespiae, whose real name was Mnesarete but who had as her nickname Sarpedion (Little fish); she was the daughter of Epicles, and the mistress of Praxiteles (cf. Ath. 13. 583c and 590d). The other bears the nicknames Clausigelos (Teary Laughter) and Sestus (Fleecer); see Raubitschek *RE* 20. 893–907. As Athenaeus does not elsewhere differentiate these two women with any consistency, I have grouped all of the references to Phryne together. All ancient references to Phryne are discussed in detail in Chapter 4; cf. also Plut. *Mor.* 125a; 336d; 401a; 759f; 849e; Alciphr. 4. 1–5; Val. max. 4. 3 ext. 3b; Lucian *Catapl.* 22; Quintil. 2. 15. 9; 10. 5. 2; Galen *Protr.* 10; Sext. Emp. *Pros Grammatikous* II. 4; Phld. *Rhet.* 1. 20. 4; Arn. *Adv. Nat.* 6. 13; Clem. Alex. *Protr.* 47; Diog. Laert. 4. 7 and 6. 6; schol. Hor. *Sat.* 2. 3. 254; schol. Lucian *Amor.* 17; Eustath. 1259. 1; Ar. *Eccl.* 1101; [Longinus] *Subl.* 34.3. The name Phryne is quite uncommon, see *LGPN* 2. 466, while Mnesarete occurs several times, see *LGPN* 2. 316.

53. Archilochus F331. 2. West also refers to a woman named Pasiphile (see above); for the name, cf. Men. *Dys.* 430, *Sam.* 630; Alciphr 4. 13. 12; *Anth. Pal.* 5. 202. The name commonly appears in Greek inscriptions, see *LGPN* 2. 368.

54. On Pythionice, see Ziegler *RE* 24. 564–66; cf. Ath. 8. 339c (her love of "fish") = Antiphanes F27. 20 KA and Timocles F16 KA; Diod. Sic. 17. 108. 5 (liaison with Harpalus); Paus. 1. 37. 5 (*mnēma*).

55. For the name Rhodopis as a vase inscription, cf. ARV² p. 1616 ('Ροδο[π]ις: kale); cf. Rhodope, *Anth. Pal.* 5. 92, 219, 228, 249.

56. According to Athenaeus, there were two Sapphos, one the archaic lyric poet and the other a hetaera from Eresus (above); cf. title of play by Timocles, Ath. 8. 339c = F32 KA; Ael. *VH* 12. 19 (distinguishes between the hetaera and *poi[emacron]tria*); *Anth. Pal.* 5. 246.

57. A pipe player (*suristēs*) bears the same name at *Anth. Pal.* 5. 206.

58. It is possible that Athenaeus refers to two different women called Sinope, one who was a procuress (595a), the owner of Bacchis the auletris; she originally practiced her trade in Aegina but later moved it to Athens. The other was involved in impiety litigation according to [Dem.] 59. 19 and is mentioned frequently in Middle and New comedy. For a comic reference to her old age, cf. 8. 338f = Antiphanes F27. 12 KA. See also *LGPN* 2. 399.

59. On the name, cf. Ar. *Thesm.* 807; Plut. *Pomp.* 36 (pallakis of Mithridates); possibly the same as the auletris or orchestris Aristonice at Plut. *Mor.* 753d.
60. For the play entitled *Synoris* by Diphilus, cf. Ath. 6. 247a (where it is said to be a hetaera's name) and FF74–78 KA.
61. Mss. C and E have Τελεσιλλα instead of ms. A's Τέλεσις. The Argive poet is also mentioned at Ath. 11. 467f.
62. For the burning of Persepolis, cf. Plut. *Alex.* 38 and Diod. Sic. 17. 72; as a character, cf. Alciphr. 4. 6, 7; 4. 14. 2; 4. 19. 19; Lucian *Dial. meret.* 1 and 3; Ter. *Eun.*; for the name, cf. *Anth. Pal.* 5. 161; Prop. 2. 6. 2; *LGPN* 2. 209.
63. References to Theano at Ath. 13. 560b and 599a do not appear to refer to a hetaera, but to two different women, the wife of Pythagoras, cf. Diog. Laert. 8. 1. 42; and a celebrated prostitute, cf. Ath. 8. 339b for her love of "fish" = Antiphanes F27. 24 KA; for vases with the same name, cf. CVA Oxford 1 pl. 40, 3–4 (c. 430 BCE); Collignon Couve 1588 (c. 425 BCE); *Anth. Pal.* 5. 283.
64. Theodote is not mentioned in any of Lysias' extant speeches against Alcibiades; in connection with the latter, cf. Ath. 12. 535b; for her conversation with Socrates, cf. Ath. 5. 220e–f (Socrates' visit); Ael. *VH* 13. 32.
65. For the name, cf. Ath. 11. 471a = Theopomp. F33. 5–6 KA.
66. Athenaeus alleges that a fragment of Sophocles alludes to her: φιλη γὰρ ἡ Θεωρίς (=*TrGF* 765); Coll. Alex. p. 99 F7, 59.
67. Cf. Alciphr. 4. 14.

Courtesans and their Lovers in Book 13 of Athenaeus' *Deipnosophistae*

Male Name	Female Name	Type of Prostitute	Passage
Alcibiades	Damasandra	hetaera	574e
	Medontis	hetaera	543f
	Theodote	hetaera	574e
Alcman	Megalostrate	poetria	600f
Alexander the Great	Thais	hetaera	576d–e
	Callixeina	hetaera	435a
Andronicus, actor	Gnathaenion	hetaera	581c–d
Antigonus, the One-Eyed	Demo	eromene	578a
Antimachus, comic poet	Lyde	hetaera	597a
Apelles	Phryne	parthenos	588d
Aristippus the Socratic	Lais of Hyccara	hetaera	588c
Aristophon, rhetor	Choregis	hetaera	577b–c
Aristotle	Herpyllis	hetaera	589c
Axiochus	Medontis	hetaera	534f
Cyrus the Younger	Aspasia the Younger	hetaera	576d
Demades	Unknown	auletris	591f
Demetrius of Phalerum	Lampito	hetaera	593f
Demetrius Poliorcetes	Demo	eromene	578b
	Lamia	auletris	577c
	Leaena	hetaera	577c–d
	Mania/Melissa	eromene, hetaera	578a
	Myrrhine	auletris, hetaera	593a

Male Name	Female Name	Type of Prostitute	Passage
Demosthenes, rhetor	Lais of Hyccara	hetaera	588c
Demophon, Sophocles' *erōmenos*	Nico	hetaera	582e
Diogenes the Cynic	Lais of Hyccara	eromene	588c
Diphilus, comic poet	Gnathaena	hetaera	579e, 583f
Epicurus	Leontion	eromene, hetaera	588b
Gyges, King of Lydia	Unnamed	eromene	573a
Harmodius	Leana	eromene	596f
Harpalus	Glycera	hetaera, porne	586c, 595d
	Pythionice	hetaera	586c, 594e
Hermesianax	Leontion	eromene	597a, 598e
Hieronymus, Tyrant of Syracuse	Peitho	*ep' oikematos*	577a
Hipparchus, actor	Neaera	eromene	593f
Hyperides	Aristagora	hetaera	590d
	Myrrhine	hetaera, auletris	590d
	Phila	pseudo-hetaera	590d
Isocrates	Lagis	hetaera	592c
	Lagisca	eromene, pallake	592b
	Metaneira	eromene, hetaera	592b
Lamynthius of Miletus	Lyde	hetaera	597a
Leocrates	Eirenis	hetaera	586f
Leontiscus, Pancratiast	Mania	hetaera	578f
Lysias, rhetor	Lagis	hetaera	592c
	Metaneira	eromene	592c
Menander	Glycera	hetaera	585d, 594d
Mimnermus	Nanno	auletris	597a, 598a
Moerichus	Phryne	hetaera	583c
Nicostratus, doctor	Anticyra	hetaera	586f
Oxyartes	Timosa	pallakis	609a
Pericles	Aspasia the Elder	he anthropos	589e
Philip of Macedon	Philinna	eromene, orchestris	578a
Philonides	Nais	eromene, hetaera	592c
Phrynion of Paeania	Naeara	eromene	593f
Phyallus, Tyrant of Phocis	Bromias	auletris	605b
Plato	Archeanassa	hetaera	589c
Praxiteles	Phryne	hetaera	591a–b
Ptolemy I Soter	Thais		576e
Ptolemy II Philadelphus	Agathocleia	eromene, hetaera	576f
	Bilistiche	eromene, hetaera	576f
	Cleino	oenochoousa	576f

Ptolemy II Philadelphus	Didyme	eromene	576f
(cont.)	Mnesis	auletris	576f
	Myrtion	eromene	576f
	Potheine	auletris	576f
	Stratonice	eromene	576f
Ptolemy IV Philopater	Agathocleia	hetaera	577a
Seleucus II Callinicus	Mysta	eromene	578a, 593e
	Nysa	eromene	593e
Pyrrhus, King of Epeirus	Tigris	eromene	590a
Pythagoras	Theano	eromene	599a
Sophocles	Archippe	eromene	592b
	Erigone		598d
	Theoris	hetaera	595a
Sophron of Ephesus	Danae	eromene, hetaera	578a–b
Stephanus	Neaera		593f
	Nicarete	eromene, hetaera	593f
Stilpo	Glycera		585c–d
	Nicarete		596b
Stratocles, orator	Leme/Phylacion		596f
Theodotus, court of Philadelphus	Hippe	hetaera	583a
Xenocleides, poet	Neaera	eromene	593f

Notes

Introduction

1. From the poem *Agrippina* by D. C. von Lohenstein (1724), quoted in Benjamin 1999: 361–2.
2. Dimakis 1988: 53, "Les orateurs recherchaient la compagnie des hetaïres—et particulière-ment des plus célèbres d' entre elles—, pour la raison qu'à cette époque classique celles-ci étaient presque les seules femmes libres disposant d'une culture plus étendue et capables de discuter sur des sujets de niveau supérieur"; see also Havelock 1995: 42–49, on the courte-san Phryne.
3. On their representation in art, see Peschel 1987; Reinsberg 1993: 80–162; Stewart, A. 1997: 177–81; for their political implications, see Halperin 1990a; Davidson 1997; Kurke 1999.
4. Athenaeus has been widely misused; readers often overlook the fact that statements made by speakers do not reflect the views of the author, and that the literary quotations must be understood in their discursive context; for further discussion, see Dalby 1996: 176–7; on the importance of context for evaluating the fragments of Theopompus, especially in Athenaeus, see Flower 1994: 7.
5. Davidson 1997: 135. For a good, brief discussion of these two terms, see Peschel 1987: 19–20.
6. Kurke 1999: 175–219. The absence of prostitution vocabulary in early literary texts makes it difficult to posit a strong distinction between the discourses of the hetaera and the prosti-tute in the archaic period, not to mention to gauge the extent to which a political agenda underlies them.
7. Marx 1979: 72. I have drawn on the work of Walter Benjamin in formulating aspects of my theoretical framework; for the social type in his *Passagen-Werk*, see Buck-Morss 1986; on the prostitute as an allegory for modernity in the work of Benjamin, see Rauch 1988. I am indebted to my colleague in the German department at the University of Wisconsin, Ger-hard Richter, for bibliographical references on the subject.
8. Benjamin 1999: 361; on p. 511 he observes, "Love for the prostitute is the apotheosis of em-pathy with the commodity." See also Buck-Morss 1986: 171, "As a dialectical image, she is 'seller and commodity in one.'"
9. Ogden 1996: 102 refers to the use of pallake in this passage as "frustratingly obscure but nonetheless maintains an absolute separation between legitimate wives and all other women"; see also Henry 1985: 3–5.
10. For a complete list of ancient Greek words for prostitute, consult Schneider 1913: 1331, who includes, in addition to hetaera and porne, the terms *apopharsis, deiktērias, dēmiour-gos, dēmia, dromas, gephuris, kapraina, kasalbas, kasalbē, kasaura, kasōris, koriskē, lesitos, leōphoros, lōgas, machlas, machlis, paidiskē, pandosia, peripolis, porneutria, pōlos, skammas, spodēsilaura, statē, stegis, tegitis, chamaitupē, chametairis.*

203

11. For an excellent discussion of prostitution terminology in this oration, see Miner 2003.
12. On the opposition of hetaera and porne, see Hauschild 1933: 7–9; Herter 1957: 1154, 1181–82, and 1960: 83; Peschel 1987: 19–20; Harvey 1988: 249; Calame 1989: 103–4; Dover 1989: 20–21.
13. Cohen 2002 similarly characterizes the terms porne and hetaera as a "complementary antithesis."
14. The table reflects searches of Greek stems for the words given in the left column in the *Thesaurus Linguae Graecae* database. The number of works in which prostitution terms appear is found in the first row (top). Given the many duplicated passages in the corpus, these statistics are somewhat inflated. Figures do not include masculine forms such as *hetairos, pornos* and *erōmenos*.
15. It is extremely doubtful, given the presence of the word *erōmenas* in the first line, that the composition dates prior to the last quarter of the fourth century.
16. I base this assertion on the adjective *ōnētē* (purchased) that modifies pallake at *Od.* 14. 202 and on the fact the term does not describe the concubines of Achilles and Agamemnon, the spear captives Briseis and Chryseis; in fact it appears only in the context of foreigners, e.g., Phoenix' narrative (Hom. *Il.* 9. 449, 452) and Odysseus' Cretan tale (*Od.* 14. 203).
17. For a detailed discussion of this poem, see Kurke 1999: 187–190.
18. For this view in connection with the pseudo-Demosthenic *Neaera*, see Miner 2003.
19. On hetaera as an all-inclusive term, see Gomme and Sandbach 1973: 30; Kapparis 1999: 422–32; and Cohen 2002; on the overlap between the two terms, and analysis of their distinctions in [Dem.] 59, see Miner, 2003; on slaves owned by the pornoboskos, a stock character in New comedy, such as Habrotonon in *Epitrepontes* and Philotis at *Kolax* 117, see Webster 1974: 32.
20. The term hetaera could be used by a women of a female friend; indeed, it appears the to have been the preferred designation of the women poets; cf. *philai . . . etairai*, Sappho F142. 1; *etairais tais emais*, 160.1; *eman hadeian hetairan*, Erinna F2. 2; *moi ha sunetairis*, F5. 7; cf. Pind. *Pyth.* 3.18, 9.19; Ar. *Eccl.* 23, 528; *Lys.* 701. Athenaeus comments that freeborn matrons and respectable girls, even in his own time, used this term in referring to their intimate friends (571d).
21. Ussher 1973 ad loc states, "the counterpart here, almost, of *hetaira*."
22. For a detailed discussion, see Kurke 1999: 175–8 and 220–7.
23. The use of *ergazomai* and cognates to refer to prostitution appears throughout classical literature; consider also the phraseology used of Neaera's profession in the Demosthenic oration: *ergazomenē men ēdē tōi sōmati*, [Dem.] 59. 22. 9–10; cf. 59. 30, 32, 37, 49. See also Davidson 1997: 84, and 112–3, for discussion of this term, and its cognate, *ergastērion* (brothel).
24. The play on hetaera and hetaeros appears to have been a standard joke; cf. Ath. 6. 260f, where a quoted passage of Theopompus describes the licentious friends of Philip as "female companions (*hetairas*), not male companions (*hetairous*), ground-beaters (*chamaitupas*) not soldiers."
25. Brown 1990: 263, n. 38; see also Gomme-Sandbach 1973: 30, 515; and Post 1940: 445. The patrons of Greek courtesans served much the same function as the *danna* of Japanese geisha; as one woman observes, "a *danna* and a customer are quite different. The *danna* is like your husband. You have a proper arrangement with him"; see Downer 2001: 174.
26. On the similarities of hetaeras to wives, especially in their control of visual economy, see Davidson 1997: 125, and 132–3; contra Ogden 1996: 102. Brown 1990: 249 argues that the hetaera could transition back and forth out of concubinage quite fluidly, while the pallake probably did not originate as a prostitute. Wolff 1944: 74, citing [Dem.] 59. 118 and Isaeus 3, claims that the hetaera who became a pallake did not cease to be a hetaera. Fantham 1975: 65 n. 47 finds the term pallake to be "archaic and technical." For a similar blurring of boundaries in Roman society, see Edwards 1997: 81 and 93, n. 61.
27. Xen. *Anab.* 4. 3. 20, 5. 4. 33; cf. also Ath. 13. 573a.
28. Cohen 2002 argues that the term porne was synonymous with doule (slave); however, a slave prostitute, as evident in Herodotus' account of Rhodopis, could become a hetaera; see also Citti 1997.
29. Frequent reference is made to the pornoboskos in Attic Middle and New comedy; cf. Diphilus FF43. 38–40 and 87 KA; Nicostratus F26 KA; Sophilus F6; Men. *Kitharista* 41

Sandbach; *Kolax* 83. 120–32 Sandbach (speech of character). There were also several plays of that title, by Anaxilas, Dioxippus (for testimonia, cf. PCG 5. 44), Eubulus FF88–89 KA. Theophr. *Char.* mentions brothel keepers in connection with *aponoias* (shamelessness, 6. 5. 1) and *aēdias* (bad taste, 20. 10. 5).

30. For the use of the phrase *ho boulomenos* to describe the clientele of prostitutes, cf. Andoc. 1. 100. 2, where the speaker accuses his opponent of "doing anyone who wants it" for not very much money at Andoc. 1. 100. 2; cf. Ath. 13. 595c in connection with the hetaera/porne Pythionice.

31. On the negative representation of prostitutes in Attic oratory, especially as symbols of extravagance, see Glazebrook 2002.

32. On the expense involved in keeping a hetaera, see Davidson 1997: 194–205; Post 1940: 445; Cohen 2002 estimates that a single evening with a high class hetaera might have cost as much as $500–1000 U.S. Downer 2001: 171–6 discusses the prohibitive cost of keeping a geisha, estimated at around $200,000 to $300,000 per year in modern U.S. currency.

33. For other examples of hetaeras as a symbol of male prodigality, cf. Lys. 14. 25; Andoc. 4. 14. 3.

34. For forms of *hetairein*, cf. Aeschin. 1. 13. 5, 13. 11; 19. 1, 20. 5, 21. 1, 21. 9, 29. 7; 42. 51. 5, 52. 7. 160. 1 and 4. 161. 7, 163. 2, 164. 3; and 5. 165. 3, 165. 6; cf. *hetairēsonta*, Lys. 3. 24. 4; *paidos hētairēkotos*, Ar. *Pax* 11; *hētairēkōs*, Dem. 22. 29. 3, 30. 7, 61. 6, 73. 5; *hētairēkasin*, Lys. 14. 41. 5; *hētairēsas*, Andoc. 1. 100. 2.

35. For cognates of *porneuein*, cf. Aeschin. 1. 29, 52. 9, 70. 5, 79. 9, 94. 3, 119. 8, 136. 3, 137. 6, 154. 9, 155. 6, 159. 9, 188. 2 and 189. 4.

36. Dover 1989: 21 observes that the terms *hetairein* and *hetairesis* "do not seem to have been used of a hetaira, but exclusively of a man or boy who played a homosexual role analogous to that of the hetaira." It is unclear whether the participles at Ar. *Pax* 11 and Lys. 3. 24 allude to citizen prostitutes or others. For fourth-century references to this verb in relation to citizen prostitution, cf. Dem. 45. 79; 46. 26; Aeschin. 1. 19. 1, 13. 5, 13. 11, 20. 5, 21. 1, 12.

37. For the phrase, cf. [Dem.] 59. 24, 25. 10, 28. 12, 48. 3, 48. 6, 12–13. Kapparis 1995: 21 points out that although the construction with the particle *an* implies a hypothetical situation, for the orator, Neaera's presence at the symposium provides "clear evidence that she was a courtesan"; he recommends deletion of *an* because it implies she was not a courtesan. Miner 2003 shows that Apollorus' use of the phrase *hōs an* with the participle indicates that Neaera was not yet a hetaera, although she behaved like one.

38. Verbal forms of porne in the fifth century only appear in Herodotus, in connection with the prostitution of girls; cf. *porneuontai*, Hdt. 1. 93.10; *kataporneuousi*, 1. 94. 2; *kataporneuei*, 1. 196. 30–31.

39. Both Athenaeus and the Hellenistic poet Machon, whom he quotes, frequently use the verb *hetairein* of women; cf. *hetairein*, Ath. 13. 581c; *hetairousēs*, 586f; *hetairizoumenē*, 593b.

40. Brown 1990: 263 n. 37 observes that pallake appears infrequently in comedy, although Alexis and Menander wrote comedies entitled *Pallake*, and Diphilus wrote one called *Pallakis*, plays that may have served as prototypes for Naevius' *Paelex*; see Arnott 1996: 512. For Menander's *Pallake*, see FF318–321 Körte. The noun pallake is also found at Men. *Sam.* 508 and *Pseud.* F453 Körte; for other fourth-century references, cf. Dem. 23. 53, 55; [Dem.] 59. 118, 122. On slave and free concubines, see Wolff 1944: 73–75; Harrison 1968: 13–15; Bushala 1969; MacDowell 1978: 89–90; Sealey 1984; and Henry 1985.

41. On the pallake as a woman kept within the household, see Bushala 1969; Patterson 1990; and Miner 2003.

42. Plut. *Per.* 24. 6; Cratinus fr. 246–48 and 259 KA; see also the discussions of Patterson 1990: 55 and n. 61; and Henry 1995: 20–2, who has made a strong case for Aspasia as a pallake, and not a hetaera. Indeed, Book 13 of the *Deipnosophistae* supports Henry's view as it never uses prostitution terminology in connection with her, nor does it deal very extensively with her stories.

43. On auletrides generally, see Davidson 1997: 80–2. Justin. 36. 4. 6 states that Aristonicus' courtesan mother was the daughter of a cithera player; Jerome *In Danielem* 11. 13–14 describes the lover of Ptolemy Philopater, Agathocleia, as a psaltria; cf. Habrotonon at Men. *Epitrep.* 621 Sandbach. According to Plut. *Mor.* 753d, Aristonica, mistress of Philopater, Oenanthe and Agathocleia, lovers of Philadelphus, were orchestrides, as was Philinna, mistress of Philip II; cf. Ath. 13. 577f–578a; Justin. 9. 8. 2. Myrtion, another courtesan associ-

ated with Philadelphus, was a mime actress (*deiktērias*, Ath. 13. 576e–f); she is also referred to as a *theatrotorunē* at Ath. 4. 157a. See Ogden 1999: 259–60. For general background, see Schneider 1913: 1341–2. On their sexual favors, see Olson and Sens 1999: 151–2; cf. Ar. *Ach.* 1197–202, 1216–7, 1220–1; *Vesp.* 1345–6; *Ran.* 543–44; Metagenes F4 KA.

44. On this term, see Olson and Sens 1999: 151.

45. On the word *thaumatopoios* generally, see Olson and Sens 1999: 142–3.

46. Cf. Ath. 13. 589f, where the courtesan Melissa is described as dressed in Peloponnesian fashion, wearing a *monochitōn* while she acting as wine-pourer for the workmen in the fields.

47. For Lamia, cf. Plut. *Demetr.* 16 and 27; Ath. 3. 101e (quoting Lynceus of Samos), 4. 128b (Lynceus), 13. 577c–f (including Machon F13) and 14. 614e–f (including Phylarchus *FGrH* 81 F12) and Alciphron 4. 16. Other auletrides in Book 13 include Mnesis and Potheine, lovers of Ptolemy Philadelphus (576e); Boa, mother of Philataerus, King of Pergamum (577b); and Bromias, mistress of Phaÿllus, tyrant of Phocis (605b). On flute players associated with the Hellenistic monarchs, see Ogden 1999: 258–9. Davidson 1997: 82 and 329 n. 27 maintains that the term auletris was synonymous with "cheap prostitute" by the end of the fourth century.

48. Davidson 1997: 81 and 328 n. 22; see also Herter 1960: 86 n. 290; cf. Metagenes F4 K-A; Theopomp. *FGrH* 115 F290; Ar. *Ach.* 551.

49. For auletris in fifth-century texts: in oratory, cf. Isoc. *Aereopagiticus* 48. 2, *Antid.* 287. 3 and Lys. 4. 7; in comedy, cf. Ar. *Ach.* 551; *Vesp.* 1219, 1368, 1369; *Ran.* 513; Archippus F27 KA; Aristagoras, *Mammacuthus* or Metagenes, *Aurae* F4 KA; and Plato Comicus F170 KA; in history and philosophy, cf. Xen. *Symp.* 2. 1. 3, 2. 2. 2, 2. 22. 8, 6. 5. 1; Pl. *Tht.* 173d; *Symp.* 176e, 212c, d, 215c; and *Prt.* 347d. For fourth-century references: in oratory, cf. Dem. 21. 36. 6, Aeschin. 1. 42. 6, 75. 9; Hyp. 4. col. 19. 18; F142 Jensen; in history and philosophy, cf. Arist. *An. Post.* 78b31; *Ath. Pol.* 50. 2. 3; Theophr. *Char.* 11. 7. 1; 19. 10. 2; in comedy, cf. Amphis, *Gynaikomania* F9; Antiphanes, FF50 (play title), 224, and 233 KA; Epicrates, *Antilais* F2 KA; Nicostratus, F27 KA; Philemon F44 KA; Men. *Pk.* 340 Sandbach; *Sam.* 730 Sandbach; *Methe* F264 Körte; as the title of a lost play, see Körte 1953: 38. For the visual evidence, see Peschel 1987: figures 189–245.

50. For *erōmenos* in the major philosophical sources, cf. Xen. *Symp.* 8. 3, 11. 2, 14. 1, 16. 1, 25. 6, 28. 1, 34. 7, 35. 3, 36. 5; *Cyr.* 5. 1. 12; *Hiero* 1. 37. 2; Pl. *Euth.* 14c; *Symp.* 178e, 180b; 183c; 184a; 185c; 204c; *Phdr.* 231b–c, 232a, c; 233b; 238e; 239a, e; 240d; 245b; 252c–e; 253a; 254a; 255b; 263c; *Rep.* 403b; *Leg.* 837c–d; Arist. *An. Pr.* 70a; *Eth. Eud.* 1233b10; 1235a15; 1238b38; 1244a19; 1246a19; *Eth. Nic.* 1157a6; 1159b16; 1164a5–7; *Rhet.* 1370b20–22; 1373a17; 1391a5. In the orators, cf. Dem. 61. 3. 1; Aeschin. 1. 159.

51. Henry 1985: 97 interprets this passage as employing the stereotype of the crafty, wicked prostitute.

52. For a discussion of this fragmentary play, see Henry 1985: 102–108.

53. Arnott 1996: 51–54 speculates about the title and plot of this lost play.

54. Webster 1974: 13–17; Fantham 1975: 56 puts it this way: "love between a youth and girl was easier to contrive if the girl, though born a citizen and eligible for marriage, had lost her identity through kidnapping or had been rescued as a foundling, and was already living as a non-citizen."

55. The women described exclusively by the term eromene in Athenaeus Book 13 include the mistresses of Seleucus the Younger, Mysta and Nysa, those of Ptolemy II Philadelphus, Didyme and Stratonice; Demo, mistress of Antigonus the One-Eyed, and possibly his son, Demetrius Poliorcetes; and Tigris, mistress of Pyrrhus.

Chapter 1

1. Sigmund Freud, on Armistice Day, 1918, quoted by J. M. Coetzee, "The Emperor of Nostalgia," *New York Times Book Review*, February 28, 2002.

2. Several discussions of the Second Sophistic have appeared in the last decade: see Anderson 1993; Woolf 1994; Swain 1996; Goldhill 2001; Alcock et al. 2001. On the name and the period encompassed by Second Sophistic, see Bowersock 1969: 8–9; Van Groningen 1965: 41.

3. Stewart, S. 1993: 145–6 discusses how nostalgic desire always involves loss and seeks to close the gap between resemblance and identity, the lived experience and its signification or copy.

4. See Whitmarsh 2000: 271 on the need for "self-definition against the past" and Porter 2001: 90 on the "shared problems of definition."

5. Bowie 1970; Swain 1996: 6–7, and *passim*.

6. Bowie 1970: 28; see also Humphreys 1997: 217, on the importance of ruins to the Greeks, "Ancient Greeks . . . were constantly renegotiating their relations with the past. Both public and sacred spaces were full of records, relics and monuments. The political process constantly generated new documents on stone, yet also singled out great moments of past history for a privileged place in discourse."

7. As Humphreys 1997: 209 observes, "fixation on material traces of the past, like fixation on fragments, is also a form of fetishism"; cf. Porter 2001; Stewart, S. 1993: 163–4; for the concept of fetishism and commodification, see Marx 1979: 72–3.

8. Bowie 1970: 22 notes that Pausanias does not deal with monuments and dedications later than 150 B.C.E.

9. In Bowie's view, Athens' new wealth only aggravated the absence of political power, even as it provoked a nostalgia for a glorious past; see Bowie 1970: 39. Although Gabba 1982: 65 is keen to advance his argument that Roman dominion paved the way for this Hellenic revival, he does in the end concede that some members of the Greek upper classes "emphasized their glorious past in defiance of Roman domination."

10. Swain 1996: 105, 113; Woolf 1994: 125.

11. The end of Dio Chrysostom's *Euboean Oration* equates prostitution with other immoral urban activities such as pederasty, adultery, and premarital sex; cf. *Orationes* 7. 133–152. The strong association of the prostitute with the city is widespread in Near Eastern and other texts: in the *Epic of Gilgamesh*, the prostitute initiates the wild man Enkidu into human society while the Hebrew Bible is filled with images of the city as prostitute; cf. Isaeus 15–16. Chapter 2 examines the Greek practice of naming prostitutes and courtesans after major cities, such as Abydus, Anticyra, Scione, Nysa, and Olympia.

12. On the hetaera as a metaphor for corrupt literary style, see Edwards 1997: 81; cf. Tac. *Dial.* 26; Sen. *Helv.* 6. 2; Plut. *Mor.* 142b.

13. McKechnie 1989: 154, in his discussion of the role of traveling specialists—courtesans, philosophers, actors, and cooks—depicted in late fourth-century literature, observes, "probably the people ensuring Athenian cultural predominance in this area were drawn largely from the outside, just a philosophers were."

14. Woolf 1994: 128 observes, "Greeks felt themselves to be Greeks, in a sense that was not wholly compatible with being Roman, while at the same time adopting much Roman material culture," and further, on p. 131, "the Romans made no assault on the defining characteristics of Hellenism"; see also Dihle 1994: 345–346; Swain 1996: 9, 327 describes this isolationism as a "a complete disregard of Roman literature, art, and culture."

15. Woolf 1994: 119; cf. Cic. *Ad Quintum fratrem* 1. 1. 27.

16. Plin. *HN* 3. 39; Swain 1996: 120.

17. As Braund 2000: 19 observes, "nowhere in the *Deipnosophistae* is there any sign of significant conflict between Greek and Roman identities." For this reason, Swain 1996: 11–12 omits him from his study. Whitmarsh 2000, on the other hand, argues that Athenaeus exemplifies the Greek need for refuge in the past, a notion implicit in Bowie 1970: 18 and explicit in Swain 1996: 49–51.

18. Bowie 1970; on *paideia* and the emergence of the Greek elite, see Swain 1996: 40 and *passim*; on the romanization of the East, see Woolf 1994; on fluctuating identities, see Whitmarsh 2001. Although Anderson 1993: 101 calls for a modification of Bowie's view, Gabba 1982 remains the most convincing alternative to Bowie.

19. Bowie 1970; Woolf 1994: 125.

20. Bowie 1970: 23; Porter 2001: 76 reframes this idea along psychoanalytical lines, as an escapist fantasy or displacement in response to the politics of the present.

21. Woolf 1994: 118; Whitmarsh 2001: 272.

22. Swain 1996: 21 and *passim* shows how linguistic practice and cultural knowledge distinguished elite Greeks from the lower classes; Gabba 1982 seems to suggest that the shared cultural heritage of educated Greeks and Romans elided other cultural distinctions. It should also be noted that a decade earlier, Bowie 1970: 4 had also emphasized the unity of the Greco-Roman upper-class during this period.

23. Van Groningen 1965: 49–50; Bowersock 1969: 1 describes these pedagogical exercises as "over-elaborated productions on unreal, unimportant, or traditional themes. . . . rhetorical showpieces."
24. Anderson 1993: 10; Dihle 1994: 346.
25. See Anderson 1993: 50–51 on the importance of the encomium in rhetorical education in the Sophistic period. On sophistic paradox generally, see Van Groningen 1965: 49–51; Anderson 1993: 171–3; on Favorinus, see Whitmarsh 2001: 295.
26. According to Bowersock 1969: 11, the professions of the philosopher and rhetor were quite "conflated and confused" in this period.
27. Philostratus *VS* 579; Bowersock 1969: 17, 20; Bowie 1970: 5.
28. Bowersock 1969: 30; Anderson 1993: 24; Woolf 1994: 125.
29. Philostratus, *VS* 484; Swain 1996: 98–9; Anderson 1993: 1 describes sophists as "established public speakers who offered a predominantly rhetorical form of higher education." While the sophists of the Roman empire continued the quarrel between philosophy and rhetoric, the two disciplines gradually became fused during this period; see Anderson 1993: 134, 142.
30. Dihle 1994: 346; see also Bowie 1970: 3.
31. I have not been able to ascertain the extent to which actual hetaeras populated Greek cities in the late second century C.E. The term very infrequently occurs in such Second Sophistic authors as Achilles Tatius (8. 3. 3; 8. 10. 2), Favorinus (F112. 1), Heliodorus (*Aeth.* 1. 10. 4), and Philostratus (*VA* 1. 13. 28; 1. 34. 30; 5. 29. 31; 8. 7. 238); the latter almost always associates her with contexts of drinking and carousing (*kōmazein; paizein*). The word does not appear at all in the New Testament, only porne and its cognates are found. In any case, this figure appears to be associated with an antiquated social and literary milieu.
32. Anderson 1993: 183–4 argues that the decline of drama led to the detachment of characters from their dramatic context and allowed them to stand independently in *ethopoeia*; because "they are the character types least likely to epitomise the genuine cultural heritage of classical Athens, there is a certain perverse sophistication in allowing them to do so."
33. Cf. Ath. 5. 187c–188d; 219d–220a and 13. 563d–566e; 605d; cf. also Pl. *Leg.* 841d.
34. Plut. *Mor.* 712c; Swain 1996: 126–7; for the shift towards heterosexuality and new attitudes towards marriage in the second century C.E., see Foucault 1988: 72–80.
35. The tiresome debate over the dating of the *Deipnosophistae* is one worthy of Ulpian. Athenaeus states in one address to Timocrates that they are living in the time of the Emperor Commodus (12. 537f), that is, between 180 and 192 C.E. Another remark refers to the death of Ulpian, which, if the famous jurist, would necessitate a dramatic date prior to 223 C.E. By the same reasoning, if Galen is also a historical personage, the conversations would have had to take place prior to his death in 199 C.E. The current view places the date of the banquet around 192 C.E., for which see Dihle 1994: 345–46; Dalby 1996: 168; and Anderson 1997. For a detailed discussion of the issues, see in particular Baldwin 1976 and 1977. Because I believe that the sophists at Athenaeus' table are meant as aggregates of both fictional and historical characters, precise dating of the text is not central to my argument.
36. On the Codex, see now Arnott 2000: 42–7; see also Kaibel 1887: 1. vii; Gulick 1927: 1. xvii–xviii.
37. Wilkins 2000: 23 convincingly argues that the text originally consisted of 15 books, rather than the 30 posited by Kaibel.
38. Dalby 1996: 174–5. Gulick's text, considered authoritative for Books 11–15 of the *Deipnosophistae*, has been adopted throughout.
39. Whitmarsh 2000: 305 bases this observation on Dupont 1977: 9–16.
40. On the *gelōtopoios* as a conventional figure of the symposium, cf. Pl. *Symp.* 189b; Ath. 5. 187c; Martin, J. 1931: 57.
41. Cf. Xen. *Symp.* 4. 28, *eskōpsan te kai espoudasan*; cf. Dio Chrys. *Or.* 55. 11; Martin, J. 1931: 4–10. Consider also the *skōmmata* between Socrates and Charmides at Xen. *Symp.* 4. 28 (*eskōpsan te kai espoudasan*) and that of Socrates and Antisthenes at 8. 4.
42. Lukinovich 1982: 230–231 argues that Athenaeus intends his work as an ironic polemic against the Socratic tradition; Relihan 1992: 220 observes that Plato's *Symposium* is in fact an aberration of the genre, since the interlocutors refuse the normal entertainments of the symposium. See also Wilkins 2000: 23–4 on Athenaeus' desire to improve upon the Platonic symposium; cf. Ath. 5. 186d–193d; 11. 504c–509d.

43. Olson and Sens 1999: 4 argue that the title of Matro's work is a "modern invention" drawn from Ath. 4. 134d–137c.
44. For a discussion of both poetic and prose versions of the *deipnon*, see Martin 1931: 156–157. On Matro of Pitane, cf. Ath. 1. 5b; 2. 62c, 64c; 3. 73d–e; 4. 134d–137c; 6. 243a; 14.656e; for a translation of the text with commentary, see Olson and Sens 1999. Henry 1995: 59 and 61 comments that the fragment of the parody preserved by Athenaeus gives "food a feminized sexuality . . . representing prostitutes and their customers prominently in the poem." The passage clearly plays on animal slang for prostitutes with words like *aphuē* (sardine), also a generic term for hetaera; see the discussion of nicknames in Chapter 2, especially pp. 72–73.
45. On Hippolochus, cf. 4. 128a; cf. 3. 100f; 101e–f; 4.128b; see also Martin 1931: 157–160.
46. For libraries and Athenaeus, see Jacob 2000; especially useful is his comparison of Athenaeus' text and genre to a Roman library.
47. Anderson 1997: 2180 argues that Rome remains characteristically at the margin of Athenaeus' world. Roman allusions include the recognition of being Greek in a Roman empire (3. 121f); Roman luxury (6. 272d–275b); peacocks at Rome (14. 654d); Roman foundation legend and Janus (15. 692d); a Latin word serves as a springboard for an Attic allusion (6. 224c); Cynulcus mentions his residence at Rome (3. 121f). For more examples and a general discussion, see Braund 2000, especially p. 21.
48. Baldwin 1977: 38; Relihan 1992: 223.
49. Entertainers in the *Deipnosophistae* include: Amoebeus (14. 622d); unnamed rhapsodes (14. 620b); unnamed *gelōtopoioi* (4. 613d); *planoi* (jugglers; 14. 615e); *philoskōpountes* (14. 616b); *hilarodists* (14. 620d). It is unclear whether *planoi* and *hilarodists* are actually present and *philoskōpountes* could simply refer to the diners; whereas rhapsodes and *gelōtopoioi* do seem to be present; see Martin, J. 1931: 51–64. On the uninvited guest, cf. 7. 307f; 14. 622d; cf. also Lucian *Symp.* 20; Pl. *Symp.* 212d; Martin, J. 1931: 64–79, 92–7; Baldwin 1977: 41; and Relihan 1992: 215. The unnamed weeper appears at 4. 129f. Heavy drinkers include Ulpian (15. 668f); Leonides (11. 504b); and Proteus (4. 129e).
50. Dalby 1996: 169; Kaibel 1887–1890, and the Budé editor, Desrousseaux 1956: xii–xix view the characters as fictional; Gulick 1927: 1. xi–xii asserts that Athenaeus' practice is "to take a well-known historical personage and attribute to him different traits from those he was known to possess." In contrast, Baldwin 1976 and 1977 argues that all of the sophists are based on historical persons. Reviving the view of Dittenberger 1903, Baldwin 1976 identifies Ulpian as the father of the celebrated jurist; on Galen, see Baldwin 1977: 38. He further argues for Larensis as "a real character with an Antonine career"; see Baldwin 1977: 37.
51. Baldwin 1977: 38; Bowersock 1969: 14 argues that the term sophist in Athenaeus has a purely honorific function. See also Anderson 1997: 2174
52. For Daphnus, cf. 2. 51a, 3. 120b–121e; 7. 276d; 8. 355a–359d; and Dionysocles, cf. 3. 96d; 3. 116d–f.
53. On doctors in Athenaeus and other symposiac works, see Martin, J. 1931: 79–92; Baldwin 1977: 43.
54. Baldwin 1977: 44. For Leonidas, cf. 3. 96d; 3. 116a; 9. 367d–368f; 11. 504b; 13. 558e–560f.
55. Lukinovich 1990: 264–5 stresses the orderly plan of the banquet; Reardon 1971: 227 characterizes it as anarchic: "Athénée se soucie peu de la forme; il ne fait qu' accumuler des faits tout particulièrement divers. Et c'est là seule 'méthode.' Véritable anti-méthode. C'est une preuve que la simple érudition plaisait." On the relation of the speeches to the sequencing of Athenaeus' symposium, see Milanezi 2000: 402. See also Relihan 1992: 22 and Pellizer 1990: 179–80.
56. Lukinovich 1982: 232; Dalby 1996: 170–1.
57. For this view, see Dihle 1994: 345; on the number of quotations from tragedy, see Collard 1969: 168; on allusions to fifth-century comedy, see Sidwell 2000: 137.
58. Cf. Aul. Gell. *NA* praef. 11, "For all of them, and in particular the Greeks, after wide and varied reading, with a white line, as the saying goes, that is with no effort to discriminate, swept together whatever they had found, aiming at mere quantity. The perusal of such collections will exhaust the mind through weariness or disgust, before it finds one or two notes which it is a pleasure to read, or inspiring to have read, or helpful to remember" (trans. Rolfe).
59. On quotation in Athenaeus, see Anderson 1997: 2174–75; on his accuracy, see Zepernick 1921; Collard 1969; Brunt 1980; Ambaglio 1990; and Arnott 2000: 41.

60. Hertz 1983: 591 in his study of Longinus, argues that the "violent fragmentation of literary bodies into 'quotations' " serves to build up one's own discourse in a continual process of disintegration and figurative restoration; on the function of quotation in literary texts, see also Stewart, S. 1993: 19–20.

61. Out of more than 180 named authors in Book 13 of the *Deipnosophistae*, 34 are comic poets, 38 are historians, 25 are biographers or prosopographers, and 13 are orators. Among the 239 titles mentioned, 104 refer to comedies, 33 to historical works, 7 to biographies and prosopographies (including those of hetaeras), 20 to oratories or rhetorical works, 10 to geographical or archaeological works. Four authors of erotic treatises are also mentioned (with titles such as *Peri tōn Erotikōn Homoiōn, Peri Erotikōn*), including Ariston of Ceos, Clearchus of Soli, Heraclides Pontus, and Theophrastus.

62. Anderson 1997: 2175–6; see also Bowie 1974: 166–209.

63. On Middle comedy as a genre, see Wehrli 1936; Webster 1970; Sandbach 1977: 55–60; Handley 1985; Nesselrath 1990.

64. The most extensive work on courtesans in ancient Greece has focused on the comic genres, starting with Hauschild 1933 and Wehrli 1936: 21–8. Most of this research has examined social status, terminology, and characterization: Fantham 1975: 49–52 discusses the social and political status of prostitutes; Henry 1985: 34 argues that their representation in Attic comedy became increasingly glamorized and humanized as the fourth century progressed; Brown 1990 argues against categorizing the hetaera as either good or bad; on the marriage plot, see Konstan 1987 and Wiles 1989.

65. Names such as Cyrene (Ar. *Ran.* 1325–28; *Thesm.* 98), Salabaccho (*Eq.* 763–66; *Thesm.* 805), and Cynna probably did refer to actual courtesans as part of comic invective (*Eq.* 763–66; *Vesp.* 1015–1035; *Pax* 1030–1037; see Henry 1985: 13–6).

66. According to Brown 1990: 254, Menander's representation of courtesans conforms to conventions already well-established by Anaxilas, Antiphanes, and others; *contra* Henry 1985; cf. also Plut. *Mor.* 712b–d.

67. Plut. *Mor.* 712b–c contrasts the crude sexuality and obscenity of Attic Old comedy with that of Menandrian New comedy; cf. Arist. *Nic. Eth.* 1128a22.

68. On the difficulty of distinguishing real persons from invented characters in comedy, see Webster 1952: 23; and Henry 1985: 15.

69. Schneider 1913; Webster 1952: 23–24: 1335. For a recent list of Middle and New comedies that took their titles from the names of hetaeras, see Ath. 5. 567c; and Hawley 1993: 88 n. 4.

70. Cooper 1995: 303 and notes 2–3 discusses biographical fictions in oratory; on the fictionality of women in the genre, see Gagarin 2001; on Neaera, see Patterson 1994: 208 and Miner 2003.

71. On Aspasia's trial, cf. Ath. 13. 589e; Plut. *Per.* 32. 1–6; Hermippus F5 KA; for a discussion of this trial and its sources, see Henry 1995: 24–5; and Cooper 1995: 315.

72. For the idea that the disrobing scene was invented after the trial of Phryne, see Cooper 1995: 312–8; and the extended discussion of this trial at the end of Chapter 4, pp. 132–136.

73. Schaps 1977: 326 n. 10. Other fragments of Hyperides include the names of the hetaeras Timandra (F164–65 Jensen); Glycera (F121 Jensen); Mica (F125 Jensen); and the freedwoman Demetria (F99 Jensen).

74. On Satyrus and his oeuvre, see Lefkowitz 1983; on the importance of his work for the study of hetaeras, see Henry 1995: 61.

75. Out of 598 lines of Theopompus' text, 412 are quoted by Athenaeus; see Flower 1994: 8 and *passim.*

76. For the fragments of Polemon, see Preller 1964.

77. For this theory, see Jacoby 1955: 3b. 113–5; Henry 1995: 61–3 and 157, n. 15; cf. Ath. 13. 567c, where Cynulcus directly links the knowledge of courtesans' names with an ability to gloss names in comedy. For the treatises mentioned in Athenaeus' Book 13, cf. *FGrH* 244 F208–12 (Apollodorus); 349 T1–2 (Antiphanes); 350 T1–2 (Ammonius); 348 TA (Callistratus); 347 T1–2 (Aristophanes of Byzantium); Gorgias of Athens 351 T1–3, F1.

78. For Brendel 1970: 64 and n. 67, these treatises reflect the Hellenistic interest in systematization and compilation; for discussion, see also Henry 1995: 61–2.

79. No fragments of this text remain; see Henry 1995: 63 and 157 n. 15.

80. On Lynceus, see Kebric 1977: 2–5; on these authors and the genre of the *apomnemoneumata*, see Henry 1995: 58–9.

81. Gow 1965: 19–21; Ogden 1999: 226 and notes 65–6.
82. For this traditional debate, cf. Thgn. 1345–50; Meleager, *Anth. Pal.* 5. 208; Rufinus, *Anth. Pal.* 5. 19. See also Martin, J. 1931: 127–139; Pellizer 1990: 182; and Hawley 1993: 82–3.
83. On the ridicule of intellectuals, cf. Ath. 4. 134b–c; see also Anderson 1993: 176–179.
84. Dio. Chrys. *Or.* 32. 9; Krueger 1996: 230; cf. Dudley 1967: 143.
85. Branham and Goulet-Cazé 1996: 10; Dudley 1998: 114.
86. Anderson 1997: 2174 argues that the relationship between Myrtilus and Cynulcus may reflect a social reality in Imperial Roman circles, that Cynic advocates could "take on the sophists"; cf. Philostratus *VS* 563f.
87. Davidson 1997: 106 borrows this term from Athenaeus to refer to "the rich and famous ones, the ones catalogued in scholarly treatises, who had plays written about them and speeches composed on their behalf, the ones whose *bon mots* were recorded in anecdotal collections."
88. On the meaning of *pornographos* in this passage, see Henry 1992: 261 and 2000: 503–4. On Aristides, cf. Plin. *HN* 35. 98; on Pausias, cf. Plin. *HN* 35. 123. Brendel 1970: 67 n. 70 discusses the scant evidence for Hellenistic erotic art catalogues and links them to the prosopographical treatises.
89. On the polygamous Macedonian kings, see Tronson 1984; Greenwalt 1989; and Carney 1991: 154–6.
90. On the mistresses of Ptolemy II Philadelphus, see Polyb. 14. 11. 2; Fraser 1972: II. 818 n. 165; Pomeroy 1984: 53–4; Ogden 1999: 221–3.
91. Didyme, according to Ptolemy Euergetes (Ath. 13. 575e–f = *FGrH* 234 F4), was a native woman, e.g., Egyptian, described as "black" in *Anth. Pal.* 5. 210; see Cameron 1990: 287–92; on his loves generally, see Ogden 1999: 73–4.
92. Diog. Laert. 5. 76 states that he received this nickname from Lamia and an unnamed courtesan.

Chapter 2

1. Hdt. 2. 135.
2. Schneider 1913: 1362–1371; several discussions of hetaeras have almost completely overlooked the importance of their names; they are only briefly mentioned by Davidson 1997: 118–9; 115 and 133; and Kurke 1999: 198, 202, 205–7. Webster 1974: 94–6 discusses names and nicknames in Middle comedy, and Ogden 1999: 247–52 has a good section on the courtesans associated with the Hellenistic monarchs. Henry 1985 makes no mention of the subject, nor does Cameron 1981: 294 in his summation of topics treated by Athenaeus in Book 13.
3. For Melissa as the name of a respectable woman, cf. Hdt. 5. 92, the wife of Periander; a hetaera named Melissa and known as the *theatrotorunē* is also mentioned at Ath. 4.157a.
4. According to Xen. *Hell.* 3. 1. 10–16, Zenis and Mania were wealthy aristocrats from Dardania in the Troad, while the latter had special favor with Pharnabazus. Many thanks to my colleague, William Aylward, for bringing this information to my attention.
5. Henderson 1991: 186 maintains that culinary terminology in Attic Old comedy frequently suggests cunnilingus; he cites the phrase *tragoi d' akratieisthe* in the scurrilous chorus of Ar. *Plut.* 295, glossed by the scholiast as a reference to the habit goats have of licking their genitals.
6. See Ogden 1999: 247–52 for a good discussion of the pitfalls of interpreting hetaeras' names.
7. Demo is associated with Demetrius Poliorcetes, his father Monophthalmos (One-eyed) and his son Antigonus Gonatas; see Ogden 1999: 247.
8. Schaps 1977; Ogden 1996: 193; but note that Sommerstein 1980 contends that the prohibition against the public naming of respectable women applied only to free citizen men, as female characters frequently name each other in Attic Old comedy, even in the presence of men.
9. Schaps 1977: 323; he adduces other classical parallels on the seclusion of Athenian women: Hyperides F205 Jensen; Lys. 3. 6; Arist. *Pol.* 4. 15 1300a4–7.
10. Information about the names of historical women in ancient Greece has been drawn from the data of *LGPN* vols. 1 and 2. Vestergaard et al. 1985 [1993]: 178 maintain in their survey

of names inscribed on gravestones in Attica that only 34% contain the names of citizen women while 41% include the names of metic and foreign women.

11. For an alphabetical list of Greek slave names, see Fragiadakis 1988: 83–101; see also Golden 1986: 250; on the difficulty of ascertaining slave names generally, see Garlan 1988: 22–3 and 28–9.

12. Golden 1986: 251; in n. 15 he observes that some common boys' names, like Lysis, also took the form of abstract nouns, but because they were feminine in gender, there would have been less of a tendency to link the meaning with the person.

13. The difficulty of evaluating the names listed in references to *LGPN* results from the large number of homonyms, spelling variants, inability to distinguish slave, citizen, or metic in every case and the large role played by literary sources and thus fictitious characters, for which see Rigsby 1995.

14. Humphreys 1983: 111–117 gives as examples Ampharete (c. 410) = IGii² 10650; Archedice = IGii² 7528; Archippe = IGii² 5374; Euphrosyne= IGii² 7263; Melitta = IGii² 6230; Nicostrate (after 350) = IGii² 6218; Nicarete (before 350) = IGii² 12254.

15. On these courtesans, see Ogden 1999: 243 and 255–56, notes 107–109. On Thais, cf. Plut. *Alex.* 38; Diod. Sic. 17. 72, Curtius 5. 7. 2–11, and Justin. 15. 2. On Lamia, cf. Ath. 4. 128b, 13. 577c–f; Clem. *Protr.* 4. 48; Diog. Laert. 5. 76. On Leaena, cf. Ath. 6. 252f–253b; 13. 577c–f.

16. The only evidence for hetaeras as citizens is found in Plutarch who states that Alcibiades consorted with hetaeras, both citizen (*astais*) and foreign (*xenais*); cf. Plut. *Alc.* 8. 3; on hetaeras and citizenship, see most recently Ogden 1996: 160–1 and Davidson 1997: 76 and 327, n. 10. The Mytilene mosaic showing Chrysis in Menander's *Samia* with the courtesan's diadem, but with the clothing of a respectable matron, supports the point that some hetaeras could have been viewed almost as citizens; I am grateful to Madeleine Henry for this observation. On fullers as members of the lower class, cf. Ar. *Eccl.* 415 and *Vesp.* 1128.

17. Both Cameron 1990: 302–3 and Ogden 1999: 244 argue that Bilistiche came from Macedon and that her claim to Argive descent was a common one among Macedonian royalty. Cameron further argues that she was an equestrian who won chariot victories at the Olympian games in 268 and 264 B.C.E. which were commemorated in an epinician poem by Callimachus; for further discussion, see pp. 298–9 and n. 31; Fraser 1972: 1. 210, n. 206.

18. Ogden 1996: 160. In Menandrian drama, hetaeras are typically foreigners, many Samian, but reside in Athens with metic status; see Webster 1974: 32.

19. Schneider 1913: 1334–1335; Reinsberg 1993: 161 actually dates the importation of hetaeras into Athens to the early sixth century B.C.E. because of an increase in long-distance trade; Kurke 1999: 181 believes the distinction between hetaera and porne was facilitated by the invention of coinage during this same period.

20. See Brendel 1970: 19–36; Sutton 1981: 74–113 and 117, Table L. 1; Peschel 1987; Reinsberg 1993: 104–112; and Stewart, A. 1997: 156–67. The depiction of hetaeras on vases functioned metasympotically as almost 80% of these representations occur on the drinking cups used at ancient symposia.

21. Herodotus also attributes the practice of prostitution to foreigners, namely the Babylonians and the Lydians; cf. Hdt. 1. 93–94, 196, 199; for a discussion of these passages, see Kurke 1999: 176–7.

22. For Rhodopis, see Hdt. 2. 134–135 and Kurke 1999: 176–77. *LGPN* 1. 398–99 shows 19 separate entries for names built on the stem *rhod**.

23. Kurke 1999: 185 refers to this ideology as the "cult of habrosyne," celebrated by lyric poets such as Anacreon and reinforced by the aristocratic symposia of the late archaic period.

24. On obscene epithets and nicknames in Attic Old comedy, see Henderson 1991: 213–219.

25. Sathon and Posthon, slang terms for penis, also appear as nicknames of male prostitutes; see Licht 1932: 416.

26. On the name, see Henderson 1991: 203; cf. Hdt. 4. 155, where a stammering youth is named Battus.

27. For the names of hetaeras inscribed on Attic vases, see Peschel 1987: 74–79; 183–185; and 326–27.

28. For this interpretation, see Peschel 1987: 75, who cites in support Pherecrates F113. 28–29 KA, *korai . . . hēbulliōsai kai ta rhoda kekarmenai.*

29. See Henderson 1991: 118, 135; cf. the hymenaios (wedding song) sung by the chorus at Ar. *Pax.* 1349–50: *tou men mega kai pachu,* / *tēs d' hēdu to sukon,* and the obscene use of the term *sukas* in connection with hetaeras at Alciphr. 4. 13. 2–3.

30. The name possibly derives from the phrase *se kline;* for two interpretations of this name, see Peschel 1987: 77–8.

31. It should be observed that Corone was not strictly a hetaera's name; in fact it appears on a black figure hydria, along with Rhodopis, in a water fountain scene of the type typically associated with respectable women (London British Museum B 329); for other examples, see Beazley 1956: 677.

32. Peschel 1987: 79; see also Kurke 1999: 205 and n. 79 .

33. This table was compiled from Schneider 1913: 1358–60.

34. On Leaena, see Gow 1965: 93 and n. 1; for the semitic origins of Lais, see *RE* 12. 514 s. v. Lais; on the lion *schēma,* cf. Ar. *Lys.* 232: *ou stēsomai leain' epi turoknēstidos.*

35. For the woman-on-top interpretation of this epigram, see Cameron 1981: 295; Gutzwiller 1998: 126 and n. 30; for this position in connection with prostitutes, see Henry 1992: 264; for a general discussion of *keltiazein,* see Heath 1986.

36. Henderson 1991: 110–111 and 131, n. 126 discusses the metaphorical term used of the female children, *choiros* (pig), and its diminutive, *choiridia,* slang words for the pudenda of a young girl. Henry 1992: 254 further discusses the link between women and food, especially fish, in Athenaeus' *Deipnosophistae.*

37. Note that Henderson 1991: 48 states that most animal metaphors refer to both genders except when they emphasize physical resemblance; it is therefore open to question whether such metaphors exclusively target women, as Henry 1985: 28–9 suggests. On birds as a metaphor for the female genitals, see Henderson 1991: 142, who mentions *neottis* (chick), a title of plays by Antiphanes, Eubulus, and Anaxilas, and *chelidōn* (swallow); on fish, see p. 142 (most of the terms refer to shellfish, however). See also Henry 1985: 28 and n. 51. The Japanese similarly referred to lower-order prostitutes as nighthawks (*yotaka*) and ducks (*ahiru*); see Downer 2001: 108.

38. *LGPN* 2. 271 contains six references to the name Corone: two are on vases (cf. c. 510 ABV p. 677 (κορωνη: Kale); and c. 510–505 BC ARV2 p. 113 no. 7); one occurs in Middle comedy and one in Machon; another attests to an Attic woman living in the fourth century B.C.E. with the same name (IG II² 11893).

39. On fish as a symbol of decadence and seduction, see Davidson 1997: 9–10.

40. Olson and Sens 1999: 90–91 discuss the use of *aphuē* in Matro's *deipnon;* for Sepia and Atherine, see pp. 96–7.

41. For courtesans as fish in Attic Old comedy, see Aristophanes, *Olcades* 409 *CAF, Vesp.* 1342; Cratinus F8 KA; Phrynicus F52 KA; for birds, see Autocrates F1 KA. On the use of nicknames to distinguish homonyms, see Cameron 1998.

42. A courtesan by the name of Ocimon is also mentioned by Anaxandrides, *Gerontomania,* F9 KA = 570e; Nicostratus, *Pandrosus* F20 KA = 587d; and by Hyperides in *Against Aristagora* = 587d, always in connection with other hetaeras. On the name Opora, see Arnott 1996: 496–500, and the discussion in Chapter 4.

43. On these commodifying nicknames that turn women into coins, see Davidson 1997: 118–119 and Kurke 1999: 198 and n. 57.

44. On *pulē* (gate) as a metaphor for the female genitals, see Henderson 1991: 137–9; cf. Ar. *Lys.* 250, 264, 423, and 1163, with the geographical pun on *tan Pulon.*

45. For the lamp as the deity of lovemaking, see Kost 1971: 126–32; and Cameron 1981: 283 and n. 36; for a comic version, see Praxagora's invocation to the lamp (*O lampron omma tou trochēlatou luchnou,* Ar. *Eccl.* 1).

46. Hornblower and Matthews 2000: 65 mention this law in passing.

47. Under Εἰρήνη, *LGPN* 2. 139 lists 35 inscriptional entries; references to feminine abstracts are also found, such as Habrosyne (*LGPN* 2. 1 = IG II² 10534), Sige (*LGPN* 2. 397 = IG II² 12600), and Opora (*LGPN* 2. 354 = SEG 37 191).

48. On the meanings of Rhodopis and the term hetaera, see Kurke 1999: 176–178 and 222–7.

49. Wiedemann 1981: 33; Garlan 1988: 23 also observes that the master thus "fixed the identity of his slaves."

50. Ogden 1996: 91–3 and 127 observes that naming played an important role in the process of legitimation for male citizens, beginning at birth and extending to the various recognition

ceremonies that involved naming, such as introduction into the phratry; cf. Plut. *Per.* 37. 2–5.

51. Pomeroy 1997: 127 takes this practice as evidence of "the woman's unseverable bond to her natal family."

52. On the use of the metronymic in women's speech, see Skinner 1987. Roth 2002 speculates that children described by the metronymic in ancient Mesopotamian cultures may have also been the offspring of prostitutes.

53. A mocking reference traces the poetic descent of Nossis to Erinna at Herod. 6. 20; see Skinner 1987: 40; Ogden 1996: 95.

54. Miner 2003 argues that Apollodorus uses the metronymic to identify Phano with Neaera in *Against Neaera*; I would also add that the orator may wish to suggest that she herself is a hetaera, a charge for which he has no concrete evidence.

55. *LGPN* 2, s.v. Γαλήνη no. 4 = CIA App. 102 b 18 (Γαλήν[η]: d. Πολυκλεία).

56. The practice of adopting a second name upon induction into the profession appears widespread: Japanese geisha adopt professional names on completion of their preliminary training, which connect them with a specific geisha "family," for which see Downer 2001: 117; for this custom in 19th century France, see Corbin 1990: 77–8. A famous example is Manet's Olympia.

Chapter 3

1. Strabo 8. 6. 20 includes this joke in his discussion of Corinth and its prostitutes; the joke puns on the double meaning of the word *histos*, in the sense of mast or pole and web-beam of the loom. Note that Gnathaena's joke at 580d plays on the verbal form, *histēs*. The connection between wool-working and brothels is discussed more fully in Chapter 4, p. 130.

2. As Henry 1992: 262 argues, "Besides their eloquence and bravado, the courtesans Myrtilus praises speak only as the self-defined objects of men's sexual pleasure"; cf. also Henry 2000: 504. Keuls 1985: 199 similarly describes the cultivated hetaera as "a fabrication of the male mind," whose witticisms consist of "male-generated jokes, hinging on puns and sexual innuendo." Faraone 1999: 156 and n. 90 views the hetaera's repartee as part of a generalized preference for male speech modes, exemplified in magical practice by their use of *agōgē* spells normally deployed by men; cf. Lucian *Dial. meret.* 4. 1; *Anth. Pal.* 5. 205; Theoc. *Id.* 2. 23–32.

3. Davidson 1997: 135 argues that the hetaera's literary allusions frequently disguise obscene propositions in a sort of verbal striptease that shows a "resistence to closed meaning, to definition."

4. A recent strand of criticism views these witticisms as a form of parodic lampooning of the philosophical tradition; see Hawley 1993: 87 and Davidson 1997: 93. For Hawley, courtesans' jokes undercut or parody the catalogues of maxims uttered by women in Plutarch, such as the *Apophthegmata Lakonika*. Similarly, Kurke 2002 argues that the courtesans' jokes of Machon's *Chreiae* provide a subversive and democratic commentary on Macedonian political rule. Thanks are owed to Leslie Kurke for showing me an early version of her essay.

5. Lukinovich 1990: 264 discusses the verbal features of sympotic entertainment, including riddles. See also Ath. 4. 162 b–e, and 10. 448b–459b; Anderson 2000: 318–9.

6. According to Webster 1974: 102, hetaeras in Menander are given to using "nursery endearments" and swearing oaths; see also Gomme and Sandbach 1973: 131; Henry 1985: 57–60.

7. Martin, R. 2001: 63; cf. Plu. *Mor.* 150e–f and *Anth. Pal.* 14. 14 (*aulos*); 14. 23, 36 (pickled fish); 14. 26 (a linen hand-towel); and 14. 52 (wine). Note that the hetaera Thais at Alciphr. 4. 7. 8 attributes riddle-telling to the philosopher-sophist Euthydemus. On riddles at the symposium, see Lukinovich 1990: 264.

8. Since many riddles revolved around aspects of the symposium, the hetaera might have served as a common subject; indeed, one solution to the riddle posed at Thgn. 861–4 is a hetaera, whose feminine identity is highlighted by adjectives, *automatē, hesperiē, orthriē*; see Martin, R. 2001: 60; see also West 1996: 11.

9. Hasan-Rokem and Shulman 1996: 5. Although he does not specifically mention riddles, Davidson 1997: 135 discusses the ambiguity of the hetaera's speech, which he characterizes as "notoriously enigmatic, parodic and punning." See also Pitts 2002: 102–9.

10. Hawley 1993: 77 inexplicably insists that "the evidence . . . for [hetaeras'] alleged 'culture' is in fact scarce (77)," a view that is directly contradicted by Ath. 13. 584a, 588b, and *passim*. Although not often described as *sophē* by Athenaeus as in other texts, the adjectives *euthik-*

tos and *asteia* suggest a type of verbal sophistication. For the adjective *sophē* and cognates as applied to prostitutes, cf. Axionicus F1 KA, where a tambourinist is described as *sophōtatē*; Theophilus F12. 7 KA = 563a calls a harpist *sophē*; the same term is applied to an Epicurean hetaera, Alciphr. 4. 7. 8. Hawley further notes that *sophisma* may refer to fellatio in Theopompus F36 KA; see also Henderson 1991: 183; cf. Ar. *Lys.* 546 and *Eccl.* 895–96.

11. Halliwell 1991: 293 and n. 55 points out that defendants in Attic oratory received acquittals through their use of *asteia*; cf. Dem. 23. 206; Lys. 24. 18; cf. Ar. *Vesp.* 567.

12. Richlin 1992b: 73. It is possible that in attributing such joking to Julia, the tradition attempts to assimilate her to a prostitute, especially given her legendary sexual misconduct; for further discussion, see McGinn 1998: 170.

13. Wilamowitz as quoted by West 1996: 22.

14. Henry 1995: 64–5 provides a valuable discussion of Socratic erotics in the Hellenistic period.

15. As Henry 1995: 14–15, 20–22, and 138–39 n. 9, argues, correctly in my view, that Aspasia was probably the pallake of Pericles, not a hetaera. In a private correspondence, Henry remarked that her biographical tradition developed a "wise woman" strand in the Hellenistic period that subsequently excluded her from the "pornographic" discourse of the Alexandrians; see also pp. 19 and 205 n. 42.

16. West 1996: 20–1 and 38, notes 21–2; he adds to this list Astyanassa.

17. Brendel 1970: 67 n. 70 discusses the scant evidence for Hellenistic erotic treatises and art catalogues.

18. Lobel 1972 and Tsantsanoglou 1973: 183.

19. For Philaenis and literary forgery, see Tsantsanoglou 1973: 192 and West 1977: 118.

20. Hawley 1993: 77 argues that Athenaeus by referring to Gnathaena's treatise parodies such works, as does Davidson 1997: 104. See Gow 1965: 107 and most recently Kurke 2002.

21. Pitts 2002: 75–123 considers the tradition linking Sappho to prostitution.

22. On the proverb, "in Charixena's day," cf. Ar. *Eccl.* 942–43 and Ussher 1973: 207; Cratin. F153 KA; Theopompus Comicus F51 KA. The Aristophanic scholium ad loc refers to her as a hetaera while Hesychius states that she composed erotic songs. See also Campell 1992: 98 and West 1996: 42.

23. Skinner 1991: 45 n. 42, following Wilamowitz, rejects this idea; for recent discussion of this issue, see Gutzwiller 1998: 75 and n. 71. As both Gutzwiller 1998: 143, and earlier, Cameron 1981: 277, argue, most of the promiscuous women of the epigrammatists are not prostitutes, but "new" women characteristic of the Hellenistic period. See also Pomeroy 1977 and Chapter 5, pp. 161–2.

24. West 1996: 29, "Das Vögelein war vielleicht eben eine Hetäere."

25. On Locrian songs, see West 1996: 21 and 38, n. 24; MacLachlan 1995: 206; on Theano, see West 1996: 22 and 47.

26. On Megalostrate, see West 1996: 12 and 45, Alcm. *PMG* F59b.

27. Cf. Ar. *Vesp.* 12366ff. = *PMG* 897; Campbell F749 and *Thesm.* 528ff. = *PMG* 903; Campbell F750; on Praxilla, see West 1996: 20 and 46–47; see also Campbell 1992: 371; cf. F749 and 750 *PMG*.

28. Campbell 1992: 371; West 1996: 20, "Aber wie konnte eine anständige Priesterin bzw. Chorlieterin in der nordöstlichen Peloponnes dazu kommen, derart anstößige Verse zu dichten?"

29. Historical priestesses include Aristocleia (Porph. *Vit. Pyth.* 41; Phot. *Lex.* τ Suda τ West 1996: 41) and Boio (Paus. 10. 5. 8; Clem. Strom. 1. 132. 3). Mythical priestesses such as Phemonoe (West 1996: 11 and 46) and Daphne, daughter of Teiresias, were credited with writing oracular verse (Diod. 6. 66. 6; West 1996: 42); cf. Xenocleia (Paus. 10. 13. 8; West 1996: 48). West 1996: 42–46 identifies number of sibyls as poets, including Athenais, Demo, Hierophile, Lampousa, and Phoito.

30. For Sempronia, see Lyne 1980: 14; Sall. *Cat.* 25; for Julia, see Richlin 1992b.

31. Halliwell 1991: 289 and n. 40; cf. also Hom. *Il.* 20. 251–2; Ar. *Eq.* 1400, 1403; *Vesp.* 496–469, 1388; *Ran.* 549, 857–858; *Plut.* 426–428, 435–6; Pl. *Resp.* 395d 6–7; *Leg.* 935a1.

32. Figs have numerous associations with genitalia in Attic Old comedy, for which see Henderson 1991: 118, 134, and n. 137; see also the discussion of the term *sukas* in Chapter 2, p. 70, and Chapter 3, p. 86.

33. Mockery of hetaeras appears to have been a common practice at symposia, as attested by one of the Attic scolia (F905 *PMG*); see also Gutzwiller 1998: 174.

34. On the aggressive function of laughter in ancient Greek culture, see Henderson 1991: 42–43; see also Halliwell 1991: 287.

35. Gnathaena abused (*eloidoreito*) Mania, who suffered from kidney stones (Machon 211–17 = 578e). The latter replied, "I should have given it to you, so that you would have been able to wipe yourself" (*edōk' an, hin' eiches, phēs', apopsasthai*). Lyncaeus records the same scatalogical joke, but changes the interlocutor to Phryne (584c–d). For quarreling hetaeras, cf. Gnathaena's mockery of Dexithea, Machon 295–99 = 580c, and Callistion and Corone, Machon 433–38 = 583a.
36. Milanezi 2000: 403 notes that the word *gelōtopoios* does not appear until Xenophon; cf. Xen. *Symp.* 1. 11, *An.* 7. 3. 33; Pl. *Resp.* 620c; and Ath. 14. 613–616. For a recent discussion of parasites in Athenaeus, see Whitmarsh 2000. Geisha parties in Japan frequently required a male master of ceremonies; the *taikomochi*, like the parasites and *gelōtopoioi* at the Greek symposium, entertained with dirty jokes, mime, dancing, and slapstick; see Downer 2001: 96–9.
37. Milanezi 2000: 405–406. The *gelōtopoios* Philip in Xenophon's *Symposium* thus plays at likenesses (6. 8 to 7.1).
38. This pronunciation joke recalls the actor Hegelochus' famous mistake while delivering a line from Euripides' *Orestes*. His breathless delivery of *galēn* instead of *galēn'* changed the intended meaning of the sentence from "I see the calm after the storm" to "I see the ferret after the storm." Cf. Eur. *Or.* 279; cf. Ar. *Ran.* 303–4; Sannyrio F8 KA; and Strattis, FF1 and 60 KA.
39. For the use of the verb in Herodotus, see Lateiner 1977 and 1989: 28 and n. 48.
40. On *progymnasmata*, see Hock and O'Neil 1986.
41. Hawley 1993: 76 observes that the *chreia* involves "a brief narrative setting, introducing at least one person, an attribution of at least one proper name as protagonist (often a famous individual), a question, and then a final capping answer, often in direct speech." He further argues that the apophthegm or anecdote, because brief, represented an appropriate speech genre for women. He does not, however, account for the anecdotal traditions surrounding women who are seen as violating or subverting in some way normative gender roles, such as the *Apophthegmata Lakōnika* of Plutarch or the hetaeras of Machon, not to mention the fact that many such apothegms are also attributed to powerful men. Hock and O'Neil 1986: 22–5 delineate the four characteristic features of the *chreia* as follows: it contains a saying or action; it is concise, often only one sentence in length; it is spoken in character and is applicable to everyday life. Gilula 2000: 429 identifies the basic structure of the *chreia* as an either/or question "to which the witty saying is an answer which completely ignores the alternatives offered in the question and surprisingly comes up with a third possibility."
42. Gow 1965: 12–14; the authors mentioned by Diogenes include: Aristippus (Diog. Laert. 2. 85, 4. 40), Demetrius of Phalerum (5. 81), Hecaton the Rhodian, a follower of Panaetius (6. 32), Metrocles (6. 33), Diogenes (6. 80), Zeno of Citium (6. 91), Persaeus (7. 36), and Ariston of Chios (7. 163).
43. Krueger 1996: 223–224 discusses the *chreiae* of Diogenes in the context of the philosopher's shameless public behavior.
44. Gow 1965: 14. On Machon's *Chreiae* as a philosophical parody, see Davidson 1997: 93 and 104 and Kurke 2002.
45. See Theon, *On the Chreia*, 1. 338; Hock and O'Neil 1986: 102–5; Krueger 1996: 239.
46. Dudley 1998: 50–1 theorizes that Hipparchia is cast as a stock figure on which to fasten *anaideia*.
47. Gow 1965: 19–21; Ogden 1999: 226 and notes 65–66; Henry 1995: 58–9.
48. Hawley 1993: 77 divides their quips into the following groups, witty puns (578e, 584d, 580 d–e, 582 a, 584b–585f); literary or political allusions (579e–580a, 582c–d); sexual double entendres (579d, 580b, 581f); and blatant obscenity (580f).
49. For a Roman parallel, consider that Julia apparently told her jokes when she was 38, on the verge of old age in the view of the ancients; see Richlin 1992b: 70. For a cross-cultural comparison, Downer 2001: 247 describes an aging geisha of 90 as saying little but laughing the loudest and the longest at the crudest jokes at a party for Japanese business men.
50. Prostitution appears to have been an intergenerational practice transmitted from mother to daughter as Athenaeus and his sources regularly refer to the matrilineal descent of courtesans; see Ogden 1996: 94–5, and the discussion in Chapter 2, pp. 76–77.
51. cf. Ar. *Lys.* 231, *ou stēsomai leain' epi turoknēstidos*, and the scholion, *schēma akolaston kai hetairikon*. The sexual position appears on vases and hand mirrors, for which Stewart, A. 1997: 177–81.

52. For another link between Lamia and Leaena, cf. Ath. 6. 253a, where according to De-mochares the Athenians built temples to Aphrodite Leaena and Aphrodite Lamia as a compliment to Demetrius. On *keltiazein*, see Heath 1986; Henry 1992: 264; on its use in this anecdote, see Davidson 1997: 196–7 and Kurke 2002.

53. For the discursive dominance of Medea in Euripides' play, see McClure 1999b; for its application to Machon, see Kurke 2002, who views it as a political declaration of "the superiority of a quintessentially Athenian poetic genre to the crude physical demands of Athens' boorish conquerer."

54. Kurke 2002 elaborates the political aspects of this joke.

55. Thanks are owed to Peter White for his trenchant clarification of this joke.

56. For this view, see Gow 1965: 124, who relates *to mēden ōphelēma* to Aesch. *PV* 613, *ō koinon ōphelēma thnētoisin phaneis*; cf. *Eur. Tro.* 703. He also notes that *stegos* commonly refers to a brothel.

57. On *psuchros* as a feature of dramatic poetry, cf. Ar. *Thesm.* 170, *ho d' au Theognis psuchros ōn psuchrōs poiei*; the frigidity of his tragedies apparently earned him the nickname Chion (Snow); cf. Ar. *Ach.* 138–140 and the scholion to v. 11. For the "frigid" jokes of parasites generally, see Theophr. *Char.* 2. 4.

58. The comic poet Philippides also pilloried Gnathaena for her gluttony in one of his plays (F5 KA); see Gow 1965: 8–9. Similarly, at Alciphr. 4. 2. 5 the hetaera Glycera fears that she will have to endure Menander's *loidoria* on the comic stage.

59. Trying solve this difficulty, Gow 1965: 107 suggests that *erōmenōn* has a middle rather than passive meaning; on p. 108, he remarks that the verb *agapaō* in these contexts normally has an active meaning and thus applies to the male, not to the hetaera, as in Anaxilas, *Neottis* F22. 1 KA, *hostis anthrōpōn hetairan ēgapēse.*

60. Similar language is found in Diphilus' extant corpus, while the lack of crudity in Glycera's joke may also reflect the linguistic style of Menander; many thanks to Madeleine Henry for this insight.

61. On the idea of the female creation talking back to her male creator, see Rosenmeyer 2001.

62. Following a scholion, Gow 1965: 128 believes this episode may have actually taken place. But the fact that such dialogues appear to have been popular during the Second Sophistic period—Musonius, for instance, similarly engages in a conversation with Euripides about slavery—militates against the idea that they ever happened; see Whitmarsh 2001: 278.

63. On this passage, see Gow 1965: 128; on the line from Euripides' *Aeolus*, cf. Ar. *Ran.* 1475, *ti d' aischron, ēn mē tois theōmenois dokēi*, and Plut. *Mor.* 33c.

64. Many thanks to C. A. Faraone for drawing this passage to my attention.

65. Gow 1965: 104 takes the phrase *automolos anthrōpos xenos* to refer to "the typical boorish solider of New Comedy." In any case, the term *anthrōpos* denotes contempt.

66. Kurke 2002 finds an allusion to political disenfranchisement in this joke: in parting the bronze smith from his gold, the hetaera symbolically "casts him out of the citizen body" and thus restores normative social hierarchies.

67. I have followed Gulick in keeping the emendation of Capps, τοι δέρος, instead of the τοιγαρ of manuscript A.

68. In Aristophanes' *Wasps*, the verb refers to anal rape (*prosagagōn pros tēn elaan exedeir' eu kandrikōs*, Ar. *Vesp.* 450), while elsewhere it denotes male arousal; cf. Ar. *Lys.* 158, 739, and 953; *Av.* 365; *Nub.* 442; on the verb generally, see Henderson 1991: 167.

69. For women's speech at the Adonia, see McClure 1999a: 216, 223, 254, and n. 165, 264.

70. Henry 1995: 49; Goldhill 1998 explores how this dialogue deploys Athenian conceptions of viewing to destabilize notions of gender and citizenship.

71. Henry 1995: 35 points out the incongruities of putting the epitaphios, a genre that celebrated Athenian *andreia*, into the mouth of a foreign woman.

72. On the sexual sense of *entugchanein*, cf. Plut. *Sol.* 20. 3, see Henry 1995: 35.

73. Apparently a famous anecdote in antiquity, for which see Brendel 1970: 33 and n. 36; cf. Diog. Laert. 10. 4; Alciphr. 4. 17 and Plin. 35. 9. On Leontion, see Castner 1982: 56 and n. 16; cf. Cic. *Nat. D.* 1. 93; *Orat.* 151; Plin. *HN* praef. 29. The figure looms large in the tradition of spurious letters attributed to Epicurus by his detractors; see Gordon 1996: 82, 85–8, 127.

74. On performative displays and the competitive culture of the period, see Gleason 1991.

Chapter 4

1. Downer 2001: 9, on the Japanese geisha.
2. For the idea of Athens as a "culture of viewing" in which citizens performed as democratic actors, see Goldhill 1998: 108 and *passim*. Chaniotis 1997: 251 discusses these spectacles, and more generally, the formation of a "culture of onlookers" in Hellenistic urban centers.
3. As Pirenne-Delforge 1994: 429 observes, "le corps est au centre de la répresentation de la courtisane et il constitue pour elle la préoccupation essentielle . . . ." Downer 2001 vividly illustrates critical role played by the costume of the Japanese geisha, the kimono, obi, elaborately coifed wig or hairstyle, make up, and clogs, in creating a fantasy of exaggerated femininity.
4. Gleason 1991: xxiv borrows Bordieu's term *habitus* to describe this phenomenon; see also Foucault 1988: 85–86; on the sophists' actual performances, see Anderson, G. 1993: 55–68.
5. Gleason 1991; see also Quint. *Inst.* 11. 3. 75; Seneca, *Ep.* 52. 12. The cinaedus is also described as having a mincing gait and feminine way of moving the body. Clement designates this motion by the term *katakeklasmenos*, cf. Clem. Al. *Paed.* 3. 11. 69; see also *CAF* F3. 470; Dio. Chrys. *Or.* 33. 52; on this gait in second century declamation, see Gleason 1991: 60–3 and notes 26, 83.
6. Most current scholarship rejects Wilamowitz's earlier view that naked courtesans played the feminine abstractions in Aristophanes' plays; for a summary of this debate, see Henry 1985: 29–30; Henderson 1987a: 195–6; Zweig 1992; Olson 1992: 313 and Taaffe 1993: 23–47. Stone 1981: 144–6 argues that the term *gumnos* does not always denote actual nudity, but can be applied figuratively to refer to scant clothing.
7. Henderson 1991: 148 and n. 208; cf. Alexis F98 KA = Ath. 13. 568a.
8. On this scene, see Henry 1985: 21–2; on the term *prōktopentetērida*, see Henderson 1991: 150; for other references to hetaeras in the play, cf. 317, 339–40, 748–60, 439–40, and 164–5 (brothel). On these characters, see further, Stone 1981: 148–50.
9. In her discussion of Socratic courtesans, Henry 1995: 34 develops the idea of the courtesan as a figure of substitution and interchangeability, as a signifier whose signification constantly changes.
10. Henry 1985: 18–27, 29–30 and n. 52 discusses the association of politicians with brothels and courtesans in Attic Old comedy.
11. At Ar. *Thesm.* 98, Euripides' manly kinsman compares the effeminate tragic poet, Agathon, to Cyrene; the scholia to this passage mentions that the name Cyrene appeared several times in Aristophanes' other comedies; for a discussion, see Henry 1985: 13, 24.
12. Japanese geisha were similarly distinguished by the extent to which they could be seen; those born in a geisha house, the highest class, were difficult to view, while young girls from humble origins could be summoned for a line-up in which the male client looked them over and made his choice (*mirare*); see Downer 2001: 134–5.
13. The prototype for the theatrical or artistic viewing of courtesans is found at Xen. *Mem.* 3. 11. 2; for further discussion, see Goldhill 1998: 114–6. For the verb in the context of erotic viewing between *erastēs* and *erōmenos*, see most recently Steiner 2001: 209–10.
14. On athletic metaphors for sexual activity, see Henderson 1991: 169–70; cf. Ar. *Pax* 894 904; Alciphr. 4. 14. 5.
15. Cf. Ar. *Eccl.* 64; for discussion, see Stone 1981: 23.
16. The earliest reference to women dragging men indoors occurs in the dispute of the two crones, figured as hetaeras, in Aristophanes' *Ecclesiazusae*; cf. Ar. *Eccl.* 1049–50; in Theophr. *Char.* 28. 3, they "kidnap" (*sunharpazousi*) their customers.
17. Studies of Greco-Roman prostitution have tended to take this anecdote as factual; see Pomeroy 1975: 57; Vanoyeke 1990: 24–5; Reinsberg 1993: 161–2. Given that coinage was not widespread during Solon's reign, these late anecdotes about the origins of Greek prostitution are improbable. Rosivach 1995 provides a much needed correction of the traditional view.
18. On this passage, see Pomeroy 1994: 304–6, who notes that no ancient author, with the exception of Ovid, writes approvingly of the female use of cosmetics, which are typically linked with drugs and deception. Ancient evidence, however, does suggest widespread use of cosmetics among Greek women: Attic *lekythoi* show women applying makeup as part of their nuptial toilette; literary evidence, such as the opening scene of Aristophanes' *Lysis-*

trata and Lys. 1. 14, attest to the use of cosmetics to enhance the attractiveness of married women. Substances used for cosmetics included highly toxic lead carbonate, or *psimuthion*, used to achieve the whitened face of leisured women not accustomed to working outdoors, for which see Shear 1937; a rouge made from the plant alkanet, *miltos*, which approximated the tanned flesh of men; and *andreikelon*, a flesh-colored foundation used for eye make up, as well as a pigment used by artists. Height also comprised a desired characteristic of feminine beauty; in Hom. *Od.* 6. 103–7, Odysseus compares Nausicaa to Artemis as she towers above her companions. Pomeroy suggests that Xenophon's denunciation of cosmetics may reflect a Spartan distaste for adornment, for which see Xen. *Lac.* 5. 8; Plut. *Lyc.* 1. 4. 4; Ath. 15. 686d–687d (on the use of perfume). On women and cosmetics, see also Goldhill 1995: 82–3, 90–1 and 1998: 114; and Bassi 1998: 111.

19. Brown 1987: 190; see also Webster 1974: 91–2, who speculates on the basis of the Mytilene mosaics and Pollux.

20. On the similarity of the makeup used by prostitutes and the comic mask, see Slater 1989. Ar. *Eccl.* 1101 speaks of the crone as having a *lekythos*, like Phryne, next to her, possibly in reference to the theatrical mask; see Slater 1989: 47; for a different interpretation, see Ussher 1973: 225–6. In any case, the passage clearly plays on the association of make up, acting, and comedy with hetaeras. For white lead and hetaeras, cf. Ar. *Eccl.* 878; *Plut.* 1065; Ussher 1973: 195; Stone 1981: 22–7.

21. Arnott 1996: 268 notes that real-life hetaeras, like Stagonion, frequently took their names from aspects of female cosmetic adornment; on F103 KA, see pp. 273–83.

22. For a recent discussion of the manufacture of Pandora and its affinities with artistic creation, see Steiner 2001: 186–7; on embellishment and *korē* statues, pp. 234–38.

23. Arnott 1986: 278. On comic padding, see Stone 1980: 135–38.

24. On painting the face in Aristophanic comedy, cf. Ar. *Lys.* 43–48, 149, 220; *Eccl.* 732, 878, 904, 1072–3 and 1101; *Plut.* 1064–5; for discussion, see Stone 1981: 26–7.

25. On *tarantinidion* = *diaphaneston huphasma*, cf. schol. Lucian, *Dial. meret.* 7; Men. *Epitr.* 489 Sandbach; Philostratus, letter 22. 16–17; Ar. *Thesm.* β F332 KA = Pollux 7. 95 (discussed in this chapter); Herod. 1 and Ath. 13. 568b–c. Stone 1981: 302–3 discusses the association of transparent garments with prostitutes in Attic Old comedy. An epigram further underscores their importance for seduction: "The folds of your thin dress cling well to you, / and all your charms are visible as if naked, and yet are invisible" (*panta de sou blepetai gumna, kai ou blepetai*, M. Argentarius, *Anth. Pal.* 5. 104; trans. Paton); cf. Theoc. *Id.* 28. For Roman equivalents, cf. Prop. 4. 5; Ov. *Am.* 1. 8.

26. For further discussion of this image, see Goldhill 1998: 117, although he overlooks the sartorial dimension.

27. On laws geared to curb licentious behavior at Locri, including the wearing of garments with purple borders, see MacLachlan 1995: 207; cf. Diod. Sic. 12. 21.

28. Cf. Ar. *Eccl.* 268, where Praxagora instructs the women to hitch up their *chitōnia*; for the women's *chitōn*, see Stone 1981: 172–4.

29. The tomb refers to the body of the aged Sophocles, 592b; cf. Plato, *Cleophon* 57 KA.

30. See White 1975: 59 (= Artem. 1. 78), "For I know of a man who dreamt that he went to a brothel and could not leave. He died a few days later, this being the quite logical result of his dream. For a brothel, like a cemetery, is called 'a place men have in common,' and many human seeds perish there." On positive dreams involving prostitutes, see p. 191 (= 4. 9), "A whore in herself indicates good luck but her 'workshop' means harm."

31. Foucault 1988: 110–113; Gal. *De loc. aff.* 3. 8.

32. White 1975: 212, "a rich man dreamed he was changed into a bridge. He was regarded contemptuously by many and thus he was, in a certain sense, trampled under foot. If a woman or handsome youth ever has this dream, they will become prostitutes and allow many to go over them." See also Foucault 1988: 27 and note. On the metaphor in Latin literature, see Edwards 1997: 82.

33. See Davidson 1997: 129, 132–3; cf. [Dem.] 59. 122; for further discussion, see the introductory chapter, with relevant scholarship.

34. On this fragment, see Brown 1990: 254 and n. 55.

35. In the Japanese tradition, the geisha were originally dancers and musical entertainers; see Downer 2001: 37–8. On the movements of prostitutes in Rome, see Sen. *Controv.* 1. 2. 5 and

Priap. 19. 1, where a whore is called a *circulatrix*, "she who walks"; on Latin terms for prostitutes, see further Adams 1983: 332.

36. Clem. Al. *Paed.* 3. 294; Anac. 458 *PMG*.
37. For the vase made in shape of a courtesan's shoe in which nails in the sole spell out *akolouth(e)i*, see Daremberg and Saglio 1877–1919: 4. 2; cf. also Fig. 4968, 3. 2l s.v. *meretrices*.
38. The word *prosaulein* meant both to pipe a tune and to commit fellatio; in connection with flute-girls and hetaeras, see Henderson 1991: 183.
39. Xen. *Symp.* 2. 8; cf. Ath. 4. 129 A–130 and passim; and Bieber 1939: 640–4.
40. Cf. Hor. *Carm.* 3. 6. 21–24; *Anth. Pal.* 9. 139. 1–2.
41. For the kordax as an erotic dance associated with drinking, see Alciphr. 3. 10. 2; Dem. 2. 18; Ath. 14. 630e; Paus. 6. 22. 1; Ar. *Nub.* 540, 555; Theophr. *Char.* 6. 3. On the drunken dancing of men, see Pl. *Leg.* 815c; Ath. 14. 628c; Hdt. 6. 126–30.
42. On the kordax as an obscene dance that involved masturbation, cf. Apul. *Met.* 2. 117; see also Henderson 1991: 168.
43. See Henderson 1991: 179; for a homoerotic parallel, cf. Theocr. 5. 117 and scholion.
44. On Aphrodite and *kallipygia*, see Henderson 1987b: 77; and Säflund 1963: 45–8. On female beauty contests, cf. Hedylus, *Anth. Pal.* 6. 292.
45. On this passage, see further Dean-Jones 1994: 116.
46. Dean-Jones 1994: 175 n. 90 observes that the fetuses of the Hippocratic texts *Nat. Puer.* and *Carn.* are said to derive from prostitutes.
47. See LSJ s. v. σχῆμα as appearance as opposed to reality, cf. Pl. *Resp.* 365c; Theogn. 8. 89; in reference to dress or manner, cf. Eur. *Ba.* 832; as a dance figure, cf. Ar. *Vesp.* 1485; Xen. *Symp.* 7. 5; as a rhetorical figure of speech, cf. Pl. *Ion* 536c; Cic. *Brut.* 37. 141.
48. Goldhill 1998: 109–12 discusses how Socrates' conversations with these craftsmen introduce some of the major themes of his exchange with Theodote.
49. Sutton 1992: 21; see also Bonfante 1989: 558–62. On the pervasiveness of male nudity in monumental sculpture during the archaic and classical periods and its meanings for the ancient Greeks, see Bassi 1998: 99–105.
50. McKechnie 1989: 155–6 discusses Praxiteles and other artisans in the context of mobile skilled workers of the Hellenistic period.
51. For a reconstruction of Phryne's biography based on the ancient sources, see Raubitschek 1941; see also Cantarelli 1885; Semenov 1935; Kowalski 1947; and the excellent analysis of Cooper 1995.
52. For this view, see Raubitschek 1941: 894.
53. Paus. 9. 27. 1 states that the Thespians honored Eros above all other deities; on the importance of Aphrodite to this city, see Pirenne-Delforge 1994: 291–3.
54. Ridgway 1987: 406 while stating that it is "not at all plausible" Phryne posed for Praxiteles, admits the authenticity of the statue at Delphi.
55. For ancient references to Phryne's beauty, cf. Plut. *Mor.* 849e; Alciphr. 4. 5. 2; Val. Max. 4. 3. ext. 3; Lucian, *Catapl.* 22; Quint. 2. 15. 9; Galen *Protr.* 10; Sext. Emp. *Math.* 2. 4; *Rhet. Gr.* 14. 64. 16 (Rabe); Philodem. *Rhet.* 1. 20. 4; *Rhet. Gr.* 4. 119 (Walz); Arnob. *Adv. Nat.* 6. 13; Clem. Alex. *Protr.* 47. Note that all of these sources are very late, and almost all of them rhetorical works.
56. In another version of the story, the hetaera reclines with the drunken philosopher as part of a wager with a group of young men. When they mocked her failure to seduce him, she quipped that she had made her bet about a man (*de homine*) not a statue (*de statua*, Val. Max. 4. 3 ext. no. 3); of course, the Greek pun is lost in the Latin translation. In a similar story, the celibate Eubatas had a portrait made of Lais to avoid consummating their union; cf. Ael. *VH* 10. 2.
57. On Phryne's immersion at Eleusis as an initiatory rite, see Havelock 1995: 23. At Aegina, the festival of Aphrodite was celebrated at the end of the Poseidonia and featured a banquet to which courtesans were invited; see Pirenne-Delforge 1994: 177 and 394. So the hetaera Lais remains for two months with Aristippus at Aegina during the Poseidonia; cf. Ath. 13. 588e.
58. Moreno 1964–65: 84 n. 11 discusses the association of Apelles with Pancaspe.
59. Bonfante 1989: 559–60. On female nudity as the sign of vulnerability or pathos, consider the uncovered breasts of Clytemnestra, Hecuba, Helen, Polyxena, and others in Greek myth.
60. On Inanna/Ishtar, see Pritchard 1943: 83–7; Bonfante 1989: 544, 548.

61. Alciphr. 4. 1; for further discussion, see Rosenmeyer 2001. Bassi 1998: 101 discusses the Herodotean story of Gyges who, as a result of gazing upon Candaules' naked wife, must choose between killing himself or Candaules; see Hdt. 1. 8–12; on the same story, see also Goldhill 1998: 114; cf. Pl. *Resp.* 359c–360b. Bonfante 1989: 545 comments, "the partial nudity or exposure of a woman's breast or genitals . . . can signify weakness or powerlessness, but it can also function as a powerful magic."
62. On male nakedness, see Osborne 1994: 83; that of women, p. 92.
63. Stewart, A. 1997: 38. For male nudity in Greek sculpture, see Ridgeway 1977: 53–54; Bonfante 1989 examines public nudity as a costume; Sutton 1992: 21 remarks "Male nudity was a common convention in Greek art which attracts little attention except when first encountered, whereas female nudes are rare in archaic and classical Greek art except in the private medium of vase painting . . . . Pervasive male nudity is one of the more peculiar conventions of Greek art, one that is not easily explained."
64. Although Brendel 1970: 32; Williams 1983: 99; and Bonfante 1989: 559 assume most nude representations of women on late archaic and classical Athenian vases depict prostitutes, Sutton 1992: 24 argues that these scenes can be taken as showing hetaeras on the grounds of nudity alone. For vase depictions of hetaeras generally, see Peschel 1987 and Reinsberg 1993: 88–146.
65. Wool-working scenes featuring nude women appear to be hetaeras; see Rodenwaldt 1932; Brendel 1970: 38–40; Williams 1983: 96; Bonfante 1989: 561. Keuls 1983 argues that the combination of the risqué and the respectable in these scenes titillated Athenian men, but I agree with the interpretation of Davidson 1997: 85–89 and 331 n. 50 that such scenes reflect the function of brothels as textile factories. He adduces as evidence the presence of loomweights in building Z of the Cerameicus, presumably a brothel, from the fifth and fourth centuries B.C.E. Cohen 2002 assumes that the female woolworkers listed in the *phialai exeleutherikai*, our primary source for the manumission of Athenian slaves, also moonlighted as brothel workers. For the debate on "spinning" hetaeras, see Rodenwaldt 1932; Keuls 1985: 258–9; and Reinsberg 1993: 122–5. A similar practice is found in medieval England, where one regulation prohibited brothel keepers from requiring workers to spin or card wool, thereby limiting their ability to exploit their prostitutes for profit, for which see Karras 1996: 39.
66. Richter 1970: 200–201; Sutton 1992: 21. On the dating of the Cnidian Aphrodite, see Havelock 1995: 9.
67. Osborne 1994: 82 also cites Cratine in Poseidippos as a model for the Cnidian Aphrodite, for which see Jacoby *FGH* 447 F1.
68. Paus. 9. 27. 5; Plut. *Mor.* 753f; Alciphr. 4. 4. 1.
69. On the statue of Eros given to Phryne by Praxiteles , see Asclepiades, *Anth. Pal.* 5. 181; on its dedication to the Thespians as the price of her labors (*misthon huper lektrōn*), see Geminus, *Anth. Pal.* 6. 260; as a metaphor for the passion of the sculptor and hetaera; see Julianus, *Anth. Pal.* 16. 203, 205; see also Raubitschek 1941: 899.
70. Sutton 1992: 23–24; Williams 1983: 97–9.
71. The statue apparently prompted viewers to masturbate; cf. Plin. *HN* 36. 4. 21; Lucian *Amores* 13–14; cf. also Alciphr. 4. 1. 9–11.
72. For a discussion of the dynamics of viewer and viewed in this letter, see Rosenmeyer 2001.
73. Similarly, Osborne 1994 argues that the modest gesture of the Cnidian's right hand shows an uncharacteristic awareness of publicity; in contrast to other scenes in which female nakedness is "realistically 'motivated,'" that is to say, placed in a normative context such as bathing.
74. Cooper 1995: 304 and 305. n. 7 discusses the sources of this story and their influence on later writers.
75. On the charges, see Cantarelli 1885; Semenov 1935; Kowalski 1947; and Cooper 1995: 306, n. 10.
76. To give just a few examples, cf. Eur. *Hec.* 271–78; *Med.* 324, 709–18.

Chapter 5

1. Nossis, *Anth. Pal.* 9. 332; trans. Paton. Many thanks to Catherine Keesling and William Aylward for their comments on earlier drafts of this chapter.

2. On prostitution in Herodotus, see Kurke 1999: 220–46.

3. Pirenne-Delforge 1994: 26–40 discusses the cult of Aphrodite Pandemos at Athens; for ancient sources, cf. Nicander of Colophon *FGrH* 271 F9 and Philemon, *Adelphoi* F3 KA = 569d–e; Paus. 1. 22. 3; Harpocr. s. v. *Pandemos Aphrodite*.

4. For the idea of dedications of hetaeras and their portrait statues as transgressive, see Keesling 2002. I am extremely grateful to Catherine Keesling for sharing her essay with me before its publication.

5. Kirshenblatt-Gimblett 1998: 72. Stewart, S. 1993: 146–7 has a similar analysis of the souvenir as a means of miniaturizing and interiorizing the experience of travel.

6. Note that Myrtilus attributes the quote to a different play by the same author, the *Cynagis*, F8 KA = 572d.

7. According to Hesychius, both male and female friends frequented the temple of the hetaera, cf. Hesych. s. v. *hetairas hieron*; see also Dillon 2002: 190–2.

8. On the Hetaerideia, cf. Hegesander *FGrH* 4 F25 = 572e; see also Dillon 2002: 198–9.

9. See Pirenne-Delforge 1994: 428; on Aphrodite Hetaera, cf. Apollodorus *FGrH* 244 F112 = 571 c; Hesych. s. v. *Hetairas hieron*; Photius s. v. *Hetairas*; Clem. Al. *Protr.* 2. 39. 2.

10. Cf. Paus. 3. 18. 1; see Pirenne-Delforge 1994: 210 and n. 89 on the statue; on importance of youth for prostitutes, see p. 429.

11. Pirenne-Delforge 1994: 428, "le patronage qu' Aphrodite accordait à la sexualité concourait à placer l' activité des filles publiques sous sa protection, l' érigeant en véritable référence divine de la 'corporation.'"

12. The cult epithet *Melainis* honored Aphrodite throughout Greece; see Pirenne-Delforge 1994: 97–8 (harbor at Corinth); 252–3 (Arcadia); 291–3 and note 114 (Thespiae); cf. Paus. 9. 27. 5. On the nocturnal nature of Aphrodite's work, cf. Eur. *Hipp.* 106.

13. On prenuptial sacred prostitution, see Pirenne-Delforge 1994 and Rudhardt 1975: 122–4: 118–9; Hdt. 1. 93; Strabo 11. 14. 16.

14. For arguments against temple prostitution in ancient Greece, see Conzelmann 1967; Calame 1989; and Pirenne-Delforge 1994: 112–113. In favor, see Vanoyeke 1990: 29–31. Dillon 2002: 199–202 takes the statements of Athenaeus, and other late writers, at face value, and assumes the existence of sacred prostitution at Corinth, as does Kurke 1996: 68–9, n. 3.

15. On the meanings of *amphipolos*, see Hiller 1987; on the passage generally, see Pirenne-Delforge 1994: 112–3, and n. 109.

16. Pirenne-Delforge 1994: 115–6; on prostitution at Corinth in comedy, see Anderson, W.S. 1986. Aristophanes of Byzantium gives two glosses of the verb κορινθιάζομαι, both implying prostitution.

17. For variations on this saying, cf. Ar. F928 KA, which states that the difficulty of Corinth resides in the sorcery (*goēteia*) of its hetaeras; Hesych. s. v. *ou pantos andros es Korinthon esth' ho plous*; for other late references, including Photius and Xenobius; cf. Strabo 8. 6. 20; 12. 3. 36; Aul. Gel. *NA* 1. 8. See also Pirenne-Delforge 1994: 115–6, nn. 119–120; a complete discussion of the phrase and its comic origins is found in Anderson, W. 1986.

18. For literary evidence of prostitutes visiting temples of Aphrodite, cf. Theopomp. *FGrH* 115 F285a–b; Timaeus *FGrH* 566 F10 = 573d; and Machon 336 = 581a. On the sanction against prostitutes entering other types of temples, see Derenne 1930: 9; Dillon 2002: 190–91 and 346, n. 5 discusses Neaera in this light; cf. [Dem.] 59. 85–86, 113–14; Is. 6. 50.

19. On the Adonia, see Deubner 1932: 222; Winkler 1990: 189; cf. Ar. *Lys.* 387–396; Men. *Sam.* 35–50 Sandbach; Diphilus F42. 38–40 KA. See also Atallah 1966; Weill 1966; and Pirenne-Delforge 1994: 21–25.

20. For other references to the Aphrodisia; cf. Ath. 3. 101f; 4. 128b; 13. 574b–c; 579e; Lucian *Dial. meret.* 14. 3; Eust. *Erot.* 3. 2; Xen. *Hell.* 5. 4. 4; Plut. *Mor.* 301f. See also Pirenne-Delforge 1994: 393–4.

21. Palladas, Anth. *Pal.* 10. 48.

22. Pomeroy 1984: 28–40; Kron 1996: 171–72.

23. For the story, cf. Lucian *Syr. D.* 17–21; cf. also Plut. *Demetr.* 38 (marriage to Antiochus, son of Seleucus I). For inscriptional evidence, see Segre 1931; Ridgway 1987: 408 and n. 56; and Kron 1996: 172 and n. 148.

24. Ridgway 1987: 407; and Kron 1996: 172.

25. On the temple of Bilistiche-Aphrodite, see Cameron 1990: 300.
26. Strab. 17. 1. 11; cf. Polyb. 14. 11. 5; Plut. *Cleom.* 33; *Mor.* 753d.
27. Python of Catana, or Alexander, *Agen* 91 F 1 *TrGF* = 595e–f, and Diod. Sic. 17. 108; see also Dillon 2002: 196
28. Symeonoglou 1985: 148; see also Pirenne-Delforge 1994: 286–7.
29. Humphreys 1983: 92. According to Keesling 2003: 76, only about 10% of archaic Attic funerary monuments commemorate women. *Mnēmata* connected with citizen women include that of Learete, c. 430–420, Mnesagora, and Nichochares; see Humphreys 1983: 92–3.
30. Dillon 2002: 197 observes that "in death prostitutes were the equal and sometimes more so of their citizen counterparts," but fails to take into account the exceedingly negative connotations of most funerary commemorations of hetaeras.
31. As a *graus*, cf. Timocles' *Orestautocleides* F27 KA = 567f; for her relationship with fish, cf. Alexis' *Agonis* or *Hippiskos* F2 KA; Antiphanes' *Halieuomene* F27 KA; Timocles' *Ikarioi* F16 KA = 8. 338f–339d.
32. On this passage and the term *basilissa* among the Macedonian dynasts, see Carney 1991: 158–60.
33. For a complete discussion of the monument and its remains, with a reconstruction, see Scholl 1994: 254–61; see also Travlos 1988: 177, 181; Dillon 2002: 196; cf. also Plut. *Phoc.* 22. 1–2; Diod. Sic. 17. 108. 5.
34. Elsewhere we learn that Demetrius levied a tax on the Athenians in the amount of 250 talents, then used the money to buy soap for his lover Lamia and her colleagues, cf. Plut. *Dem.* 27. 1.
35. On the grave of Lais, see Dillon 2002: 196–7; Paus. 2. 2. 4; Plut. *Mor.* 767f–768a; Polemon F44 Preller = 589a–b; for Lais generally, cf. Plut. *Nic.* 15. 4; Hyp. F13 Jensen; Strattis F27 KA; Nymphadorus *FGrH* 572 F1 = 588f; Timaeus *FGrH* 566 F14 = 589a–b.
36. Ath. 6. 264c; according to Plut. *Mor.* 397f, the crown belonged to the Cnidians.
37. Of the seventeen female names, only two identified themselves as citizen wives by inscribing their husband's names and demotics; two women who made a joint dedication were non-Attic sisters from Argos; and another identified herself as a washerwoman. It has been commonly assumed that the others were prostitutes; for further discussion, see Keesling 2003: 76; Ridgway 1987: 401; Aleshire 1989: 76; and Kron 1996: 160–1.
38. On the offerings of hetaeras, see Rouse 1975: 355 and p. 92; and Dillon 2002: 197–8. Keesling 2002 examines the physical evidence for Rhodopis' dedication and shows how it transgressed dedicatory norms; see also the excellent discussions of Ridgway 1987: 406; Reden 1997: 173–4 and Kurke 1999: 220–5. Kron 1996: 161–2 suggests that Iphidice, who dedicated a contemporary votive column to Athena on the Athenian Acropolis, may have been a wealthy Ionian hetaera; see also Ridgway 1987: 401–402.
39. For a list of tithes made by various professionals, see Rouse 1975: 58–60.
40. Keesling 2002 and n. 13; cf. Plut. *Lys.* 17. 1–3; against this view, see Reden 1997: 160.
41. Steiner 2001: 268–9 and n. 66; cf. Paus. 10. 9. 7; Thuc. 1. 132. 2–4.
42. On the statue of Conon, see Boardman 1995: 103; the reputedly realistic traits of a statue of Themistocles were probably exceptional (see fig. 246).
43. See Ridgway 1987: 405 and Kron 1996: 142–3. A survey of Greek dedicatory inscriptions, including not only large-scale dedications, from the eighth to late fifth century yields a total of 884, of which only 80 can be ascribed to females; see Kron 1996: 161; and Keesling 2003: 75–77. For honorific images of priestesses placed in sanctuaries, cf. Paus. 2. 7. 3; 2. 35. 8; 7. 25. 7.
44. On the statue of Niceso, see Kron 1996: 147–7; on sacerdotal votives and female independence, see pp. 149 and 155.
45. Lysimache, priestess of Athena, represents a female version of this type of statue; see Ridgway 1987: 405. See also Keesling 2002; on the subject generally, see Rouse 1975: 372–3.
46. On this statue and its violation of conventions regarding portrait statues, see Keesling 2002 on the portrait of royal women, see Gauthier 1985: 74–75 and Kron 1996: 171–82.
47. Kaibel's emendation of the manuscript reading of καὶ περιορᾷ to καθάπερ θεὰν ὁρᾷ clearly shows he also had a similar interpretation in mind.
48. A woman named Melissa, daughter of Procles, ruler of Epidaurus, dons this garment at 589f, while pouring wine for the workmen. Note that the name Cleino crops up elsewhere in connection with two little gold pots offered at Delos, for which see Rouse 1975: 93.

49. On the specifics of this statue, see Raubitschek 1941: 900–901. Ridgway 1987: 406 states that it is "indisputable" that the hetaera dedicated her own portrait, along with other statues of Praxiteles in various sanctuaries.
50. The story of Thais' burning of the city was popular among later writers, both Greek and Roman; cf. Plut. *Alex.* 38; Arrian 3. 18. 10; Quint. Curt. 5. 7. 3–7.
51. On the lion as a funerary monument, see Rouse 1975: 144 and Boardman 1995: 114–15 and fig. 114.
52. Keesling 2002 observes that "oral traditions tended to fill the gaps left by inscriptions, and in this case the connection with Leaina effectively explained why there was a statue of a lioness standing next to one of Aphrodite."
53. Contrary to what one might expect, ancient Greek women could found cults and sanctuaries; in Pausanias, we find numerous *hieroi logoi* about female founders; see Kron 1996: 153.
54. Theopomp. *FGrH* 115 F285a–b; Timaeus *FGrH* 566 F10 = 573d. For the ritual use of *pinakes* more generally, see Rouse 1975: 135 and n. 3; MacLachlan 1995 discusses votive tablets at Locris. As Keesling 2002 notes, inscribed catalogues of exclusively women's names, as well as representations of groups of women in votive sculpture, would have been quite rare in fifth-, and even fourth-century, Greece. Ridgway 1987: 405 notes that depictions of groups of worshipers confronting a divinity became increasingly common by the early and mid-fourth century.
55. The plaque may have shown a visual representation of a group of supplicating courtesans, for which, see Dillon 2002: 201, or may have contained an inscribed list of their names; according to see Pirenne-Delforge 1994: 109, and van Groningen 1956: 13–4, 22, the participle *grapsantōn* does not permit anything more precise. See also Keesling 2002.
56. Pirenne-Delforge 1994: 104–6 discusses the ancient sources for the prayers of the Corinthian women.
57. Gutzwiller 1998: 80–82 discusses *Anth. Pal.* 6. 275 in the context of the collection; in her view, "The portraits all show forth a beauty that belongs both to the artistic object and to the woman it represents."
58. Gutzwiller 1998: 143 and *passim*; Pomeroy 1977; Cameron 1981: 277.
59. On this type of dedication, see Rouse 1975: 72; on the epigrams, see Olson and Sens 1999: 150, and the discussion of Leonidas in Gutzwiller 1998: 88–97.
60. On mirror dedications and women, see Ridgway 1987: 402–3; and Kron 1996: 159.
61. Keesling 2002, and n. 21.
62. Votive offerings often marked any change in professional status, for which see Rouse 1975: 74, and n. 4.
63. On this type of dedication, see Rouse 1975: 249 and n. 11.

Conclusion

1. Lucian *Rhet. praeceptor* 12.
2. For the effeminization of sophists, cf. Philostr. *VS* 570–1 (arranging hair, polishing nails, myrrh); and Philostr. *VS* 623 (on the offensive gait, unsuitable attire, effeminate voice, and indolent language of Philiscus).
3. Kirshenblatt-Gimblett 1998: 149 describes heritage as "a new mode of cultural production in the present that has recourse to the past."

Bibliography

Adams, N. 1983. "Words for 'Prostitute' in Latin." *RhM* 126: 321–58.

Alcock, S., J. Cherry, and J. Elsner. 2001. *Pausanias: Travel and Memory in Roman Greece*. Oxford and New York.

Aleshire, S. 1989. *The Athenian Asklepieion: The People, Their Dedications, and the Inventories*. Amsterdam.

Ambaglio, D. 1990. "*I Deipnosophisti* di Ateneo e la tradizione storica frammentaria." *Athenaeum* 78: 51–64.

Anderson, G. 2000. "The Banquet of Belles-Lettres: Athenaeus and the Comic Symposium." In Braund and Wilkins 2000: 316–26.

———. 1997. "Athenaeus: the Second Sophistic Environment." *ANRW* II:34:3: 2173–2185.

———. 1993. *The Second Sophistic: A Cultural Phenomenon in the Roman Empire*. London and New York.

Anderson, W. 1986. "Corinth and Comedy." In *Corinthiaca. Studies in Honor of Darrell A. Amyx*, 44–9. Columbia, MO.

Apter, E. and W. Pietz (eds.). 1993. *Fetishism as Cultural Discourse*. Ithaca, NY.

Arnott, W. G. 2000. "Athenaeus and the Epitome: Texts, Manuscripts and Early Editions." In Braund and Wilkins 2000: 41–52.

———. 1996. *Alexis: The Fragments. A Commentary*. Cambridge.

Atallah, W. 1966. *Adonis dans la littérature et l' art grecs*. Paris.

Bagnall, R. 1991. "The Prostitute Tax in Roman Egypt." *Bulletin of the American Society of Papyrology* 28: 5–12.

Bakhtin, M. 1984. *Rabelais and His World*. Trans. H. Iswolsky. Bloomington, IN.

Baldwin, B. 1977. "The Minor Characters in Athenaeus." *Acta Classica* 20: 37–48.

———. 1976. "Athenaeus and his Work." *Acta Classica* 19: 21–42.

Bassi, K. 1998. *Acting Like Men: Gender, Drama, and Nostalgia in Ancient Greece*. Michigan.

Beard, M. and J. Henderson. 1997. "With This Body I Thee Worship: Sacred Prostitution in Antiquity." *Gender & History* 9: 480–503.

Beazley, J. D. 1963. *Attic Red-figure Vase-painters*. 2nd ed. Oxford.

———. 1956. *Attic Black-figure Vase-painters*. Oxford.

Bechtel, F. 1902. *Die Attischen Frauennammen nach ihrem Systeme dargestellt*. Göttingen.

Benjamin, W. 1999. *The Arcades Project*. Trans. H. Eiland and K. McLaughlin. Cambridge, MA.

Bernheimer, C. 1993. "Fetishism and Decadence: Salome's Severed Heads." In E. Apter and W. Pietz (eds.), *Fetishism as Cultural Discourse*, 62–83. Ithaca, NY.

———. 1989. *Figures of Ill Repute: Representing Prostitution in Nineteenth-century France*. Cambridge, MA.

Bieber, M. 1939. "Mima Saltatricula." *AJA* 43: 640–4.

———. 1928. *Griechische Kleidung*. Berlin.

Bloedow, E. 1975. "Aspasia and the 'Mystery' of the *Menexenos*." *Wiener Studien* 9: 32–8.

Boardman, J. 1995. *Greek Sculpture: The Late Classical Period*. London.

————. 1986. "Leaina." In H. Brijder, A. Drukker, and C. Neeft (eds.), *Enthousiasmos: Essays on Greek and Related Pottery Presented to J. M. Hemelrijk*, 93–6. Amsterdam.

————. 1976. "A Curious Eye Cup." *Archaeologisher Anzeiger*: 281–91.

Bompaire, J. 1958. *Lucien écrivain. Imitation et création*. Bibl. des Écoles franç. d' Athènes & de Rome 190. Paris.

Bonfante, L. 1989. "Nudity as Costume in Classical Art." *AJA* 93: 543–70.

Bowersock, G. 1969. *Greek Sophists in the Roman Empire*. Oxford.

Bowie, E. L. 1994. "The Readership of Greek Novels in the Ancient World." In J. Tatum (ed.), *The Search for the Ancient Novel*, 435–52. Baltimore.

————. 1985. "Athenaeus." In P. E. Easterling and B. M. W. Knox (eds.), *Cambridge History of Classical Literature*, 1. 682–3. Cambridge.

————. 1982. "The Importance of Sophists." *YClS* 27: 29–59.

————. 1970. "Greeks and their Past in the Second Sophistic." *P&P* 46: 3–41 [= 1974. In M. I. Finley (ed.), *Studies in Ancient Society*, 166–209. London and Boston.]

Branham, R. 1989. *Unruly Eloquence: Lucian and the Comedy of Traditions*. Cambridge, MA.

Branham, R. and Goulet-Cazé. M. 1996. *The Cynics: The Cynic Movement in Antiquity and its Legacy*. Berkeley.

Braund, D. "Learning, Luxury and Empire: Athenaeus' Roman Patron." In Braund and Wilkins 2000: 1–22.

Braund, D. and J. Wilkins (eds.). 2000. *Athenaeus and His World*. Exeter.

Brendel, O. 1970. "The Scope and Temperament of Erotic Art in the Graeco-Roman World." In T. Bowie et al. (eds.), *Studies in Erotic Art*, 3–107. New York.

Brown, P. G. McC. 1990. "Plots and Prostitutes in Greek New Comedy." *Papers of the Leeds International Seminar* 6: 241–66

————. 1987. "Masks, Names and Characters in New Comedy." *Hermes* 115: 181–203.

Brunt, P. 1980. "On Historical Fragments and Epitomes." *CQ* 30: 477–94.

Buck-Morss, S. 1986. "The Flaneur, the Sandwichman and the Whore: The Politics of Loitering." *New German Critique* 39: 99–140.

Bushala, E. 1969. "The *Pallake* of Philoneus." *AJP* 90: 65–72.

Butler, J. 1993. *Bodies that Matter: On the Discursive Limits of 'Sex.'* New York.

Byrne, S. and M. Osborne (eds.). 1994. *Lexicon of Greek Personal Names. Volume II. Attica*. Oxford.

Calame, C. 1989. "Entre rapports de parenté et relations civique: Aphrodite l'hetaire au banquet politique des hetaîroi." In *Aux Sources de la Puissance: Sociabilité et Parenté*, Actes du Colloque de Rouen 12–13 Novembre 1987: 101–9.

Cameron, A. 1998. "Black and White: A Note on Ancient Nicknames." *AJP* 119: 113–7.

————. 1990. "Two Mistresses of Ptolemy Philadelphus." *GRBS* 31: 287–311.

————. 1981. "Asclepiades' Girlfriends." In H. P. Foley (ed.), *Reflections of Women in Antiquity*, 275–302. New York.

Campbell, D. (ed. and trans.). 1992. *Greek Lyric. Volume 4*. Cambridge, MA.

Cantarelli, L. 1885. "Osservazioni sul processo di Frine." *RIFC* 13: 465–82.

Carey, C. 1992. *Apollodoros Against Neaera: [Demosthenes] 59*. Warminster.

Carney, E. 1991. "'What's in a Name?': The Emergence of a Title for Royal Women in the Hellenistic Period." In Pomeroy 1991: 138–54.

Castner, C. 1982. "Epicurean Hetairai as Dedicants to Healing Deities?" *GRBS* 23: 51–7.

Chaniotis, A. 1997. "Theatricality Beyond the Theater. Staging Public Life in the Hellenistic World." *Pallas* 47: 219–259.

Citti, V. 1997. "Una Coppia Nominale in Lisia." In M. Moggi and C. Cordiano (eds.), *Schiavi e dipendenti nell' ambito dell 'oikos' e della 'familia'*, 91–6. Pisa.

Cohen, B. (ed.). 2000. *Not the Classical Ideal: Athens and the Construction of the Other in Greek Art*. Leiden.

Cohen, E. 2002. "Salaried Whores and Entrepreneurial Courtesans: An Economic Analysis of Athenian Prostitution." Paper delivered at the conference, "Prostitution in the Ancient World," held at the University of Wisconsin, Madison, Wisconsin, April 12–14, 2002.

Collard, C. 1969. "Athenaeus, the Epitome, Eustathius and Quotations from Tragedy." *RFIC* 97: 157–79.

Conzelmann, H. 1967. "Korinth und die Mädchen der Aphrodite: Zur Religionsgeschichte der Stadt Korinth." *Nachrichten der Akademie der Wissenschaften im Göttingen*. Phil.-Hist. Kl. 8: 247–61.

Cooper, C. 1995. "Hyperides and the Trial of Phryne." *Phoenix* 49: 303–18.

Corbin, A. 1990. *Women for Hire: Prostitution and Sexuality in France after 1850.* Trans. A. Sheridan. Cambridge, MA.

Crome, J. 1966. "Spinnende Hetairen?" *Gymnasium* 73: 245–7.

Dalby, S. 2000. "Lynceus and the Anecdotists." In Braund and Wilkins 2000: 372–94.

———. 1996. *Siren Feasts: A History of Food and Gastronomy in Greece.* London and New York.

Daremberg, C. and E. Saglio. 1877–1919. *Dictionnaire des antiquités.* vol 4. 2. Paris.

Davidson, J. 1997. *Courtesans and Fishcakes: The Consuming Passions of Classical Athens.* New York.

Dean-Jones, L. 1994. *Women's Bodies in Classical Greek Science.* Oxford.

Derenne, E. 1930. *Les procès d' impieté.* Liège and Paris.

Desrousseaux, M. (ed.). 1956. *Les deipnosophistes.* Paris.

Detienne, M. 1977. *The Gardens of Adonis.* Trans. J. Lloyd. New York.

Deubner, L. 1932. *Attische Feste.* 2nd ed. Berlin.

De Vries, K. 1973. "East Meets West at Dinner." *Expedition* 15: 32–9.

Dihle, A. 1994. *Greek and Latin Literature of the Roman Empire: From Augustus to Justinian.* Trans. M. Malzahn. London and New York.

Dillon, M. 2002. *Girls and Women in Classical Greek Religion.* London and New York.

Dimakis, P. 1988. "Orateurs et Hetaïres dans l'Athènes Classiques." In P. Dimakis (ed.), *Éros et droit en Grèce classique.* Paris.

Dittenberger, W. 1903. "Athenaeus und sein Werk." In *Apophoreton.* 47. Versammlung deutscher Philologen und Schulmänner. Berlin.

Dover, K. 1989. *Greek Homosexuality.* 2nd ed. Cambridge, MA.

Downer, L. 2001. *Women of the Pleasure Quarters: The Secret History of the Geisha.* New York.

Dudley, D. 1998. *A History of Cynicism: From Diogenes to the 6th Century A.D.* 2nd ed. Bristol. [Reprint of 1937 Methuen edition.]

Dupont, F. 1977. *Le plaisir et la loi: du Banquet de Platon au Satiricon.* Paris.

Edwards, C. 1997. "Unspeakable Professions: Public Performance and Prostitution in Ancient Rome." In Hallett and Skinner 1997: 66–95

Egger, B. 1994. "Women and Marriage in the Greek Novels: The Boundaries of Romance." In J. Tatum (ed.), *The Search for the Ancient Novel,* 260–82. Baltimore.

Ehlers, B. 1966. *Eine vorplatonische Deutung des sokratischen Eros: Der Dialog Aspasia des Sokratikers Aischines.* Munich.

Ehrenberg, V. 1951. *The People of Aristophanes: A Sociology of Old Comedy.* Oxford.

Fantham, E. 1975. "Sex, Status, and Survival in Hellenistic Athens: A Study of Women in New Comedy." *Phoenix* 29: 44–74.

Faraone. C. 1999. *Ancient Greek Love Magic.* Cambridge, MA.

Featherstone, M., M. Hepworth and B. Turner (eds.). 1991. *The Body: Social Process and Cultural Theory.* London.

Flower, M. 1994. *Theopompus of Chios.* Oxford.

Ford, J. 1993. "Bookshelf on Prostitution." *Biblical Theory Bulletin* 23: 128–34.

Foucault, M. 1988. *The Care of the Self.* Trans. R. Hurley. New York.

Fragiadakis, C. 1988. *Die attischen Sklavennamen von der spätarchaischen Epoche bis in die römische Kaiserzeit: Eine historische und soziologische Untersuchung.* Inaugural dissertation. Mannheim.

Fraser, P. M. 2000. "Ethnics as Personal Names." In Hornblower and Matthews 2000: 149–57.

———. 1972. *Ptolemaic Alexandria.* 3 vols. Oxford: Clarendon Press.

Fraser, P. M. and E. Matthews (eds.). 1987. *Lexicon of Greek Personal Names. Volume I. The Aegean Islands, Cyprus, Cyrenaica.* Oxford.

Gabba, E. 1982. "Political and Cultural Aspects of the Classicist Revival in the Augustan Age." *CA* 1: 43–65.

Gagarin, M. 2001. "Women's Voices in Attic Oratory." In Lardinois and McClure 2001: 161–76.

Garlan, Y. 1988. *Slavery in Ancient Greece.* Trans. J. Lloyd. Ithaca, NY.

Gauthier, P. 1985. *Les cités grecques et leurs bienfaiteurs.* Athens and Paris.

Gilula, D. 2000. "Stratonicus, the Witty Harpist." In Braund and Wilkins 2000: 423–33.

———. 1977. "The Mask of the Pseudokore." *GRBS* 18: 247–50.

Glazebrook, A. 2002. "The Bad Girls of Athens: The Image and Function of *Hetairai* in Judicial Oratory." Paper delivered at the conference, "Prostitution in the Ancient World," held at the University of Wisconsin, Madison, Wisconsin, April 12–14, 2002.

Gleason, M. 1991. *Making Men: Sophists and Self-Presentation in Ancient Rome.* Princeton.

Glenn, C. 1994. "Sex, Lies, and Manuscript: Refiguring Aspasia in the History of Rhetoric." *CCC* 45.2: 180–199.

Golden, M. 1986. "Names and Naming at Athens." *Echos du monde classique/ Classical Views* 30: 245–69.

Goldhill, S. (ed.). 2001. *Being Greek under Rome: Cultural Identity, the Second Sophistic and the Development of Empire.* Cambridge.

———. 1998. "The Seductions of the Gaze: Socrates and His Girlfriends." In P. Cartledge, P. Millett, and S. von Reden (eds.), *Kosmos: Essays in Order, Conflict and Community in Classical Athens*, 105–24. Cambridge.

———. 1995. *Foucault's Virginity.* Cambridge.

———. 1992. Review of Reinsberg, *Ehe, Hetärentum und Knabenliebe im antiken Griechenland,* and Winkler, *Contraints of Desire, JHS* 112: 196–8.

Gomme, A. W. and F. H. Sandbach. 1973. *Menander: A Commentary.* Oxford.

Gordon, P. 1996. *Epicurus in Lycia: The Second-Century World of Diogenes of Oenoanda.* Ann Arbor.

Gow, A. S. F. 1965. *Machon: The Fragments.* Cambridge.

Greenwalt, W. 1989. "Polygamy and Succession in Argead Macedonia." *Arethusa* 22: 19–45.

Griffin, A. 1982. *Sicyon.* Oxford.

Gulick, C. B. (ed.). 1927–1941. *Athenaeus: The Deipnosophists.* 7 vols. Cambridge, MA.

Gutzwiller, K. 1998. *Poetic Garlands: Hellenistic Epigrams in Context.* Berkeley and Los Angeles.

Hallett, J. and M. Skinner (eds.). 1997. *Roman Sexualities.* Princeton.

Halliwell, S. 1991. "The Uses of Laughter in Greek Culture." *CQ* 41: 279–96.

Halperin, D. 1990a. "The Democratic Body: Prostitution and Citizenship in Classical Athens." In *One Hundred Years of Homosexuality and Other Essays on Greek Love*, 88–112. New York and London.

———. 1990b. "Why is Diotima a Woman?" in D. Halperin, J. Winkler, and F. Zeitlin (eds.), *Before Sexuality.* Princeton.

Halperin, D., J. Winkler, and F. Zeitlin (eds.). 1990. *Before Sexuality.* Princeton.

Handley, E. W. 1985. "From Aristophanes to Menander." In P. E. Easterling and B. M. W. Knox (eds.), *Cambridge History of Classical Literature*, 1. 398–413. Cambridge.

Harrison, A. 1968. *The Law of Athens.* 2 vols. Oxford.

Harvey, D. 1988. "Painted Ladies: Fact, Fiction and Fantasy." In J. Christiansen and T. Melander (eds.), *Proceedings of the 3rd Symposium on Ancient Greek and Related Pottery*, 242–54. Copenhagen.

Hasan-Rokem, G. and D. Shulman (eds.). 1996. *Untying the Knot: On Riddles and Other Enigmatic Modes.* New York.

Hauschild, H. 1933. *Die Gestalt der Hetäre in der griechischen Komödie.* Leipzig.

Havelock, C. 1995. *The Aphrodite of Knidos and her Successors.* Michigan.

Hawley, Richard. 1993. " 'Pretty, Witty and Wise': Courtesans in Athenaeus' *Deipnosophistae* Book 13." *International Journal of Moral and Social Studies* 8. 1: 73–89.

Heath, J. 1986. "The Supine Hero in Catullus 32." *CJ* 82: 28–36.

Henderson, J. 1991. *The Maculate Muse: Obscene Language in Attic Comedy.* Oxford.

———. 1987a. "Older Women in Attic Comedy." *TAPA* 117: 105–29.

———. 1987b. *Aristophanes* Lysistrata. Oxford.

Henry, M. 2000. "Athenaeus the Ur-Pornographer." In Braund and Wilkins 2000: 503–10.

———. 1995. *Prisoner of History: Aspasia of Miletus and her Biographical Tradition.* New York.

———. 1992. "The Edible Woman: Athenaeus' Concept of the Pornographic." In Richlin 1992a: 250–68.

———. 1985. *Menander's Courtesans and the Greek Comic Tradition.* Frankfurt.

Hering, E. 1967. *Angeklagt ist Aspasia.* Leipzig.

Hershatter, G. 1999. *Dangerous Pleasures: Prostitution and Modernity in Twentieth Century Shanghai.* Berkeley and Los Angeles.

Herter, H. 1960. "Die Soziologie der antiken Prostitution im Lichte des heidnischen und christlichen Schrifttums." *Jahrbuch für Antike und Christentum* 3: 70–111.

———. 1957. "Dirne." In *Realexikon für Antike und Christentum* 3: 1149–213.

Hertz, N. 1983. "A Reading of Longinus." *Critical Inquiry* 9: 579–96.

Hiller, St. 1987. "A-PI-QUO-RO AMPHIPOLOI." *Minos* 20–22: 239–55.

Hirzel, R. 1962. *Der Name. Ein Beitrag zu seiner Geschichte im Altertum und Besonders bei den Griechen.* Abhandlungen der Philologische-Historischen Klasse der Sächsischen Akademie der Wissenschaften 36, 2. 2nd ed. Amsterdam.

Hock, R. and E. O'Neil (eds.). 1986. *The Chreia in Ancient Rhetoric: Volume 1, The Progymnasmata.* Atlanta, GA.

Hornblower, S. 2000. "Personal Names and the Study of the Ancient Greek Historians." In Hornblower and Matthews 2000: 129–43.

Hornblower, S. and E. Matthews (eds.). 2000. *Greek Personal Names: Their Value as Evidence*. Proceedings of the British Academy. vol. 104. Oxford.

Humphreys, S. 1997. "Fragments, Fetishes, and Philosophies: Towards a History of Greek Historiography after Thucydides." In G. Most (ed.), *Collecting Fragments/ Fragmente sammeln*, 207–24. Göttingen.

———. 1983. *The Family, Women and Death*. London and New York.

Hunter, R. 1989. *The New Comedy of Greece and Rome*. Cambridge.

Hunter, V. 1994. *Policing Athens: Social Control in the Attic Lawsuits, 420–320 B.C*. Princeton.

Immerwahr, H. 1990. *Attic Script: A Survey*. Oxford.

Jacob, C. 2000. "Athenaeus the Librarian." In Braund and Wilkins 2000: 85–110.

Jacoby, F. 1923—. *Fragmente der griechischen Historiker*. Leiden. [=*FGrH*]

Jansen, W. 1987. *Women without Men: Gender and Marginality in an Algerian Town*. Leiden.

Jocelyn, H. 1980. "A Greek Indecency and Its Students: LAIKAZEIN." *PCPS* n.s. 26: 12–66.

Just, R. 1989. *Women in Athenian Law and Life*. London and New York.

Kaibel, G. 1887–1890. *Athenaei Naucratitae, Dipnosophistarum Libri XV*. 3 vol. Leipzig.

Kampen, N. 1996. *Sexuality in Ancient Art*. Cambridge.

Kapparis, K. 1999. *Apollodoros "Against Neaira" [D.59]*. Berlin.

———. 1995. "Critical Notes on D. 59 'Against Neaira.'" *Hermes* 123: 19–27.

Karras, R. 1996. *Common Women: Prostitution and Sexuality in Medieval England*. Oxford.

Kebric, R. 1977. *In the Shadow of Macedon: Duris of Samos*. Historia Zeitschrift für alte Geschichte. Heft 29. Wiesbaden.

Keesling, C. 2003. *The Votive Statues of the Athenian Acropolis*. Cambridge.

———. 2002. "Heavenly Bodies: Monuments to Prostitutes in Greek Sanctuaries." Paper delivered at the conference, "Prostitution in the Ancient World," held at the University of Wisconsin, Madison, Wisconsin, April 12–14, 2002.

Keuls, E. 1985. *The Reign of the Phallus*. New York.

———. 1983. "The Hetaera and the Housewife: The Splitting of the Female Psyche in Greek Art." *Mededelingen van het Nederlands Instituut te Rome* 44/45: 23–40.

King, H. 1998. *Hippocrates' Woman: Reading the Female Body in Ancient Greece*. London and New York.

Kirshenblatt-Gimblett, B. 1998. *Destination Culture. Tourism, Museums, and Heritage*. Berkeley and Los Angeles.

Klein, W. 1898. *Die griechischen Vasen mit lieblingsinschriften*. Leipzig.

Konishi, H. 1986. "Euripides' *Medea* and Aspasia." *LCM* 11: 50–2.

Konstan, D. 1987. "Between Courtesan and Wife: Menander's *Perikeiromene*," *Phoenix* 41: 122–39.

Kost, M. 1971. *Musaios: Hero and Leander*. Bonn.

Kowalski, G. 1947. "De Phrynes Pectora Nudato." *Eos* 42: 50–62.

Krenkel, W. 1988. "Prostitution." In M. Grant and R. Kitzinger (eds.), *Civilization of the Ancient Mediterranean: Greece and Rome*, 2: 1291–7. New York.

Krieter-Spiro, M. 1997. *Sklaven, Köche und Hetären: Das Dienstpersonal bei Menander*. Stuttgart and Leipzig.

Kron, U. 1996. "Priesthoods, Dedications and Euergetism: What Part Did Religion Play in the Political and Social Process of Greek Women?" In P. Hellström and B. Alroth (eds.), *Religion and Power in the Ancient Greek World*, 139–82. Proceedings of the Uppsala Symposium, 1993. Uppsala.

Krueger, D. 1996. "The Bawdy and Society." In Branham and Goulet-Cazé 1996: 222–39.

Kurke, L. 2002. "Gender, Politics, and Subversion in the *Chreiai* of Machon." *PCPS* 48: 20–65.

———. 1999. *Coins, Bodies, Games, and Gold*. Princeton.

———. 1997. "Inventing the *Hetaira*: Sex, Politics and Discursive Conflict in Archaic Greece." *CA* 16: 106–53.

———. 1996. "Pindar and the Prostitutes, or Reading Ancient 'Pornography.'" *Arion* 3rd series, 4 2: 49–75.

Laqueur, T. 1990. *Making Sex: Body and Gender from the Greeks to Freud*. Cambridge, MA.

Lardinois, A. and L. McClure (eds.). 2001. *Making Silence Speak: Women's Voices in Greek Literature and Society*. Princeton.

Lateiner, D. 1989. *The Historical Method of Herodotus*. Toronto.

———. 1977. "No Laughing Matter: A Literary Tactic in Herodotus." *TAPA* 107: 173–82.

Lawler, L. 1978. *Dance of Ancient Greece*. Middletown, CT.

230 · Bibliography

———. 1950. "Ladles, Tubs, and the Greek Dance." *AJP* 71: 70–2.

———. 1947. "A Mortar Dance." *CJ* 43: 34.

Le Barillier, B. 1913. *Aspasie et Phryne.* Paris.

Lefkowitz, M. 1983. "Satyrus the Historian." In *Atti del xvii Congresso Internazionale di Papirologia*, 339–43. Naples.

———. 1981. *The Lives of the Greek Poets.* Baltimore.

Lerner, G. 1986. "The Origin of Prostitution in Ancient Mesopotamia." *Signs* 11: 236–54.

Licht, H. 1932. *Sexual Life in Ancient Greece.* Trans. J. Freese. New York.

Lind, H. 1988. "Ein Hetärenhaus am Heiligen Tor?" *Mus. Helv.* 45: 158–69.

Lissarrague, F. 1990. *The Aesthetics of the Greek Banquet: Images of Wine and Ritual.* Trans. A. Szegedy-Maszak. Princeton.

Lobel, E. (ed.). 1972. *The Oxyrhynchus Papyri.* vol. 39. London.

Lonie, I. 1981. *The Hippocratic Treatises:* On Generation, On the Nature of the Child, Diseases IV. Berlin and New York.

Lukinovich, A. 1990. "The Play of Reflections between Literary Form and the Sympotic Theme in the *Deipnosophistae* of Athenaeus." In Murray 1990: 263–71.

———. 1982. "Tradition Platonicienne et Polemique Antiphilosophique dans les Deip-nosophistes d' Athenée." Proceedings of the 16th International Eirene Conference, P. Oliva and A. Frolíková (eds.), 1: 228–33. Prague.

Lyne, R. O. A. M. 1980. *Latin Love Poets: from Catullus to Horace.* Oxford.

MacDowell, S. 1978. *The Law in Classical Athens.* Ithaca, NY.

MacLachlan, B. 1995. "Love, War and the Goddess in Fifth-Century Locri." *Ancient World* 26: 205–23.

Martin, J. 1931. *Symposion: Die Geschichte einer literarischen Form.* Paderborn.

Martin, R. 2001. "Just Like a Woman: Enigmas of the Lyric Voice." In Lardinois and McClure 2001: 55–74.

Marx, K. 1979. *Capital.* Ed. F. Engels. vol. 1. New York.

McClure, L. 1999a. *Spoken Like a Woman: Speech and Gender in Athenian Drama.* Princeton.

———. 1999b. "*The Worst Husband*: Discourses of Praise and Blame in Euripides' *Medea*." *CP* 94: 373–94.

McClure, L. and A. Lardinois (eds.). 2001. *Making Silence Speak: Women's Voices in Greek Literature and Society.* Princeton.

McGinn, T. 1998. *Prostitution, Sexuality and the Law in Ancient Rome.* Oxford.

McKechnie, P. 1989. *Outsiders in the Greek Cities in the Fourth Century B.C.* London and New York.

Milanezi, S. 2000. "Laughter as Dessert: On Athenaeus' Book 14, 613–616." In Braund and Wilkins 2000: 400–12.

Miner, J. 2003. "Courtesan, Concubine, Whore: Apollodorus' Deliberate Use of Terms for Prosti-tutes." *AJP* 124: 19–37.

Montuori, M. 1988. "Aspasia of Miletus." In *Socrates: An Approach*, 201–26. Trans. M. de la Pae Beresford. Amsterdam.

Moreno, P. 1964–65. "Il realismo nella pittura Greca del IV secolo AC." *Rivista d' archeologia e sto-ria d' arte* 13–14: 84–96.

Mulvey, L. 1987. "You Don't Know What Is Happening, Do You Mr. Jones?" In Parker and Pollock 1987: 127–31.

Murray, O. (ed.). 1990. *Sympotica: A Symposium on the Symposion.* Oxford.

Neils, J. 2000. "Others within the Other: An Intimate Look at Hetaerai and Maenads." In Cohen 2000: 203–26.

Nesselrath, H. 1990. *Die attische mittlere Komödie : Ihre Stellung in der antiken Literaturkritik und Literaturgeschichte.* Berlin and New York.

Ogden, D. 1999. *Polygamy, Prostitutes and Death.* London.

———. 1996. *Greek Bastardy.* Oxford.

Olson, S. D. 1992. "Names and Naming in Aristophanic Comedy." *CQ* 42: 304–19.

Olson, S. D. and A. Sens (eds.). 1999. *Matro of Pitane and the Tradition of Epic Parody in the Fourth Century BCE : Text, Translation, and Commentary.* Atlanta, GA.

Osborne, R. 1994. "Looking on—Greek Style. Does the Sculpted Girl Speak to Women too?" In I. Morris (ed.), *Classical Greece: Ancient Histories and Modern Archaeologies*, 81–96. Cam-bridge.

Parker, R. and G. Pollock (eds.). 1987. *Framing Feminism: Art and the Women's Movement 1970–1985.* London.

Patterson, C. 1994. "The Case against Neaira and the Public Ideology of the Athenian Family." In A. Boegeheld and A. Scafuro (eds.), *Athenian Identity and Civic Ideology*, 199–216. Baltimore.

———. 1990. "Those Athenian Bastards." *Classical Antiquity* 9: 40–73.

Patterson, O. 1982. *Slavery and Social Death: A Comparative Study*. Cambridge, MA.

Pelling, C. 2000. "Fun with Fragments: Athenaeus and the Historians." In Braund and Wilkins 2000: 171–90.

Pellizer, Ezio. 1990. "Outlines of a Morphology of Sympotic Entertainment." In Murray 1990: 177–84.

Peschel, I. 1987. *Die Hetäre bei Symposion und Komos in der attisch-rotfigurigen Vasenmalerei des 6.—4. Jahrhunderts vor Christus*. Frankfurt.

Pirenne-Delforge, V. 1994. *L' Aphrodite grecque*. Centre International d' Étude de la Religion Grecque Antique. Kernos Suppl. 4. Athens-Liège.

Pitts, A. 2002. "Prostitute, Muse, Lesbian: The Biographical Tradition of Sappho in Greek and Roman Literature." Ph.D. diss. University of Wisconsin–Madison.

Pollitt, J. 1986. *Art in the Hellenistic Age*. Cambridge.

Pollock. 1987a. "What's Wrong with 'Images of Women'?" In Parker and Pollock 1987: 132–8.

———. 1987b. "Feministry." In Parker and Pollock 1987: 238–43.

Pomeroy, S. 1997. *Families in Classical and Hellenistic Greece: Representations and Realities*. Oxford.

———. 1994. *Xenophon Oeconomicus. A Social and Historical Commentary*. Oxford.

———. (ed.). 1991. *Women's History and Ancient History*. Chapel Hill, NC.

———. 1984. *Women in Hellenistic Egypt*. New York.

———. 1977. "Technikai kai Mousikai." *American Journal of Ancient History* 2: 51–68.

———. 1975. *Goddesses, Whores, Wives, and Slaves. Women in Classical Antiquity*. New York.

Porter, J. 2001. "Ideals and Ruins: Pausanias, Longinus and the Second Sophistic." In Alcock, Cherry, and Elsner 2001: 63–92.

———. (ed.). 1999. *Constructions of the Classical Body*. Michigan.

Post, L. A. 1940. "Woman's Place in Menander's Athens" *TAPA* 71: 420–59.

Pritchard, J. B. 1943. *Palestinian Figurines in Relation to Certain Goddesses Known through Literature*. New Haven.

Radermacher, L. 1925. "Zur Geschichte der grieschischen Komödie." *SAWW* 202: 13–4.

Raubitschek, A. 1941. "Phryne." *RE* 20. 1: 893–901.

Rauch, A. 1988. "The *Trauerspiel* of the Prostituted Body, or Woman as Allegory of Modernity." *Cultural Critique* 10: 77–87.

Reardon, B. 1971. *Courants littéraires grecs du II et IIIieme siecles après J.-C*. Paris.

Reinsberg, C. 1993. *Ehe, Hetärentum und Knabenliebe im antiken Griechenland*. 2nd ed. Munich.

Relihan, J. 1992. "Rethinking the History of the Literary Symposium." *ICS* 17: 213–44.

Richlin, A. (ed.). 1992a. *Pornography and Representation in Greece and Rome*. Oxford.

———. 1992b. "Julia's Jokes." In B. Garlick, S. Dixon, and P. Allen (eds.), *Stereotypes of Women in Power*, 65–91. New York.

Richter, G. 1970. *Kouroi: Archaic Greek Youths. A Study of the Development of the Kouros Type in Greek Sculpture*. London and New York.

Ridgway, B. 1987. "Ancient Greek Women and Material Evidence." *AJA* 91: 399–409.

———. 1977. *The Archaic Style in Greek Sculpture*. Princeton.

———. 1970. *The Severe Style in Greek Sculpture*. Princeton.

Rigsby, K. 1995. Review of M. Osborne and S. Byrne, *A Lexicon of Greek Personal Names*. Volume II, *Attica*. (Oxford, 1994). *BMCR* 95. 05. 02.

Robinson, D., and E. Fluck. 1937. *A Study of the Greek Love Names*. Baltimore.

Rodenwaldt, G. 1932. "Spinnende Hetären." *AA* 47: 7–22.

Rosenmeyer, P. 2001. "(In-)Versions of Pygmalion: The Statue Talks Back." In Lardinois and McClure 2001: 240–60.

Rosivach, V. 1995. "Solon's Brothels." *Liverpool Classical Monthly* 20: 2–3.

Roth, M. 2002. "Marriage, Divorce and the Prostitute in Ancient Mesopotamia." Paper delivered at the conference, "Prostitution in the Ancient World," held at the University of Wisconsin, Madison, Wisconsin, April 12–14, 2002.

Rouse, W. 1975. *Greek Votive Offerings*. New York.

Rousselle, A. 1988. *Porneia: On Desire and the Body in Antiquity*. Trans. F. Pheasant. Oxford.

Rudhardt, J. 1975. *Chypre des origines au moyen âge.* Geneva.
Rudolph, F. 1891. "Die Quellen und die Schrifstellerei des Athenaios." *Philologus* Suppl. 6: 111–61.
Säflund, G. 1963. *Aphrodite Kallipygos.* Stockholm.
Sandbach, F. 1977. *The Comic Theater of Greece and Rome.* New York.
Schaps, D. 1977. "The Woman Least Mentioned: Etiquette and Women's Names." *CQ* 27: 323–30.
Schmidt, K. "Die griechischen Personennamen bei Plautus." *Hermes* 37: 173–209; 353–89; 607–26.
Schneider, K. 1913. "Hetairai." *RE* vol. 8. 2, 1331–72.
Scholl, A. 1994. "ΠΟΛΥΤΑΛΑΝΤΑ ΜΝΗΜΕΙΑ. Zur literarischen und monumentalen Über-lieferung aufwendiger Grabmäler im spätklassischen Athen." *JdAI* 109: 239–71.
Scott, S., and D. Morgan (eds.). 1993. *Body Matters: Essays on the Sociology of the Body.* London.
Sealey, R. 1984. "On Lawful Concubinage in Athens." *CA* 3: 111–33.
Segre, M. 1931. "L' asilia di smirne." *Historia* 5: 241–53.
Semenov, A. 1935. "Hypereides und Phryne." *Klio* 28: 271–9.
Shear, T. 1937. "Psimythion." In *Classical Studies Presented to E. Capps*, 314–6. Princeton.
Sidwell, K. 2000. "Athenaeus, Lucian and Fifth-century Comedy." In Braund and Wilkins 2000: 136–52.
Skinner, M. A. 1991. "Nossis Thēlyglōssos: The Private Text and the Public Book." In Pomeroy 1991: 20–47.
———. 1987. "Greek Women and the Mētronymic: A Note on an Epigram by Nossis." *Ancient History Bulletin* 19: 39–42.
———. 1983. "Corinna of Tanagra and her Audience." *Tulsa Studies in Women's Literature* 2: 9–20.
Slater, N. 1989. "Lekythoi in Aristophanes' *Ecclesiazusae.*" *Lexis* 3: 43–51.
Sommerstein, A. 1980. "The Naming of Women in Greek and Roman Comedy." *QS* 11: 393–418.
Stallybrass, P. and A. White. 1986. *The Politics and Poetics of Transgression.* Ithaca, NY.
Steiner, D. 2001. *Images in Mind: Statues in Archaic and Classical Greek Literature and Thought.* Princeton.
Stewart, A. 1997. *Art, Desire and the Body in Ancient Greece.* Cambridge.
Stewart, S. 1993. *On Longing: Narratives of the Miniature, the Gigantic, the Souvenir, the Collection.* Durham, NC and London.
Stone, L. 1981. *Costume in Aristophanic Comedy.* New York.
Sutton, R. 1992. "Pornography and Persuasion on Attic Pottery." In Richlin 1992a: 3–35.
———. 1981. *The Interaction between Men and Women Portrayed in Attic Red Figure Pottery.* Ph.D. diss. University of North Carolina at Chapel Hill.
Swain, S. 1996. *Hellenism and Empire.* Oxford.
Symeonoglou, S. 1985. *The Topography of Thebes: From the Bronze Age to Modern Times.* Princeton.
Taaffe, L. 1993. *Aristophanes and Women.* London and New York.
Thesleff, H. 1965. *The Pythagorean Texts of the Hellenistic Period.* Acta Academiae Aboensis, Ser. A. 30.1, Abo.
Travlos, J. 1988. *Bildlexicon zur Topographie des antiken Attika.* Tübingen.
Tronson, A. 1984. "Satyrus the Peripatetic and the Marriages of Philip II." *JHS* 104: 116–26.
Tsantsanoglou, K. 1973. "The Memoirs of a Lady from Samos." *ZPE* 12: 183–95.
Ussher, R. 1973. *Aristophanes* Ecclesiazusae. Rochelle, NY.
van Groningen, B. A. 1965. "Some General Literary Tendencies in the Second Century A.D." *Mnemosyne* 18: 41–56.
———. 1956. "Théopompe ou Chamaeléon? À propos de Simonide 137 B, 104 D." *Mnemosyne* 9: 11–22.
Vanoyeke, V. 1990. *La prostitution en Grèce et Rome.* Paris.
Vermeule, C. 1958. "Socrates and Aspasia: New Portraits of Late Antiquity." *CJ* 54: 49–55.
Vernant, J.P. 1980. *Myth and Society in Ancient Greece.* Tr. J. Lloyd. London.
Vestergaard, T., L. Bjertrup, M. Hansen, T. Nielsen, and L. Rubinstein. 1985 [1993]. "A Typology of Women Recorded on Gravestones from Attica." *American Journal of Ancient History* 10: 178–190.
von Reden, S. 1997. "Money, Law and Exchange: Coinage in the Greek Polis." *JHS* 117: 154–76.
———. 1995. *Exchange in Ancient Greece.* London.
von Wilamowitz-Moellendorff, U. 1924. *Hellenistische Dichtung in der Zeit des Kallimachos.* 2 vols. Berlin.
Webster, T. B. L. 1974. *An Introduction to Menander.* Manchester.
———. 1970. *Studies in Later Greek Comedy.* 2nd ed. Manchester.

———. 1952. "Chronological Notes on Middle Comedy." *CQ* n. s. 2: 13–26.

Wehrli, F. 1974. *Hermippos der Kallimacheer: Die Schule des Aristoteles.* Suppl. 1. Basel and Stuttgart.

———. 1936. *Motivstudien zur griechischen Komödie.* Zurich and Leipzig.

Weill, N. 1966. "Adōniazousai ou les femmes sur le toit." *BCH* 90: 664–98.

West, M. L. 1996. *Die griechische Dichterin: Bild und Rolle.* Stuttgart and Leipzig.

———. 1977. "Erinna." *ZPE* 25: 95–119.

White, R. 1975. *The Interpretation of Dreams: Oneirocritica by Artemidorus.* Park Ridge, NJ.

Whitmarsh, T. 2001. "Greece Is the World: Exile and Identity in the Second Sophistic." In Goldhill 2001: 269–305.

———. 2000. "The Politics and Poetics of Parasitism: Athenaeus on Parasites and Flatterers." In Braund and Wilkins 2000: 304–15.

Wiedemann, T. 1981. *Greek and Roman Slavery.* Baltimore, MD.

Wiles, D. 1989. "Marriage and Prostitution in Classical New Comedy." In J. Redmond (ed.), *Themes in Drama 11: Women in Theatre*, 31–48. Cambridge.

Wilkins, J. 2000. "Dialogue and Comedy: The Structure of the *Deipnosophistae*." In Braund and Wilkins 2000: 23–38.

———. 1987. "Aspasia in *Medea*?" LCM 12" 8–10.

Williams, D. 1983. "Women on Athenian Vases: Problems of Interpretation." In A. Cameron and A. Kuhrt (eds.), *Images of Women in Antiquity*, 92–106. Detroit, MI.

Winkler, J. 1990. *The Constraints of Desire: The Anthropology of Sex and Gender in Ancient Greece.* London and New York.

Wolff, H. 1944. "Marriage Law and Family Organization in Ancient Athens: A Study of the Interrelation of Public and Private Law in the Greek City." *Traditio* 2: 43–95.

Woolf, G. 1994. "Becoming Roman, Staying Greek: Culture, Identity and the Civilizing Process in the Roman East" *PCPS* 40: 116–43.

Wyke, M. (ed.). 1999. *Parchments of Gender: Deciphering the Body in Antiquity.* Oxford.

———. (ed.). 1998. *Gender and the Body in the Ancient Mediterranean.* Blackwell.

Zepernick, K. 1921. "Die Exzerpte des Athenaeus in den Deipnosophisten und ihre Glaubwürdigkeit." *Philologus* 77: 311–63.

Zweig, B. 1992. "The Mute Nude Female Characters in Aristophanes' Plays." In Richlin, 1992a: 73–89.

Index